A BRIEF HISTORY
OF THE
GREAT WAR

THE MACMILLAN COMPANY
NEW YORK · BOSTON · CHICAGO · DALLAS
ATLANTA · SAN FRANCISCO

MACMILLAN & CO., LIMITED
LONDON · BOMBAY · CALCUTTA
MELBOURNE

THE MACMILLAN CO. OF CANADA, LTD.
TORONTO

A BRIEF HISTORY

OF THE

GREAT WAR

BY

CARLTON J. H. HAYES

PROFESSOR OF HISTORY IN COLUMBIA UNIVERSITY
AUTHOR OF "A POLITICAL AND SOCIAL
HISTORY OF MODERN EUROPE"

New York

THE MACMILLAN COMPANY

1920

All rights reserved

TO

THOSE STUDENTS OF HIS WHO LOYALLY LEFT THEIR
BOOKS AND PROUDLY PAID THE SUPREME SACRI-
FICE IN THE CAUSE OF HUMAN SOLIDARITY
AGAINST INTERNATIONAL ANARCHY
THE AUTHOR INSCRIBES
THIS BOOK

PREFACE

THE following pages constitute a connected story of the late war from its origins to the conclusion of the Peace of Versailles, not for the edification of "experts," military or other, but rather for the enlightenment of the general reader and student. A "definitive" history of the war will never be written; it is much too early, of course, even to attempt it. All that the author has here essayed to do is to sketch tentatively what seem to him its broad outlines — domestic politics of the several belligerents no less than army campaigns and naval battles, — and in presenting his synthesis to be guided so far as in him lay by an honest desire to put heat and passion aside and to write candidly and objectively for the instruction of the succeeding generation.

The author is under special obligation to Messrs. Dodd, Mead and Company for the kind permission which they have accorded him of drawing freely upon the articles on "The War of the Nations" which he wrote in 1914, 1915, and 1916 for their invaluable *New International Year Book*. In the opening chapter of the present work the author has also incorporated a few paragraphs from the last chapter of his *Political and Social History of Modern Europe*, to which, in a way, the BRIEF HISTORY OF THE GREAT WAR is supplementary.

CARLTON J. H. HAYES.

AFTON, NEW YORK,
April 5, 1920.

CONTENTS

CONTENTS

A BRIEF HISTORY
OF THE
GREAT WAR

EUROPE, 1914

Scale of Miles
0 100 200 300 400 500 600

Cities with over 1,000,000 .... **London**
Cities with 500,000 to 1,000,000 ...... **Naples**
Cities with 200,000 to 500,000 .... **Leipzig**
Smaller Places .... Venice
Capitals with less than 200,000 .... BERNE

Capitals ⊙   Other Cities ○

A BRIEF HISTORY OF
THE GREAT WAR

CHAPTER I

THE GREAT WAR COMES

THE GENERAL CAUSE: INTERNATIONAL ANARCHY

SELF-INTEREST was the dominant note of the years immediately preceding the outbreak of the Great War. In economics and in politics, among individuals, social classes, and nations, flourished a self-interest that tended more and more to degenerate into mere cynical selfishness. Pseudo-scientists there were to justify the tendency as part of an inevitable "struggle for existence" and to extol it as assuring the "survival of the fittest."

Economic circumstances had provided the setting for the dogma of self-interest. The latest age in world history had been the age of steam and electricity, of the factory and the workshop, of the locomotive, the steamship, and the automobile. It had been the age of big competitive business. Between the capitalists of the new era had developed the keenest rivalry in exploiting machinery, mines, raw materials, and even human beings, with a view to securing the largest share of the world's riches and the world's prestige. It was a race of the strong, and "the devil take the hindmost."

Competition in big business gave manners and tone to the whole age. It inspired a multitude of mankind to emulate the "captains of industry." It furnished the starting-point and the main impulse for the development of the doctrines of Socialists and of Anarchists and of all those who laid stress upon "class consciousness" and "class struggle." It even served to set farmers against manufacturers and to pit "producers" against "consumers." To secure power and thereby to obtain wealth, or to secure wealth and thereby to obtain power, became the more or less conscious end and aim of individuals and of whole classes.

B   I

Trade — the veritable red blood of modern industrial life
— has not been, and from its nature cannot be, narrowly national.
Not only must there be commerce between one highly civilized
nation and another, but there must likewise be trade between
an industrialized nation and more backward peoples in tropical
or semi-tropical regions. The modern business man has need
of raw materials from the tropics; he has manufactured goods
to sell in return; most important of all, he frequently finds
that investments in backward countries are especially lucrative
in themselves and stimulative of greater and more advantageous
trade. So self-interest has been pursued abroad as well as at
home, and usually with the most calamitously anarchical results.
Whatever restrictions might be imposed by a strong national
state on the selfish activities of its citizens at home were either
non-existent or ineffective in restraining them wherever governments were unstable or weak. In backward countries the
foreign exploiter often behaved as though "getting rich quick"
was the supreme obligation imposed upon him by the civilization
whose representative and exponent he was. The natives suffered
from the unregulated dealings of the foreigners. And the
foreigners, drawn perhaps from several different nations, carried
their mutual economic rivalries into the sphere of international
competition and thereby created "danger zones" or "arenas of
friction."

After 1870 this aspect of capitalistic imperialism was increasingly in evidence. Any one who would follow an outline story
of the exploitation of backward regions by business men of Great
Britain, Germany, France, Italy, Russia, Japan, and the United
States would perceive the process and would appreciate its
attendant dangers. Any one who is at all familiar with the
"arenas of friction" in Egypt, in China, in Siam, in the Sudan,
in Morocco, in Persia, in the Ottoman Empire, and in the Balkans would be in possession of a valuable clew to a significant
cause of every war of the twentieth century, particularly to
the chief cause of the Great War.

What had complicated the situation was the fact that trade,
though in essence international, had been conducted in practice
on a national basis, and that foreign investors had been perpetually appealing for support not to an international conscience
and an international police but to the patriotism and armed
forces of their respective national states. In other words,
anarchy had continued to characterize international politics as
well as domestic economics.

There was no international organization. There was no general authority for the determination of disputes and for the regulation of world interests. There were at the opening of the twentieth century some *fifty* states, in theory absolutely independent, sovereign, and equal. In fact, the fifty were very unequal and even the strongest among them was not strong enough to maintain its independence should the others unite against it. Yet each proceeded to act on the assumption in most cases that it was self-sufficient and that its own self-interest was its supreme guide.

Running through the whole anarchic state-system, as woof through warp, was the doctrine of nationality. It is a commonplace to us that a compact people speaking the same language and sharing the same historical traditions and social customs should be politically united as an independent nation. To the nineteenth century, however, nationalism was a revolutionary force. At its dawn there was no free German nation, no free Italian nation. But the all-conquering armies of the French Revolutionaries brought to the disjointed and dispirited peoples of Europe a new gospel of Fraternity, that men of the same nation should be brothers-in-arms to defend their liberties against the tyrant and their homes against the foreign foe. Poetry glorified the idea of national patriotism, religion sanctioned it, and political theory invested it with all the finality of a scientific dogma. Within a century, the spirit of nationality produced an independent Greece, a Serbia, a Rumania, a Bulgaria, a Belgium, a Norway, an Italy, a Germany. Each nation— old and young — was proud of its national language, its national customs, its frequently fictitious but always glorious national history, and above all, of its national political unification and freedom.

Everywhere the doctrine of nationality has brought forth fruits in abundance. It has awakened all peoples to national self-consciousness. It has inspired noble and glorious deeds. It has stimulated art and literature. It has promoted popular education and political democracy. It should have led, not backwards to eighteenth-century indifferent cosmopolitanism, but forwards to twentieth-century *inter-nationalism*, to a confederation of all the free nations of the world for mutual cooperation and support. Hither, on the eve of the Great War, it had not led. And this was the tragedy of nationalism.

Nationalism was utilized too often to point citizens to what was peculiar to their own nation rather than to what was common

to all mankind. It served to emphasize the exclusiveness of each
state and to promote selfishness in a new and national form. It
led nations which had not yet achieved complete unity and independence, like the Irish, the Poles, the Czechs, the Serbs, and the
Rumans, to combat more fortunate nations; and among the perfected nations it aroused such selfish intolerance as to render them
tyrannical over dissident minorities and to cause them to entertain the notion that they were manifestly destined to impose their
own brand of civilization or *Kultur* upon, if not arbitrarily to
rule over, "inferior" races.

Nationalism, moreover, prompted whole peoples to give patriotic support to the pretensions of their relatively few fellow-citizens who in less favored lands were seeking profits at the expense
of natives and perhaps of neighbors. The foreign tradesman or
investor was under no obligation to an impartial international
tribunal: he had only to present his international grievances to
the uncritical and sympathetic ears of his distant fellow-nationals,
with the usual result that his cause was championed at home and
that redress for his real or fancied wrongs was forthcoming from a
single one of the fifty sovereign states. And when tradesmen or
investors of other nationalities appealed from the same distant
regions to their several states, what had been an arena of economic
friction between competing capitalists in backward lands speedily
became an arena of political friction between civilized sovereign
states.

In this fashion the spirit of nationalism operated to reënforce
the anarchy both of international politics and of international
economics. Modern imperialism, curiously enough, became an
arc on the circle of exclusive nationalism. It was a vicious circle,
and the only way to break it seemed to involve the method most
terribly anarchic — employment of brute force — war! It had
been in view of this grim eventuality that in the nineteenth century every sovereign state had been arming itself and utilizing
every landmark in the progress of civilization in order to forge
instruments of destruction. Imperialism — Nationalism — Militarism — these three stalked forth hand in hand.

Armed force was comparatively little used; its mere existence
and the mere threat of its use ordinarily sufficed. Indirectly, if
not directly, however, force and power were final arbitrament between each two of the fifty sovereign states. And it was no eu-
phemism that every such state was styled a "Power," and that
certain states on account of the thickness and weight of their armor and the success that customarily attended their threats were

popularly dubbed "Great Powers." In a world like this there was little chance for international order and security. It was international anarchy — and that was all.

For many generations before the Great War the delicate relations between the jealously sovereign states — aptly called the "balance of power" — had been manipulated by a professional class of "diplomatists" with the aid of military and naval *attachés* and of spies and secret service. The customs and methods of diplomacy had been determined in large part at a time when they conformed quite nicely to the purposes and ideals of the divine-right dynasts of the seventeenth and eighteenth centuries, but in the nineteenth and twentieth centuries, when democracy was constantly preached and increasingly practiced, they might have seemed old-fashioned and anachronistic. To be sure, there were some modifications both in the objects and in the methods of diplomacy: as a result of the industrial changes in our own day, economic questions provided a larger and more attractive field for tortuous diplomatic negotiation than mere dynastic problems; and by the use of the telegraph, the telephone, and the cable the individual diplomatist was kept in closer touch than formerly with his home government. Still, however, the diplomatists were mainly persons of a class, elderly, suave, insinuating, moving mysteriously their wonders to perform. Democrats who in many countries had laid violent hands upon innumerable institutions of despotism and had brought most matters of public concern to the knowledge of a universal electorate, hesitated to assail this last relic of divine-right monarchy or to trust the guidance of international relations to an enfranchised democracy which might by the slightest slip upset the balance of power and plunge an anarchic world into an abyss.

So the diplomatists in our own day continued to manage affairs after their old models. They got what they could for their fellow-nationals by cajolery or by threats. If they thought they could do more for their fellow-nationals by making special "deals" with diplomatists of other Powers, they did so, and presto! a "convention," an "entente," or a "treaty of alliance" defensive or offensive or both. The game had become quite involved and absorbing by 1914, and quite hazardous. Germany thought she needed aid to enable her to retain the loot which she had taken from France; Austria-Hungary thought she needed assistance in the development of her Balkan policy; Italy thought she must have help in safeguarding Rome and in defending herself from possible French or Austrian aggression. So German and Austrian diplomatists formed a "defensive alliance" in 1879, and Italy, joining them in 1882, transformed it into the "Triple Alliance." This was the beginning of the alignment of the Great Powers in our own generation. Diplomatists of republican France and autocratic Russia cemented the secret defensive "Dual Alliance" in 1892. Diplomatists of democratic Great Britain and oligarchical Japan formed a Far Eastern "alliance" in 1902. Diplomatists of Great Britain and France effected a *rapprochement* and an "entente" in 1904. To this "entente" the diplomatists of Russia were admitted in 1907. And between Triple Alliance and Triple Entente the balance of power was so neatly adjusted that from 1907 to 1914 one trivial occurrence after another almost upset it.

Of course, the smaller states — the "lesser powers" — were mainly at the mercy of the "Great Powers" and their delicate balance. On the very eve of the Great War diplomatists of Germany and Great Britain were secretly negotiating the virtual partition of the colonial empire of Portugal. On the other hand, changes among the lesser powers might produce prodigious danger to the balance of the Great Powers. The defeat of Turkey by four little Balkan states in 1912–1913 appeared on the surface to be slightly more advantageous to Russia than to Austria-Hungary, with the result that Germany and her Habsburg ally were thrown into a paroxysm of fear, and one Power after another consecrated the year 1913 to unprecedented armed preparedness. By 1914 it actually required nothing less trivial in itself than the assassination of an archduke to exhaust the imagination and endeavor of the professional balancers between the Powers and to send the diplomatists scurrying homewards, leaving the common people of the several nations to confront one another in the most formidable and portentous battle-array that the world in all its long recorded history had ever beheld.

Those last years before the storm and the hurricane were indeed a strange, nightmarish time. Man had gained a large measure of control over his physical environment and a very small amount of knowledge about his true political, social, and economic needs. In most countries democracy and nationalism were growing by leaps and bounds. In other countries there was more or less mute protest against interference with national right and democratic development. Everywhere the Industrial Revolution was providing an economic foundation for international federation. Yet the spirit of the age seemed incapable of expression save in institutions which had been distantly inherited and which in most

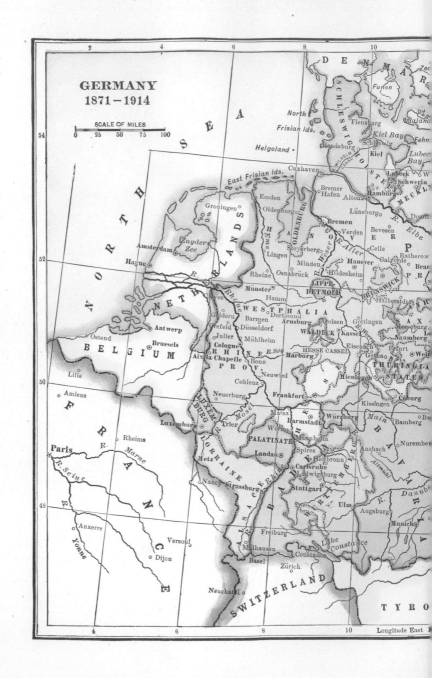

GERMANY
1871–1914

SCALE OF MILES
0   25   50   75   100

SWEDEN

BALTIC SEA

Bornholm

Rixhoft

Memel

Memel

Tilsit

Gulf of
Danzig

Königsberg

Braunsberg

R. Pregel

Friedland

Preuss. Eylau

Moen
Falster

Rügen

Stolpe

Danzig

Elbing

Marienwerder

Bartenstein

Lotzen

54

Stralsund

Coslin

Colberg

Butow

Rostock Wolgast

Usedom I.

Wollin I.

Allenstein

Johannisberg

Swinemünde

Rummelsburg

Elbing

Graudenz

BURG
argun

Anklam

Regenwalde

Marienwerder

Narew

Waren

Golinow

Neu Stettin

R. Vistula

R. Brahe

Strelitz

Stettin

Peterswalde

Thorn

Pritzwalk
tenberge

Arnswalde

Wirsitz

Bromberg

Woclawek

Plock

R. Bug

Liebenwald

FINOW
CANAL

Kreutzo

R.

Netze

Warsaw

52

BRANDENBURG

Landsberg

Wronke

Mogilno

Spandau

Custrin

R. Warthe

Gnesen

POLAND

Berlin

Potsdam Gr. Beeren

Frankfurt

Posen

POSEN

Trebbin

Zullichau

Schrimm

Lübben

Luckau

Grünberg

Fraustadt

Pleschen

Spremberg

R. Spree

Glogau

Rawicz

R. Warthe

Meissen

R. Neisse

Liegnitz

Kempen

Dresden

Görlitz

Breslau

SILESIA

Chemnitz

Reichenberg

Schweidnitz

Brieg

R. Vistula

Zwickau

Reichenback

50

BOHEMIA

Glatz

Neustadt

Cracow

GALICIA

Prague

Jägerndorf

Pilsen

Troppau

BÖHMER

MORAVIA

Waag

Gran

WALD

tisbon

R. Moldau

Brünn

R. March

A U S T R I A

shut

Passau

Linz

Danube R.

Pressburg

Miskolcz

48

ar
Muhldorf

Salzburg

Vienna

Inn

Odenburg

Budapest

A U S T

Danube

R.

R.

Greenwich

ENGRAVED BY BORMAY & CO., N.Y.

instances had outlived their usefulness.   Recurring crises between sovereign states and increasing social unrest in every country were alike signs of the passing of a worn-out age and of the coming of a new age which should more perfectly square institutions with vital popular needs and longings.   Those three shibboleths of the nineteenth century, — Nationalism, Imperialism, Militarism, — as interpreted in the traditional language of the exclusive state-system, were producing the utmost confusion.   Together they embodied the spirit of Anarchy, a spirit that could not permanently endure on a shrinking globe or among social animals.   Together they were operating to produce a cataclysm which should stand forth as one of those great crises in Man's historic evolution, such as the break-up of the Roman Empire, the Reformation, and the French Revolution.   And the cataclysm came in the Great War.   Its underlying cause was international anarchy.   Its stakes were the perpetuation or the destruction of that anarchy.

THE IMMEDIATE CAUSE: GERMANY

The vices of modern political and economic life might be exemplified in greater or less degree by reference to the history of any Power or any country.   Obviously they were more developed in the "Great Powers" than in the "Lesser Powers"; and of all the "Great Powers" the most perfect exemplar of nationalism, imperialism, and militarism, and therefore the most viciously anarchic in international relations, was Germany.   It was Germany which precipitated the Great War.

Militarism is not merely the possession of large armed forces; it involves also the exaltation of such armed forces to the chief place in the state, the subordination to them of the civil authorities, the reliance upon them in every dispute.   In explaining why a given nation may be peculiarly predisposed to militarism, at least four factors should be taken into account: (1) geographical situation, (2) historical traditions, (3) political organization, and (4) social structure.   In every country one or another of these factors has worked toward militarism, sometimes two or three.   In Germany all four have been fully operative in that direction.

For centuries German lands had been battlefields for aggressive neighbors.   Situated in the center of Europe, with weak natural frontiers, these lands had been the prey of Spaniards, Swedes, Frenchmen, Poles, and Russians.   From the Thirty Years' War, in the first half of the seventeenth century, down to the domination of Napoleon Bonaparte, in the first decade of the nineteenth century, most of the German states were at the mercy of foreigners. What international prestige Germans retained throughout that dreary period was credited to the military prowess of Austria and more particularly to the waxing strength of Prussia.   Prussia had no easily defensible boundaries, and her rise to eminence was due to the soldierly qualities of her Hohenzollern sovereigns — the Great Elector, King Frederick William I, and Frederick the Great. When, in the nineteenth century, the German Empire was created, it was the work of the large, well-organized, well-equipped army of Prussia, and it was achieved only at the price of French military defeat and of diplomatic concessions to Russia.   After the creation of the German Empire in 1871 most of its citizens continued to believe that its geographical position between populous Russia and well-armed France required the guarantee of militarism for its future maintenance.

Despite the drawback of their geographical situation the Germans had finally achieved national unification, and among a people zealously worshiping the spirit of nationalism the process by which they had secured national union became their most hallowed historical tradition.   It will be recalled that the first serious attempt to achieve the political unification of the Germanies was made by the democratic Frankfort Assembly in the stormy days of 1848–1849; that it represented a combination of nationalism and liberalism, of the German nation with the German democracy. But this first attempt failed.   The second attempt, Bismarck's attempt "by iron and blood," was crowned with success.   Bismarck's three wars of 1864, 1866, and 1870–1871, solidly established the united German Empire.   "Nothing succeeds like success," and the three wars simultaneously sanctified the union of nationalism and militarism, of the German nation with the Prussian army.   Moreover, as Prussia henceforth embraced two-thirds the area and three-fifths the population of the Empire and as the Hohenzollern king of Prussia was henceforth the German Emperor, the whole Empire was inevitably Prussianized, and Prussian history and Prussian tradition supplied the patriotic impulse to all Germans.   In this way the tradition of militarism — the most important one that Prussia had — gradually supplanted the more cosmopolitan and cultural traditions which had once flourished in southern and central Germany, and in the pantheon of national heroes all German patriots inscribed tablets to the long line of warlike Hohenzollern monarchs, to the valorous Queen Louise, to Scharnhorst, Gneisenau, Moltke, and Roon, to the unscrupulous and forceful Bismarck — a veritable galaxy of Thors and Wodens.

With this tradition the political organization of the German Empire was in perfect harmony. Chief authority in the central government was confided to the *Bundesrat*, a close corporation of diplomatists representing the hereditary princes of the German states, meeting in secret session, and largely controlled by the chancellor, an official appointed by, and responsible to, the king of Prussia. Only secondary authority was intrusted to the popularly elected *Reichstag*. Prussia, as the dominant state in the confederation, retained her oligarchical and plutocratic form of government, with her parliament elected by the absurd and thoroughly undemocratic three-class system of voting. The Emperor, in training and profession a soldier rather than a civilian, was commander-in-chief of the army and navy, and his tenure was for life. Under the constitution of Prussia, whose contingent comprised the greater part of the German army, the Emperor-King might apply indefinitely from year to year to the support of the army the amount last voted by the parliament, instead of being obliged to depend upon annual financial grants. The German soldier took an oath of allegiance to the Kaiser and not to the Constitution. In Germany, finally, the military authorities were accountable for their acts only to military tribunals. Such an affair as that at Saverne in Alsace in 1913–1914 [1] was a clear illustration of the disregard of the military for civilian rights and of the inability of civilians under German political institutions to obtain redress for their just grievances against the military.

Most potent of all factors in predisposing Germany to militarism was the structure of her society. In Germany more nearly than in any other highly industrialized country, agriculture has held its own and the agricultural classes have suffered less in purse and in prestige through competition with manufacturers and tradesmen. Not only have the German farmers preserved their economic independence, but a conspicuous group of them have continued to our own day to enjoy the greatest social prestige and to exert the greatest influence in politics. These are the

---

[1] Saverne, or Zabern as the Germans called it, was the scene throughout 1913–1914 of the harshest and most offensive conduct of the German garrison toward the native civilian population, culminating in the slashing of a lame cobbler by a Junker lieutenant. In vain did the local authorities and even the Reichstag endeavor to establish the supremacy of the civil courts in handling the situation; the army proved itself superior to the law, and the responsible officers received no part of the punishment which they richly deserved. For a detailed account of the Saverne Affair, see C. D. Hazen, *Alsace-Lorraine under German Rule* (1917), ch. viii.

landholding nobles and the country gentlemen of Prussia — the squirearchy, or *Junkerthum*. From time immemorial they had divided their attention between oversight of their extensive estates and the service of their Hohenzollern overlord in his civil bureaucracy or in his army. Unlike their fellows in France no mighty revolution had wrested their lands from them and no republican régime had deprived them of their offices and privileges. In our own generation the efficient civil service in Prussia and throughout Germany was still largely recruited from them; most commissioned officers in the large Prussian army were still appointed from their number; and they were still utilizing their positions of trust and power in order to serve their own class-interests. The Junkers could afford to be most intensely loyal and patriotic. They extolled militarism, and the extolling of militarism exalted them.

Second only to the Junkers in significance and influence were the capitalists, the product of that amazing industrial and commercial evolution through which Germany had passed in the last forty years. Not a country in the world had witnessed in so brief a time an economic transformation of such prodigious dimensions as the German Empire had experienced. Cities had grown rapidly; factories had been reared overnight; mine-shafts had been quickly sunk into the bowels of the earth; an ever expanding fleet of merchant vessels had put to sea, carrying German manufactures to the uttermost parts of the globe; traders, suddenly gorged with gold, had speedily turned investors, and, imitating the example of older foreign industrialists, had rushed to exploit Africa and South Sea Islands and China and South America and the Ottoman Empire.

The capitalists, and the middle classes generally, might have been expected to come into sharp collision with the Junkers, so divergent were the natural interests of the two classes. As a matter of fact they did collide repeatedly in shaping domestic policies, and much of the internal history of the German Empire from 1870 to 1914 was the story of the conflicts and compromises between them. One sacred German institution, however, kept the class-struggle within patriotic bounds, and that institution was militarism. German traders and investors, arriving late in foreign and backward lands, usually found the keenest economic competition already proceeding between business-men of Great Britain, France, or some other industrialized Power; and were they to have an equal or a better chance in the international scramble for economic exploitation they would have to invoke the armed forces of Germany, their own "Great Power." At home a huge military machine was ready to aim and fire. Admitting that the German army of the 1870's was relied upon chiefly for defense against potential attacks of neighboring France and Russia, it may be affirmed that twenty and thirty years later it had become the standing threat by means of which German citizens were prosecuting their unregulated economic activities abroad and by means of which the whole German Empire was championing unrestrained anarchy in international relations. To the existing army, the capitalistic interests of Germany added the rapidly expanding navy with the threats therein implied. The Junkers officered all the armed forces and naturally extolled militarism. Militarism proved serviceable to the capitalists, and they in turn extolled militarism. By the iron ring of militarism were agricultural and industrial interests wedded. The Junkers were now serving the capitalists, and the capitalists were honoring the Junkers. The promise "to obey" was left out of the covenant, for both contracting parties had freely given that pledge to the high priest who solemnized the nuptials, to the Kaiser himself.

Even in Germany protests were raised from time to time against the extent of militarism and against some of the uses to which it was put. The numerically important party of the Social Democrats were particularly vocal in their denunciations. The Center, or Catholic, party had not always taken kindly to militarism. There were various groups of radicals who had inveighed against it. It was naturally viewed with dislike by dissident nationalities within the German Empire, such as the Poles, the Danes, and the Alsatians. Yet over these parties and factions the Junker and capitalistic patriots always managed to keep the upper hand, and in course of time the opposition dwindled rather than increased. The dissident nationalists and the pacifist radicals were relatively few and quite impotent. The Catholics grew more resigned to militarism when they discovered that it was being used to bolster up Austria-Hungary, Germany's Catholic ally. And the Social Democrats were never given to violence; as time went on, they were too intent upon rolling up electoral pluralities to take a positive stand that might shock the patriotic instincts of their fellow-countrymen. The militarists in Germany were having their own way.

Forcefully the militarists cleared the way for German capitalists abroad. The German fist was shaken in the face of Japan in 1895 and in the face of China in 1897 and again in 1900. In 1896 there were threats against Great Britain in connection with affairs in South Africa. In 1898 there were veiled threats against the United States in connection with affairs in the Philippines, and in 1903 America was concerned with German threats against Venezuela. In 1896 the Kaiser himself, on a spectacular visit to Turkey, declared at Damascus that "at all times he was the friend and protector of the three hundred million Mussulmans who honored Sultan Abdul Hamid as Caliph" — an assertion not only of German political and economic interests in the Ottoman Empire but also of German opposition to British rule in India and in Egypt and to French rule in northern Africa. In 1904 the Kaiser encouraged Russia to fight Japan, and in the following year he utilized Russian military defeats in order to compel France, Russia's ally, to alter her Moroccan policy. In 1908–1909 he stood "in shining armor" beside his own ally, Austria-Hungary, enabling her coolly and calmly to tear up an international treaty and to appropriate the Serb-Turkish provinces of Bosnia and Herzegovina despite the entreaties of the states of Serbia and Montenegro and despite the lively sympathy of the Russians with their South Slav (Jugoslav) brethren. In 1911 Germany unsheathed the sword at Agadir, and put it up again only on condition of receiving a hundred thousand square miles of French colonial dominion in equatorial Africa. In 1912 and 1913, during the Balkan Wars, Germany proved herself a brilliant second to Austria-Hungary in preventing Serbian egress to the Adriatic, in driving the Montenegrins out of the town of Scutari which they had captured from the Turks, in erecting the petty principality of Albania, and otherwise in strengthening the Austro-German strangle-hold on Turkey and the Balkans. From 1895 to 1914 Germany pursued without cessation the policy of employing force and threats and bluff in order to win economic advantages and political prestige. "It is only by relying on our good German sword," wrote Crown Prince Frederick William in 1913, "that we can hope to conquer that place in the sun which rightly belongs to us, and which no one will yield to us voluntarily. . . . Till the world comes to an end, the ultimate decision must rest with the sword."

Militarism has been most frequently excused on the ground that it guarantees order and security. Paradoxical as it may seem, German militarism from 1895 to 1914 produced no such happy results. Not only was there a renewed epidemic of wars and rumors of war between states but there was the most astounding lack of a sense of security in Germany. The more

Germany affronted Russia, France, and Great Britain, the higher rolled the wave of fear, even of panic, within Germany. Patriotic militaristic societies came into being by the score, societies like the Navy League, the Pan-German League, the Security League, performing the twofold function of preparing the mind for additional deeds of aggression and of instilling in the same popular mind the basest sort of fright and terror. Under the auspices of these leagues what might be termed a "psychology of suggestion" was communicated gradually and skillfully to the German masses. Russia was "menacing," and as formerly there had been a "Yellow Peril" so now there was a "Slavic Peril." France was thirsting for "revenge," was "vengeful," but also the French were "decadent." The English were insanely "jealous" and Great Britain was "the vampire of the Continent." Moreover, when "menacing" Russia and "vengeful" France and "jealous" Britain tended to draw together, the German professors of suggestive psychology began to exploit the word "encirclement" and to expatiate upon the ring of dangerous, greedy neighbors by which the Fatherland and child Austria were surrounded. As the ring best known to the German mind was of iron, this foreign "encirclement" was naturally termed the "iron ring."

One step further went the terrifying phrase-makers of Germany. Now that they had made up their own minds and had gone far toward fashioning the conviction of the bulk of their fellow-countrymen that sooner or later Germany and Austria-Hungary would be crushed to death by the inevitable pressure of the encircling "iron ring," they began to suggest and then to preach the necessity of a speedy open attack before the iron ring should become so strong as to be irresistible. Such an attack upon nominally peaceful neighbors could not be construed as "defensive war." Yet from the German standpoint it would not be "offensive war." The psychologists escaped from the dilemma by urging the plausible slogan of "preventive war." And to the problem of finding the most favorable opportunity for inaugurating the "preventive war," German militarists and German patriots turned their attention. In 1914 Germany was ready, and her governing class of Junkers and capitalists were willing, to precipitate war.

THE OCCASION: THE ASSASSINATION OF AN ARCHDUKE

On June 28, 1914, the Archduke Francis Ferdinand, nephew of the aged Emperor-King Francis Joseph and heir to the Habsburg crowns, was assassinated, together with his wife, in the

streets of the Bosnian city of Serajevo by youthful Serb conspirators. The outrage caused an instantaneous outburst of indignation throughout Austria-Hungary and Germany. For on
Francis Ferdinand many hopes had been pinned. His piety had
made him a favorite with Catholics; his loyalty to the German
alliance augured well for the future maintenance of the international solidarity of the two great Teutonic Powers; his vigorous
patriotism and his conscientious fulfillment of administrative
duties were harbingers of the continued integrity and stability
of the Dual Monarchy after the demise of Francis Joseph. Moreover, Francis Ferdinand was supposed to favor a special policy
on the part of Austria-Hungary toward the Slavs of Southern
Europe: to him was attributed the leadership in a scheme to
transform the Dual Monarchy into a Triple Monarchy, in
which the Serbs of Bosnia and the Serbo-Croats of Croatia-
Slavonia and probably the Slovenes would constitute an autonomous entity resembling Austria and Hungary; and to him,
therefore, was imputed by patriotic Serbians and Montenegrins
the inspiration of the hostile attitude which Austria-Hungary,
with Germany's powerful backing, had taken, especially since
1908, toward the territorial expansion of the two independent
Serb kingdoms.

Certainly the Serbs disliked Francis Ferdinand immensely and
certainly from 1908 to 1914 they organized secret societies in
Bosnia as well as in Serbia and Montenegro and conducted a deliberate propaganda with the more or less avowed object of wholly
detaching the South Slav peoples from the Habsburg Empire.
Naturally, then, when the official Austrian investigation into the
archduke's assassination indicated that the plot had been executed by Bosnian youths animated by the revolutionary secret
societies of the Serbs and with the connivance of at least two officials of the kingdom of Serbia, the indignation of both Germans
and Magyars was aroused. The government of Austria-Hungary
solemnly affirmed that the very existence of the Dual Monarchy
depended upon putting an end once for all to Serbian machinations, and with practical unanimity the responsible press of Germany declared that Austria-Hungary's welfare was Germany's
welfare. But by the same token and with equal unanimity the
press of Russia declared that Serbia's welfare was Russia's welfare. A new crisis, and a most serious one, had arisen in the
Balkans.

One week after the Serajevo assassination, a conference of
German and Austrian dignitaries was held at Potsdam. Pre-

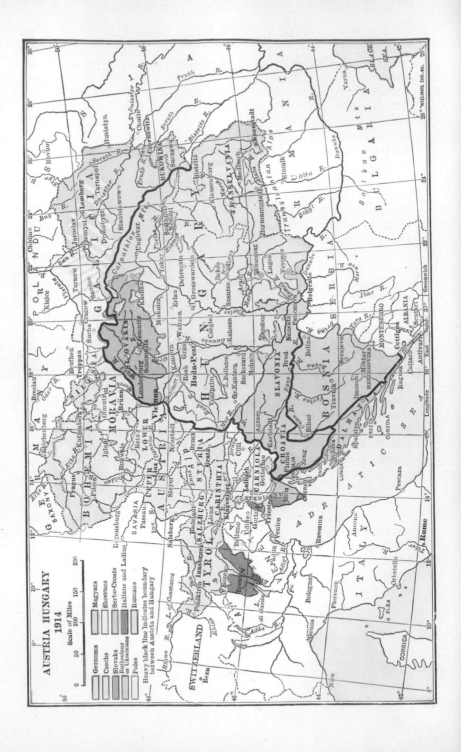

AUSTRIA HUNGARY
1914

Scale of Miles

0   50   100   150   200

Germans

Czechs

Slovaks

Italians and Ladins

Poles

Magyars

Slovenes

Serbo-Croats

Ruthenians
or Ukrainians

Rumans

Heavy black line indicates boundary
between Austria and Hungary

cisely what was there discussed and determined upon we do not
know.   There is little doubt, however, that the Austro-Hungarian government received *carte blanche* to use the archduke's
murder as the pretext for dealing drastically with the one obstrep-
erous Balkan state which had been thwarting the full realization
of Teutonic political and economic aims in southeastern Europe.
As recently as August, 1913, Austria had formally invited Italy
to coöperate with her in crushing Serbia.   At that time no good
excuse existed for such a use of force and Italy had declined the
invitation, but now the occasion was propitious and the ruling
classes in Germany were favorably disposed.[1]   Perhaps the German dignitaries, mindful of the success of their former military
threats in 1908–1909 and in 1912–1913, entertained the idea that
if Germany were now again to stand "in shining armor" beside
her ally, Russia would once more back down and leave Serbia to
the tender mercy of Austria-Hungary.   It would be Germany's
rôle by threats and intimidation to keep the Balkan conflict "lo-
calized."   Assuredly the German dignitaries must have foreseen
the possibility of Russia's not backing down and of the resulting
precipitation of a general and truly Great War.   But such a war,
precipitated by Austria's act and Germany's threat, might be
the heralded "preventive war," through which Germany would
break the "iron ring" of her jealous and greedy neighbors and
assume in the wide world a position to which her might and her
Kultur destined her.   It was a peculiarly opportune moment for
provoking the "preventive war," for at that very moment each
one of the Entente Powers was embarrassed by domestic difficulties — Russia by a serious and violent strike of workingmen
in Petrograd, France by an alarming popular opposition to the
new three-year military law and by a scandalous murder trial of
political importance at Paris, and Great Britain by the menace
of civil war in Ireland.   It was time to cast the die, and whether
strained peace or vast war would eventuate was a minor consideration to the Imperial German Government.   If Russia simply
blustered, Germany would gain her point; if Russia fought,
Germany would succeed even better.   It would be another instance of "heads, you lose; tails, I win."

Such at any rate is the burden of the testimony of a conspicuous German diplomatist, Prince Lichnowsky, the Kaiser's ambassador at London during those decisive days.   In a private

---

[1] Italy, though an ally of Austria-Hungary and Germany, was not represented
at the Potsdam Conference and was not privy to the Teutonic plot of 1914.   Italy's
refusal to coöperate with Austria-Hungary in 1913 probably made the latter quite
wary of her in 1914.

memorandum prepared in 1916 and indiscreetly published in
March, 1918, Prince Lichnowsky gives the most damning lie to
the official contention of his government that it had had no prior
knowledge of Austria's plans against Serbia and that it had been
most anxious to preserve peace and thereto had counseled moderation at Vienna.   Referring to the Potsdam conference of July 5,
1914, he affirms that "an inquiry addressed to us by Vienna found
positive assent among all personages in authority.   Indeed, they
added that there would be no harm if war with Russia were to
result."   Prince Lichnowsky, who from personal acquaintance
with the members of the British government had come to believe
implicitly in the pacific purposes and policy of Great Britain, was
greatly perturbed by what he deemed the mistaken policy of his
own government in backing Austria-Hungary's selfish Balkan
policy, and he accordingly besought Herr von Jagow, the German
foreign secretary, to recommend moderation to the Austrians.
"Herr von Jagow answered me that Russia was not ready, that
there doubtless would be a certain amount of bluster, but the
more firmly we stood by Austria the more would Russia draw
back.   He said Austria already was accusing us of want of spirit
and we must not squeeze her; and that, on the other hand, feeling in Russia was becoming more anti-German and so we must
simply risk it."   If any confirmation of this point of Prince Lichnowsky's memorandum is required, it is provided by the revelations of Dr. Mühlon, an ex-director of the Krupps, who learned
from high German officials in the middle of July, 1914, that the
Kaiser was fully cognizant of the Austrian purpose and that it
was not the intention of the German government to maintain
peace.

Provided, as we now know, with secret assurances of Germany's
unqualified support, Austria-Hungary presented to Serbia, on
July 23, 1914, an ultimatum couched in the most peremptory
terms; it breathed a ruthless determination to crush all Pan-
Serb plotting regardless of international usage or of constitutional
formalities.   The ultimatum alleged that, by failing to suppress
anti-Austrian conspiracies, Serbia had violated her promise of
1909 to "live on good neighborly terms" with Austria-Hungary,
and had compelled the government of the Dual Monarchy to
abandon its attitude of benevolent and patient forbearance, to
put an end "to the intrigues which form a perpetual menace to
the tranquillity of the Monarchy," and to demand effective guarantees from the Serbian government.   As definite guarantees of
good behavior Serbia was called upon to suppress anti-Austrian

publications and societies, to discharge such governmental employees as the Austro-Hungarian government should accuse of anti-Austrian propaganda, to exclude anti-Austrian teachers and textbooks from the Serbian schools, "to accept the collaboration in Serbia of representatives of the Austro-Hungarian government for the suppression of the subversive movement directed against the territorial integrity of the Monarchy," and to signify unconditional acceptance of these and the other Austro-Hungarian demands within forty-eight hours.

Thenceforth events marched fast. Russia, France, and Great Britain at once endeavored to obtain from Austria an extension of the time-limit of the ultimatum in order that the whole question might be submitted to general international negotiation, but to international anarchy rather than to international coöperation Austria-Hungary was committed and she sharply declined the request. On July 25, Serbia replied to the ultimatum, promising to comply with such demands as did not seem to impair her independence and sovereignty and offering to refer all disputed points to the Hague Tribunal or to a conference of the Great Powers. The Austrian government pronounced the reply evasive and unsatisfactory, broke off diplomatic relations with Serbia, and started the mobilization of her army. The Serbians removed their capital from Belgrade to Nish and began a counter-mobilization. War was clearly impending between Austria-Hungary and Serbia.

But a much vaster and more terrible war was impending. To the Russian view it was obvious that Austria-Hungary was planning to deprive Serbia of independence and to annihilate Russian influence in southeastern Europe. On the other hand the German government insisted that the quarrel was one which concerned Austria-Hungary and Serbia alone: it consistently and pertinaciously opposed the repeated efforts of Russian, British, French, and even Italian, diplomatists to refer the quarrel to an international congress or to the Hague Tribunal. Unequivocally Germany declared that if Russia should come to the assistance of Serbia, she would support Austria-Hungary with all the armed forces at her command. The last resort of an anarchic world was in a test of physical strength, and the most powerful of all the Great Powers, thoroughly possessed of the demon of militarism, was deaf to all suggestions of negotiation and compromise and by threats and imprecations was pushing the whole civilized world to that ultimate anarchic test.

On July 28, 1914, — exactly one month after the archduke's

c

assassination, — Austria-Hungary formally declared war against Serbia. On the next day the Russian government decreed the mobilization of its army. On August 1, the frantic endeavors of various diplomatists to arrive at some peaceful solution of the Serbian problem were rudely arrested by the outbreak of war between Germany and Russia. Germany had presented a twelve-hour ultimatum to Russia, demanding immediate and complete demobilization; Russia had refused to comply; and Germany had declared war.

The German government knew that war with Russia was likely to involve France. France was the sworn ally of Russia. There was popular feeling in France that common cause must be made with Russia if France were to preserve her own prestige and re-cover Alsace-Lorraine. Accordingly, on the very day of deliver-ing the ultimatum to Russia, the German government demanded to know within eighteen hours what would be the attitude of France; if the French government should repudiate its alliance with Russia and promise to observe neutrality, the German am-bassador at Paris was instructed to demand that the powerful French fortress of Toul and Verdun be handed over to Germany for the duration of the war. Apparently the German government was resolved thoroughly to humiliate, if not to crush, France. The French government, however, gave a non-committal answer to the German ultimatum, and began mobilization. On August 3 Germany declared war against France.

Thus, within a week of the declaration of hostilities by Austria-Hungary against Serbia, four Great Powers were in a state of war — Germany and Austria-Hungary against Russia and France. The attitude of the other two Great Powers of Europe — Great Britain and Italy — did not long remain in doubt. Italy promptly proclaimed her neutrality, on the ground that the war waged by her allies was not defensive, but offensive, and that therefore she was not bound to give assistance to them. Great Britain, how-ever, appeared more hesitant. The English people certainly had sympathy for France and little love for Germany, and the British government, though liberal and pacifistic, had already in-formed Germany that, while their country was not formally en-gaged to help France or Russia, they could not promise in case of war to observe neutrality. By August 2, the British govern-ment had gone further and had announced that they would not tolerate German naval attacks on the unprotected western coast of France. And on the next day occurred an event which decided Great Britain to enter the war on the side of Russia and France.

On August 2, — twenty-four hours before the formal declaration of war by Germany against France, — German troops were set in motion toward the French frontier, not directly against the strong French border fortresses of Verdun, Toul, and Belfort, but toward the neutral countries of Luxemburg and Belgium, which lay between Germany and less well-defended districts of northern France. Both Germany and France had signed treaties to respect the neutrality of these "buffer states," and France had already announced her intention of adhering loyally to her treaty engagements. But on August 2 German troops occupied Luxemburg in spite of protests from the grand-duchess of the little state; and on the same day the German government presented an ultimatum to Belgium demanding within twelve hours the grant of permission to move German troops across that country into France, promising, if permission were accorded, to guarantee Belgian independence and integrity and to pay an indemnity, and threatening that, if any resistance should be encountered, Germany would treat Belgium as an enemy and that "the decision of arms" would determine the subsequent relations between the two Powers. The Belgian government characterized the ultimatum as a gross violation of international law and not only refused categorically to grant Germany's request but appealed at once to Great Britain for aid in upholding the neutrality of Belgium.

The neutrality of Belgium had long been a cardinal point in the foreign policy of Great Britain. The British had fought against Napoleon I in part because of the annexation of Belgium by France, and they had opposed the threatened aggression of Napoleon III against the little kingdom; they were not likely to view with favor German attacks upon Belgium or its possible incorporation into the German Empire. On August 4, therefore, when news was received in London that German troops had actually crossed the border into Belgium, Sir Edward Grey, the British foreign secretary, dispatched an ultimatum to Germany, requiring assurance by midnight that Germany would respect Belgian neutrality. Germany refused, on the ground of "military necessity," and Bethmann-Hollweg, the German chancellor, with evidence of anger and disappointment, rebuked Great Britain for making war for "a scrap of paper." The next day, Mr. Asquith, the British prime minister, announced that a state of war existed between Great Britain and Germany.

On August 6, Austria-Hungary declared war on Russia. On the following day little Montenegro joined her fellow-Serb state of Serbia against Austria-Hungary. On August 9, a state of war was proclaimed between Montenegro and Serbia, on one hand, and Germany, on the other ; on August 13, between France and Great Britain, on one hand, and Austria-Hungary, on the other. This completed the first alignment of the European Powers in the Great War : Germany and Austria-Hungary, on the one side, against Russia, France, Great Britain, Serbia, Montenegro, and Belgium, on the other.   It was speedily evident that the opposing combinations were fairly evenly matched in resources, in prowess, and in determination, and that the war would be not only terribly expensive but horribly destructive and long drawn out.   There was no sign that either Germany or Austria-Hungary would consent to make peace separately ; and on the other side, Great Britain, France, and Russia mutually engaged by the Pact of London, of September, 1914, not to conclude peace separately nor to demand terms of peace without the previous agreement of each of the others.

CHAPTER II

GERMANY CONQUERS BELGIUM AND INVADES FRANCE

MOBILIZATION AND STRATEGY

In precipitating the Great War, the German militarists had dictated to the governments and the diplomatists; in waging it, they dictated to the nations. No European people was advised of the actual situation until war had been declared, and every popular demonstration against war was inexorably suppressed. At Berlin meetings of Social Democrats and pacifistic radicals were broken up, and as soon as war was proclaimed a most rigorous censorship of the press was enforced. So skillful were the German Government's pleas "that the sword had been thrust into its hands," so densely ignorant of the real facts were the bulk of the German people, so patriotic were they all, that there was a pathetically general and speedy acquiescence in the decision of the militarists. With the formal order for mobilization, issued in Germany on August 1, 1914, crowds surged through the streets of Berlin cheering and singing patriotic songs. The war found the German nation superbly confident and tremendously loyal. On August 4 the Reichstag unanimously passed all the necessary war bills and authorized extraordinary war credits. This time the Social Democrats joined with the other parties in applauding the Kaiser.

If an aggressive Power could so instantly command the enthusiastic support of all its citizens, it is not surprising that the peoples obviously attacked should rally immediately and whole-heartedly to the military aid of their governments. This was what happened in Serbia, Russia, Belgium, and France. Even in Great Britain, though the resignation of three members of the cabinet on the eve of hostilities indicated opposition to entering the struggle, the appointment of Lord Kitchener as secretary of war and the popular favor accompanying it subsequently signalized the triumph of the war-spirit. From German sources emanated reports that a serious pacifist and Laborite resistance was being encountered by the British government;

on the contrary, a statement issued by representatives of all sections of the labor movement in October, 1914, pledged the loyal support of the British working classes for the war against German militarism, since the victory of the German army "would mean the death of democracy in Europe." All the independent peoples of Europe were loyal to their several Governments. Truly the Great War was to be a War of the Nations.

Before military operations could be inaugurated on a large scale in any theater of the war, the millions of men composing the "citizen armies" of the various Continental belligerents had to be collected, equipped, and sent to the front, that is "mobilized." In time of peace each nation had troops scattered in towns and camps all over the country. Take Germany for example. Germany's standing, or "peace," army was composed of about 800,000 officers and men, organized in twenty-five army corps. On a peace footing, an army corps numbered about 20,000. For war each army corps was raised to a strength of about 43,000 men by the inclusion of "active reserves," *i.e.* men who had recently served and were still under twenty-eight years of age. This gave Germany a field army of over 1,100,000 young trained men. Next, the *Landwehr* or second line, consisting of trained men between twenty-eight and thirty-nine years of age, was called up to reënforce the first line. The *Landwehr* numbered about 2,200,000. The third line or *Landsturm* included 600,000 trained men of middle age, who would be called upon for special aid behind the front and for defense against invasion. In addition Germany had at least 500,000 able-bodied men of military age who had been excused from regular military service and could be used in case of war to replace the wounded and killed. Thus there were military forces in Germany, already trained, amounting to 4,400,000, and of the untrained enough more potential soldiers to bring up the grand total to nearly seven million men. War, therefore, meant military service for some member of almost every family.

The word of mobilization, flashed by telegraph to every corner of the German Empire on August 1, brought the active reserves to the appointed mobilizing center of each army corps. Some German corps were mobilized at frontier towns, such as Strassburg, Metz, Saarburg, and Coblenz. Others had to be transported by rail from the interior. The immensity of this movement may be faintly appreciated when one considers that an army corps required more than one hundred trains, each composed of fifty-five cars, for its transportation. Guns, rations, ammunition, artillery, clothing, hospital supplies, trucks, and horses went with the troops. In many cases the rations and horses had to be purchased from farmers at the beginning of mobilization, and motor trucks and clothing from merchants. The whole railway system was operated by military authorities on a special schedule calculated to bring the troops to the front in the shortest possible time. The huge national army was a perfect mechanism whose delicate adjustments might be thrown into fatal confusion by the blunder of one stupid official or the delay of one special train. Travelers who witnessed the German armies concentrating on the French frontier affirm that the marvelous German mobilization progressed with the precision of clockwork.

In France, in Austria-Hungary, and in Russia, mobilization was slower and less perfect in its appointments. But most reports confirm the impression that both the French and the Russian armies were put in the field with greater celerity and with far less confusion than could have been expected. Great Britain, alone of the belligerents, did not have the general compulsory military service, but her small standing army of 250,000 men was already in a state of high efficiency and preparedness; a hundred thousand volunteers appeared in a day or two; another army of half a million was recruited with little difficulty; and it was estimated that Britain, with her colonies and dependencies, could within three years send four million men to the theater of war.

No less perfect than the organization and movement of the enormous armies was the equipment with which they fought. The Great War was to be a war of machines, waged with the help of every deadly device science could invent. A feature of the conflict in the Franco-Belgian theater was the new Krupp 11-inch howitzer,[1] weighing about seven tons, hauled by powerful motors, and capable of throwing an 11-inch shell at any object within a radius of five miles. But the surpassing achievement of the Krupp gun-factory at Essen in the early stage of the war was the production of a 16-inch (42-centimeter) siege-piece which could be transported by rail and readily emplaced on a concrete foundation. From this mortar, discharged by electricity, a shell one meter in length, weighing almost a ton, and filled with high explosives, could be hurled some fifteen miles.

[1] A "gun" throws its projectile in almost a straight line; a "howitzer" discharges its shell at an angle of elevation varying from fifteen to forty-five degrees; a "mortar" is fired at a still greater angle of elevation, the object being to drop a shell on the top of a fortification or behind the earthworks of the enemy.

In the field much smaller guns were ordinarily used. The German army employed a three-inch gun capable of throwing twenty 15-pound shells a minute at an enemy three miles away. The French field gun (the famous "75") was of slightly smaller bore than the German, but of greater power and weight. Machine guns were used on both sides with telling effect. A machine gun is light enough to be packed on the back of a horse or drawn on a light carriage; it fires from five hundred to seven hundred shots a minute. The regular arm of the infantry was, of course, the rifle, tipped with the bayonet for hand-to-hand encounters; of the various makes, the German Mauser possessed the greatest muzzle velocity, although the French Lebel had a longer effective range.

Airplanes, whose value in warfare had long been discussed, now rendered priceless service, not only for general reconnaissance but also in locating the hostile force so that the artillery officers could instruct their gunners at what angle to fire at the unseen enemy. Even more important than the airplane was the automobile. Motor cars incased in steel and armed with rapid-fire guns accompanied the German cavalry on its swift advance. Speedy automobiles and motorcycles were invaluable for communication where telephone, telegraph, or airplane was not available. Enormous motor trucks, often provided with monster searchlights, were ceaselessly employed in conveying incalculable quantities of foodstuffs.

The Great War originated as a struggle on the part of Austria-Hungary and Germany against the "Slavic Peril," against the great Slav empire of Russia and the small Slav kingdoms of Serbia and Montenegro. But from the very beginning of hostilities, Teutonic defense against Russia was of minor interest as compared with the attack on Belgium and France. The reason was quite simple. The German General Staff had planned to hurl the bulk of the German army first against France and then, having crushed France, to transfer it to the east to turn back the tide of Russia's slow-mobilizing multitudes. For Russia, with all her 180 millions of inhabitants in Europe and in Asia, was spread over so vast an area and was so deficient in railways that ten of her thirty-six army corps could not arrive on the scene within two months, and the remaining twenty-six were not expected to begin a serious attack within the first few weeks of the war. Germany would leave a small force of her own to coöperate with Austro-Hungarian armies in holding back the

Russian advance-guard, while with the rest she would overwhelm France. The German armies in the west would sweep across Belgium — with its network of convenient railways and smooth highways — turning the flank of the strong line of French fortifications along the Franco-German frontier, and swoop down upon Paris with irresistible might. The French army annihilated, the German troops could be shifted from the west to the east (it is less than 600 miles from Belgium to Russia, that is, about the distance from New York to Cleveland), and reserves could be brought up to defeat the oncoming Russians.

The French plan of defense had originally been based on the assumption that the neutrality of Belgium and Luxemburg would be respected. To appreciate the importance of the neutrality of these "buffer" states, one needs only to observe that with Belgium and Luxemburg neutral, approximately half of the northern frontier of France was immune from attack. The eastern half of that frontier, from Luxemburg to Switzerland, was defended by the Vosges mountains and by a line of fortified towns from Verdun through Toul and Épinal to Belfort. French mobilization, moreover, was directed so as to place the main strength of the French army in the trenches and forts along the Franco-German frontier proper, if not actually to take the offensive in this region. If the Germans endeavored to strike into France from Lorraine, they would encounter the bulk of the French army intrenched along a strong line of defense.

As events proved, the German military authorities had determined to deliver the chief attack not from Lorraine but from Belgium and Luxemburg. By adopting this course, Germany brought 150,000 Belgians into the field as enemies and three British army corps whom Lord Kitchener dispatched as an Expeditionary Force to aid the French and Belgians. But the immediate advantages to be gained were considered more important by the Germans than the addition of 300,000 soldiers to the enemy's ranks. The Belgian forces were of the nature of militia rather than of a perfect military machine; and the small British Expeditionary Force — all that un-military Great Britain could at that time put in the field — was referred to by the Kaiser as a "contemptible little army." As yet the Germans had formed no idea of the dogged determination and enormous resources of the British, and they failed utterly to comprehend the strength of the moral indignation with which the whole world would view the violation of Belgium's neutrality. It was the price they must pay for intrusting all decisions to the militarists and for basing all actions on "military necessity."

Meanwhile the attack on France by way of Belgium appealed irresistibly to the German military mind. In the first place, through Belgium and Luxemburg, German armies would have two natural routes leading into the heart of France. The northern route, leading from the German military bases at Cologne and Aix-la-Chapelle through Liège, Namur, and Maubeuge, was that of the main railway between Berlin and Paris; the network of roads and railways in Belgium and northern France would facilitate the transportation of troops and supplies, and the comparatively level country would admit of the extensive use of the famous Krupp howitzers. The other route followed the Moselle valley from the German base of Coblenz on the Rhine through Trier up to Luxemburg and thence entered France at Longwy and passed south to Verdun.

In the second place, the French did not possess such formidable defenses along the frontier opposite Belgium and Luxemburg as those opposite Lorraine and Alsace: Dunkirk, Lille, and Maubeuge could not compare with Verdun, Toul, Épinal, and Belfort. In the third place, the use of routes through the "buffer" states would enable the German General Staff to put its entire effective forces immediately in the field and to use them in decisive flanking movements rather than in protracted frontal attacks. Finally, and perhaps this was the most important consideration, a swift incursion of German armies by way of Belgium and Luxemburg would compel the French army to change the front of its mobilization from the Lorraine frontier to the Belgian; and in attempting to re-form its lines the French army might conceivably be thrown into such confusion and disorder that a gigantic victory — a Sedan on a colossal scale — might be won by the Germans. This was the supreme purpose of German strategy, to demoralize and break up the French field army. Paris could be taken later.

The nineteen army corps which Germany had immediately available for the invasion of France were grouped in seven great armies; three were detailed to cut a swath through central Belgium, past Maubeuge, and down the Oise; two were sent through Luxemburg and southeastern Belgium (Belgian Luxemburg); and two were stationed in Alsace-Lorraine. The seven main armies were: (1) General von Kluck's army, north of the Meuse; (2) General von Bülow's, south of the Meuse; (3) General von Hausen's, directed against Givet; (4) Duke

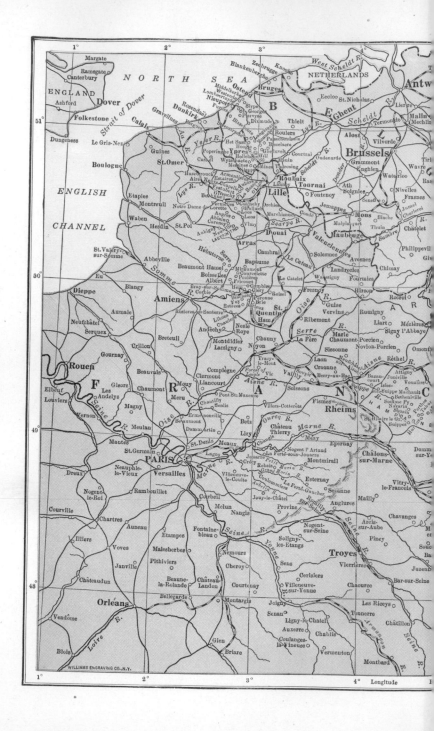

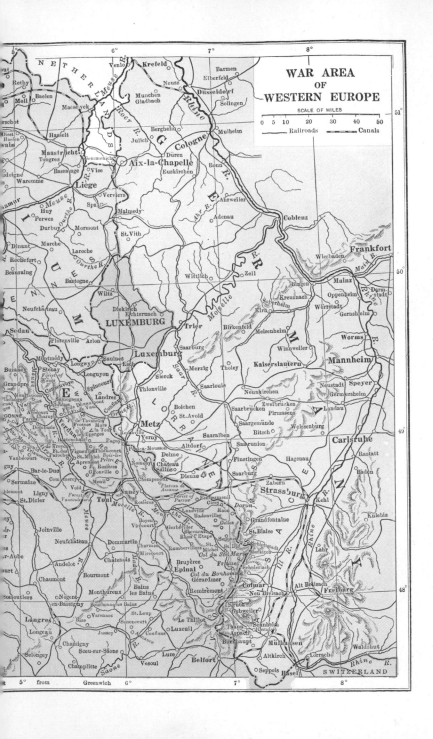

WAR AREA
OF
WESTERN EUROPE

SCALE OF MILES

0 5 10   20   30   40   50

Railroads   Canals

Albert of Württemberg's, directed against southeastern Belgium; (5) the Prussian Crown Prince's, occupying Luxemburg; (6) the Bavarian Crown Prince's, based on Metz; (7) General von Heeringen's, based on Strassburg. It seemed a happy omen that over all these armies the supreme German commander, the chief of the General Staff, was Helmuth von Moltke, a nephew of that illustrious Moltke who had overwhelmed France in 1870. A detachment of the first army was intrusted to General von Emmich for the immediate task of seizing Liège.

THE CONQUEST OF BELGIUM

From the German frontier, opposite Aix-la-Chapelle, to the gap of the Oise, on the Franco-Belgian frontier, it would be six days' march for an unresisted German army. But the Belgians were unanimously and heroically determined to resist Germany's outrageous violation of their country's neutrality. In the face of national disaster, and in an unparalleled outburst of national patriotism, even the most fundamental party differences and social distinctions were swept aside. "Irreconcilable" Socialists sprang to the support of their plucky King; and the Socialist leader, Émile Vandervelde, entered the Catholic cabinet on August 4. Belgium had nothing to gain from the war; she was resolved that it should not take from her the most priceless treasure of her plighted word and national honor.

Situated just across the Belgian frontier and directly in the path of the German advance from Cologne up the valley of the Meuse was the strongly fortified city of Liège. Against Liège the detachment of General von Emmich struck on August 4. So anxious were the German military authorities not to lose time, that Emmich recklessly sacrificed his men in futile attempts to carry the city by assault. Compact masses of German soldiery were hurled against the Belgian forts, only to be mowed down by murderous artillery fire or annihilated by exploding mines. Assault failing, Emmich brought up giant 42-centimeter howitzers which speedily demolished some of the forts encircling the city and enabled the Germans to enter the town on August 7. It was not until eight days later, however, that the last of the encircling forts was silenced.

After the fall of Liège, the German cavalry swept over the neighboring country and the German armies penetrated Belgium. Constant skirmishing marked the retirement of the main Belgian force to its principal line of defense at Louvain. There, on August 19, the Belgian army made its last important stand against overwhelming odds, was defeated, and the greater part of it was driven back in a northwesterly direction on Malines and Antwerp. General von Kluck, after dispatching a force to press the retreat of the Belgians northward, entered Brussels on August 20, and then, with the principal part of his army, swung southward in the direction of Mons and Maubeuge. Meanwhile, the armies of General von Hausen and Duke Albert of Württemberg were striking into the hilly country of the Ardennes in southeastern Belgium; and between the forces of Kluck and Hausen, General von Bülow was pursuing a small Belgian detachment up the Meuse to the fortress of Namur. On August 22 Namur succumbed to Bülow's siege howitzers, and the way was at length cleared for a German invasion of France. Belgian resistance had meant that the German march across Belgium had taken eighteen days instead of six and that both the French and the British had been given a longer respite in which to prepare their defense.

The French were unable to come to the immediate assistance of the Belgians, because their mobilization, as the enemy anticipated, was proceeding along the Franco-German frontier proper, and General Joffre, the French commander-in-chief, was unwilling to risk too sudden a disarrangement of his plans. As some relief to the hard-pressed Belgians, however, General Joffre ordered a counter-offensive against Alsace-Lorraine. In the extreme south, an army stepped over into Alsace at Altkirch, carried the German trenches there on August 7, and on the next day occupied the city of Mülhausen. Driven out, the French reëntered Mülhausen on August 19. General Paul Pau was in actual charge of this invasion of Alsace and was hailed as a liberator by a large part of the population, which had never ceased to long for reunion with France, although more than a generation had passed since Alsace-Lorraine was appropriated by German conquerors. General Pau's forces penetrated as far north as Colmar.

Simultaneously other troops mastered the difficult passes of the Vosges mountains and descended from the west into the Alsatian valleys. Further north, General Castelnau with five army corps invaded Lorraine, and took Saarburg on August 18. But here the French advance was halted. With slower mobilization, Joffre was unable to reënforce the army corps in Alsace-Lorraine and at the same time to take needful measures of precaution against the rapidly growing German menace from

Belgium and Luxemburg. French armies had to be moved up to face the Duke of Württemberg and the Prussian Crown Prince in the region of the forest of the Ardennes in southeastern Belgium. Another French army, under General Lanrezac, had to be dispatched to the Belgian border, for the two or three British corps which had been hurried to France and which by August 21 had managed to take up a defensive position north of Maubeuge on a line from Condé in France to Mons in Belgium, were far too few to make a decisive stand against the German hordes; General Lanrezac took position, on the British right flank, in the angle formed between the Sambre and Meuse rivers south of Namur.

In the four days, August 20–23, the advanced Franco-British lines made an unsuccessful attempt to stay the German conquest of Belgium, and the French counter-offensive in Alsace-Lorraine definitely failed. In Lorraine, General Castelnau's invading army was attacked from three sides at once by General von Heeringen, the Bavarian Crown Prince, and garrison forces from Metz. For the first time under fire, one French corps suddenly gave way, and Castelnau was able to extricate his defeated army only with the greatest difficulty. He now took the defensive before Nancy. In southern Alsace, the French invaders were compelled to retreat as rapidly as they had advanced and to abandon nearly all the ground they had won. The French counter-offensive had been politically advantageous in that it had strengthened French morale and had stirred up all France to seek the reconquest of the "lost provinces," but from a strictly military standpoint it had been unsuccessful if not disastrous.

There remained the principal business of giving aid to the hard-pressed Belgians and of checking the flood of German invasion before it had rolled quite to the French frontier. On August 20, with the arrival of the British Expeditionary Force under Field Marshal Sir John French and with the posting of a French army south of Namur and of two other French armies in the Ardennes, General Joffre gave orders for an offensive.

On the next two days the French offensive in southeastern Belgium broke down completely. "There were imprudences committed under German fire, divisions ill-engaged, rash deployments, a premature waste of men, and a notable incompetence of certain French troops and their commanders." [1] The French were soon in precipitate retreat from the Ardennes toward Sedan,

[1] From the French official report.

Montmédy, and Longwy, across the border. To the west, the Allies still had a chance of success if General Lanrezac's army and the British could obtain a decisive result.

This was unfortunately not the case. General Lanrezac's right flank was too exposed as a result of the French retirement from the Ardennes, and by the fall of Namur on August 22 he was exposed to the powerful blows of Bülow's army. After a savage struggle at Charleroi on August 22–23, he retired up the Meuse to the French border towns of Givet and Maubeuge. Now the British army was endangered: it lacked support on its right, and in front and on the left appeared four German army corps. Obviously General von Kluck intended to overwhelm the two British corps and turn the flank of the allied line. Unwilling to be either outflanked or overwhelmed, General French abandoned his precarious position after a hot contest at Mons, August 23–24, and conducted a hasty retreat — an orderly flight, one might say — back into France. Trenches had been prepared at the line Cambrai-Le Cateau-Landrecies; but the continued pressure of Kluck's superior numbers forced the British to continue their flight. In six days' retreat, hotly pursued by Kluck's cavalry and armored motor cars, struggling desperately to prevent its artillery and supplies from falling into the enemy's hands, the little British army lost 230 officers and 13,413 men.

Most of Belgium was conquered by the Germans and the route to France was now cleared.

THE INVASION OF FRANCE

The sensational retreat of Sir John French from Belgium far back into France should be regarded as but one detail of the general strategic retreat ordered by General Joffre after the French defeats of August 20–23. The fate of the whole French army depended upon avoiding a decisive battle until the French forces could be concentrated upon an advantageous battle-line and could confront the Germans with equal or superior numbers. It would have been folly to rush troops northward to sure defeat. General Joffre, therefore, ordered a strategic retreat southward.

Into France poured the German armies. Occasionally they were obstructed for a few hours by a fortress-garrison or by the allies' turning at bay in order to save the retreat from becoming a rout. Past the border towns of Lille, Valenciennes, Maubeuge, Mézières, Montmédy, and Longwy swept the German forces down over northern France. By September 2 the invasion had progressed far. General von Kluck's army had passed Compiègne; General von Bülow had reached Laon; General von Hausen had crossed the Aisne near Attigny; the duke of Württemberg and the Prussian Crown Prince had advanced to the upper Aisne and taken positions between Vouziers and Verdun; to the east, the sixth and seventh German armies faced the French fortresses of Verdun, Toul, Épinal, and Belfort.

Hastily the French government-offices were removed from Paris to Bordeaux; General Galliéni began to prepare the metropolis for siege; and as General von Kluck, on the extreme German right, swiftly pursued the British and a newly organized French army southward, until the din of battle could be heard by the Parisians, the prediction seemed about to be verified that the Germans would be in Paris six weeks after the declaration of war. By September 5, though the eastern fortresses of France were still holding, the Germans were threatening them from the rear and were already in possession of St. Menehould, Châlons, and Esternay.

After their long and exhausting retreat the French armies stood with their left resting on Paris, their right holding Verdun, and their center sagging south of the Marne. In reality Verdun was a central salient extending far into the German lines rather than the extreme right of the French lines, for in the east French and German armies faced each other from Verdun to the Swiss border in a line almost at right angles with the Paris-Verdun line. The French armies had now reached the ultimate points of retreat; for the first time they and the British army were in touch with one another all along the line; and on September 5 General Joffre issued his famous order for commencing the battle of the Marne. "The hour has come," he wrote, "to advance at all costs, and to die where you stand rather than give way."

On the eve of the battle of the Marne, the German General Staff was preparing to deliver a crushing blow against the French armies. On the extreme right of the German line, General Kluck had suddenly swerved from north of Paris toward the southeast and was marching on Meaux and Coulommiers. Obviously it was planned for him to coöperate with Generals Bülow and Hausen in concentrating the force of a gigantic and decisive blow against the center of the Paris-Verdun allied line, between Sézanne and Vitry-le-François. If the Germans could break through the center, the French armies would be separated; those in the west might be driven into Paris and obliged in time to surrender, while those in the east would be ground to pieces on the Verdun-Belfort line of fortresses between the armies of the Prussian Crown Prince, and the Bavarian Crown Prince, and General von Heeringen.

The French center stood firm against the German onset, however, and the battle of the Marne, September 6–12, marked the culmination and the decline of the German invasion. As a matter of fact, the "battle of the Marne" is merely a conventional name to designate a whole series of desperate battles that were waged almost simultaneously along the entire line from Paris to Belfort. On the extreme west of the line a brilliant manœuver of the allies led to a serious German reverse. Here a newly organized French army under General Maunoury, moving out eastward from Paris, fell upon the right of Kluck's exposed forces. Turning west to confront these new assailants, Kluck was attacked from the south by Sir John French's British army and from the southeast by a French army under General Franchet d'Esperey. By dint of desperate fighting he escaped from the jaws of the Anglo-French trap and gradually shifted his army northwards to shake off the French forces which clung to his right flank. The harder Kluck was pressed, the fiercer were the attacks which the Germans directed at the French center, particularly in the neighborhood of Sézanne and Fère-Champenoise. Here was the most critical position, and here was the most furious fighting. That the French were able at this crucial point not only to hold their own but to force the Germans back was due to the heroism and *élan* of the common soldiers and to the remarkable military genius of their commanding officer, General Ferdinand Foch. Foch's brilliant qualities were supremely tested at Fère-Champenoise. Without his army and his generalship, the battle of the Marne might have been a signal disaster to France.

Even the allied manœuver against Kluck and the success of Foch might not have availed the French in the extended battle of the Marne if the Germans had been able in the east to turn the line of French fortresses extending from Verdun to Belfort. The Germans did their best to turn this line. While the armies of the Bavarian Crown Prince and General von Heeringen endeavored to batter the fortifications from the direction of Lorraine and Alsace, the Prussian Crown Prince was struggling to penetrate south through the region of the Argonne, between Verdun and the rest of France, and thereby to complete, from the west, the surrounding of the fortified line. The fate that had already overtaken Liège, Namur, and the fortresses of northern France made the French properly apprehensive of trusting to the protection of forts against heavy German artillery. The French understood that the defense of Verdun and the other eastern fortresses would have to be undertaken in the field. Thus it transpired that, at the very moment when at the west Kluck was being forced back and in the center Foch was valiantly gaining ground, French armies were fighting equally decisive battles in the Argonne and before Nancy. In the Argonne, General Sarrail finally stopped the advance of the Prussian Crown Prince. Before Nancy, General Castelnau, with superb tenacity, held his position against the superior numbers of the easternmost German armies and even forced them back to the Vosges mountains.

Against the solid wall of French resistance, German attacks were everywhere unavailing. Everywhere the French advanced: they recrossed the Marne; they retook Châlons and Rheims; they were not halted until they had reached the Aisne and had delivered the eastern fortresses from immediate danger.

Such was the seven days' battle of the Marne, in which more than two millions of men were engaged. It was won by troops who for two weeks had been retreating and who had to meet practically the whole German army. In spite of the fatigue of the allied forces, in spite of the German heavy artillery, the victorious armies captured an enormous quantity of supplies and thousands of prisoners. The battle of the Marne completely upset the strategy of the German General Staff. It signified that while France might be invaded, France was not to be crushed and conquered.

When the French and British pushed north after the battle of the Marne, they were halted abruptly on September 12 at the Aisne. It was soon clear that the Germans were not simply pausing in their retreat but were occupying a battle-line of great natural strength, prepared with trenches for infantry and with concrete foundations for the big German guns. From the hills of Noyon, just north of where the Aisne flows into the Oise, the line followed the heights on the northern bank of the Aisne as far as Berry-au-Bac and then, leaving the Aisne, it bent southward almost to Rheims and extended across the forested ridge of the Argonne to the region of Verdun. A French drive was directed northward against Laon; a German drive, southward against Rheims. Both were checked. After an excessively

D

vigorous and destructive bombardment of Rheims on September
19–20, the battle along the Aisne practically came to a close,
although the opposing armies viewed each other fiercely from
their parallel lines of trenches.

While the armies in the center were coming to a deadlock,
events of great interest were transpiring on both wings.   On
the east, the Prussian Crown Prince sent large forces to cut in

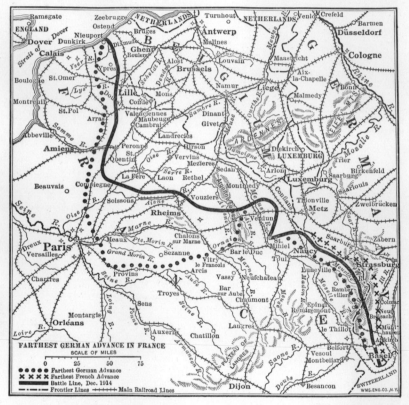

FARTHEST GERMAN ADVANCE IN FRANCE
SCALE OF MILES

0   25   50   75

●●●● Farthest German Advance
×××× Farthest French Advance
▬▬▬ Battle Line, Dec. 1914
——— Frontier Lines ++++++ Main Railroad Lines

south of Verdun.   The Germans had already reduced the fort
of Troyon, just south of Verdun, and had reached St. Mihiel,
a little further south on the Meuse, thus threatening to surround
Verdun, when the French reënforced their line at this point.   St.
Mihiel continued, however, to be an additional outer defense for
Metz and a possible starting point for a strong German offensive.
In upper Alsace the French managed to cling to the town of
Thann as a base for further operations in the "lost provinces."

On the west of the long battle-line, the Germans and the French engaged in a "race to the sea." French troops were hurried northward by way of Amiens in the hope of enveloping the right wing of General von Kluck's army, and German troops were hastily marched northward to frustrate the French flanking movement. The net result was the extension of the battle-line, almost at right angles with the Aisne sector, from Noyon to Flanders and the Channel coast. The Germans possessed themselves of Cambrai, Douai, and Lille; the French saved Amiens, Arras, Ypres, and Dunkirk.

Since the last days of August the small Belgian army had been annoying the Germans by occasionally sallying forth from its positions at Malines and Antwerp. So long as these cities remained in Belgian hands, they constituted potential points of support for a large Franco-British expedition which might be landed on the northern Belgian coast and thence harass the rear of the German line. On September 27 the Germans bombarded and occupied Malines, and on the following day began in earnest to attack the supposedly impregnable stronghold of Antwerp. A small force of British and French bluejackets was sent to the aid of the defenders, but too small to be of any avail. The German artillery pounded the Belgian fortifications to bits. During the night of October 8 the allied forces forsook the doomed city, and on the following day the Germans entered in triumph. The survivors of the heroic little Belgian army were transferred to the extreme left flank of the allied line in Flanders.

Had the Allies been able to retain Antwerp, they might conceivably have stretched their long line in a northeasterly direction from Ypres past Ghent to the stronghold of Antwerp itself and thereby have retained the whole Belgian coast and been in a strategically ·favorable position from which to launch a huge offensive against the Germans. The sorry loss of Antwerp was due in part to mismanagement on the part of the British authorities in London, and in greater part to the hard, cold fact that the Allies were not prepared either in men or in equipment for such an extension of their battle-line as the retention of Antwerp would involve. As it was, the Germans were enabled not only to occupy Antwerp but also to appropriate Ghent, Bruges, and the coast towns of Zeebrugge and Ostend.

German possession of coast towns would menace England by providing bases for submarines and perhaps by cutting England's communications with France. For these reasons the

Germans desired to capture the French towns of Dunkirk, Calais, and Boulogne, as well as the Belgian ports of Zeebrugge and Ostend. Consequently, as soon as they had taken Antwerp, they massed three armies under the duke of Württemberg, the Bavarian Crown Prince, and General von Bülow, respectively, for a drive towards the Straits of Dover. In the last week of October, almost simultaneously, these armies furiously assailed the Allied line along the Yser, at Ypres, at La Bassée, and before Arras. The terrific battle of Flanders was on. At first the brunt of the conflict was borne by the battered Belgian army, which held Duke Albert of Württemberg back of the Yser until British warships could draw into range and open fire with their heavy guns, forcing the Germans to desist. Further inland, between Nieuport and Ypres, the German advance was checked, after other means had failed, by the desperate expedient of cutting the dikes and flooding the country. The town of Dixmude, in this region, was finally won by the Germans. Further south, the Bavarian Crown Prince managed after five days' intense fighting to advance the few miles from La Bassée to Neuve Chapelle, but no nearer the coast could he go. Still further south General von Bülow drove hard against Arras, but the French, under General Maud'huy, held their ground most tenaciously. Near Ypres, however, the Germans delivered their most savage and protracted assaults. The brave British army, reënforced by colonials and French troops, was beaten back a little, but its line was not broken. The Germans' effort to reach the Channel ports was as much a failure in October and November as had been their attempt to smash the whole French army in August and September.

By the middle of November, the battle of Flanders, like the battle of the Aisne, had lost its fury and become a dreary process of trench-digging with intermittent cannonading. Here and there a few hundred yards could be gained by one side or the other by hurling masses of infantry at the opposing trenches, but for such sacrifice the strategic gain was small. The rigors of winter, moreover, now added to the sufferings of the soldiers, who had to settle down in trenches filled with mud and water if not with ice and snow.

The battle-line established after the struggles on the Aisne and in Flanders extended some six hundred miles from the coast of the Channel to the border of Switzerland; of this long line the Belgians at the close of 1914 held about eighteen miles and the British about thirty-one, while the French armies, two and a half millions strong, defended. the remaining 543 miles. By this time the line had become almost stationary, and was so

ALLIES' WESTERN FRONT, DECEMBER, 1914

formidably intrenched and fortified that it could not possibly be broken except at a terrible cost of life and with an enormous expenditure of shells.

GERMAN GAINS IN THE WEST — AND FAILURE

What had the Germans gained by their attack upon Belgium and France? In the first place, they were in military occupation of the whole kingdom of Belgium except a tiny strip in the southwest corner extending from Nieuport to Ypres. The Belgian government was exiled to Havre in France, and the Belgian people were ruled by a German military governor at Brussels. To the already great industrial resources of Germany were now added those of Belgium, and by forced levies the conquerors obtained goods and money from the vanquished as aids to the prosecution of the war. The invasion of Belgium, however, had contributed directly to bringing Great Britain into the war, and the horrors amid which the conquest of Belgium was consummated aroused the liveliest enmity of the whole Belgian people and the keenest sympathy of neutral nations as well as of the Allies. The Germans had won Belgian territory but no Belgian hearts.

A large part of the city of Louvain, including the famous

Catholic university and church of St. Peter, was deliberately razed by the Germans, because, said the German official report, the civilian population had concerted an attack on the German troops which occupied the town. The vandalism at Louvain especially shocked the consciences of civilized men, but it was only one of numerous similar instances where towns or villages had been ruthlessly burned and many of their inhabitants shot or outraged. The spirit which prompted these acts may be judged by an extract from the proclamation of General von Bülow to the citizens of Liège: "The inhabitants of the town of Ardennes, after having declared their peaceful intentions, have made a surprise attack on our troops. It is with my approval that the commander has ordered the whole town to be burned and that about a hundred persons have been shot. I bring this to the knowledge of the city of Liège so that its citizens may realize the fate with which they are menaced if they adopt a similar attitude." In the town of Wavre, the German general demanded a war levy of three million francs as a fine for the resistance offered by the inhabitants, and threatened: "The town will be burned and utterly destroyed if the levy is not paid in due time, without regard for anyone; the innocent will suffer with the guilty." This was precisely the most distressing circumstance, that the innocent were made to suffer with the guilty. Evidence collected on oath by French and British commissions of inquiry tended to show that in countless cases the worst horrors of war had been inflicted on innocent women and children. For instance, at Sommeilles, which was burned by the Germans on September 6, two women, and four children aged respectively eleven, five, four, and one, were afterwards discovered lying in a pool of blood in a cellar where they had been cruelly butchered. For such heinous crimes, for such violation of international law and common decency, the Germans offered the curious pleas of "military necessity" and "war is war."

Against German perfidy and German "frightfulness," the Belgians found a courageous and able advocate in Cardinal Mercier, archbishop of Malines and primate of the Catholic Church in Belgium. He was indefatigable in protesting against the German conquest, in comforting his compatriots, and in appealing to the Vatican and foreign Powers for aid. In vain the German administration sought to silence him or to nullify his efforts. In a famous pastoral letter addressed to his priests on Christmas Day, 1914, the venerable prelate wrote: "I have traversed the greater part of the districts most terribly devastated in my diocese, and the ruins I beheld, and the ashes, were more dreadful than I, prepared by the saddest forebodings, could have imagined. . . . Churches, schools, asylums, hospitals, convents, in great numbers, are in ruins. Entire villages have all but disappeared. . . . God will save Belgium, my brethren, ye cannot doubt it. Nay rather, He is saving her. . . . Is there a patriot among us who does not know that Belgium has grown great? Which of us would have the courage to tear out this last page of our national history? Which of us does not exult in the brightness of the glory of this shattered nation?"

To the eloquent words of Cardinal Mercier should be added the work of the special commission dispatched by the Belgian government from Havre to the United States and the active Belgian propaganda carried on in England. The wrongs done Belgium were ceaselessly reviewed. One noteworthy result was the organization of relief, chiefly under American auspices; for two years and a half, Mr. Brand Whitlock, the United States minister at Brussels, coöperated with various Belgian and foreign societies, in attempting to lessen the misery and suffering of millions of men and women in Belgium. Another result was the increasing fervor of the British in prosecuting the war. The "assassination of Belgium" became one of the most effective aids to Lord Kitchener in securing volunteers for his armies. The British Expeditionary Force, which in August, 1914, amounted to but 150,000, was thenceforth steadily augmented until by April, 1915, it numbered at least 750,000, to say nothing of colonial troops that were arriving from Canada, Australia, New Zealand, and even India.

What had the Germans gained? In the first place, they had gained Belgium — but also the hatred of the Belgian people, the ever greater and more determined hostility of the British at home and overseas, and the suspicion and horror of nearly the whole world. Incidentally, they had opened up a more strategically suitable route for their major attack upon France. In the second place, they had invaded France and possessed themselves of a fairly large strip of northern French territory, including the populous towns of Lille, St. Quentin, Douai, Valenciennes, Maubeuge, Sedan, Montmédy, Vervins, and Laon. Though the occupied territory constituted only about one-twentieth of the total area of European France, it was a fraction which, because of its industrial and mining wealth, was of great importance for the successful conduct of the war. It included ninety per cent. of France's iron ore, eighty per cent. of her iron and steel manufactures, and seventy per cent. of her coal resources. Despite this serious handicap, however, France was not crushed. Her armies were intact. Her government had returned from Bordeaux to Paris in December, 1914. Her national spirit was quickened. Her confidence in ultimate victory was superb. The strategy of the German General Staff on the Western Front had failed. The Germans had not attained their objectives.

The invasion of France in the late summer of 1914 had exposed a momentous fallacy. The belief that before the terrific on-slaught of the German armies, with their swift mobilization, their unrivaled discipline, and their ponderous howitzers, the French people would prove themselves cowardly, decadent, and excitable, and the armed resistance of France would wither and crumple up, was definitely relegated to the realm of fancy by the absolutely calm and heroic conduct of the French during the crisis and by the battle of the Marne. The magnificent holding battle fought by the French along the line from Paris to Verdun, after a long and discouraging retreat, effectually dispelled the illusion that the swift Prussian victory over France in 1870 could be repeated in 1914. That the omens had fickly changed was evidenced in the autumn of 1914 by the supersession of Helmuth von Moltke as Chief of the German General Staff by Erich von Falkenhayn, the Prussian minister of war.

The German General Staff had planned to overcome France quickly and then turn its whole force against Russia. Unable to overcome France, what would it do with Russia?

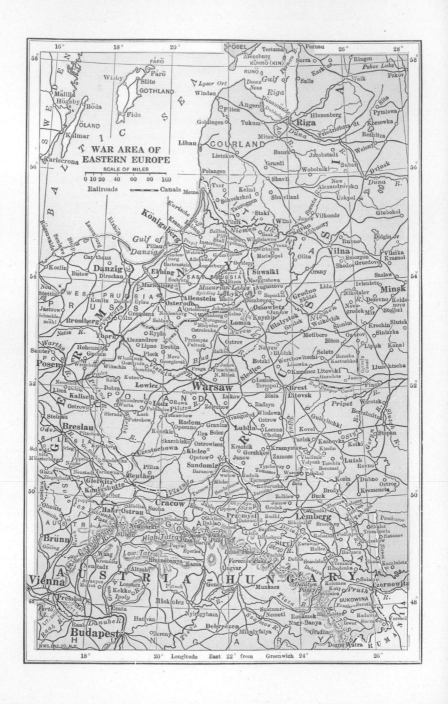

CHAPTER III

RUSSIA FAILS TO OVERWHELM GERMANY

THE RUSSIAN INVASION OF EAST PRUSSIA

ONE significant effect of the German failure speedily to crush France was the inability of the German General Staff to transfer its main forces from the west to the east before the first Russian armies had been mobilized. As a matter of fact the mobilization of the Russian "hordes" proceeded practically unhindered and with unexpected rapidity. By the third week of August, some two million Russian soldiers were under arms; and of the twenty-six Russian army corps then available, eight were assigned to deal with the five left in the east by Germany, and eighteen were massed against the Austrians' twelve.

As the gigantic battles in northern France assumed more and more the character of a deadlock between intrenched troops, the Allies looked to Russia to invade Germany with her vast armies and compel Germany to turn attention to the east. It was generally assumed that the Russians would sweep like a tidal wave toward Berlin, while the weakened German battle-line in the west would be beaten back out of France and Belgium. But month after month dragged by, and although the fighting forces surged back and forth on the eastern frontier of Germany there was little sign of the "tidal wave."

In order to understand the failure of the Russians in the early stages of the war to overwhelm Germany in the east, one must realize that Russia had to battle not only against the well-trained and perfectly equipped soldiers of Germany, and the somewhat less efficient soldiers of Austria-Hungary, but also against geography. European Russia, it should be observed, formed a huge wedge, with Russian Poland as the rather blunt point of the wedge, thrust in between German East Prussia on the north and Austrian Galicia on the south. The point of the wedge was less than two hundred miles from Berlin, but before the wedge could be driven into Germany, the Germans would have to be crowded out of East Prussia and the Austrians out

of Galicia.   In other words, no army would be safe in proceeding
from Russian Poland against Berlin so long as the Germans from
the north and the Austrians from the south could close in and
cut off the communications of that army with its sources of supply
in Russia.   For this reason the Russian generalissimo, the Grand
Duke Nicholas, instead of marching his chief armies straight
westward from Warsaw to Berlin, deflected them to the north
and to the south.

To the north lay East Prussia, and hither the Russians penetrated about the middle of August.   In invading East Prussia,
the Russians would have to overcome three serious obstacles.
First there was a chain of almost impassable lakes, marshes,
and rivers, stretching from Johannisberg to Insterburg.   Behind this lake barrier lay the fortified camp of Königsberg with
one German army corps, in the north, and Allenstein, with another army corps, in the south.   Still further west was the strong
line of the Vistula river, defended by Danzig, Marienburg,
Graudenz, and Thorn.   The main bodies of Russian invaders
avoided the lake country near the eastern frontier of East
Prussia.   One Russian army, under General Rennenkampf,
proceeded directly westward from Kovno, defeated the Germans
at Gumbinnen on August 17–20, pressed on to Insterburg, and
drove the Königsberg army corps to the shelter of its fortifications.   Simultaneously another and larger Russian army invaded East Prussia from the south, between the lake barrier
on the east and the Vistula on the west, and with dash and vigor
took Allenstein and pressed back a second German army corps.

But suddenly, as they turned westward, the Russians discovered on their flank three fresh German army corps which
had hastily been brought up by rail and detrained near Allenstein.   In the battle that then took place, August 26–31, in
the neighborhood of Tannenburg and the Masurian lakes, the
Russian army was enveloped and completely routed.   At the
end of the contest, the German commander, General von Hindenburg, could report the capture of 90,000 Russians, including two
generals, besides the equipment and supplies of three whole
army corps.   The news reached Berlin in time to transform the
anniversary of Sedan (September 1) into a triumphal celebration
of Hindenburg's great victory.   The German general followed
up his success by driving the Russians out of East Prussia.   The
Russian invasion of East Prussia had definitely failed.   Hindenburg was the "man of the hour"; he was to all the German
people both savior and hero; and the Kaiser promptly raised

him to the rank of Field Marshal and made him generalissimo of the armies in the East.

On September 15, Hindenburg passed the East Prussian border on a wide front and carried the war into the Russian district of Suwalki. Rennenkampf retired before him, fighting rearguard actions, until the Niemen river was reached. Here the Russian commander, reënforced from Kovno and Vilna, turned at bay. In vain did the Germans struggle to effect a crossing of the Niemen. Unable to make further headway, Hindenburg late in September ordered a retreat to the East Prussian frontier. This time it was the Russian army which followed and harassed a retiring foe. In the vicinity of Augustovo Rennenkampf inflicted a serious defeat upon Hindenburg early in October; and the Germans found no rest or safety until they were again on their own soil. If the Russians had failed to conquer East Prussia, so too had the Germans failed to invade Russia from East Prussia.

It had been proved alike to the Russians and to the Germans that East Prussia was an isolated area splendidly fitted by nature for defense but poorly adapted as a base for offense. Between Russian Poland and Austrian Galicia, however, there were no such natural barriers. Galicia was not an isolated area, nor was it defended by a Hindenburg or by perfectly disciplined German troops. To Galicia, therefore, the Russians directed their major attention.

THE RUSSIAN INVASION OF GALICIA

At the outbreak of the Great War it had fallen to the lot of the Austrians to bear the brunt of the struggle with Russia, while the Germans were conquering Belgium and France. It was a hard lot, for Austria-Hungary as a military Power was far less efficient than Germany; she was a hodge-podge of quarrelsome nationalities; and now she had to wage war on the Bosnian front against Serbia and Montenegro and keep a reserve force at Trieste and in the Trentino against the possible intervention of Italy as well as to defend Galicia. Galicia belonged naturally and geographically to Russia and Poland, for from Austria proper and from Hungary it was separated by the range of the Carpathians. To be sure, an invading army would have to cross numerous rivers with which Galicia was provided, and would have to encounter very strong fortifications which Austria had erected at Lemberg, at Jaroslav and Przemysl, and at

Cracow. But after all, the best means of defending Galicia would probably be an attack upon Russian Poland before the Russians were fully mobilized.

Accordingly, two Austro-Hungarian armies, numbering 300,000 men each, were collected in Galicia early in August, 1914. The one, commanded by General Dankl, was based on the fortresses of Przemysl and Jaroslav and was destined for an invasion of Russian Poland on a front east and west from Tomasov to the Vistula. The other, under General von Auffenburg, was based on Lemberg and extended north and south from the upper waters of the Bug to the town of Halicz, at right angles with General Dankl's. On August 10 General Dankl crossed the frontier, captured Krasnik, won successes near Lublin, and pressed the Russians under General Ivanov back over the Bug river.

The Russians had not planned to attack Galicia from the north. Their mobilization was proceeding more to the east, especially at Lutsk, Dubno, and Kiev. Their real plans were gradually disclosed when they at once retired before Dankl and assailed Auffenburg in full force. On August 14, General Ruzsky, with a large Russian army, based on Lutsk and Dubno, moved over the northeastern boundary of Galicia, captured Sokal, and in six days marched to within thirty miles of Lemberg. Simultaneously another large Russian army, under General Brussilov, had come westwards from Kiev and was advancing against Auffenburg's right flank by way of Tarnapol and the valley of the Sereth. Brussilov took Tarnapol on August 27, then Halicz, and then wheeled north against Lemberg.

On September 1–2, the critical battle of Lemberg was fought. While Brussilov fiercely attacked the Austrian right and carried the line of the Gnila Lipa, Ruzsky swept to the north of the city, drove in the Austrian left, and threatened Auffenburg's communications. Austrian generalship proved defective, and some of the Slav contingents in the Austrian army abandoned their posts and threw down their arms at the first favorable opportunity. The Russians took at least 100,000 prisoners, and on September 3 entered Lemberg in triumph, giving the city the genuinely Slavic name of Lvov.

After the battle of Lemberg, Brussilov sent a detachment of his army to occupy Czernowitz, the capital of Bukowina, and to seize the passes through the Carpathians, and with his main force, in company with Ruzsky, advanced toward Przemysl on a front from Stryj to Rawaruska. The Russian advance in

Galicia seriously menaced General Dankl's operations in Russian Poland. Two German army corps were dispatched to the aid of Auffenburg; Austrian reënforcements were hastily brought up; and a new Austrian army, under the Archduke Joseph Ferdinand, was put in the field, from the Vistula to Lublin. Thus, early in September, the three Austrian armies were drawn up in the form of a quarter arc extending from the Vistula, past Lublin, Rawaruska, and Grodek, to the Dniester.

On this extended front a great battle was fought, September 6–10. The Archduke Joseph was decisively beaten and driven in ignominious retreat southward toward the San. Dankl fought well, but failed to maintain his position. Auffenburg was worse battered than before. This time there was a rout along the entire Austrian front. This time there was a head-long flight to Jaroslav and Przemysl, and the vanguard of the vanquished halted only under the protecting guns of far-away Cracow. The synchronizing of this great Russian victory with the battle of the Marne on the Western Front gave new courage and delight to the Allies: Austrians could be overcome by Russians as decisively as Germans could be defeated by French and British. Teutonic "invincibility" was a myth.

Onward in Galicia pressed the Russians. On September 23, they captured Jaroslav and invested the fortress of Przemysl. By the end of September they reached Tarnow, less than a hundred miles from Cracow. Nearly all of Galicia was in their possession, and could they but seize Cracow they would have in their grasp the most important base for either an advance through Silesia toward Berlin or a direct thrust at Vienna. Occupation of Cracow would afford them a means of turning the flank of the strong German positions in East Prussia and Posen and of seriously interfering with the economic resources of the Teutonic Powers.

But the Russians were too optimistic. Early in October, Field Marshal von Hindenburg was put in command of all the German and Austro-Hungarian forces in the East. Leaving a small army in East Prussia, he immediately set to work to prepare a counter-offensive against the Russians in Poland. Now that the contest on the Western Front had assumed the character of trench warfare, fewer men were needed there to defend the trenches than had been required to conduct field operations. Consequently several army corps were transferred to the East, and with these and with army corps and reservists already in Silesia and Posen, Hindenburg massed an army of at least

750,000 Germans between the fortress of Thorn and the town of Lublinitz in southern Silesia. At the same time he superintended the organization, near Cracow, of two Austrian armies, which, bolstered up with several German officers and including a liberal interspersing of German soldiers, aggregated close to one million.

In the second week of October, Hindenburg struck out all along his extended line. The Grand Duke Nicholas, the Russian generalissimo, at once perceiving the danger to his armies operating in western Galicia, ordered a general withdrawal to Warsaw, the Vistula, and the San. By the middle of October, Hindenburg's left wing was at Plock on the lower Vistula; his center was east of Lowicz and nearing Warsaw; his left was between Radom and Ostrowiecs; while Dankl with one Austrian army was at the junction of the San and Vistula, and the other Austrian army was recapturing Jaroslav and raising the siege of Przemysl.

A fight for Warsaw raged on October 16–19. The German left flank was turned by a Russian reserve army unexpectedly brought up from Novo Georgievsk by General Rennenkampf, and Hindenburg's left and center were compelled to retire. But the most determined fighting took place on his right as the result of a desperate attempt of the Germans to cross the Vistula at Ivangorod and at the narrows near Josefov. The Russians under General Ruzsky successfully held Ivangorod and allowed only such divisions to cross at Josefov as could be captured or annihilated in the roadless country behind the town. On October 22, the German right wing was compelled to retire from the Vistula; on November 3, Ruzsky drove it from Kielce. Hindenburg's first great offensive against Warsaw had failed. He withdrew his forces behind the Warthe river near the German frontier, and the Austrians were again back on Cracow. Again the Russians occupied Jaroslav and invested Przemysl; again they advanced upon Cracow.

The Russians were determined to possess themselves of all Galicia. In spite of renewed counter-offensives conducted by the Germans in Poland and by the Austrians in the Carpathians, they clung doggedly to their task throughout the winter of 1914–1915. On December 8, 1914, a Russian army under Radko Dmitriev, formerly chief of staff of the Bulgarian army but now in the service of the Tsar, fought an indecisive battle almost at the outskirts of Cracow. A few days later the Austrians' capture of the Dukla Pass in the Carpathians obliged him to withdraw from the vicinity of Cracow, but he intrenched himself near Tarnow and held this position throughout the winter.

Meanwhile another Russian army was overrunning Bukowina, which commanded the southeastern end of the Carpathian barrier. On January 6, 1915, it captured the town of Kimpolung, at the southern extremity of the province, and on January 17, it gained the pass of Kirlibaba, leading westward into Hungary, and threatened Transylvania. If the Russians could successfully occupy both Bukowina and Transylvania, — provinces peopled mainly by Rumans, — Rumania would be likely to enter the war and coöperate with the Russians, turning the eastern flank of the Carpathian ridge, while the Russians swarmed over the central Carpathian passes.

The situation called for strenuous and immediate action on the part of Austria-Hungary. The supersession of Count Berchtold as foreign minister of the Dual Monarchy by Baron Stephan Burian, a friend and compatriot of Count Tisza, the Hungarian premier, on January 13, 1915, was interpreted as a sign of the Emperor's determination to protect Magyar interests at all costs. While Hindenburg prepared to distract the attention of the Russians by new attacks in Poland, Archduke Eugene of Austria marshaled his forces in three great armies for a supreme effort to secure the Carpathian ridge, relieve the hard-pressed garrison of Przemysl, free Bukowina, and intimidate Rumania.

In the second half of January the Austrian counter-offensive was launched. The first Austrian army, under General Boehm-Ermolli, moved up into the three central Carpathian passes (Dukla, Lupkow, and Uzsok) with the object of advancing north to the relief of beleaguered Przemysl. The second army, under the command of the German General von Linsingen, operated from Munkacs northward in the passes east of Uzsok. The third army, comprising both German and Austro-Hungarian troops, was led by General von Pflanzer against the Russians in Bukowina. General von Pflanzer made rapid progress. Kirlibaba Pass was retaken; the weak Russian defense of Czernowitz succumbed on February 18; and the Austro-Germans turned northward into Galicia, passing Kolomea, and holding the important railway center of Stanislau for a brief space, until they were forced back on Kolomea, March 3. General von Linsingen, however, failed dismally in his attempt to advance from Munkacs toward Lemberg. Even more disappointing was the result of General Boehm-Ermolli's campaign against the central passes : after two months of bitter battles in the snow-bound mountain defiles, the Russians at the end of the third week in March held the Dukla Pass and the northern entrance to Lupkow.

The culminating failure of the Austrian counter-offensive and the crowning success of the Russian Galician campaign was the surrender, on March 22, of the Austrian fortress of Przemysl, which had been besieged by the Russians ever since November 12. The situation of the garrison had become alarming early in March. After provisions were well-nigh exhausted and a breach had been effected by the Russians in the outer ring of defenses, General von Kusmanek had ordered a last desperate sortie, March 18. This failing disastrously, he destroyed a considerable quantity of ammunition and then surrendered the city. By the capture of Przemysl the Russians won 120,000 prisoners, about a thousand guns, and less important stores of small arms. More significant still, the railway leading westward from Lemberg through Przemysl to Tarnow and Cracow was at last cleared, and the investing army of 100,000 men was released for aggressive operations elsewhere. The Russians profited by their improved position to renew the offensive in the Carpathian passes, and by the end of April they were in possession of the Carpathian crest for seventy-five miles, commanding Dukla, Lupkow, and Rostok passes, and they were fiercely attacking Uzsok Pass.

Thus, from August, 1914, to April, 1915, the Russians struggled to conquer Galicia. They had met with some setbacks, but on the whole their gains had been steadily augmented and solidified. Their generals had committed few mistakes or blunders and the rank and file had fought courageously and stubbornly. They were in complete possession of all eastern Galicia, and at its capital city of Lemberg (Lvov) they had installed a Russian administration. They now occupied Jaroslav and Przemysl; they controlled most of the Carpathian passes; they threatened Bukowina and Hungary at one end of their Galician conquest; and at the other end they menaced Cracow and with it the most direct routes to Berlin and Vienna.

To many publicists of Western Europe it seemed high time that the long-heralded Russian "tidal wave" or "steam roller" should sweep out of the comparatively restricted province of Galicia and descend with magnificent might and irresistible force over the plains of Austria and Hungary, on one side, and over the rich valley of the Oder, on the other. It had been for this spectacular *dénouement* that French and British and Belgians had been pouring out their blood upon the Western battlefields; for this they had been impatiently waiting in their trenches throughout the long, dreary winter-months.   It was now spring, and the Russians were still a goodly number of miles away from Cracow.   Until Cracow should be captured and Galicia entirely cleared of the enemy, the Russian commander-in-chief knew it would be suicidal to undertake an invasion of Germany.

As the event proved, there had been a fallacy in the reasoning of Western publicists concerning the Russian "masses" and "hordes."   These publicists had at first underestimated the speed and efficiency with which the early mobilization was effected.   Then, knowing that Russia comprised a population almost three times as large as that of the German Empire, they had proceeded to underestimate the difficulties of continued military activity on the part of Russia and therefore to overestimate the momentum of the "steam roller."

The Russian armies, in fact, were not "steam rollers" and were not likely to be.   The lines of communication upon which they had to depend were wretchedly inadequate.   Most of the soldiers were distressingly ignorant not only of the rudiments of reading and writing but also of why they were fighting.   The officers and men alike were woefully dependent upon an autocratic régime at Petrograd, which at its best was clumsy, inefficient, and capricious, and which at its worst was tyrannical, cruel, and corrupt.   Corruption had eaten into the very vitals of the military administration, as well as of the civil bureaucracy, and in the critical year 1914–1915 signs were plenty that large funds which should have bought guns and rifles and ammunition and airplanes and motor cars had shamefully disappeared in the pockets of grafting officials and contractors.   A war that was to be waged by weight of armor and projectiles even more than by weight of numbers found the Russians peculiarly short of heavy artillery.   To be sure, the lack of ammunition and other military equipment was gradually supplied, at least in considerable part, by importations from Japan and America, but such supplies had to be transported over the long, light Siberian railway (much of it single track); and imports from western Europe could enter only through the port of Archangel, which was blocked by ice six months of the year.   Throughout Russia the few, ill-equipped railways were congested with foodstuffs and army supplies going to the troops in Poland and Galicia. The more troops there were at the front, the greater was the con-

E

gestion on the railways; the greater the congestion, the more difficult it was properly to take care of the troops at the front or to bring up reënforcements of men. In other words, the preliminary mobilization in August, 1914, was Russia's best. For Russia it was physically impossible to mobilize all her fighting men and get them to the front for effective service. If Russia could not overwhelm Germany in the early stages of the war, her chances of doing so as time went on grew less rather than greater. Despite what was said at the time in western Europe, it is probable that in the spring of 1915 the combined forces of Germany and Austria-Hungary in the East already outnumbered the effectives of Russia.

In view of these facts it is wonderful that the Russian armies achieved what they did. They were unable successfully to invade Germany, but they wrested most of Galicia from Austria-Hungary. They might conceivably have gone further, taken Cracow, and entered Silesia, had not the Germans transferred large forces from Flanders and France to Poland and Galicia. This gave the Allies some respite in the West; and it compelled Germany to wage the war simultaneously on two fronts, shifting her troops back and forth as occasion required, and finding her magnificent strategic railways of incalculable value. Skillful distribution of forces, able generalship, and superior equipment enabled the Germans, with Austrian assistance, to hold back the early Russian invasions and later to take up an advanced position in Russian Poland.

That the Russian invasion of Galicia was finally halted early in the spring of 1915 and that it never reached the all-important city of Cracow, is to be explained not only by reference to corruption and inefficiency in the Russian government but also by the series of counter-offensives which Hindenburg directed against Russian Poland in the winter of 1914–1915.

THE GERMAN INVASION OF RUSSIAN POLAND

In October, 1914, Field Marshal von Hindenburg, as we have seen, had undertaken the first German invasion of Russian Poland. Though he had failed on that occasion to capture Warsaw or to compel the permanent withdrawal of Russian forces from western Galicia, he had utilized his retreat from the Vistula so as to pave the way for a second invasion. As he retired to the trenches which he had constructed behind the Warthe, he systematically tore up the railways and laid waste the broad belt of country in southwestern Poland between the Vistula and the Warthe, so that the Russians who followed him to his trenches were without adequate means of communication in their rear. Then, Hindenburg, leaving a small force to man the trenches in front of the desolated Polish region, commissioned General von Mackensen to collect a large army at Thorn and to advance with it up the Vistula into the still flourishing district of northwestern Poland.

Early in November, Mackensen collected an army of at least 800,000, based on the fortress of Thorn ; and the second German drive against Warsaw began. Aided by Mackensen from the northwest, Hindenburg struck out from the Warthe, and on November 23–24 pierced the hostile lines near Lodz and captured some 90,000 Russians. Reënforcements came up and the battle continued nearly two weeks, but at length, on December 6, the Russians abandoned Lodz and fell back to within thirty-five miles of Warsaw. Here, another great battle was waged until Christmas, by which time the Russian defenders and the German assailants were facing each other in parallel lines of trenches not unlike those from which Germans and Allies were viewing each other on the Western Front. The second German invasion of Russian Poland, like the first, had failed to reach Warsaw ; unlike the first, it had not caused the Russians even temporarily to withdraw from western Galicia. Yet this second invasion secured the permanent possession of western Poland for Germany and inaugurated on a large scale in the East the system of trench warfare.

At the beginning of 1915, the Russian armies were strung out in a battle-line almost nine hundred miles long. The center of the Russian line, under General Ruzsky, was strongly intrenched in Russian Poland, behind the Rawka and Bzura rivers, and in front of the powerful fortresses of Novo Georgievsk, Warsaw, and Ivangorod. The right of the Russian line, likewise under Ruzsky's general command, stretched northeastwards of the Narew river, through the Masurian lake region of East Prussia, to the Niemen river. The left of the Russian army, under General Ivanov, included General Ewarts's army on the Nida river, west of Kielce ; General Radko Dmitriev's army in Galicia, holding Tarnow ; General Brussilov's army, holding the northern approaches to the Carpathian mountain passes ; and General Alexeiev's army, operating in Bukowina. Opposing the Russian right wing were four German army corps in East Prussia ; the Russian center was confronted by strongly in-

trenched German forces under General von Mackensen; on
the left wing was General Dankl's Austrian army west of the
Nida river; south of that and west of Tarnow, General Woyrsch's
Austro-German army; and the extreme Russian left flank in
the Carpathians was harried by the Austrian Archduke Eugene
from the south.

Throughout the winter of 1914–1915, Hindenburg's strategy
was to direct powerful blows, now from East Prussia against
the Russian right, now from Mackensen's front in middle Poland
against the Russian center, in the hope that thereby the Russian
right or the Russian center would be so weakened as to admit
of a deep penetration by the Germans. In this fashion Warsaw
and its protecting positions might either be taken by a frontal
attack or be turned by a flanking movement from East Prussia.
In December, 1914, Mackensen tried a gigantic frontal attack,
and failed. During the first week of February, 1915, he attempted another vast frontal attack: under cover of a terrific
bombardment, and in the face of a blinding snowstorm, his
troops carried three lines of Russian trenches east of the Rawka
river, only to be met by the fiercest and bravest resistance and
ultimately to be pushed back on the Rawka. In the middle of
February, Hindenburg tried a huge flanking movement from
East Prussia : in the north a German army annihilated a Russian
corps at Suwalki, won a foothold on the eastern bank of the
Niemen near Grodno, and reached a point only ten miles from
the Petrograd-Warsaw railway; simultaneously, another German army advanced to the Bobr river and began a bombardment
of Ossowietz, while a third swiftly struck at Przasnysz, sixty
miles north of Warsaw, in a determined effort to cross the Narew
and cut the lines of communication with the Polish capital.
But the flanking movement, like the frontal attacks, failed. By
the end of February, the assaults on the Niemen, on the Bobr,
and on the Narew had been stopped, and the Germans were in
full retreat towards the East Prussian frontier. In March and
April there was a lull — the lull before the great storm.

By April, 1915, the Russians were in possession of the greater
part of Austrian Galicia, but the Germans were secure in East
Prussia and were in occupation of one-third of Russian Poland.
The Russians still held Warsaw and the main strongholds of
Poland, and they had brilliantly resisted drive after drive of
Hindenburg and Mackensen. As time went on, however, it
became apparent that the offensive was passing more and more
from the Russians to the Germans. It was believed in the West

that time was on the side of the Russians. Events were soon to demonstrate that time was on the side of the Germans.

In reading the story of the military operations in the Polish theater of war, one should not entirely forget the tragic plight of the Polish nation. The once glorious kingdom of Poland, it will be remembered, had been partitioned toward the close of the eighteenth century by Russia, Prussia, and Austria. Consequently, although the Poles constituted a homogeneous nation of twenty-three millions, possessing a national language and literature and in Roman Catholicism a common religion, dwelling in the plains of Russian Poland, Prussian Posen, and Austrian Galicia, and passionately desiring to restore their political unity and freedom, they were now compelled to fight in opposing armies and to furnish the battleground for Russia, Germany, and Austria-Hungary. The march and counter-march of millions of soldiers, and the havoc caused by hundreds of howitzers, to say nothing of systematic destruction wrought by German orders, devastated Poland more completely than Belgium. Without food or homes the Polish peasants perished miserably.

Yet for the future, perhaps, a slight ray of hope could be discerned. Russia, long the cruel oppressor of the largest section of Poland, now feared a Polish revolt and promised Poland autonomy in return for loyalty. Early in August, 1914, the Grand Duke Nicholas, generalissimo of the Russian forces, issued the following eloquent manifesto to the Poles: "The hour has sounded when the sacred dream of your fathers and your grandfathers may be realized. A century and a half has passed since the living body of Poland was torn in pieces, but the soul of the country is not dead. It continues to live, inspired by the hope that there will come for the Polish people an hour of resurrection, and of fraternal reconciliation with Great Russia. The Russian army brings you the solemn news of this reconciliation which obliterates the frontiers dividing the Polish peoples, which it unites conjointly under the scepter of the Russian Tsar. Under this scepter Poland will be born again, free in her religion and her language, and autonomous. Russia only expects from you the same respect for the rights of those nationalities to which history has bound you. With open heart and brotherly hand Great Russia advances to meet you. She believes that the sword, with which she struck down her enemies at Grünewald,[1]

---

[1] The battle of Grünewald, or Tannenberg as it is more usually called, was fought in 1410 between the Teutonic Knights of Prussia, on one side, and the Poles and Lithuanians on the other. It was a decisive victory for the latter and marked the emergence of Poland as a Great Power.

is not yet rusted. From the shores of the Pacific to the North Sea the Russian armies are marching. The dawn of a new life is beginning for you, and in this glorious dawn, is seen the sign of the cross, the symbol of suffering and of the resurrection of peoples."

Similar appeals to the Poles were made by Austria-Hungary, who undoubtedly had accorded the Poles within her borders far better treatment than was received by the unfortunate Poles in Russia or in Prussia. In respect of Germany, no promise could efface from Polish memory the wrongs suffered under the harsh Prussian administration, which had pursued a deliberate policy not only of denying the Poles the use of their mother-tongue but also of depriving them of their lands.

Had the Russian Tsar given immediate effect to the fair words of his generalissimo, it is probable that the Russian Poles would have rallied enthusiastically to his banner and that serious sedition would have ensued in the Polish legions of the Austro-German armies. So long as the Russians remained in military occupation of Warsaw and Galicia, however, "Polish autonomy" remained but a hope and a promise, until, as months passed by, it seemed to an increasing number of Poles to be but a mirage. The less enthusiastically the Russian Poles fought for the Auto-crat of All the Russias and the less frequently their kinsmen deserted Teutonic service, the more quibbling became the Russian promises even of "autonomy." The longer the Russians, still in possession of most of Poland, delayed to make real con-cessions to the Poles, the more expectantly did the Poles turn to the prospect of Austro-German conquest. They certainly did not love the Germans; they certainly did not desire an overwhelming German victory. Yet they were becoming con-vinced that they had nothing — perhaps less than nothing — to gain from an overwhelming Russian victory.

Imperialistic autocracy in Russia was storing up great future tribulations for itself. Its inefficiency and corruption were gradually paralyzing the might of the Russian armies in the field. Its overweening pride and arrogance were perceptibly weakening the loyalty not only of Poles but of other subject nationalities within the Russian Empire — Ukrainians, Lithu-anians, and Finns. It was utilizing the temporary heat of national altruism and patriotism in order to forge enduring iron links in the chain of social inequality and political abso-lutism. Liberals in Russia were depressed, and revolutionaries desperate. Well-wishers of Russia and of the Allied cause throughout the world should have been alarmed and should have made energetic representations at Petrograd that this war was a war in behalf of small nationalities, that it was "a war to end war."

Nothing of the sort happened. On the contrary, the Russian conquest of Galicia and the stubborn Russian defense of Warsaw deceived the diplomatists of France and Great Britain as to the true strength of their Russian ally. On the Western Front, the Allies were fully holding their own, and on the Eastern Front the Russians seemed to be more than holding their own. What merely "seemed," was taken as proved reality; and the diplomatists of all the Allied Powers, instead of urging moderation and unselfishness upon the Tsar's government, devoted the late winter and early spring of 1915 to making secret treaties with one another whereby some of the worst features of German and Russian imperialism were consecrated as guiding principles for the peace which, in their optimistic opinion, was about to follow a speedy Allied victory. Russia not only was to annex Galicia and Posen and exercise her own sweet will over all Poland but she was to appropriate Constantinople and realize her age-long imperialistic dream of succeeding to the destinies of Byzantium. France not only was to regain Alsace-Lorraine but she was virtually to establish a protectorate over the entire left bank of the Rhine. Great Britain was to appropriate Egypt and Mesopotamia and, in conjunction with France and Japan, to partition all the German colonies. It was the supreme blunder of the Allies. It was a blunder that eventually was to constitute the worst indictment of professional diplomatists.

THE SECURITY OF SERBIA

It will be recalled that in July, 1914, Austria-Hungary had set out to "punish" Serbia. The task was not altogether an easy one. The little Slav state, poor and small as it might appear, could boast a war army of 250,000 men, mostly seasoned veterans, besides a territorial reserve of 50,000; moreover, Serbia's ally, Montenegro, could put in the field about 50,000 hardy mountaineers, renowned for their valor. In spite of the fact that the Serbs were deficient in heavy artillery, airplanes, and sanitary service, they enjoyed the immense advantage of recent experience in war and the courageous confidence imparted to them by their victories of 1912–1913 over Turks and Bulgars.

Nevertheless, short shrift would undoubtedly have been made

of Serbia, had not Austria-Hungary been much engaged during the year of 1914-1915 with large Russian armies in Galicia and Poland. With such forces as could be spared from the Eastern theater of war, the Dual Monarchy undertook to preserve its southern lands from Serb invasion and to attempt incursions into Serbian territory.

About the middle of August, Austrian columns were thrown across the Drina and Save rivers. Obviously the intention was to invade the northwestern corner of Serbia simultaneously from the west and from the north, and to converge on the Serbian military depot at Valievo. With frantic haste the Serbian Crown Prince brought his main armies by forced marches westward to meet the Austrian invasion. In the mountainous northwest district of their country, between the Save and the Drina, the Serbians fought the battles of Shabatz and the Jadar, August 16-23, to prevent the junction of the invading columns. So successful were the Serbian tactics that the Austrians were defeated at all points and compelled to retreat into their own territory. In repelling the 200,000 Austrians, the Serbians had lost 3000 killed and 15,000 wounded; but they had killed some 8000 of the enemy, wounded perhaps 30,000 and captured 4000; they had, in addition, captured much needed supplies of rifles and ammunition.

It was now the turn of Austria-Hungary to suffer invasion. Early in September, the Serbians took Semlin, across the river from Belgrade, while another Serbian army struck into southern Bosnia in the direction of Serajevo. These forces had to be speedily withdrawn, however, for Austria-Hungary again assumed the offensive, massing 250,000 men against the same northwest corner of Serbia.

In the second week of September the Austrians advanced a second time on Valievo. Though fierce resistance was encountered, and though another Austrian army crossing the Danube east of Belgrade was routed at Semendria, the main Austrian offensive was continued and Valievo was taken on November 15. Belgrade, which had been besieged and intermittently bombarded since July 29, capitulated to the Austrians on December 2.

Just when Serbia's complete collapse was momentarily expected, news came that the Serbians had broken through the center of the advancing Austrian army, recaptured Valievo, and inflicted a crushing defeat on two Austrian corps, capturing 40,000 prisoners, fifty cannon, and munitions in immense quantity.

The Austrian right wing was driven back in disorder across the Drina, where it was still further punished by the Montenegrins at Vishegrad. On December 15, the Serbians recaptured Belgrade, and King Peter was able to reënter his former capital at the head of his victorious army, while all Serbia rejoiced over the announcement that not a single Austrian invader remained on Serbian soil.

After the exhausting campaign of December, 1914, a period of inaction ensued in the Serbian theater of war. Serbs and Austrians alike had suffered heavily and needed time to repair their losses. Inclement weather and impassable roads added to the disinclination of either party to renew active operations. On the Austrian side, there was talk of undertaking a decisive offensive in February, 1915, but this time the Italian government warned Austria-Hungary that any military action undertaken in the Balkans without previous agreement regarding the compensation to be granted Italy, would lead to grave consequences. Relations were already becoming strained between Italy and Austria-Hungary, and the latter was not inclined to draw her ally into the circle of her enemies just for the sake of "punishing" Serbia. Meanwhile, profiting by the inactivity of Austria-Hungary in the south, Serbia sought as best she could, with some foreign aid, to repair the horrible ravages which the typhus, in combination with the past year's campaigns, had wrought in her army and among her civilian population.

With the exception of minor frontier engagements and rather desultory bombardments of Belgrade, the Serbian front remained comparatively quiet until October, 1915. Austria-Hungary had as yet failed to "punish" Serbia, but, on the other hand, the Serbs had as yet been unable to take advantage of the Dual Monarchy's discomfiture in Galicia in order to free their kinsfolk of Bosnia-Herzegovina and of Croatia-Slavonia from Habsburg rule. Serbian despair and Serbian rejoicing alike waited on the outcome of the tremendous battles in progress between Russians and Austro-Germans along the nine-hundred mile line from the Niemen river through Russian Poland and Galicia to the Carpathian mountain passes and Bukowina. To a lesser degree they waited on the outcome of a contest of wit which at the very time was being carried on between Teutonic and Allied diplomatists in the several Balkan capitals. But this story belongs to a later chapter.

CHAPTER IV

GREAT BRITAIN MASTERS THE SEAS

IMPORTANCE OF SEA POWER

AT the beginning of the Great War it was confidently believed in Allied countries that France and Russia would be able to hold in equipoise the military forces of Germany and Austria-Hungary, while Great Britain, by means of the weight of her enormous naval superiority, could tip the balance against the Teutonic Powers. Little was expected from unmilitary Britain in the way of armed intervention on the continent of Europe, but much was expected from her naval power and her naval prowess.

The Great War was far more than a conflict over Serbia and Alsace-Lorraine; it was a struggle for world dominion. And world dominion depended quite as much on the mastery of the seas as upon a conquest of Belgium or an invasion of Galicia.

From the time she entered the war on that fateful day in August, 1914, Great Britain used her naval superiority both for defense and for offense. Of the two, defense was the more vitally necessary. From the very nature of things, the command of the seas was even more essential to Great Britain's preservation than it was injurious to Germany's welfare. To be sure, the German merchant marine and German commerce would be swept from the seas, involving thereby the partial inability of Germany to import foodstuffs, copper, or munitions of war, or to market the products of her industry. All this would entail direct financial losses of alarming size. But Germany might make her food supply last by strict economy; she had large stores of most materials requisite for war; and the effectiveness of her army did not depend absolutely upon control of the sea. To Great Britain, however, the loss of the seas would have spelled ruin. Her people would have been starved, her industries throttled, and her army prevented from engaging in the battles of France. The very fact that Germany was a large country combining agriculture and manufacture, surrounded by contiguous neutral countries, as contrasted with the insularity and almost complete industrialization of Great Britain, explains the secondary importance of naval power to Germany, and its primary importance to Great Britain.

Though the paramount purpose of the British navy was defense, the Germans shuddered perceptibly when they fell to thinking of the purposes of offense for which it would now be employed. In the first place Great Britain undertook a drastic "war on German trade," which threatened to deprive the manufacturer of his business, the workingman of his employment, and the statesman of his country's prosperity. In the second place, the control of the high seas by Great Britain would make it increasingly difficult for Germany to carry on the war successfully; it would enable Great Britain to scour the four quarters of the globe for recruits and to bring back negroes from Africa, Asiatics from India, Malays, Australians, New Zealanders, and Canadians, to fight in Europe against Germany; it would make possible the landing in France of a million British soldiers already in training in England; it would create bitter hardship for the civilian population of Germany through lack of sufficient food. Finally, even should the German armies crush France and Russia, the British fleet could still stand between Germany and her dreams of world empire, for as long as the British fleet sailed the seas it could prevent Germany from becoming the greatest colonial and commercial Power and could assure to Great Britain the possession of the most valuable colonies and "spheres of influence" throughout the world. It was this naval superiority of Great Britain and the thought of its significance that caused the Germans forthwith to take up the chanting of hymns of hate as a national pastime.

Early in the war the British fleet achieved much. Though it could not altogether prevent the Germans from planting mines and torpedoes along the coasts of the North Sea and bombarding Russian ports in the Baltic, it compelled the German battle squadron to lie idle at its moorings in Wilhelmshaven, Cuxhaven, and Kiel. Admiral von Tirpitz, the director of the German navy, was so much inclined to consider discretion the better part of valor that the English comic papers appropriately styled him the "Admiral of the Kiel Canal." The only hostile warships which proved embarrassing to the British were two in the Mediterranean and a squadron in the Far East.

At the outbreak of the war one of Germany's swiftest and most powerful battle-cruisers, the *Goeben*, and a light cruiser, the *Breslau*, happened to be in the western Mediterranean, where they might conceivably interfere with the transportation of

French troops from Algeria to France, but were much more likely to fall in with superior French or British naval units. British and French warships immediately gave chase to the two German cruisers, which, however, eluded pursuit and made port first at Messina and then at Constantinople. From the refuge of these cruisers in Turkish waters led the causal chain of circumstances which subsequently lugged the Ottoman Empire into the Great War.

In the Far East Germany possessed a squadron of eight cruisers, which early in the war managed to escape from the naval base of Kiao-chao and for some time to elude capture or destruction. Five of the number, the *Scharnhorst, Gneisenau, Nürnberg, Leipzig,* and *Dresden,* under command of Admiral von Spee, were at last sighted by Admiral Cradock's smaller British squadron on the evening of November 1, 1914, off the coast of Chile near Coronel. As the sun sank behind the horizon, and the heavy seas dashed against the bows of the British ships, the British gunners experienced serious difficulty in training their guns on the German ships and were unable to make any impression upon the heavier armor of the Germans. Fifty minutes after the first shot was fired, the *Good Hope* blew up, shooting a column of fire two hundred feet in the air. Shortly afterwards the *Monmouth* was sunk, and the two other British ships were making off to escape destruction.

The British had their revenge a little more than a month later. On December 8 a powerful British squadron, which had been sent out under Vice-Admiral Sturdee to search for the five German cruisers, sighted them off the Falkland Islands. According to the laconic statement of the British admiralty, "an action followed, in the course of which the *Scharnhorst,* flying the flag of Admiral Count von Spee, the *Gneisenau,* and the *Leipzig* were sunk. The *Dresden* and the *Nürnberg* made off during the action and are being pursued. Two colliers also were captured. The Vice Admiral reports that the British casualties are very few in number. Some survivors have been rescued from the *Gneisenau* and the *Leipzig.*" The *Nürnberg* was overtaken and destroyed the same night, but it was not until March, 1915, that the *Dresden* was wrecked.

The three swift German cruisers in the Far East not included in Admiral von Spee's fleet had spectacular careers for some time as commerce raiders and managed to inflict considerable injury on Allied shipping. One of these cruisers, the *Emden,* commanded by the intrepid Captain Karl von Muller, cruised the waters about the East Indies for three months, destroying twenty-five merchant vessels valued, exclusive of their cargoes, at ten million dollars, firing the oil tanks at Madras, sinking four British steamers in Rangoon harbor alone, and stealing into the harbor of Penang disguised by the addition of a false smokestack to sink a Russian cruiser and a French torpedo boat. The *Emden* was not a powerful ship; her displacement was only 3350 tons, her speed less than 25 knots, and her largest guns only 4.1 inches. Again and again more powerful warships were on the *Emden's* trail, but each time she escaped, until one day Captain Muller decided to destroy the wireless station at Cocos Islands, southwest of Java. There the *Emden* was discovered by an Australian cruiser and driven ashore in flames after a sharp battle. The career of the second German raider, the *Königsberg*, had come to an end a few days earlier, when, after destroying about a dozen merchantmen, she was caught hiding in shoal waters up a river in German East Africa.

Once in a while a cruiser would slip out of a German home base and commit depredations on the high seas, but such a raider would ultimately be detected and lost. Thus the *Prinz Eitel Friedrich* was obliged to take refuge in Newport News, Virginia, on March 10, 1915, after a destructive cruise of more than 30,000 miles. Similarly, the *Kronprinz Wilhelm*, after sinking nine British, four French, and one Norwegian merchantmen, entered Newport News on April 11, 1915, and was interned. But after all, the number of these German raiders was too small and their life too precarious to constitute any grave menace to British naval supremacy or even to affect British commerce seriously. The exploits were spectacular rather than significant, and the most they accomplished was to dwarf in popular esteem the quieter and more substantial achievements of the British navy.

The fact remains that the German merchant marine was swept from the seas swiftly and methodically within a week of the outbreak of war. In every quarter of the globe British warships, in conjunction with the fleets of France and Russia, spread their net and caught virtually the whole sea-borne trade of Germany. German merchantmen in the ports of the Allies were detained, and hundreds were made prizes of "in the high and the narrow seas." Some escaped to the shelter of ports still neutral, especially to those of the United States, but none got back to Germany. By the sheer threat of naval superiority, the British had annihilated German commerce and protected their own and that of their allies.

From British naval superiority it resulted, moreover, that the French could transport colonial troops to the battle-line in Western Europe, that the British Expeditionary Force under Sir John French could be safely landed in France in August, 1914, and that munitions and supplies could flow freely from the United States to France and England while their entrance into Germany was effectually barred.

Spectacular deeds were not entirely confined to the Germans. As early as August 28, 1914, Sir David Beatty, a promising aspirant for naval fame, led a British fleet, accompanied by a flotilla of submarines and destroyers, into the bight of Heligoland and engaged part of the German fleet almost under the guns of the great German naval base. Three German armored cruisers and one destroyer were sunk, and 700 German sailors were killed and 300 taken prisoners; the British casualties were thirty-two killed and fifty-two wounded.

No other important naval engagement was fought until the battle off Dogger Bank on January 24, 1915, in which a German battle-cruiser squadron raiding the coast of England was severely punished for its temerity. Three powerful German cruisers were seriously injured by a British fleet under Beatty, but made their escape to Heligoland, thanks to the dense screening smoke of a destroyer flotilla and to the timely appearance of German submarines. A fourth cruiser, however, the slower and less powerful *Blücher*, fell an easy victim and was first crippled by gunfire, then torpedoed and sunk. The engagement was a conclusive demonstration of the value of big guns and high speed in modern naval warfare.

THE PARTICIPATION OF JAPAN

In mastering the seas and the German colonies Great Britain enjoyed the special assistance of Japan. On August 15, 1914, — less than two weeks after the declaration of war between Great Britain and Germany, — the Japanese ambassador in Berlin handed to the German Foreign Office an ultimatum, demanding that Germany should immediately withdraw all warships from Chinese and Japanese waters and deliver up the entire leased territory of Kiao-chao before September 15, "with a view to the eventual restoration of the same to China."

Kiao-chao, it should be remembered, was a bay on the northern Chinese coast, with 117 square miles of surrounding territory, which had been seized in 1897 and then leased for ninety-nine years by Germany as compensation for the murder of two German missionaries in China. At Tsing-tao, on the leased ground, the German government at great expense had erected strong fortifications, commanding the bay; under the shelter of frowning forts the Germans had constructed a magnificent floating dock which made Tsing-tao a splendid naval base. Leading back from Tsing-tao the Germans had built the Shantung railway. Germany had invested heavily in her Kiao-chao venture, and her imperial position in the Far East depended largely upon its security.

Upon the refusal of the German government to comply with the terms of the ultimatum, Japan forthwith declared war, August 23. The reasons for this step were set forth by Baron

JAPAN'S POSITION IN RELATION TO
KOREA, KIAO-CHAO AND CHINA

Kato, the Japanese foreign minister: "Early in August the British government asked the Imperial (Japanese) government for assistance under the terms of the Anglo-Japanese agreement of alliance. German men-of-war and armed vessels were then prowling the seas of eastern Asia to the serious menace of our commerce and that of our ally, while in Kiao-chao Germany was busy with warlike preparations, apparently for the purpose of making a base for warlike operations in eastern Asia. Grave anxiety was thus felt for the maintenance of the peace of the Far East. As all are aware, the agreement of alliance between Japan and Great Britain has for its object, the consolidation and maintenance of the general peace in eastern Asia, insuring the independence and integrity of China as well as the principle of equal opportunities for the commerce and industry of all nations in that country, and the maintenance and defense respectively

of the territorial rights and of the special interests of the contracting parties in eastern Asia. . . . Germany's possession of
a base for powerful activities in one corner of the Far East was
not only a serious obstacle to the maintenance of permanent
peace, but also was in conflict with the more immediate interests
of the Japanese Empire. The Japanese government, therefore,
resolved to comply with the British request, and, if necessary,
to open hostilities against Germany."

In addition to her desire to fulfill her obligations as Great
Britain's ally, Japan was undoubtedly actuated also by the
lingering resentment which had been aroused by the Kaiser's
references to the "Yellow Peril" and by the part Germany had
played in preventing Japan from retaining Port Arthur in 1895
after the Chino-Japanese War.

Four days after the declaration of war, the Japanese navy
established a blockade of Kiao-chao ; and on September 2, 10,000
Japanese troops were landed on the Shantung peninsula outside
the German leased territory. This landing, and the subsequent
seizure of the Shantung railway in the Chinese hinterland, constituted a technical violation of China's neutrality and called
forth formal protests from Berlin and from Pekin. A small
British East Indian force of 1360 men arrived in September to
coöperate with the Japanese landing party, which was raised to
the strength of 23,000 men under the command of General Kamio.

On September 28, Tsing-tao was fully invested by the Anglo-
Japanese expedition and the siege begun. Bombardment by
two German cruisers in the harbor and a sortie by the garrison
failed to dislodge the assailants. Prince Heinrich hill, easily
carried by assault, was crowned with Japanese guns which on
the last day of October opened the final attack with the aid of
Japanese and British warships. The German forts, powerful
though they were, could not withstand the terrific fire. By
November 6 the forts had been silenced, and the word for an
infantry assault was given by General Kamio. Early the next
morning the attacking party discovered that white flags had been
hoisted in the city. The articles of capitulation were soon
signed, and on November 10, 1914, the German governor formally handed over Kiao-chao to Japan. In addition to the
valuable naval base, Japan had captured 3000 German prisoners.
The Japanese landing party had lost 236 killed and 1282
wounded ; the British, 12 killed and 61 wounded.

In the meantime Japanese naval forces were coöperating with
the British in the conquest of Germany's island possessions in the

Pacific.   Japan sent no troops to Europe, but her participation
in the Great War served the cause of the Allies in several ways.
It deprived the swift German commerce-raiders of a most important base in the Far East; it hastened the conquest of the German
colonies; it enabled Great Britain to rest easier about her Indian
Empire and her Chinese interests while she was centering her
military efforts in western Europe; and it secured protection for
Russia from attacks in the rear and a steady, uninterrupted flow
of munitions of war from Japan and from America.

THE CONQUEST OF THE GERMAN COLONIES

It had been recognized that in case of war between Germany
and Great Britain, the latter's naval superiority would normally
admit of the conquest of the former's colonies and "spheres of
influence" in Asia, Africa, and the Pacific Islands.   When the
war actually came in 1914, the Germans trusted to two factors
which, they hoped, might delay, if not altogether prevent, the
reduction of their colonies.   In the first place, mindful of an old
dictum that the destinies of the world are settled upon the battlefields of Europe, they planned to strike their enemies on the
Continent with such overwhelming military might that Great
Britain could not spare soldiers from Europe for expeditions
overseas and with such decisive results that any colonies which
might temporarily have been occupied by hostile forces would
be permanently restored as compensation for concessions from
the conqueror of Europe.   In the second place, the Germans had
long cherished the notion that the whole British Empire was
seething with discontent and sedition and that when war came
Great Britain would be too embarrassed by revolts of her own
subjects in Ireland, Canada, India, and South Africa, to bother
about the conquest of new and foreign troublesome areas.

Obviously the first of these factors on which the Germans
depended was not quite operative even after a whole year of war
had gone by.   Germany had not yet won a decision on the battlefields of Europe; France and Great Britain were fully holding
their own on the Western Front, and in the East Russia was
putting up an unexpectedly stubborn resistance.   It might well
be that the old dictum was fallacious, and that a greater measure
of truth was contained in the argument that while other Powers
wore themselves out on the battlefields of Europe the nation
possessing superior sea power would conquer the four Great
Continents.   A protracted war had not been counted on by

F

Germany, but by the summer of 1915 the Great War promised to be protracted.

Nor did the domestic politics of the British Empire during the critical first year of the war conform to German expectations. There were no serious and all-absorbing revolts anywhere. Many Irishmen were disgruntled that the Home Rule Act, passed in 1914, was not immediately put into effect; but John Redmond, the Catholic leader of the Nationalist party, joined with Sir Edward Carson, the fiery Ulster Unionist, in promising united Irish defense against German aggression, and thousands of Irishmen, including several Irish members of Parliament, volunteered for active service in the British army. In Canada, there were many bickerings between English-speaking and French-speaking colonists over the language question in the schools, but early in the war French Canadians vied with British Canadians, and Liberal followers of Sir Wilfred Laurier with Conservative partisans of Sir Robert Borden, in offering their lives and their goods to the Empire; by October, 1915, the Dominion of Canada, with a population less than that of the state of New York, had obtained a volunteer army of 200,000 men, of which the larger part was already in overseas service. From the outset no disloyalty was expected from Newfoundland, Australia, or New Zealand; but as time went on, these self-governing British dominions surpassed expectations. Up to July, 1915, Australia had furnished 100,000 troops to the Allies; New Zealand, 20,000; and Newfoundland, 3000. All these had contributed funds beyond their proportional share; and the two South Pacific dominions had, in addition, given valuable naval assistance to the Anglo-Japanese fleets. India was the more amazing. In spite of systematic attempts on the part of German agents and spies to fan the persistent spark of native unrest into the flame of widespread rebellion, India remained comparatively calm and loyal; numerous Indian princes contributed to British armies and to British funds; in January, 1915, Lord Hardinge, the viceroy, declared that 200,000 Indian troops were then serving in the active British forces at the front. Only in South Africa was there anything resembling armed revolt.

In South Africa, especially in the Transvaal and the Orange Free State, the resentment which some of the Boers still cherished against their British conquerors combined with the prevalence of acute industrial disquiet to pave the way for the insurrection headed by three veteran generals of the Boer War — Beyers, Maritz, and DeWet. However, General Louis Botha, the prime

minister of the South African Union, who himself had once
borne arms against Great Britain, now remained unflinchingly
loyal, and with him the ablest of the Boer commanders, General
Smuts.   The English-speaking South Africans and a majority of
the Boers supported General Botha's attitude of loyalty to the
Empire; only a Boer minority sympathized with the rebellion.
The efforts of the rebels had to be confined to guerrilla warfare,
and by the close of 1914 had proved fruitless.   Beyers had been
drowned, DeWet taken prisoner, and Maritz pursued into German Southwest Africa.   Late in December, 1914, the Union
minister of justice stated that 4000 ex-rebels were in prison and
1000 on parole.   Leniency was uniformly shown the rank and
file in the trials which ensued; and in 1915 Generals Botha and
Smuts were aiding the British powerfully in the conquest of
German Southwest Africa and German East Africa.   In Great
Britain General Smuts was received as a conquering hero.

Under such actual circumstances, the British, with their undisputed mastery of the seas, had no great difficulty in mastering
the German colonies.   German Samoa surrendered to an expeditionary force from New Zealand on August 28, 1914.   Australian troops occupied Herbertshöhe, the seat of government
for the Bismarck Archipelago and the Solomon Islands, on
September 11, and captured Kaiser Wilhelmsland, September
24–25.   In October a Japanese fleet took possession of the Mar-
shall, Marianne, and Caroline Islands.   By an arrangement
effected in November, 1914, the islands north of the equator were
to be administered by Japan; Samoa, by New Zealand; and the
other islands south of the equator, by Australia.   The German
flag had vanished from the South Seas.

In Africa slower progress was made in reducing the German
colonies, for they were defended by fairly strong garrisons of
German and native troops.   To be sure, Togo, the narrow strip
on the northern coast of the Gulf of Guinea, was conquered on
August 27, 1914, by Anglo-French forces from the adjacent British colony of Gold Coast and the French protectorate of Dahomey.
But elsewhere serious obstacles were encountered. German
Southwest Africa was invaded by forces from the Union of South
Africa, and Lüderitz Bay was occupied in September, 1914; but
the outbreak of the Boer rebellion in the Union necessitated the
recall of the South African troops and temporarily delayed military operations against the Germans.   In July, 1915, however,
the conquest of German Southwest Africa was carried to completion by General Botha.   Meanwhile, a French expedition

from Equatorial Africa and British expeditions from Nigeria had been penetrating into the jungles and fastnesses of Kamerun; it was not until February, 1916, that they were able to overcome both the natural difficulties and the German commander's stubborn defense and to put the whole area under Anglo-French rule.

In East Africa the German flag waved longest. Though German East Africa bordered on two British colonies and on Belgian Congo, its conquest proved difficult by reason of its inaccessibility from the hinterland and also by reason of the marked resourcefulness and real ability of the German commander, General von Lettow-Vorbeck, and the loyal and efficient aid which the native troops rendered their German officers. At the end of 1914 the coast was under blockade, but a British advance from South Africa waited on the crushing of the Boer rebellion and the subjugation of German Southwest Africa, and an attempted invasion from British East Africa along the shores of Victoria Nyanza had been checked. In 1916, after long and difficult campaigning on the part of a South African expeditionary force under the tireless and energetic leadership of General Smuts, the Germans were driven out of the northern and central portions of the colony. In June, 1917, a new offensive was begun and carried on relentlessly, so that in November von Lettow-Vorbeck with a slender column fled into Portuguese East Africa. Here, in 1918, incessantly chased, he made his way south nearly as far as the Zambesi; then, retracing his steps, he came again in September into German East Africa, whence he sought refuge in northern Rhodesia and finally surrendered to the British on November 14, 1918. The surrender of von Lettow-Vorbeck ended the last phase of German overseas control.

The conquest of the whole German colonial empire was more than a proof of the naval superiority of Great Britain. It was clear evidence of the fact that the British Empire was less a family relationship of mother-country and subject colonies than an alliance, defensive and offensive, between Great Britain and British commonwealths beyond the sea. Australians and New Zealanders who by force of arms had secured an imperial domain from Germany in the South Seas, and South Africans who had subjugated the vast tracts of German Southwest Africa and German East Africa, would be even less likely than their British kinsfolk in Europe to view with favor the return of their conquests to Germany after the war; they were now by self-interest as well as by sentiment thoroughly committed to the fight with Germany, to the settling once for all, as between Teuton and

Anglo-Saxon, of the leadership not merely of Europe but of the whole world. To English-speaking peoples the globe over, it seemed as if the stakes in the old historic conflict for commercial and colonial supremacy between Englishman and Spaniard or between Englishman and Frenchman were pitiful indeed in comparison with these mighty universal stakes of the twentieth century between British and Germans.

TURKEY'S SUPPORT OF GERMANY

For at least twenty years prior to the outbreak of the Great War, German influence had been steadily growing in the Ottoman Empire. German military officers had reorganized, trained, and equipped the Turkish army. German business-men had exploited the natural resources and trade of Turkey. German capitalists were constructing the Anatolian and Bagdad railways, which stretched from the Bosphorus to the Persian Gulf. German ambassadors and foreign secretaries had repeatedly posed as champions of the integrity of the Ottomon Empire and had exerted themselves on many occasions to bolster up the declining fortunes of the Sultan and to apologize for acts of the Turkish government which outraged the conscience of Christian Europe. In fact, by the year 1914 Turkey was regarded both politically and economically as a German "sphere of influence," and distinguished German publicists, like Friedrich Naumann and Paul Rohrbach, were extolling the mission of Germany as the leading Power in a federation of *"Mittel-Europa,"* a federation that would include Austria-Hungary, Turkey, and certain Balkan states, and would dominate the economic and political life of the varied peoples from the Baltic and North Seas to Bagdad and ports on the Persian Gulf.

Many Englishmen had come to feel before the war that the scheme of a Germanized *Mittel-Europa*, especially the scheme for the Bagdad railway, was not only a promise of great economic gain to Germany but a threat against British ascendency in India and in Egypt. Russian imperialists, also, grew fearful, as they beheld the strengthening of German influence at Constantinople, lest their ancient dream of restoring an Eastern Empire under a Muscovite Tsar would never be realized. It was primarily against Germany's designs in Turkey and in Persia that Russia and Great Britain had concluded their *entente* in 1907; and thenceforth, the Entente Powers, including France, had been arrayed against the Teutonic Powers in nearly all diplomatic manœuvers involving Turkey. On most occasions the Teutonic Powers professed to champion the Turks, while the Entente Powers were represented as the enemies of Turkey. Such was certainly the case in the Balkan War of 1912–1913: at London, Paris, and Petrograd rejoicing marked the receipt of news of Turkish defeats and of the shrinkage of Ottoman territory; regret and grief marked the receipt of the same news at Berlin and at Vienna. This distinction the Ottoman government speedily perceived; and Enver Pasha, the most conspicuous and influential leader of the dominant Young Turk Party since the Turkish revolution of 1908 and the national Turkish hero in the Balkan war of 1912–1913, became an ardent Germanophile. Turkey, under the guidance of Enver Pasha, was predisposed to support Germany in the crisis of the Great War.

Soon after the declaration of war, two German cruisers in the Mediterranean, the *Goeben* and the *Breslau*, took refuge, as we have seen, in the harbor of Constantinople. There their German officers and crews coöperated with German agents and with Enver Pasha and other Germanophile Turks in inflaming popular sentiment against the Allies. Some members of the Turkish ministry hesitated to hazard an actual war with Britain and Russia, but they could not act independently while their capital was honeycombed with German propaganda and threatened by two powerful German cruisers cleared for action. The officers and men of the cruisers refused to put to sea or to be interned; the Turkish government, even if it so desired, did not have adequate means of enforcing its international obligations in this respect; the Allies protested; the Turks answered by abrogating the "capitulations," under which foreigners on Ottoman soil had been tried by judges of their own nationality; again the Allies protested; the Turks under German pressure replied by closing the Dardanelles to commerce, thereby cutting Mediterranean communication with Russia; again the Allies protested; and the Turks joyfully received a fresh batch of officers from Berlin to prepare them for war.

On October 29, 1914, the *Breslau*, now masquerading as a Turkish cruiser, shelled Russian towns on the Black Sea, and three Turkish torpedo-boats raided the port of Odessa. Finding the responsible Turkish authorities unwilling or unable to make reparation for these hostile acts or to take steps to prevent their repetition, the Allied ambassadors asked for their passports and left Constantinople. On November 3, Russia proclaimed hostilities, and two days later Great Britain and France declared

war against the Ottoman Empire.   Turkey had definitely cast
her lot with Germany and Austria-Hungary.

Turkey could not be of immediate, direct military value to the
Teutonic Powers, for from them she was separated by Bulgaria
and Rumania, both of which were still neutral, and by Serbia,
which was hostile.   Turkish armies could not be brought to the
Teutonic battle-lines in France or in Poland.   Yet the Germans
welcomed the support of Turkey for two reasons.   In the first
place, the Mohammedan Turks were counted upon to stir up the
fellow-Moslem populations of Morocco, Algeria, Egypt, and
India, to engage in a "Holy War" against Great Britain and
France.   In the second place, the Turkish army was expected to
require the attention of a considerable body of Russian and
British troops, who would thus be prevented from participating
in the battles of Galicia and Flanders.   Neither of these expectations was fully realized.   The "Holy War," it is true, was
solemnly proclaimed at Constantinople on November 15, 1914,
but despite some spasmodic uprisings in Morocco against French
rule and a certain amount of general Moslem unrest elsewhere,
in the main the Mohammedan subjects of Great Britain and
France gave little heed to the Chief of the Faithful at Constantinople.   No general insurrection ensued, and the hoped-for
diversion from the conquest of German colonies overseas was not
forthcoming.   Nor were the Allied forces in Europe seriously
weakened by Turkey's entry into the war.   The Russians utilized such forces as they could not easily transport to Poland to
inaugurate their campaign from the Caucasus into Armenia;
the British could depend largely on colonial troops to defend
Egypt and to invade Mesopotamia; and the Allies might even
count on a timely Mohammedan diversion in their favor within
the Ottoman Empire itself, for the Arabs of the Hedjaz, under their
respected chieftain, the Sherif of Mecca, were disgusted with the
Young Turk régime at Constantinople and were ripe for revolt.

In one way Turkey's entry into the war was a boomerang
against Germany.   To Germany the "sphere of influence" in
Turkey was of far greater economic and political importance
than all her "colonies" in Africa and in the South Seas put together.   The latter, under the German flag, were an obvious and
quick prey to Great Britain's naval superiority, but so long as
Turkey remained out of the war the German sphere of influence
in Anatolia and Mesopotamia was protected by the neutral
Crescent flag.   As soon as Turkey entered the war, however,
Great Britain's naval superiority could be brought to bear upon

Germany's interests in the Near East as well as upon her interests in Africa and Oceanica. If German imperialists were devoted to a Berlin-to-Bagdad *Mittel-Europa* project, there were British imperialists whose hearts and minds were set upon a Suez-to-Singapore South-Asia project. The Ottoman Empire occupied a strategic position in both schemes. A neutral Turkey, on the whole, was favorable to German imperialism. A Turkey in armed alliance with Germany presented a splendid opportunity for British imperialism.

Coincident with Turkey's entry into the war, the British formally annexed the Greek-speaking island of Cyprus, in "military occupation" of which they had been since 1878. On December 17, 1914, the legal status of Egypt was changed by a decision of the British government: "In view of the state of war arising out of the action of Turkey, Egypt is placed under the protection of His Britannic Majesty, and will henceforth constitute a British protectorate. The suzerainty of Turkey is thus terminated. His Majesty's government will adopt all the measures necessary for the defense of Egypt and the protection of its inhabitants and interests." At the same time the khedive of Egypt, Abbas II, who had thrown in his lot with Turkey, was deposed, and the Egyptian crown was given, with the title of sultan, to Hussein Kemal Pasha, an uncle of the khedive. Already a British force from India had landed at the head of the Persian Gulf, had taken Basra on November 23, and was preparing for an invasion of Mesopotamia, with Bagdad, three hundred miles up the Tigris, as the objective. In vain the Turks struggled against their foes on many fronts: their efforts to invade Russian Caucasia and to drive the Russians from northwestern Persia were frustrated in January, 1915, and their attacks on the Suez Canal failed dismally in February, 1915.

An opportunity of another kind was afforded the Allies by Turkey's entry into the war. It might now be possible to disintegrate the whole Ottoman Empire and to utilize the extensive spoils as inducements for strengthening and enlarging the armed alliance against the Teutonic Powers. Here was an opportunity for Great Britain and France to undo the work which they had accomplished in the Crimean War, and by pledging Constantinople to Russia to bind their Eastern ally more closely to themselves. Here, too, was an opportunity for the Entente Powers to draw Italy into a firm alliance with themselves: Italy had long been angling in the troubled waters of Near Eastern diplomacy; she could now be promised Albania and attractive imperialistic concessions in Asiatic Turkey. From Turkish spoils, moreover, sufficient territorial rewards might be dangled before the eyes of Balkan statesmen to actuate them to put aside their mutual jealousies, to reconstitute the Balkan League of 1912, and to add the considerable weight of their joint armaments to the forces of the Allies. Of the Balkan states, Serbia and Montenegro had the least to gain from making war on Turkey, but they were already serving manfully the Allied cause. Bulgaria, however, after conquering Adrianople in the First Balkan War, had been despoiled of that rich prize by the Turks in 1913; now, if she would espouse the cause of the Allies, she might recover what she had lost. Greece, likewise, might be rewarded for timely aid by securing the Greek-speaking cities of Asia Minor, which were still oppressed by foreign, Turkish rule, but toward which the free Greeks turned ever longing eyes. A grand alliance cemented between the Balkan States, Italy, Russia, France, and Great Britain, would admit of the crushing not only of Turkey but of Austria-Hungary and Germany. The prospect was alluring.

Turkey had gone to the support of Germany in October, 1914. This action, however, did not serve, as the Germans expected, to stay the conquest of the German colonies by Great Britain. Rather, it widened the area which the British might master and the opportunity which British naval superiority could seize. Nay more, it offered the Allies a chance to terminate the Great War favorably to their own interests by a noteworthy *coup* in the Near East.

GERMANY'S COUNTER–OFFENSIVE ON THE SEAS

It was apparent soon after the outbreak of the Great War that England was mastering the seas and vast dominions beyond the seas. Neither rebellion within the British Empire nor the struggle on the continent of Europe was staying the rapid loss of German commerce, German colonies, and German "spheres of influence." Japan was assisting Great Britain, and to Germany Turkey was rapidly becoming a hindrance rather than an aid. Could not some counter-offensive be undertaken against the Mistress of the Seas, some measures that would terrify her merchants and paralyze her industry? Could not Teutonic "frightfulness" succeed where Teutonic force failed?

In attempting to answer these questions, the German authorities from the beginning of the war utilized such weapons of "frightfulness" as floating mines, naval raids on unprotected English coast towns, and the bombardment of populous cities by Zeppelins and other aircraft. Allusion has already been made to the planting of mines by the Germans along the North Sea coasts; these mines caused considerable loss to British and Allied shipping.

Moreover, it was occasionally possible for a few very swift German cruisers to elude the powerful British squadrons in the North Sea and to conduct a sudden raid along the English and Scottish coasts. Thus, for example, on November 3, 1914, German warships threw shells at the towns of Yarmouth and Lowestoft; and in a second raid, on December 16, they inflicted a good deal of damage on three other coast towns. At Hartlepool, the only one of the three towns which could be called a fortified place, 119 persons were killed and over 300 were wounded. Scarborough suffered less severely, losing eighteen killed, mostly women and children, and about seventy wounded. Whitby, the third town to be bombarded on this occasion, reported the destruction of many houses, but only three persons killed and two wounded. These raids called forth angry protests from the English press, on the ground that the shelling of unfortified places, and the killing of unsuspecting civilians, was a needless barbarity and could serve no military purpose. But obviously the German government considered it as important to strike terror into the heart of the civilian as to disarm the soldier.

This was probably the major purpose of the frequent attacks made by German aviators on cities like London and Dover, to say nothing of Paris and Antwerp. Bombs dropped from a Zeppelin or from an airplane might demolish a building or two and kill a few women and children, but they would hardly destroy extensive fortifications. Undoubtedly German air-raids compelled the British to maintain a large defensive air-force at London and thereby hampered Allied air-offensives on the fighting front in France, but as a rule they were spectacular and attracted attention out of all proportion to their real importance. They were significant, however, in that they brought the Great War directly home to England's civilian population and aroused a national rage against the "Huns." It was the first time since the Norman Conquest that the soil of England had been violated by foreign foes; never before had there been in England such enthusiastic volunteering for naval defense at home and for military offense overseas.

The chief weapon of the German counter-offensive remains to be mentioned — the submarine. From the outset Germany recognized that it would be idle to risk its "supermarine" fleet in a conflict with the far more powerful British navy. But her submarines she could use to destroy not only belligerent warships but enemy merchantmen, and even neutral vessels of the latter sort if they were thought to carry contraband. All the Great Powers had fleets of submarines at the beginning of the war, but from the very nature of things only the Teutonic Powers found general use for submarines. As German warships and German merchantmen were speedily driven from the seas by British naval superiority, British submarines had little or nothing to do. On the other hand, German submarines now had much to do. France and Russia might be invaded by German armies, but the only way for Germany to strike directly at Great Britain was by means of the submarine. The inhabitants of Great Britain, to live, had to import large quantities of foodstuffs; to finance their government and their allies in the Great War, they had to keep their industries going, import raw materials, and ·export manufactured goods; to provide themselves with sufficient munitions of war to cope with militaristic Germany, they had to rely in part upon the United States. Hence uninterrupted sea-trade was essential to Great Britain's prosecution of the war. To most Germans it seemed as if the submarine was providentially placed in their hands to enable them to achieve what a Napoleon had not achieved, the breaking of Britain's sea power. By means of the submarine they would stop the flow of munitions from America, they would deprive England of her foreign markets, they would halt the turning of her factory-wheels, they would bankrupt and starve her, they would oblige her to lift the blockade she had imposed on Germany, they would ultimately vanquish her. Germany would then regain a colonial empire and secure naval superiority. Thereby would the "freedom of the seas," in a German sense, be established.

The Germans imagined that they could count on some aid from the United States in forwarding their counter-offensive on the seas. Early in the war the American government, like the governments of other neutral countries, was strenuously engaged in controversy with Great Britain over questions of contraband, blockade, and interference with mails. Most of the historic claims of the United States for the right of neutral trade in time of war had been sanctioned by a declaration drawn up at London in 1909 by authorities on international law, but as it had not been formally ratified by all the maritime Powers the United States could not get Great Britain to observe it in letter or in spirit. In fact, the British government, in its endeavors to "starve out" Germany, arbitrarily lengthened the contraband list, detained and seized cargoes in transit from America to Germany, even from America to neutral Denmark and Holland, and systematically intercepted and inspected neutral mail. The result was a notable depression in many American, as well as German, industries, a rising wave of ill-feeling against England, and the dispatch of an energetic note of protest by the United States to Great Britain on December 26, 1914.

On the same day the German government contributed to the complications of the situation by placing under public control all of the food supply of the Empire. This meant that no distinction could henceforth be made between foodstuffs imported into Germany for military use and similar imports for the use of non-combatants. Wherefore the British government at once declared that all foodstuffs intended for consumption in Germany would be treated as contraband. Neutral trade with Germany was thus practically prohibited, and American grievances against Great Britain towered higher. A test case was made with the steamship *Wilhelmina*, which reached England early in February, 1915, from the United States, loaded with grain for Germany. She was seized by the local authorities and condemned by a British prize court. It seemed an auspicious moment for the launching of the German counter-offensive.

So far the operations of German submarines had been restricted to attacks on enemy warships and on a few enemy merchantmen. Now, on February 4, 1915, Germany announced that from February 18 onward the waters around the British Isles would be considered a "war zone," that every enemy merchant vessel found there "would be destroyed without its always being possible to warn the crew or passengers of the dangers threatening," and that "even neutral ships would be exposed to danger in the war zone." This proclamation heralded the beginning of the great German counter-offensive on the seas, unrestricted submarine warfare.

Grave dangers lurked in the counter-offensive, for the submarine was a novel weapon for the purpose and one whose status was not at all explicitly established by international usage. According to recognized rules of international law the procedure for capture of merchantmen at sea was fairly simple: the merchantman must first be warned and ordered to undergo search; if then the merchantman resisted, she might be sunk; otherwise the enemy warship might place a prize crew on the captured merchantman and take her to port, or might sink her provided the safety of her passengers and crew was assured. But this procedure, quite applicable to an ordinary warship, was

strikingly inapplicable to a submarine. In the first place, a submarine had to attack quickly and without warning, for its frail construction would make it an easy prey, if observed, even for merchantmen. Secondly, the crew of a submarine was so small that members could not be spared to constitute a prize crew on a captured merchantman. And thirdly, a submarine was so slight that it could not itself provide for the safety of the passengers and crew of a merchantman which it might sink. To sink a merchantman by a first shot and to leave all persons on board to shift for themselves as best they could, was the only practicable method of "capture" by German submarines. For this kind of "capture" there was absolutely no authority in international custom or wont.

A twofold embarrassment now confronted the United States and other neutral countries. On the one hand, trade with Germany was cut off by the British. On the other hand, trade with Great Britain was menaced by German submarines, and not only trade but lives of neutral citizens also. On February 10, 1915, the American government sent a communication to the German government, calling attention to the serious difficulties that might arise if the contemplated policy of waging unrestricted submarine warfare were carried out, and declaring that it would hold Germany to a "strict accountability" if any merchant vessel of the United States was destroyed or citizens of the United States lost their lives.

American expostulations elicited from Berlin as well as from London only nicely-worded "explanatory" and "supplementary" notes. The situation grew ever more embarrassing to neutrals. On the one hand, Mr. Asquith, the British premier, declared on March 1 that Great Britain and France, in retaliation for Germany's declaration of the "war zone" around the British Isles, would confiscate all goods of "presumed enemy destination, ownership, or origin"; no neutral vessel sailing from a German port would be allowed to proceed, and no vessel would be suffered to sail to any German port. On the other hand, Germany proceeded to carry out her threats in the "war zone." In March, 1915, an American citizen lost his life in the sinking of a British steamship; on April 28 an American vessel was attacked by a German airplane; and three days later an assault upon an American steamer by a submarine caused the death of three American citizens.

Before the government of the United States had formulated any action in connection with these cases, the whole civilized world was shocked at the terrible news that the unarmed Cunard Line steamship *Lusitania* had been sunk on May 7, 1915, by a German submarine off Old Head of Kinsale at the southeastern point of Ireland, with the loss of 1195 lives, of whom 114 were known to be American citizens. The first feeling of horror at the catastrophe was succeeded in the United States by a feeling of bitter resentment at what was certainly a ruthless sacrifice of innocent civilians. It appeared at first as if a break between the United States and Germany was immediately inevitable. President Wilson, however, was resolved to act "with deliberation as well as with firmness," and there ensued a protracted interchange of diplomatic notes between the American and German governments, interspersed now and then with new submarine outrages and with new crises. The United States was not the only neutral Power which suffered from Germany's counteroffensive; the Scandinavian countries, Holland, Spain, and Latin America suffered serious losses, too. But the United States was a Great Power, and one whose friendship Germany could ill afford to lose.

In spite of widespread German propaganda in America, the grievances of the United States against Germany came to weigh more heavily than those against Great Britain. Property rights alone were involved in the latter, and they could be redressed after the war in accordance with the arbitration treaty in force between Great Britain and the United States. Between the United States and Germany there was no general arbitration treaty, and even if there were it would be impossible to arbitrate the loss of human life, in addition to property, which the submarine warfare involved. Germany had counted on American sympathy, if not active assistance, in her counter-offensive. She soon found that in practice it aroused American enmity. How far could she go with it and still keep the United States neutral?

During the year 1915 Germany did not press her counteroffensive on the seas to the utmost. She was "feeling her way" with neutral Powers. Yet the sinkings of Allied merchantmen in that experimental year were sufficient to convince the German admiralty that a perfectly ruthless and unrestricted submarine campaign would compel Great Britain to sue for peace "in six months at the most." Before undertaking such a final holocaust, it would be best, in German opinion, to crush the British allies on the Continent. This done, all the resources of Germany and Austria-Hungary, all their raiding cruisers, all their Zeppelins and airplanes, all their subtle submarines, could be brought to bear upon the task of disputing with Britain the mastery of the seas and of dominions beyond the seas.

CHAPTER V

THE ALLIES ENDEAVOR TO DOMINATE THE NEAR EAST

ALLIED OPTIMISM IN THE SPRING OF 1915

THE events narrated in the three preceding chapters, occurring simultaneously in the autumn of 1914 and the winter of 1914–1915, gave the Allies confidence in ultimate victory. Germany had counted upon a speedy, decisive crushing of France and upon the ability of Austria-Hungary to hold the Russians in check until the joint forces of the Teutonic Powers could overwhelm the Muscovite "hordes." Germany had also scoffed at England's "contemptible little army" and had relied upon uprisings within the British Empire to prevent Great Britain from giving timely aid to France or Russia. All these calculations had been upset. France was not crushed. Austria had suffered a Russian invasion of Galicia. No serious revolt had broken out in the British Empire, and Britain's army in Flanders was growing less and less "contemptible" as the days went by.

In the West the fighting had been taken out of the open field and confined to trenches, and the allied French, British, and Belgians were conducting a "war of attrition," gradually "nibbling" at the German lines and gradually depleting the German forces. In the East, it is true, the Russian invasion of Galicia had been offset by a Teutonic invasion of Poland; several disastrous defeats had overtaken Russian armies; and it was already obvious that without adequate railway facilities, without proper training and equipment, and without sufficient ammunition, the Russian "hordes" could not immediately menace Germany. In short, by the spring of 1915 it had become reasonably clear that neither the efficiency of the Germans nor the numbers of the Russians would suffice to achieve a quick victory. The Great War was to be a long war. It was to be an endurance-test, in which mere battles might play a far less decisive rôle than political and economic factors.

A long war, an endurance-test, appealed more to the Allies than to the Germans. The outcome of such a struggle would depend

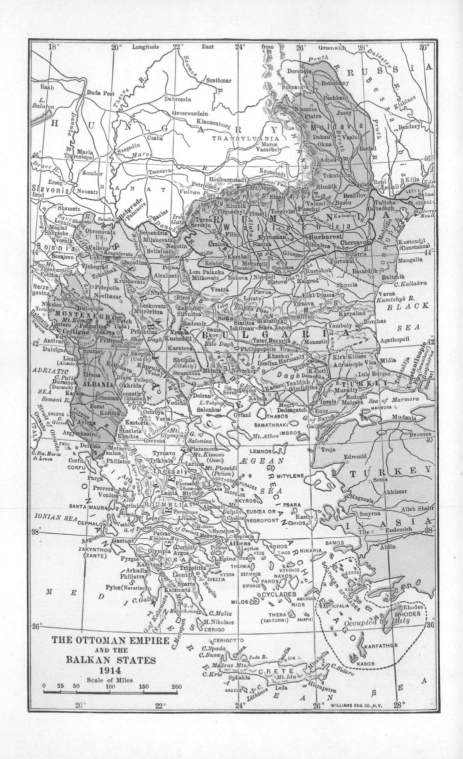

THE OTTOMAN EMPIRE
AND THE
BALKAN STATES
1914
Scale of Miles

not upon the military might of the moment but upon collective national resources of men, munitions, and money. And the Allied Powers were conceded to be vastly superior to the Teutonic Powers in latent resources. As Mr. Winston Churchill, the English statesman, put it: "It is not necessary for us to win the war to push the German line back over all the territory they have absorbed, nor to pierce it. While the German lines extend far beyond their frontiers, while their flag flies over conquered capitals and subjected provinces, while all the appearances of military success greet their arms, Germany may be defeated more fatally in the second or third year of the war than if the Allied armies had entered Berlin in the first year." The factors upon which Mr. Churchill, in common with other Allied and pro-Ally observers, counted to insure the Entente's final victory, may be indicated in five brief paragraphs.

(1) *Resources of Men*. The population of Germany, Austria-Hungary, and Turkey amounted to 140 millions, while that of the Entente Powers and Belgium exceeded 295 millions. Even this obvious disparity did not tell the whole tale, for in the latter figure were not included the teeming millions of India and other subject states of the British Empire or the population of the French colonies or of Japan. At the beginning of the war, the Teutonic Powers, by virtue of their elaborate military preparedness, could put a relatively larger number of men in the field than their enemies; as time went on, however, their initial advantage would be outweighed and obliterated by the mere weight of numbers which the Entente Powers could train and dispatch to the front.

(2) *Economic Resources*. Even should the Allies fail to overwhelm the Central Empires by sheer weight of numbers, it was believed that the failure of Germany's economic resources would bestow the final victory upon the financially invincible coalition of London and Paris. To the student of finance elaborate statistical reviews professed to prove the inevitable bankruptcy of Germany and the financial solidity of France and England. German economists, it is only fair to remark, published similar arrays of figures to demonstrate the ability of Germany to endure to the end, thanks to the willingness of her patriotic citizens to invest in the government's war loans, and thanks to more efficient management of resources.

(3) *Naval Supremacy*. With increasing frequency as the war progressed, allusion was made to the historic parallel between the present struggle and that of Napoleon with Britain's sea power. As sea power at the beginning of the nineteenth century had

overcome invincible armies then, so it was assumed that England's superdreadnoughts would overcome Germany's armies in the twentieth century. Command of the seas enabled the Allies to utilize their own resources to the full, to preserve their own trade, to "capture" German trade, and to institute a virtual blockade of Germany. Germany's attempt to break the blockade by means of submarines was still in its incipient stage and as yet promised to achieve little except to anger the United States and other neutral Powers. It remained to be seen whether German efficiency, which had already staved off a food crisis, could so wisely regulate the economic life of the nation, and so advantageously exploit the resources of Belgium, Poland, and Turkey, that the British navy would be unable to reverse the victories of German armies.

(4) *Prospect of Domestic Disturbances*. In measure as the Germans lost hope of Moslem rebellions in India, in Egypt, and in Morocco, and of popular uprisings against the British and French governments, the Allies grew more optimistic about the chance of revolution within the Teutonic countries. It became known that a group of "Minority Socialists" in Germany was opposing the war and that serious mutinies were developing among the Czechoslovak and Jugoslav subjects of Austria-Hungary. It was also thought that the Arabs would rebel against the Turks, and that the more conservative and reasonable elements in the Ottoman Empire would become disgusted with Enver Pasha's Young Turk clique. It was believed that appeals to the cause of "liberty, democracy, and humanity," against Prussian "militarism" and Turkish "barbarism" would gradually enlist the sympathy of the "oppressed masses" in the Central Powers and Turkey. Time would be required for the disillusionment of the Teutonic people, and time was on the side of the Allies.

(5) *Diplomacy*. Allied diplomacy was supposed to be more adroit and more sympathetic than that of Germany. The Balkan states, because of their hereditary enmity towards the Ottoman Empire, and Italy, because of her traditional rivalry with Austria-Hungary, could readily be cultivated by the superior Allied diplomatists and induced to cast in their lot with the Entente Powers. With such an accession of strength and resources to the Allies, the defeat of Germany would be a foregone conclusion.

Such were the factors which inspired Allied optimism in the spring of 1915. To be sure, Germany still had the advantage of waging the war on "interior" lines and of utilizing more efficiently and economically her available resources. But already France and Great Britain were taking steps, if not to unify all their military efforts, at least to reform and strengthen their respective internal administrations with a view to securing some part of the "efficiency" which Germany enjoyed. In France, as early as August, 1914, a non-partisan war cabinet had been formed under the premiership of René Viviani, including two Socialists and such well-known statesmen as Théophile Delcassé, Alexandre Millerand, Aristide Briand, and Alexandre Ribot. In Great Britain, Mr. Asquith constituted a "coalition cabinet" in May, 1915, including twelve Liberals, eight Unionists, one Labor member, and Lord Kitchener; and David Lloyd George, the ablest of Mr. Asquith's co-laborers, was put in charge of a newly created ministry of munitions.

In the summer of 1914, Germany had taken the offensive against France. By the spring of 1915 it seemed to France and Great Britain that the time had arrived for an offensive on their part. The Balkans were a field ripening for harvest. From the Balkans might be inaugurated that final offensive which would put the Teutonic Powers decisively on the defensive. To the Balkans the Allies turned their attention.

THE ATTACK ON THE DARDANELLES

The key to the Near East was thought to be the Dardanelles, the long, narrow straits connecting the Ægean and the Sea of Marmora. Once through the Dardanelles, a victorious Allied fleet would have Constantinople at its mercy, and Turkey, if not wholly eliminated from the war, would at the very least be cut in two and gravely crippled. All serious danger of Ottoman attacks on Egypt, Persia, or India would be obviated. The Germans would be deprived of any control of the Bagdad railway. The Russian armies in the Caucasus could be largely withdrawn and sent to reënforce the line in Poland. Moreover, the straits being opened, Russia would at last find a free outlet for her huge stores of grain; and the guns and ammunition of which the Russians were in sore need could be freely and cheaply imported by way of the Dardanelles and the Black Sea, as fast as the factories of France, England, and America could produce them.

The moral effect of the capture of Constantinople by the Allies would be tremendous. Not only would it put new life into the forces of France, Russia, and Great Britain; not only would it be an awe-inspiring lesson to the Mohammedan millions in Egypt and in India; it would also, by increasing the probability of the Entente's ultimate victory, hasten the decision of wavering neutral nations to join the winning side.   Italy was already seeking important concessions from Austria-Hungary as the price of her continued neutrality; the Allies would presently be in a position to make her better offers as the price of belligerency.   Most important of all, a successful attack upon the Dardanelles would probably bring the Balkan states into the war on the side of the Entente.   Both Greece and Rumania had Germanophile kings and military castes that were under the spell of German military prestige; in both countries, however, there were popular parties already favorably disposed to the Allied cause, and in Greece, the able prime minister, Eleutherios Venizelos, was known to be enthusiastically pro-Ally; only a victory at the Dardanelles was needed to convince Greece and Rumania that it would be safe for them to join the Entente.   Bulgaria, smarting under the injuries inflicted upon her by her fellow Balkan states in the war of 1913 and restless under her wily King Ferdinand, was suspected of secret leanings toward the Central Empires [1]; but in case of an Allied victory at the Dardanelles, Bulgaria would not dare to oppose the Entente Powers, for Greece, Serbia, Rumania, and the Allied forces at Constantinople could completely encircle and crush her; the cession to her of Adrianople and Turkish Thrace might readily resign her to her fate.

Forcing the Dardanelles, the Allied naval authorities had every reason to believe, would be a difficult and hazardous operation. To be sure, a British squadron had accomplished the feat in 1807; but that was long ago, and since then the ineffective, antiquated fortifications in the straits had been replaced by the most modern and scientific defensive works; expert German advisers had directed the emplacement of formidable batteries to command the approaches by land and sea; and 14-inch Krupp guns could now be trained on an attacking fleet.   But if the hazard was great, the stakes to be won were still greater.

For the sake of a momentous victory the British and French risked a powerful fleet in the attack on the Dardanelles.   During February, 1915, the warships which had been watching the entrance to the straits since the outbreak of the war were reënforced by new arrivals, until, at the time the principal assault was de-

[1] What was then merely suspected was subsequently established by the disclosure of a secret treaty concluded between Bulgaria and Austria in September, 1914, whereby Bulgaria agreed not to enter into any alliance or arrangement with the Entente Powers but to attack Rumania, if Rumania, on her part, should side with the Allies.

livered, there were fifteen British battleships under command of Vice-Admiral DeRobeck and four French battleships under Rear-Admiral Guépratte. Altogether the Franco-British fleet mounted, besides the immense 15-inch guns of the superdreadnought *Queen Elizabeth*, almost seventy 12-inch guns and an even greater number of secondary guns.

On February 19, 1915, the Allied fleet began a heavy bombardment of the forts at the entrance to the Dardanelles. On the tip of the Gallipoli peninsula, constituting the northern side of the entrance, were the fortifications of Sedd-el-Bahr, and on the southern or Asiatic side, two and three-eighths miles opposite, were the forts of Kum Kale. After repeated bombardments, the big guns of the forts were put out of action, and, although landing parties were beaten off by intrenched Turks, the Allied battleships could venture early in March into the lower end of the straits in order to bombard the forts situated fourteen or fifteen miles from the entrance. These forts, Kilid Bahr on the western shore and Chanak on the eastern shore, commanding the channel where it narrowed to about three-quarters of a mile in width, were the cardinal defenses of the Dardanelles. Here the German advisers of the Turkish government had planted their 14-inch Krupp guns. The forts at the entrance had been mere outposts, designed to delay rather than to stop the invader. The decisive battle would be the battle for the Narrows.

By March 18, all was ready for the supreme naval effort which might carry the Anglo-French fleet past the menacing Narrows and on into the Sea of Marmora. It was thought that the guns at Chanak had been silenced by a long-range bombardment conducted on previous days from the Gulf of Saros by the *Queen Elizabeth* and other British battleships. Now the Allied fleet steamed toward the Narrows and aimed their fire at Kilid Bahr. Suddenly forts which were supposed to have been dismantled blazed forth again, and floating mines were let loose against the assailants. Three large shells and a mine simultaneously struck the French ship *Bouvet*, which immediately sank with all on board. Another mine destroyed the British ship *Irresistible*. And a third demolished the *Ocean*. Meanwhile Turkish guns from shore batteries had set the *Inflexible* on fire, opened an ugly gap in the armor-plate of the *Gaulois*, and inflicted severe punishment on other ships. At twilight the great fleet quietly steamed out of the straits, followed by a salvo of parting shots from the forts which it had striven to annihilate. Three first-class battleships and more than two thousand men had been sacrificed in vain. The naval attack on the Dardanelles had failed. The most modern battleships had been proved helpless against up-to-date land batteries.

Instead of admitting defeat and abandoning the Dardanelles campaign entirely, however, the Allies decided to disembark

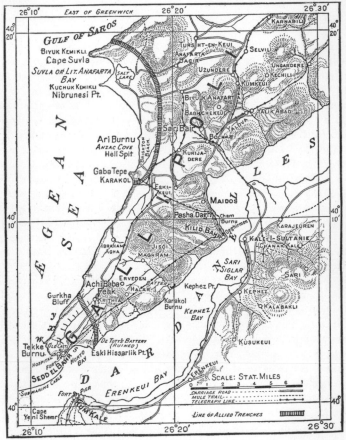

THE DARDANELLES CAMPAIGN, 1915

troops on the Gallipoli peninsula in the hope that a land attack might succeed where the navy had failed. From March 18 to April 25, 1915, the fleet passively awaited the arrival of troops on the scene, contenting itself with preventing the Turks from repairing the ruined forts at Kum Kale and Sedd-el-Bahr. It was a long wait, fraught with serious consequences. The Allies at first hoped they could prevail upon Greece and Bulgaria to furnish the necessary troops for the land attack upon the Dardanelles and Constantinople, but neither Power was particularly heartened by the Anglo-French naval failure, and both Powers made seemingly exorbitant demands as the price of their assistance.   Bulgaria would not content herself with Adrianople and Thrace ; she must also obtain Kavala from Greece and Macedonia from Serbia.   Greece would not be satisfied with Smyrna and its hinterland ; she must have Cyprus, all the Ægean islands, and half of Albania ; and the idea of making any cessions to Bulgaria was most distasteful to her.   Were the Allies to grant all the requests of Bulgaria, they would antagonize their faithful friend Serbia ; were they fully to satisfy Greek ambitions, they would outrage those of Italy, for Italy actually held twelve Aegean islands and had definite designs on Albania and parts of Asia Minor.   Italy, as a Great Power, would eventually be more of an asset to the Allies than Greece or Bulgaria, and Italy must not be alienated. Despite this difficulty, Venizelos, the Greek premier, would have accepted the rather vague offer of Cyprus and other territories and would have ceded Kavala to Bulgaria and given invaluable military aid to the Allies on the Gallipoli peninsula, had not King Constantine sternly forbidden and dismissed him from the ministry.   As for Bulgaria, King Ferdinand dilly-dallied, played politics at home and abroad, and sent no troops to Gallipoli.

Unable to procure troops from any of the Balkan states for a land attack upon the Dardanelles and Constantinople, the Allies proceeded to collect an army of their own as best they could. General Joffre, still fearful lest the Germans might break through his own lines, would spare no troops from the Western Front. Russia had no means of getting forces to the Dardanelles.   Great Britain's relatively small army at home was needed to offset the wastage in France.   The Allies were not grasping the full significance of the Dardanelles enterprise ; they were most unfortunately underestimating the results both of success and of failure. Either they should have abandoned the whole undertaking in March, 1915, or they should have moved heaven and earth to push it to a speedy and decisive result.   They did neither.

Late in April, 1915, an Anglo-French expeditionary force of 120,000 men under the command of Sir Ian Hamilton was at last ready for a land attack upon the Gallipoli peninsula.   A motley force it was.   There were a few British regulars, an Australian division, a New Zealand division, a detachment of Indian troops, a division of British Territorials, and some French colonials and marines. This heterogeneous aggregation, amounting in all to three army corps, was destined to attack a much stronger Turkish army, commanded by a skillful German general, Liman von Sanders, and ensconced in practically impregnable positions. The long delay had enabled the Turco-Germans to prepare a most redoubtable defense.

During the last week of April, the expeditionary forces managed to effect landings in two different regions of the Gallipoli coast, one at Suvla Bay and "Anzac Cove," [1] on the Ægean shore, north and across the peninsula from Kilid Bahr, and the other in the vicinity of Sedd-el-Bahr, at the tip of the peninsula. From the two regions it was planned that the attackers should advance respectively southeastwards and northwards, join forces, and capture Kilid Bahr from the rear. On the tip of the peninsula, in a three-day battle, May 6–8, the Anglo-French line made a supreme attempt to expel the Turks from Krithia. By dint of desperate infantry charges, covered by field and naval artillery, the Allies were barely able to advance a thousand yards. To their intense disappointment and chagrin they discovered that the terrain had been carefully prepared by expert engineers ; wire entanglements, concealed trenches, and hidden batteries were encountered at every turn. Turkish guns on the heights overlooking Krithia commanded the whole position and were so well protected that even the heavy guns of the British battleships, which assisted in the attack, could not disable them. In the other theater, the "Anzacs" fought most gallantly and heroically, but, though they stood their ground against savage Turkish assaults, they were unable to make any appreciable advance to the south or to the east. Meanwhile, the fleet, which had been coöperating with the land forces, was further weakened by the destruction in May of three more battleships — the *Goliath*, *Triumph*, and *Majestic* — so that the British Admiralty, thinking discretion the better part of valor, withdrew the *Queen Elizabeth* and the other large battleships from the Ægean. Glory was added to the British navy by exploits of two submarines which had passed the Narrows and penetrated into the Sea of Marmora, but glory was small recompense for the general naval failure at the Dardanelles.

On June 4, a third offensive against Krithia was ordered by Sir Ian Hamilton. Five hundred yards were gained at one point, but an equal distance was lost at another. This battle marked

---

[1] Ari Burnu, called "Anzac Cove" because the Australasians landed there, the word "Anzac" being composed of the initials of "Australian and New Zealand Army Corps."

the failure of the Allies' campaign on the tip of Gallipoli : three bloody battles had been fought, ammunition had been wasted in terrific bombardments, and some 55,000 men had been sacrificed ; yet the principal Turkish positions remained untaken and the way to Kilid Bahr blocked.   The land attack on the Dardanelles was an even more costly failure than the naval attack.

From February to June, 1915, the Allies endeavored by a *coup* at the Dardanelles to dominate the Near East.   In their immediate purposes they failed : the straits were still closed ; Constantinople was still a Turkish possession ; Bulgaria and Greece evinced fewer signs of submitting to Allied arrangements for their future welfare.   But as the strain between Balkan states and Entente Powers increased, Italy perceived an opportunity to drive a hard bargain with the Allies.   The latter, with Italian aid, might overawe the Balkans; and thus the domination of the Near East would be realized, if not through conciliatory diplomatic negotiations direct with Bulgaria and Greece, at least by means of the might and prestige of the kingdom of Italy.   Despite the failure of the Allies at the Dardanelles, they still had a good chance of dominating the Near East.   Nay more, if France and Great Britain stubbornly maintained the defensive on the Western Front, and Russia pressed her offensive in Galicia, the Allies had a capital chance, with the added weight of Italy's strength and resources, of dominating all Europe.

ITALY'S ENTRY INTO THE WAR

The optimism of the Allies in the spring of 1915 was shared by several neutral Powers, notably by Italy.   The failure of Germany to crush France and of Austria-Hungary to defend Galicia against Russian invasion served in Italy to reawaken the Irredentist agitation for the annexation of Italian-speaking districts of the Dual Monarchy and to quicken imperialistic ambitions for a share of Balkan and Near Eastern spoils.   Belligerent speeches by Italian patriots during the winter and early spring, when the general situation seemed most favorable to the Allies, had stimulated popular enthusiasm for war to such a degree in May, 1915, that the momentum of anti-Austrian feeling carried Italy into the war.

From the *Green Book* published by the Italian government to justify its participation in the war, from the information given out on the other side by the Teutonic governments, and from disclosures made by the revolutionary Russian government in November, 1917, it is now possible to reconstruct at least the main outlines of the diplomatic manœuvers which preceded the Austro-Italian break. A secret treaty, it will be recalled, first negotiated in 1882, when Italy was full of resentment against France for seizing Tunis, renewed in 1887, in 1891, in 1903, and most recently in 1912, bound Italy to the Central Powers in the defensive Triple Alliance. From what we have learned of the provisions of this secret treaty, it appears that if either or both of her allies, "without direct provocation on their part," should be attacked by another Power, Italy would be obliged to join in the war against the attacking Power. If either ally should be forced to declare defensive war against a Great Power which menaced its security, the other members of the Triple Alliance would either join in the war or "maintain benevolent neutrality towards their ally."

At the outbreak of the Great War in August, 1914, Italy had remained neutral, announcing that, since Germany and Austria-Hungary were engaged in an offensive war, the *casus foederis* did not exist. At the same time the foreign minister, the Germano-phile Marquis San Giuliano, had construed Italian neutrality as benevolent toward Germany. As the war progressed, however, and especially after the death of San Giuliano in December, 1914, and the accession to the foreign office of Baron Sidney Sonnino, in whose ancestry were both Jewish and British elements, the spirit of Italy's neutrality became less and less "benevolent," and the Italian government began to accuse Austria-Hungary of violating a clause of the Triple-Alliance treaty which stipulated that as far as the "territorial *status quo* in the East" was concerned, the members of the alliance "will give reciprocally all information calculated to enlighten each other concerning their own intentions and those of other Powers." "Should, however, the case arise that in the course of events the maintenance of the *status quo* in the territory of the Balkans or of the Ottoman coasts and islands in the Adriatic or the Ægean Sea becomes impossible, and that, either in consequence of the action of a third Power, or for any other reason, Austria-Hungary or Italy should be obliged to change the *status quo* for their part by a temporary or a permanent occupation, such occupation would take place only after previous agreement between the two Powers, which would have to be based upon the principle of a reciprocal compensation for all territorial or other advantages that either of them might acquire over and above the existing *status quo*, and would have to satisfy the interests and rightful claims of both parties." This clause had been invoked by Austria-Hungary in the Turco-Italian war of 1911–1912 to restrict Italy's operations against Turkey. In December, 1914, it was invoked by Italy to justify a demand for "compensation" for the advantages which the attack on Serbia would probably give the Dual Monarchy. As "compensation" Italy demanded not only the port of Avlona on the Albanian coast, whither an Italian expedition was dispatched late in December, 1914, but also direct cessions of Habsburg territory to Italy.

The Austro-Hungarian government, directed since January by Baron Burian, naturally objected to the Italian interpretation of the treaty, yet it could ill afford, in view of the Russian advance in Galicia, to alienate Italy. Negotiations were therefore carried on, but with the utmost procrastination on the Austrian side. At length, on February 21, 1915, Italy forbade further Austrian operations in the Balkans until an agreement should have been reached as to compensations; and on March 9, Austria-Hungary acceded in principle to Italy's threat. The German government, which had consistently urged the conciliation of Italy and had sent Prince von Bülow to urge moderation in Italy, offered to guarantee the execution of whatever terms should be agreed upon.

The Italian demands on Austria-Hungary, as formulated finally on April 8, 1915, embraced (1) the cession of Trentino up to the boundary of 1811, the towns of Rovereto, Trent, and Bozen; (2) an extension of the eastern Italian frontier along the Isonzo river to include the strong positions of Tolmino, Gorizia, Gradisca, and Monfalcone; (3) the erection of Trieste into an autonomous state; (4) the cession of several Dalmatian islands; (5) the recognition of Italian sovereignty over Avlona, and the declaration of Austria-Hungary's disinterestedness in Albania and in the twelve Ægean islands. Austria-Hungary absolutely refused the second, third, and fourth demands, and modified the first by reserving Bozen. Besides, Austria-Hungary was averse from making any cessions to Italy until the end of the war; and she set up a counter-demand that Italy should promise perfect neutrality in respect of herself and Germany so long as the war might last. The Italian government, on its side, felt that it had been dallied with and rebuffed by Austria and that Germany's "guarantees" were not very impressive. Germany had once guaranteed the neutrality of Belgium and had then rebuked Great Britain for minding a "scrap of paper." Germany now promised to guarantee cessions of Austrian territory at the conclusion of hostilities, but if she should be defeated, as seemed probable, she would be in no position to fulfill her engagements, and if by chance she should win, she most likely would laugh at Italy's "scrap of paper."

All this transpired just at the time when the Entente Powers were conducting their Dardanelles campaign and were encountering serious difficulties in obtaining support from Greece and Bulgaria. It was a splendid opportunity for Italian diplomatists. The latter were in a position to utilize Allied offers to raise the offer of Austria, and then to utilize Austrian concessions to raise the offers of the Allies. Italy was apparently willing to sell to the highest bidder, and the Entente could bid higher than the Teutonic Powers. The Entente Powers could promise large slices of Austria to Italy without hurting themselves in the least, and in the Near East, in the existing emergency, they could promise enormous imperialistic profits. The fulfillment of the Entente's promises would be like that of Germany's, "at the conclusion of the war," but the Entente had every motive for keeping its word which Germany lacked, and the Entente was more likely in the long run to win the war than were the Teutonic Powers. The more protracted were the Austro-Italian negotiations, the more zealously the Allied diplomatists courted Italy and the harder was the bargain which Italy drove with the Allies.

On May 4, 1915, Italy denounced her treaty of alliance with Austria-Hungary. Already, on April 26, Italy had signed a secret agreement at London with representatives of Great Britain, France, and Russia, whereby she was to receive Trentino, all southern Tyrol to the Brenner Pass, Trieste, Gorizia, and Gradisca, the provinces of Istria and Dalmatia, and all the Austrian islands in the Adriatic. Italy, moreover, was to annex Avlona and its neighborhood although she was not to object if it were later decided to apportion parts of Albania to Montenegro, Serbia, and Greece. Besides, Italy was to strengthen her hold on Libya, and, in the event of an increase of French and British dominion in Africa at the expense of Germany, she was to have the right of enlarging hers. Finally, Italy was to retain the twelve Greek-speaking islands in the Ægean and to secure on the partition of Turkey a share, commensurate with those of France, Great Britain, and Russia, in the basin of the Mediterranean and more specifically in that part of it contiguous to the Turkish province of Adalia. By an additional article, "France, England, and Russia obligate themselves to support Italy in her desire for the non-admittance of the Holy See to any kind of diplomatic steps for the conclusion of peace or the regulation of questions arising from the present war."

While this amazing treaty was being signed, Italy was preparing for war.   Before the final rupture, Austria-Hungary, unaware
of the Entente agreement, made a last attempt to purchase Italy's
neutrality.   According to a statement made by Bethmann-Hollweg, the German chancellor, on May 18, the Dual Monarchy

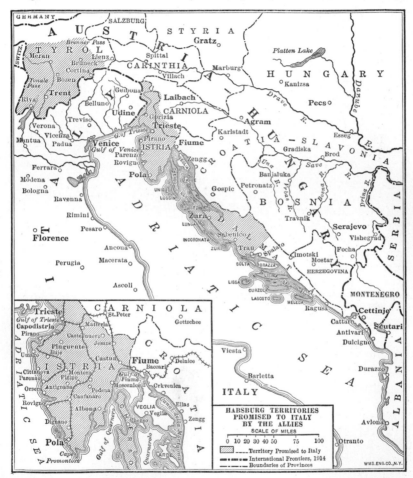

HABSBURG TERRITORIES
PROMISED TO ITALY
BY THE ALLIES
SCALE OF MILES

offered: (1) The Italian part of Tyrol; (2) the western bank
of the Isonzo, "in so far as the population is purely Italian," and
the town of Gradisca; (3) sovereignty over Avlona and a free
hand in Albania; (4) special privileges for Italian-speaking subjects of Austria-Hungary; (5) "Trieste to be made an imperial

free city, with an administration giving an Italian character to the city, and with an Italian university." Moreover, the Austro-Hungarian government accepted the previous Italian demand that the cessions should be made as soon as the new boundaries could be delimited, instead of awaiting the conclusion of the war. Signor Salandra, the Italian premier, was already committed to the Allies, and now, having tested the strength of the war-spirit in Italy by tentatively resigning, was so confident of popular support that he abruptly broke off further bargaining. On the evening of May 23, 1915, the Italian government announced that war against Austria-Hungary would begin the following day.

Italian intervention in the war must not be regarded simply as the culmination of the government's haggling over patches of territory. Italy went to war first of all because the people had been aroused by wild enthusiasm for a war of emancipation to redeem the Italian populations of Trentino and Trieste from the hereditary enemy of Italian national unity. At the same time chauvinistic journals had begun to preach the doctrine that Italy as a great and growing Power, as the modern heir to "the grandeur that was Rome," must establish an hegemony of the Adriatic and reach out for imperial dominion in the East. While chauvinists were frankly urging an aggressive war for colonial expansion, humanitarians and liberals and radicals were exhorting the Italian nation to join in the defense of civilization, democracy, and liberty, against Austro-German militaristic imperialism. These three powerful sentiments — anti-Austrian nationalism, aggressive imperialism, and anti-German liberalism — enabled a majority of the Italian people to accept with approval, if not with jubilation, the result of the diplomatic manœuvers. The Socialists objected; Giolitti and a few other pro-German politicians were pacifistic; some clericals at the outset were opposed to war with Catholic Austria. The opposition was composed of numbers too few and of elements too diverse to affect the course of events.

The Italian declaration of war, as might have been expected, was received with delight in France and England, with deep resentment in the Teutonic countries. It is significant, however, that notwithstanding its abhorrence of Italy's "treachery," the German government did not declare war against Italy [1]; probably Germany thought that thereby the way would be left open for Italy in the future to desert the Entente Powers and to make a separate peace with Austria-Hungary. As a precaution against

[1] Italy, however, declared war against Turkey on August 21, 1915.

such a contingency, the Allies prevailed upon Italy to adhere on September 5, 1915, to the Pact of London ; and by the adherence of Japan on October 19, five Great Powers — Great Britain, France, Russia, Italy, and Japan — were then bound individually not to make peace except in concert.

Italy's entry into the war added to the Allied forces a field army of one million men and some two million reservists, under the nominal command of King Victor Emmanuel, and the actual command of Count Luigi Cadorna, and a navy comprising four dreadnoughts, ten older battleships, and numerous smaller craft, under the direction of the Duke of Abruzzi. It was anticipated by publicists in Allied countries that an attack of the large Italian army upon Trentino and Trieste, synchronizing with a Serb offensive in Bosnia and with a big Russian thrust from Galicia, would effectually grind Austria-Hungary between upper and nether millstones and would speedily compel the Dual Monarchy to sue for peace. It was expected, moreover, that without lessening the efficacy of this major blow Italy would have troops enough to spare to reënforce the Allies in the Near East. Italy might help the Anglo-French expedition at the Dardanelles, might aid the Serbians, and by means of her diplomatic influence at Bucharest might prevail upon Rumania to enter the war and participate in the division of Habsburg spoils.

The publicists were altogether too optimistic. They failed to recognize the grave handicaps to the Allied cause inherent both in Italy's military position and in the nature of the secret agreement by which Italy's services had been secured. The secret agreement, as we know, promised to Italy Ægean islands and territory in Asia Minor which Greece coveted, and Dalmatia, which was peopled largely by Jugoslavs and to which for national and economic reasons Serbia aspired. The result was embarrassing to Allied diplomacy. The Allies were already having trouble enough with King Constantine of Greece, and in taking sides with Italy in the Græco-Italian rivalry they were strengthening the pro-German Greek king against Venizelos, the pro-Ally Greek statesman. At the same time, they were endeavoring to satisfy Bulgarian ambitions by obtaining from Serbia the cession of Macedonia to Bulgaria, but now that Dalmatia was pledged to Italy the Allies had to be pretty vague in promising "compensations" to Serbia for the great self-sacrifice they expected from her. The Serbian government consequently grew more intransigeant about ceding territory to Bulgaria ; Bulgaria grew more hostile to the Allies ; and the Jugoslavs of southern Austria-

Hungary, kinsfolk of the Serbians, gradually feeling that they were being left in the lurch by the Allies, temporarily evinced an unseemly loyalty to the Dual Monarchy.   Italy's entry into the war kept Greece neutral, rendered Bulgaria hostile, and made Serbia and Montenegro lukewarm.   As for Rumania, secret negotiations were known to have been carried on between that enterprising state and Italy, and it was confidently believed that Italy's declaration of war heralded Rumania's.   As we shall see in the next chapter, however, Rumania's conduct in 1915 was conditioned less by Italy's declaration of war than by Russia's overwhelming defeat.   With flanks exposed to Teutonic attacks, Rumania kept the peace.

Temporary diplomatic embarrassment would not have signified much to the Allies had effective military support come speedily from the Italians.   That it was not forthcoming was most disconcerting to optimistic publicists, but it was not the fault of Italy or of the Italian people.   It was the fault of nature and

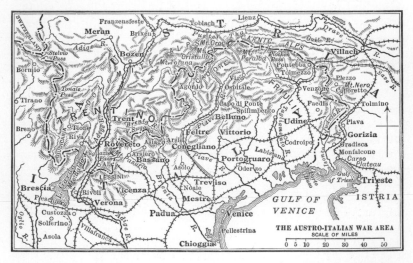

THE AUSTRO-ITALIAN WAR AREA

geography and of the strategic frontier which Austria-Hungary had cunningly held for many years as protection against a possible Italian attack.   The boundary between Italy and Austria lay across precipitate snow-clad Alpine peaks, across deep narrow ravines, across mountain torrents and swiftly flowing streams, and all the highest points and most accessible passes were on the Austrian side.   To the Italian General Staff was presented the problem of conducting a campaign on one of the most difficult

terrains in Europe.   The Austrians required a minimum of troops
to hold positions that both by nature and by artifice were admirably adapted to defense; the Italians needed a maximum of
force to take the offensive.   This geographical difficulty explains
better than anything else the seemingly long delay of the Italians
in invading Austria.   It likewise explains the unwillingness of
the Italian government to dispatch troops to Serbia or to the
Dardanelles.   Under the circumstances, Italy undoubtedly did
the best she could.

   General Cadorna concentrated the main strength of his armies
at the railheads along the southeastern portion of the Austro-
Italian frontier, for an attack in force on positions along the Isonzo
river, just east of the border; within a week of the declaration
of war the Isonzo had been reached, but there the Italians were
confronted with strongly fortified heights east of the river, from
Monte Nero in the north to Monfalcone and the Carso plateau
on the coast.   All summer the Italians struggled bravely but
vainly to master these heights.   Meanwhile, against the middle
sector of the Austro-Italian frontier, which is simply a north-
ward-bulging mountain-ridge, General Cadorna sent only a comparatively thin line of troops, with instructions to guard the passes
and prevent an Austrian counter-invasion.   The third, or western, sector of the frontier was formed by the irregular triangle
of Trentino, jutting southward into Italy.   The strong popular
sentiment demanding the liberation of the Italian inhabitants
of Trentino, taken in conjunction with the military necessity of
forestalling an Austrian offensive from the commanding heights
of the district, furnished ample justification for an Italian movement against Trentino.   With this object, one Italian army penetrated the blunt apex of the triangle, following up the valley of
the Adige and the basin of Lake Garda towards Rovereto, while
small parties of Italian mountaineers assailed the mountain passes
along both sides of the triangle, threatening Trent from the east
and from the west.   It was slow and difficult campaigning, and
great or decisive results were not speedily manifest.

   Early in the spring of 1915 the Allies endeavored to dominate the Near East.   Their first attempt — the naval attack on
the Dardanelles — had failed.   Then their efforts to obtain military assistance from Greece and Bulgaria had been fruitless.
Their next attempt — the land attack on the Gallipoli peninsula
— had netted them no considerable gain.   Then they had prevailed upon Italy to enter the war.   But Italy could not spare

H

troops from her own difficult frontiers for immediate operations in the Near East.   At the outset the domination of the Near East had seemed to the Allies a relatively easy, minor affair.   By the summer of 1915 it had assumed a major importance but had enormously increased in difficulty.   Could the Allies dominate the Near East?   There was still a chance.

Perhaps, though, it was not necessary for the Allies to dominate the Near East.   With intense pressure exerted simultaneously by Russia and by Italy against the Dual Monarchy, the quickest and best way of defeating Germany might lie in the collapse of Austria-Hungary rather than in the fate of the Ottoman Empire and the Near East.   To that end it was imperative, however, that Russia as well as Italy should fight victoriously.   The summer of 1915 beheld Russia in retreat.   It was a critical time.

CHAPTER VI

RUSSIA RETREATS

MACKENSEN'S DRIVE: THE AUSTRIAN RECOVERY OF GALICIA

Up to the end of April, 1915, the Russian situation seemed most promising to the Allies. The Grand Duke Nicholas had failed to invade East Prussia, but he had successfully defended Warsaw and other fortified positions in Russian Poland against repeated Austro-German assaults, while in Galicia he had conducted a brilliant offensive. The Carpathian passes and the fortresses of Lemberg, Jaroslav, and Przemysl were in his possession. Cracow was not far from his advanced lines along the Biala river. All this had been achieved by the Russians during the autumn of 1914 and the winter of 1914–1915. Surely, sufficient time had elapsed to enable the full utilization of Russia's vast reserve of man-power, and the Allies naturally expected decisive results in the campaign to be waged on the Eastern Front during the summer of 1915. The "military experts" of English and French journals optimistically debated the question whether Silesia or Hungary would constitute the field of the final victories. And the imminent entry of Italy into the war on the side of the Allies promised to complete the dissolution of the Dual Monarchy, so gloriously begun by Russian prowess.

In a way the campaign of 1915 on the Eastern Front was decisive, but it was decisive in a manner wholly unforeseen by the Allies. In the Allies' calculations, too much emphasis had been put upon man-power and not enough upon machine-power, too much importance had been attached to numbers and not enough to efficiency. In an earlier chapter [1] it has been pointed out that the Russians were fearfully handicapped by a clumsy, corrupt government, by poor means of communications, and by a woeful shortage of supplies, and that the Germans not only had plentiful supplies, excellent railways, and a phenomenal

[1] See above, p. 54.

military organization, but also were in a geographical position which permitted them, as soon as the fighting on the Western Front assumed the character of trench-warfare, to transfer large forces with dispatch and efficiency to the Eastern Front. But, above all, Russia was predominantly an agricultural country, while Germany was a veritable hive of manufacturing and industry; and it cannot be stated too insistently that the Great War was a war of machines, that a highly industrialized State was bound to enjoy a tremendous advantage when pitted against a peasant-state.

All winter long the factories of Germany had worked day and night, turning out guns and howitzers and airplanes and rifles and bombs and shells, preparing with skill and ingenuity for a great day of reckoning with the Russians. For the Russians no such preparedness was possible. More men might be brought up, but what could mere men do empty-handed? Guns and ammunition could be supplied in relatively small quantities by Russian factories, and Russia geographically was almost cut off from foreign assistance: during the winter of 1914–1915 the English and French could ship no supplies to Archangel or other White Sea ports because of ice, and none to Black Sea ports because of the Turks; supplies from Japan and the United States could be brought only over sea and then over thousands of miles of a single rickety railway.

So it is explicable to us now, though it then amazed and startled the Allies, that just when Italy entered the war, the Russian armies, instead of continuing their offensive, were suddenly put on the defensive and were compelled hurriedly to retreat from Galicia. With marvelous secrecy and speed Austro-Hungarian and German armies, aggregating at least two million men, had been concentrated in April, 1915, for a prodigious blow in Galicia. In Hungary the armies of General Boehm-Ermolli and General von Linsingen were ready for a new assault upon the Carpathian passes. In Bukowina, General von Pflanzer was prepared to resume his advance into southeastern Galicia. The main strength of the Austro-German concentration, however, was directed against the advanced Russian line in western Galicia along the Donajetz and Biala rivers from the Vistula through Tarnow to Gorlice and the Carpathians: here were the Teutonic armies of General von Woyrsch, the Archduke Joseph Ferdinand, and General von Mackensen, the guiding genius of the whole Galician movement. These armies were provided with at least 1500 heavy guns, thousands of lighter field-pieces, and unlimited supplies of ammunition.

By sending Linsingen into the Carpathian passes to threaten Stryj and the railway to Lemberg, Mackensen kept the Russians in uncertainty as to the point at which the principal attack was to be delivered, if indeed the Russians realized at all the grave danger in which they stood. Then quickly, on May 1, 1915, the main Austro-German attack began along the Biala river with an artillery bombardment of unprecedented magnitude. The opposing Russian trenches were blasted out of existence, and on the next day Mackensen occupied Gorlice and Tarnow. After their first reverse in western Galicia, the Russians fell back some twenty miles to the eastern bank of the Wisloka. From this line, too, despite desperate resistance, they were dislodged on May 7. Dukla Pass, now menaced from both sides, was abandoned, and large bodies of fugitive Russian troops were made captive. By the middle of May the Russians were defending the line of the San in central Galicia.

The battle of the San, one of the most momentous engagements of the war, began on May 15 with a Russian counter-attack, and ended two days later with the Austro-Germans crossing the river at Jaroslav, under the personal observation of the German Emperor. Przemysl, farther south on the San, held out until June 2. Meanwhile, Linsingen, striking north through the Carpathians, captured Stryj on June 1 and advanced across the Dniester. Although Linsingen was temporarily checked by General Brussilov, the Austro-German advance continued to make headway. On June 20, Mackensen captured Rawaruska, north of Lemberg. Mackensen's victory at Rawaruska rendered Lemberg untenable and compelled the Russians to evacuate the strong line of lakes, river, and marshes which constituted the "Grodek position," just west of Lemberg. On June 22 the Austrians under General Boehm-Ermolli triumphantly reëntered the city which the Russians had taken nine months before. The fall of Lemberg may be taken as the crowning achievement of Mackensen's great drive. The Russians had been driven out of the Carpathian passes in headlong rout; Tarnow, Jaroslav, Przemysl, and Lemberg had been reconquered; and within an incredibly brief space of time the Russians had been all but expelled from Galicia (they still held a strip of eastern Galicia, including Sokal, Brody, and Tarnapol). During June alone the Teutonic forces captured 145,000 prisoners, 80 heavy guns, and 268 machine guns. In recognition of his brilliant success, Mackensen was appointed a Field Marshal. Archduke Frederick, commander-in-chief of the Austrian army, was similarly honored.

Mackensen's honors were deserved. In less than two months he had undone what had taken the Russians nine months to do. Moreover, with combined German and Austrian armies, he had succeeded where the Austrians alone had failed. Thereby was the Austro-German alliance cemented. The Habsburg Emperor received back his "lost province" from the hands of a German general, and thenceforth the Dual Monarchy was absolutely dependent upon the military support and dictation of the German General Staff. The recovery of Galicia was of incalculable benefit to the Teutons not only for sentimental and moral reasons but also for economic and political reasons. The one substantial conquest of the Allies was lost, and with it were lost oil-wells, mines, and other natural resources that were greatly needed by the Germans; with it, too, was lost any immediate chance of bringing Rumania into the war on the side of the Allies. The Teutonic recovery of Galicia rendered Italy's ultimate success in Istria and Trentino slower and more problematical; at the same time it guaranteed the security of the Hungarian grain-fields and appeased Count Tisza, the Hungarian premier. It was to have far-reaching effects upon the diplomatic duel then proceeding between Teutons and Allies in the Balkans.

But the most important benefit which the resources of Galicia conferred immediately upon the Teutons was strictly military. It exposed Russian Poland to an attack on both flanks. Mackensen's Drive was but a phase of a grandiose scheme to put Russia entirely out of the war. The German plan of campaign in August, 1914, had been to crush France and then to turn against Russia. Failing to crush France, the German General Staff in April, 1915, had altered their plan; they were now going to overwhelm Russia and then turn against France.

HINDENBURG'S DRIVE: THE GERMAN CONQUEST OF POLAND

As soon as Mackensen had cleared the Russians out of the greater part of Galicia, Field Marshal von Hindenburg launched a gigantic offensive against them in Poland. "Hindenburg's Drive," as the movement was popularly called, was the mightiest effort yet put forth in any theater of war. Its aim was obviously

(1) to push the Russians back to a safe distance from Galicia and East Prussia, (2) to conquer Russian Poland, which the Teutonic coalition desired for military, economic, and political reasons, and (3) either to shatter the Russian field armies completely, or to drive them in a badly battered condition to a strategically disadvantageous position where they would be obliged to remain comparatively inactive.

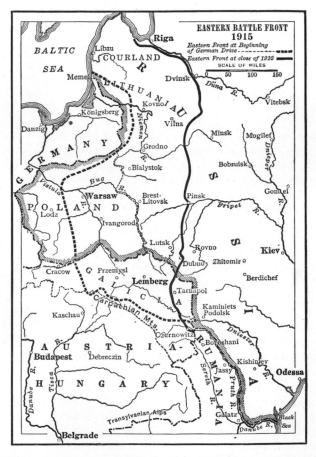

To follow the course of Hindenburg's Drive, the reader must grasp the cardinal significance of Poland's geographical situation and of her railway system. Russian Poland, it must be remembered, was a blunt wedge inserted between German East Prussia and Austrian Galicia; and just as the Russians at the beginning of the war had recognized that they could not safely advance on Berlin until the Teutons had been expelled from East Prussia or Galicia or both, so now Hindenburg fully appreciated the fact that a German offensive simultaneously begun from Galicia and from East Prussia would imperil the whole Russian position in Poland. The first objectives of such an offensive would be the side of a westward-pointing wedge of railways — the most important means of communication for the Russian armies in the field. Of this sharp railway wedge, Warsaw, the capital of Russian Poland, was the apex; the northern side was the railway running northeast from Warsaw through Bialystok, Grodno, Vilna, and Dvinsk to Petrograd; the southern side, the railway extending southeast from Warsaw through Ivangorod, Lublin, Cholm, Kovel, and Rovno to Kiev. Between the northern and southern sides, the only useful railway links behind Warsaw were (1) from Bialystok to Cholm, by way of Brest-Litovsk, and (2) from Vilna to Rovno.

The importance of defending Warsaw and its converging railways was fully realized by the Russian General Staff. The city itself was strongly fortified, and to the north and northeast a line of fortresses — Novo Georgievsk, Pultusk, Ostrolenka, and Ossowietz — made the natural line of the Narew river an artificially stronger protection against any attack from East Prussia aimed at the northern side of the railway-wedge; while to the southeast the broad line of the Vistula with its heavy fortifications at Ivangorod had been deemed sufficiently strong to repel a flanking movement from the southwest. It was reassuring that Hindenburg in his two earlier offensives [1] in Russian Poland had been unable to penetrate beyond these major lines of defense.

Late in June, 1915, just after the fall of Lemberg and the loss of most of Galicia, the Russians were still in possession of the railway salient centering in Warsaw. Their long battle-line stretched from Windau on the Baltic southward in front of Kovno and Grodno; bent westward through Ossowietz, Lomza, Ostrolenka, and Przasnysz; curved southward again in front of Pultusk, Novo Georgievsk, and Warsaw; and swept southeast near Radom, Krasnik, Zamosc, Sokal, Brody, and Tarnapol.

But already the blackest kind of storm-clouds were gathering on the whole Russian horizon. Mackensen's Drive in Galicia had served to divert the attention and chief energies of the Russians to that quarter, and Hindenburg utilized the diversion

[1] See above, pp. 50–52.

to strengthen the whole Teutonic battle-line from the Baltic to the Vistula. It is estimated that, including Mackensen's forces in Galicia, not less than forty-one German and twenty-six Austrian army corps were disposed for the crowning stroke. Russia could produce equal numbers, but she did not have the rifles, and above all she did not have the heavy guns and the shells. Hindenburg's armies were equipped for sledge-hammer blows.

The recovery of Galicia made it possible for Hindenburg to direct his great offensive quite differently from the manner in which he had conducted his earlier and smaller offensives in Russian Poland. Warsaw would no longer have to be assailed from the west; it could now be flanked from the southeast. Mackensen's Drive would be merged into Hindenburg's Drive. In fact, in the last week of June, Field Marshal von Mackensen, leaving General von Pflanzer to complete the reconquest of easternmost Galicia, turned the main group of armies under his command northward and crossed the border into Russian Poland. By the middle of July he himself had captured Zamosc and advanced to within ten miles of Cholm on the southern side of the Polish railway-wedge, while farther west his lieutenant, the Archduke Joseph, took Krasnik and threatened the same railway at Lublin, and still farther west another lieutenant, General von Woyrsch, obtained Radom and drove the Russians back on their fortress of Ivangorod.

Simultaneously the northern groups of German armies began to press the Russians. All the way from Novo Georgievsk to Kovno the pressure was hourly intensified. On July 14, a German army captured the town of Przasnysz and crossed the Narew near Pultusk. In the extreme north, Windau fell on July 20 and the Germans advanced toward Riga. At the south it was the same story. On July 28 Woyrsch forced the passage of the Vistula between Warsaw and Ivangorod, and on the next day Mackensen cut the Warsaw-Kiev railway between Lublin and Cholm.

The simultaneous attacks on the northern and southern sides of the Polish railway-wedge, and the interruption of rail communication toward the southeast rendered the position of the Russian center at Warsaw and Ivangorod extremely precarious. At any moment the Teutonic armies might bite into the salient behind Warsaw, and the Russian center would then be caught between the jaws of the great German offensive. The Grand Duke Nicholas, realizing this peril, chose to sacrifice the city of Warsaw and the fortress of Ivangorod. With feverish haste guns and supplies were dragged out of the doomed places, and on August 4 the Russians evacuated both Ivangorod and Warsaw. On the morning of August 5, 1915, a German army under the command of Prince Leopold of Bavaria entered the Polish capital.

The fall of Warsaw marked the success of the first phase of Hindenburg's Drive; within a month the Russians had been forced to abandon the apex and western sections of their railway-wedge. An isolated garrison at Novo Georgievsk, it is true, held out for a fortnight longer; but the main body of the Russian center during the first week of August raced back madly toward eastern Poland. For a time it seemed as though the bulk of the Russian field army would be entrapped. But the able generalship of the Grand Duke Nicholas and the stubborn defense of Ossowietz, which guarded the northern flank of the retreating center, enabled the Russians to preserve some form and order in their ranks.

Despite the loss of Warsaw, the converging point of the main northern and southern railways in Poland, it might still be possible for the Russians to maintain communications between the major portions of these railways by means of the connecting link through Brest-Litovsk. This, in fact, was the purpose of the secondary line of Russian defense, to hold the railways from Petrograd and Riga, through Dvinsk, Vilna (protected by Kovno), Grodno, Bialystok, Brest-Litovsk, Kovel, and Rovno, to Kiev. If the Russians could hold this line, they would be in good defensive position from which in course of time they might start a successful counter-offensive. This line the Russians were holding by the middle of August.

The second phase of Hindenburg's Drive consisted of efforts to drive the Russians from their secondary line before they had time to organize its defense. In the far north of the long battle-line the Teutonic invaders encountered the most stubborn resistance and, though they reached the Düna river, they were unable to capture either Dvinsk or Riga. At Riga a desperate attempt to land a marine expedition was foiled on August 20 by a naval victory of the Russians over the Germans in the Gulf. But the more southern parts of the secondary line speedily proved as untenable as the Warsaw line.

Already, on August 17, the Brest-Litovsk line was threatened both to the north and to the south. To the north, the fortress of Kovno, inadequately prepared against attack, was surrendered by a Russian general who subsequently was brought up on charges of criminal neglect of duty. In the south, the line was menaced by Mackensen's continued advance east of Cholm toward Kovel. On August 18 a German force cut the railway between Bialystok and Brest-Litovsk. Ossowietz fell five days later. Both Bialystok and Brest-Litovsk were evacuated on August 25, and Grodno on September 2. In vain the Russians launched a counter-offensive near Tarnapol, in Galicia. In vain was their desperate and imprudent defense of the important railway junction of Vilna. Here, while they heroically held in check the German advance from Kovno, other German armies were concentrating north, south, and east. Finally, on September 18, the Russians evacuated Vilna and by means of brilliant holding battles managed to extricate themselves with the greatest difficulty from an impossible position.

With the fall of Vilna, the whole secondary line of Russian defense, except the northernmost sector from Riga to Dvinsk, was in Teutonic hands. By the first of October, 1915, Hindenburg's Drive had come virtually to a standstill, and the Russians rested from their exhausting and demoralizing retreat. The Russian right wing now held the Düna river from Riga to Dvinsk and the lake region from Dvinsk to Smorgon (on the Vilna-Minsk railway); the center maintained an almost straight north-and-south line from Smorgon to the Pripet marshes east of Pinsk; the left wing was fighting for possession of the Lutsk-Dubno-Rovno fortress-triangle near the Galician border and was annoying the Austrians in the vicinity of Tarnapol. All Poland, together with most of Courland and a strip of Lithuania, was a Teutonic conquest.

REVIVAL OF POLITICAL UNREST IN RUSSIA

The rapid expulsion of the Russian armies from Galicia and Poland produced a marked effect upon the political situation in Russia. No sooner was Mackensen's Drive well under way than patriots began to speak out against the incompetence of the military leaders and the inefficiency and corruption of the government; and as Mackensen's Drive broadened into Hindenburg's, these voices of protest grew more numerous and louder and angrier. On all sides demands were made for an early assembling of the Duma and the formation of a really "representative" national government.

An autocracy, such as the Russian, might endure through long periods of piping peace; it might even acquire new vigor and lease of life by means of military victory. But military defeat was almost certain to discredit, if not to destroy, it. In the last war in which Russia had been engaged — the Russo-Japanese War of 1904–1905 — foreign defeats of the Tsar's troops had been a prelude to domestic revolts against the Tsar's government. Now, ten years later, would Russian history repeat itself? That was the question.

In one important respect the situation in 1914–1915 was fundamentally different from that in 1904–1905. The Great War had a significance to the Russian people far greater than the Russo-Japanese War. The latter, strictly speaking, had never been a *popular* war: it had been fought against "yellow men" in far-off eastern Siberia, and its stakes had been the Tsar's imperialistic domination over Korea and China; its reverses had been defeats of the Tsar rather than of the Russian people.

The Great War, on the other hand, was distinctly a national war which appealed alike to the reason and to the imagination of the Russian people: it was being fought at home to defend fellow-Slavic states from Teutonic imperialism; and in the alliance between the Tsar and the democracies of France, Italy, and Great Britain, Russian liberals perceived a means of working in their country a reformation without a revolution. Early in the war, all the political parties of Russia, save only an extreme group of Social Democrats, had pledged unanimous and cordial support to the Tsar's government.

Nevertheless no country can suffer as Russia suffered from May to September, 1915, without a strong reaction. The crowds of homeless peasants pouring eastwards along every highway, the troops tattered and torn and driven backwards frequently in confusion, the endless stream of wounded, were most oppressive reminders of a huge national calamity. The mere problem of relief, to say nothing of the problem of preparing new defensive positions, was enough to strain the capacity of the country to the utmost. The refugees alone by the first of October were estimated at two millions. These men had enormous distances to travel on foot, and shelter had to be provided along the roads as well as relief at the end of the journey. Of the armed forces the casualties were appalling. It was estimated in October, 1915, that to date Russia had lost half a million men killed, a million wounded, and another million in prisoners, — a frightful loss exceeding two and a half million able-bodied young Russians. Worse than all else, there was some justification for the popular impression that much of this loss and most of its attendant miseries might have been prevented if the Tsar's ministers and agents had been as solicitous for their country's welfare as for court-favor and their own pockets.

Already in June, following Mackensen's Drive, but before the full extent of the Russian disaster was manifest, Premier Goremýkin had so far yielded to popular criticism of the government as to dismiss several officials of proved inefficiency or corruption. Makarov, the unpopular minister of the interior, was succeeded by the more liberal Prince Cherbatov; and General Soukhomlinov, the boastful and thoroughly dishonest minister of war, was compelled to make way for General Polivanov. These and other changes were in the right direction, but reform was not drastic enough to satisfy popular critics. And as Hindenburg's Drive succeeded Mackensen's, popular unrest and criticism increased.

On August 1, 1915, the anniversary of the outbreak of war, the Duma was convened to listen to speeches, at once inspiriting and apologetic, by Rodzianko, president of the Duma, and by Premier Goremýkin. In the eloquent opening address of Rodzianko, two themes were dominant. First, he gave voice to the tremendous loyalty and patriotism of the Russian people, and expressed his belief that "the steel breasts of her sons" would unfailingly protect "Holy Russia" from the enemy. However, and this was his second theme, the government must collaborate with the people in a more democratic spirit. "A change of the spirit itself and of the administration of the existing system is necessary." The premier seemed to meet Rodzianko halfway, for he declared it his policy "to unite in a single institution and materially to extend the participation of the representatives of legislative assemblies, public offices, and Russian industry, in the business of supplying the army with munitions and in the coördination of measures for the feeding of the army and the country."

The central feature of Premier Goremýkin's plan to enlist the coöperation of the nation by the creation of advisory boards including experts and delegates from the towns, from the zemstvos, from the Duma, and from the Council of the Empire, to assist the ministers of war, commerce, communications, and agriculture, was readily assented to by the Duma. The Premier's concessions were not enough, however, to satisfy the more democratic of the nation's representatives, who demanded that the ministry itself should be reorganized so as to coöperate more closely with the Duma. To this course the liberals were impelled not so much by the actual German victories as by amazing revelations of the corruption in Russian officialdom. It became known that German influence was at work in Petrograd offices as well as on Polish battlefields. It was astounding that various Russian banks under German manipulation were endeavoring to "corner" certain commodities and hamper the manufacture of munitions for the Russian army, that the Putilov Armament Company, half of whose stock was controlled by Krupp, was dismissing workmen or limiting them to a five-hour day, and that the Russian ministry was taking no effective steps against these abuses.

Late in August, 1915, the leaders of the moderate groups in the Duma finally agreed upon a program of reforms; the first week in September witnessed the organization of a *bloc*, including all the groups of the Duma with the exception of the Reactionaries at one extreme and the Social Democrats at the other, on a platform calling for (1) the reconstruction of the ministry with a view to the appointment of persons able to command the nation's confidence, (2) the adoption of a governmental program calculated to reconcile discontented nationalities and conciliate aggrieved classes, (3) the reform of local administration, (4) the punishment of criminally inefficient commanders and officials, and (5) the vigorous prosecution of the war. Professor Paul Milyukov, the leader of the group of Constitutional Democrats, became the spokesman of the reform movement.

Here obviously was the golden opportunity for the Tsar to adopt a moderate program of political reform and thereby to heighten the loyalty to his person and the enthusiasm for the war which, despite the most painful military reverses, still characterized the Russian body-politic. For a brief moment it appeared as though the Tsar understood the situation and was resolved to act upon it. On September 5, 1915, in the darkest hour of Russian defeat, the Tsar signed an army order announcing that he himself had taken supreme command.[1] "To-day I have taken supreme command of all the forces of the sea and land armies operating in the theater of war. With firm faith in the clemency of God, with unshakable assurance in final victory, we shall fulfill our sacred duty to defend our country to the last.

---

[1] The order transferred the Grand Duke Nicholas to the Caucasus. Subsequently the action of the Tsar appeared in a less favorable light. The Grand Duke Nicholas was a very able general, and his removal was later interpreted as the result less of the Tsar's patriotic initiative than of a sinister court intrigue. See below, p. 226.

We will not dishonor the Russian land." By the appointment of the popular General Alexeiev as chief of staff, the new generalissimo gave sign to the whole Russian people that so far as the Autocrat himself was concerned German intrigue and Russian corruption would not prevail against his purpose to wage the war to a triumphant end.

As the event proved, the Tsar understood only the military aspect of the difficult situation in which Russia found herself. The German Drive speedily came to a standstill, and the Tsar, taking undeserved credit to himself for this surcease of imminent military danger, promptly shut his ears to the reforming clamor in the Duma and throughout the country. The reactionaries breathed more freely, and a certain sullenness possessed the souls of the liberals. It was a crisis whose distant effects no foreigner and hardly any Russian fully perceived.

Scarcely had the progressive *bloc* formulated its program of reform when an imperial ukase was issued, September 16, unexpectedly proroguing the Duma. Protests were voiced throughout the country, especially in Moscow, where a congress of the zemstvos was in session, against this arbitrary exercise of the Tsar's prerogative. Yet this was only the beginning of a pronounced political change in Russia, guided by the autocrat and his ministers, not toward reform and democracy, but straight in the direction of unqualified reaction. Early in October Prince Cherbatov was superseded as minister of the interior by Alexis Khvostov, a member of the party of the Extreme Right in the Duma, who declared emphatically and repeatedly that "we must strengthen the machinery of authority." One ministerial change followed another during the autumn and winter, always more reactionary, until on February 1, 1916, the very acme of reaction was reached with the retirement of the octogenarian premier Goremýkin and the succession to the chief ministry of Boris Stürmer, who was known to be not only an ultra-conservative and an oppressive landlord but a man of German descent, and who besides was reputed to be pro-German in his personal sympathies.

Around the German conquest of Galicia and Poland in the summer of 1915, and even more around the unwillingness or inability of the Tsar's government in the ensuing autumn and winter fully to understand the resulting feelings and emotions of the Russian people, were gradually gathering storm-clouds of popular misery and popular discontent. Russian losses were already greater than those of any other country; Russians had bled and died more numerously than any other nationality. Yet what had it all signified?   The loss of Russia's one conquest and the loss of her richest provinces, the adjournment of the Duma, and the rise of Boris Stürmer!   The great bulk of the Russian people were still enthusiastic about the war and still resolved to pour out treasure and blood to win it.   But they were coming to care less for the winning of provinces than for the winning of political and social freedom.   They still respected the Tsar, but against his corrupt and inefficient reactionary ministers they were growing bitter.   The storm-cloud of revolution, no bigger in September, 1915, than a man's hand, loomed gradually larger throughout 1916, until by the end of the year it promised to overspread the whole Russian sky.

Revolution in Russia would be bound to have marked effects upon the fortunes of the Great War.   As yet, however, in the autumn of 1915 revolution was not menacing, and in Allied countries fears of Russian defection were not expressed.   It was generally recognized that for some time to come Russia would be quite unable to recover Poland, much less to threaten Vienna or Berlin.   The "tidal wave" was stayed.   But the Allies did not yet despair of ultimate aid from Russia.   Russia was not crushed, and even if the Germans should overwhelm her and precipitate revolution and chaos in Eastern Europe, they would still have to deal on their Western Front with France and Great Britain.

FAILURE OF THE ALLIES TO RELIEVE RUSSIA

At the Marne, in September, 1914, France and Great Britain had administered a decisive defeat to Germany.   In May, 1915, Italy had entered the war on the side of the Entente Powers. In view of these facts, it may seem strange that from May to September, 1915, Germany should have been able to win a series of spectacular victories in Russia, driving her Eastern enemy out of Galicia and Poland and out of a large section of Lithuania, and threatening Russia's internal order and security.

The story of German successes against Russia could doubtless have been differently told if in 1915 the Italians had been able to dispatch large forces to the Balkans and simultaneously to capture Trieste and thence march towards Vienna.   In that case Rumania would probably have entered the war immediately on the Allied side; and Germany, instead of being free to chastise Russia, would have been obliged to come to the assistance of her own ally, Austria-Hungary, encompassed on three sides by enemies and struggling for her very existence. But the Italians, as we have seen in an earlier chapter,[1] were held back by a most difficult terrain, and they did well in 1915 to reach the Isonzo: they could spare no troops for a Balkan expedition and they not so much as threatened Trieste. Under the actual circumstances, Rumania preserved a troubled neutrality; Austria-Hungary was not seriously menaced on any side; and Germany could devote her energies to offensive, rather than defensive, war.

But, even so, the fate of Russia was not wholly dependent on an Italian drive. On a 600-mile Western Front were French and British veterans of the victories of the Marne, the Aisne, and Flanders, and a forward movement of these valorous hosts in 1915 might serve independently to bring respite and relief to hard-pressed Russians on the Eastern Front. This had been the chief of Allied calculations, that Germany, compelled to stand on the defensive in the West, would be unable to take the offensive in the East.

Such calculations were purely academic. Despite a lessening of German numbers on the Western Front, a great Allied advance in France and Belgium failed to materialize in 1915. Germany experienced no special difficulty in holding her own in the West at the very time when she was more than holding her own in the East. Why the Western Allies failed to relieve Russia requires some explanation.

It will be recalled that by the end of 1914 the fighting on the Western Front had assumed the character of trench warfare. Allies and Germans faced each other in parallel ditches, from thirty to two hundred yards apart, extending continuously from the Alps to the North Sea. Behind the Allied front there were second and third rows of trenches, and further positions at intervals in the rear. But the Germans had these, and something more. Ever since their defeat at the Marne and their failure to force France to a speedy peace, they had expended immense ingenuity and labor in preparing defensive positions whereby with the least possible effort they might be enabled to retain permanently their first conquests — Belgium and the rich iron and coal regions of northern France. The ramifications of their trenches were endless, and great redoubts, almost flush with the ground, consisting of a labyrinth of trenches and machine-gun "nests," studded their front. In natural defensive

[1] See above, p. 96.

I

areas, such as the mining districts about Lille and in Lorraine, every acre contained a fort. "The German lines in the West were a fortress in the fullest sense of the word. The day of manœuver battles had for the moment gone. There was no question of envelopment or outflanking, for there were no flanks to turn. The slow methods of fortress warfare — sap and mine, battery and assault — were all that remained to the offensive." [1]

In 1915 the burden of the offensive was on the Allies. They knew it, and throughout the preceding winter they had been planning for it. Even before the Germans had begun their great drives against Russia, the Allies undertook to follow up their own victories of the autumn of 1914 by "breaking through" the formidable new German trench-lines.

The efforts of the Allies on the Western Front will be more readily evaluated if their front is considered as comprising three sectors: (1) the northern sector, extending over a hundred miles from the Belgian town of Nieuport, east of Ypres and Armentières, west of Lille, east of Arras, west of Péronne, east of Roye, and through Noyon to a point on the Oise river a few miles north of Compiègne, and held by Belgian and French troops from Nieuport to Ypres, by British from Ypres to Béthune, and by French alone from Béthune to the Oise; (2) the central sector, exclusively French, from the Oise to Soissons on the Aisne, following the northern bank of the Aisne for perhaps twenty miles, then swinging southeast through the Champagne country, northeast of Rheims, through Perthes across the forested ridge of the Argonne to the Meuse River, just northwest of Verdun; (3) the eastern sector, swinging around the great fortifications of Verdun, bending back sharply to the Meuse at St. Mihiel (about ten miles south of Verdun), turning east again from St. Mihiel to strike the Moselle river at a point near the Lorraine frontier, thence extending southeast and crossing over the crest of the Vosges into Upper Alsace, where Thann was still retained by the French.

Early in 1915 attempts were made by the Allies in each of these sectors to carry opposing German lines. In the central sector, the French managed to capture Perthes and fought valiantly but vainly in the vicinity of Soissons. In the eastern sector, the French made a desperate effort to wipe out the St. Mihiel salient: small gains were secured on the northern and southern sides of the wedge, but the main objective was not

[1] *Nelson's History of the War*, Vol. x, p. 107.

achieved. The most ambitious offensive, however, was undertaken in the northern sector by the British, who by this time numbered well-nigh half a million. Early in the morning of March 10, 1915, a terrific bombardment of the German trenches west of Neuve Chapelle (about two-thirds of the distance from Arras to Armentières) and of the village itself prepared the way for an infantry attack. Before noon the village of Neuve Chapelle, now a smouldering heap of ruins, was completely in British possession. In the afternoon, however, and on the two succeeding days, the British were unable to push their advantage with energy; the Germans were allowed to recover from the surprise and demoralization of the sudden bombardment; and consequently the British failed to gain the commanding ridge east of Neuve Chapelle. At the cost of 13,000 lives, Sir John French had advanced his line a mile or so, on a front of three miles, but the great city of Lille, his main objective, was still securely in German hands.

By the middle of April the Allied offensive in the West had made small local gains "nibbling" at the German lines, but had failed to accomplish any strategically important object, either in the movement toward Lille, in the advance in Champagne, or in the attack on the St. Mihiel salient. Shortly after the British offensive had come to a standstill, the British minister of war, Lord Kitchener, told the House of Lords that the shortage of munitions was causing him "very serious anxiety," and Sir John French's official report of the battle of Neuve Chapelle likewise referred to the pressing need of "an almost unlimited supply of ammunition."

Herein lay the real explanation of Allied failure in 1915. The Great War was a war of machines and ammunition as well as of men. Not only were the Russians deficient in ammunition and artillery and airplanes, but in 1915 the French and British also. To make the first dent on the heavily armored German trenches of the Western Front required, as the British and French learned from sorry experience, the employment of all their reserve cannon and all their reserve shells; to carry any considerable section of the enemy lines and to "break through" would require greater reserves than they then possessed.

To add to the discomfiture of the Allies, the Germans actually undertook a counter-offensive against Ypres in April and May, 1915. The Germans did not prepare the way for their attack by artillery but by a cloud of greenish vapor which a gentle breeze wafted towards the Allies' trenches. The vapor, as the

Allied troops soon discovered to their amazement and consternation, was chlorine gas, which chokes and asphyxiates with horrible effect. The French troops holding the line north of Ypres broke and fled before this novel and diabolically cruel form of attack, and Ypres itself was saved only by the gallant and dogged

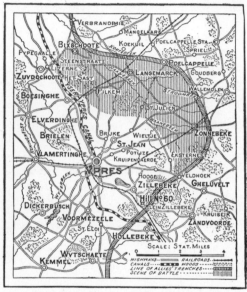

THE SECOND BATTLE OF YPRES, APRIL–MAY, 1915

resistance of Canadian troops. After a month's incessant fighting, the battle of Ypres died down : the Allies had prevented the Germans from "breaking through," but the Germans had greatly reduced the Allied salient in front of Ypres and above all had put new fear and new terror into the hearts of the Allies.

Thenceforth the Allies, and above all the British, labored zealously and anxiously to supply an equipment of hand-grenades, bombs, high-explosive shells, machine guns, airplanes, and respirators (for protection against gas attacks), that would be adequate for the new needs of trench-warfare. But such an equipment could not be supplied by day-and-night output of all the available factories of France and Great Britain, in a week, or in a month, or even in several months. Meanwhile decisive engagements on the Western Front must pause. But meanwhile the Germans, satisfied that they had little to fear from French or British during the next few months and that their own superior equipment and technique would offset any superiority of Allied numbers, hastened to fight decisive engagements on the Eastern Front. Russia must pay for the unpreparedness of Great Britain and France.

Chlorine gas — the latest novelty in German "frightfulness" — was emitted against the Allies at Ypres in April, 1915. On May 1, Mackensen's Drive into Galicia began. And from May to September occurred that series of sensational thrusts and triumphs which, as we have already seen, carried German conquest into the heart of Russia.

Immediately after the first Russian reverses in Galicia, General Foch, commanding the northern sector of the Western Front, sought a diversion by directing his forces again to take the offensive. On May 9, the French just north of Arras and the British farther north in the vicinity of Neuve Chapelle simultaneously assailed the German trenches. The immediate objective of the French attack was the important railway center of Lens; that of the British was the Aubers ridge east of Neuve Chapelle; if successful, from Lens and Aubers the Allies might push on toward Lille. But after a month's most sanguinary struggle the offensive broke down. The British had won "the entire first-line system of trenches" on a front of 3200 yards and the first and second lines on a front of two miles or more, but they had not reached Aubers. The French had mastered the so-called "Labyrinth," an intricate maze of trenches and subterranean tunnels, but Lens remained uncaptured. No relief was afforded the Russians — and none could be afforded.

In fact the Allies in the summer of 1915 grew very fearful lest by spending their small reserve of shells in fruitless assaults on the German trenches they would be so impoverished of supplies that they would be unable to hold their own against a later great German Drive in the West.[1] So the best they could do was to husband their resources, to hurry munition-production, to harry the besieging Germans, and to suffer their enemy to inflict upon their Eastern ally one defeat after another. They wished to help Russia, but they were impotent.

It was not until late September, when Hindenburg's Drive was practically completed, that the Allies on the Western Front felt themselves sufficiently supplied with munitions to undertake

[1] This fear was rendered acute in July by the success of the German Crown Prince in advancing his lines in the Argonne some four hundred yards despite his supposed inferiority of numbers and his recognized deficiency in commanding qualities.

a forward movement. During the summer many thousands of British soldiers, who before the war had been skilled mechanics, had been released from active service in France and sent home for munitions work. In Great Britain, the purchase of raw materials and the employment of labor had been organized; every machine-tool factory was under control of a governmental Ministry of Munitions; and, in addition to the twenty national shell factories already in operation, eleven new projectile works had been established. In France the situation was even better: the hope expressed in the summer, that by October the full complement of French shells would be attained, seemed likely to be realized.

In September, 1915, intense activity of Allied aviators and furious bombardment of the German trenches in France heralded the beginning of a forward movement. The infantry attack began on September 25. While unimportant assaults were delivered near Ypres, and at other points along the line, the main attacks were concentrated at two points, the one in Artois just north of Arras, the other in Champagne midway between Rheims and Verdun.

In the Artois region the initial onset met with brilliant success. A French army under General d'Urbal, north of Arras, captured Souchez and reached the ridge dominating the town of Vimy. Sir John French reported that coöperating British troops "carried the enemy's first and most powerful line of intrenchments, extending from our extreme right flank at Grenay (just west of Lens) to a point north of the Hohenzollern redoubt — a distance of 6500 yards. The position was exceptionally strong, consisting of a double line, which included some large redoubts and a network of trenches and bomb-proof shelters. Dugouts were constructed at short intervals all along the line, some of them being large caves thirty feet below the ground." British troops succeeded, moreover, in occupying the village of Loos and the outskirts of Hulluck between Lens and La Bassée. "The enemy's second line posts were taken, the commanding position known as Hill 70 in advance [east] of Loos was finally captured, and a strong line was established and consolidated in close proximity to the German third and last line."

Meanwhile, in Champagne, according to an official report, the French under General Castelnau, during September 26–27, "succeeded north of Souain and Perthes in occupying a front facing north, and in contact with the German second line, along a stretch of seven and a half miles. The ground thus conquered represented an area of some fifteen and a half square miles, and was traversed by lines of trenches graduated to a great depth. The borders of the woods were organized for defense, and innumerable passages, trenches, and parallels facilitated resistance foot by foot."

After the shock of the initial attack, however, the Allies failed to press on, as popular critics expected, to capture the German

THE ALLIED OFFENSIVE
IN SEPTEMBER, 1915
SCALE OF MILES
0   10   20   30   40   50

railway connections at Lens in Artois and at Somme-Py in Champagne. In Champagne, to be sure, the French captured the village of Tahure, October 6, and further slight gains were made in Artois, but the whole movement reached a standstill by the middle of October. It was patent that, despite feverish activity of Allied factories throughout the summer, the Germans still enjoyed a superiority in munitions-production besides an almost impregnable defensive position, and that to drive the Germans out of France and Belgium would be a terribly difficult task.

Though France and Great Britain by their repeated failures in 1915 had displayed their inability to prevent Germany from administering decisive defeats to Russia, they had more than held their own. They had learned some valuable lessons in trench-warfare by sad experience. They had, with severe losses to themselves, considerably depleted Germany's man-power, — and in the long run they could afford depletion of man-power better than Germany. Most important of all, they had utilized the lull in Germany's attacks upon them in order to forge new weapons in constantly augmenting quantities. They had failed to relieve Russia, but the great Drives of Mackensen and Hindenburg against Russia had absorbed Germany's attention and energies and had prevented her from crippling France and Great Britain in their weakest hour.[1] As the event subsequently proved, Russia had relieved Great Britain and France.

In the meantime bitter criticism was heard in England, and profound disappointment was expressed in France. In Germany the latest forward movement of the Allies was regarded as a costly failure, and a clear proof of the ability of the Germans, with their superior technique, to hold their lines in France against heavy numerical odds. Of the September movement alone a Berlin report estimated the French casualties at 130,000, the British at 60,000, and the German at 40,000.[2] Sure of themselves in the West and elated at their continuous triumphs in the East, the Germans were now quite obsessed by the mad genius of "grandeur." The Kaiser and the General Staff looked about for new worlds to conquer.

[1] In Great Britain, especially, zeal for recruiting and determination to win the war were immeasurably heightened, despite Russian reverses, by continued German outrages in Belgium, notably by the "judicial murder," on October 12, 1915, of Edith Cavell, a brave English nurse in Brussels, who had aided the escape of wounded British prisoners.

[2] The French General Staff estimated the German losses at 200,000.

CHAPTER VII

GERMANY MASTERS THE NEAR EAST

DECLINE OF ALLIED PRESTIGE

THE year 1915 marked the height of Teutonic triumph and the nadir of Allied defeat. To the optimism of the Allies at the beginning of the year rapidly succeeded a profound pessimism which speedily affected neutral countries, especially the wavering Balkan states. In the spring of 1915 the Allies had set out with high hopes to dominate the Near East, but a series of mistakes and misfortunes dashed their hopes and loosened their hold.

Turkey's entry into the war on the side of the Central Empires had appeared almost providential to the Allies; if properly exploited, it might have provided a powerful motive and a favorable opportunity for reviving the Balkan League and for employing it not only to dissolve the Ottoman Empire but also to disintegrate Austria-Hungary and bring Germany to terms. But the failure of the Anglo-French naval attack on the Dardanelles in March and the repeated failures of the Anglo-French land forces on Gallipoli in May and June signified for the Allies a falling barometer in the Balkans. Thenceforth the barometer fell rapidly.

In May, Italy was prevailed upon to enter the war on the side of the Allies, but only by means of the most extravagant promises of eventual territorial compensations, and territorial compensations in considerable part at the expense of the Balkan states. Yet Italy sent no aid to Serbia or to the Dardanelles, and the progress of her arms against Austria-Hungary in the summer of 1915 was not such as to inspire enthusiasm or confidence.

Meanwhile the Russian campaign in Galicia, so promising in March, met with terrible disaster in May; and from May to September the Russians abandoned to the Austro-Germans one city after another, one province after another. All of Galicia, all of Poland, large strips of Lithuania and Courland, became Teutonic conquests.

And meanwhile, too, on the Western Front one Allied offensive after another broke down. Apparently the French and British could barely hold their own; certainly they could not relieve Russia in her hour of supreme need. How could they hope to aid the Balkan states, if these were minded to declare war against Turkey and the Central Empires and thereby incur the risk of invasion by Turco-Teutonic hosts?

To regain some of their rapidly waning prestige in the Balkans the Allies resolved to put forth one supreme effort to clear the Gallipoli peninsula of Turkish defenders and open the way to Constantinople. If the heights called Sari Bair, back of Anzac Cove, could be carried by storm, an attack on the European defenses of the Dardanelles might be undertaken with reasonable probability of success. The great effort was made early in August, just after the Russians had lost Warsaw. While re-enforcements were landed at Suvla Bay, north of Sari Bair, Australasian and Indian troops with reckless gallantry charged up the slopes of the hill. Indians actually succeeded in reaching a point on the heights whence they could look down upon the Dardanelles, but they were compelled to fall back for lack of support. With valor quite equal to that shown by the British colonials, the Turks swept down the slopes, in the face of a murderous artillery and machine-gun fire, to dislodge the British from the footholds which had been gained. On August 10, at the close of the battle, the British still held some of their gains, but two commanding positions, which had been won by daring assaults, had been lost again to the Turks, and the supreme effort had failed with a loss of 40,000 British troops. In the trenches at the tip of the Gallipoli peninsula, the Anglo-French troops were decimated by disease; before Sari Bair the British colonials were maddened by thirst in consequence of unpardonable inefficiency in the management of the water supply. The whole Dardanelles and Gallipoli exploit was worse than a failure; it was a disgrace. All things considered, it was small wonder that by September, 1915, the Allied barometer in the Balkans had fallen until it indicated storms and tempests.

Throughout the spring and summer of 1915 the diplomatists of the Entente Powers had essayed to reconcile Bulgaria with Serbia, Greece, and Rumania, and to bring about the joint intervention of the three neutral states — Bulgaria, Greece, and Rumania. But Bulgaria would not be reconciled unless her neighbors should relinquish what she believed they had robbed her of in the Balkan War of 1913: she must have the Bulgarian

Dobrudja from Rumania, the towns of Drama and Kavala from Greece, and from Serbia a wide extent of Macedonia including Monastir. Serbia, however, after long negotiations, was willing to give only partial satisfaction to Bulgaria's Macedonian aspirations, for since Italy's entry into the war she had discovered an unwonted chariness on the part of the Entente about pledging compensations on the Adriatic for sacrifices she might make in Macedonia.

In Greece were divided counsels. On one hand, the party of Premier Venizelos, which controlled the majority of the Greek Parliament, was ardently in favor of the Entente and eager to enter the war; Venizelos felt that concessions might profitably be made to Bulgaria in view of the prospect of Greece's securing Smyrna and Cyprus. King Constantine, on the other hand, with the support of his German-trained army officers, and with the approval of a popular element, was stubbornly determined not to join forces with the Entente. The king's refusal to intervene in the war was perhaps partly ascribable to the influence of his wife, Queen Sophia, a sister of the German Emperor; doubtless also the admiration for German military methods, to which he had frequently given outspoken expression before the war, now made him extremely reluctant to hazard his own army in a struggle against the Central Empires, particularly since the Entente armies had given no convincing proof as yet of their ability to win the war. At any rate King Constantine positively declined to approve any territorial cessions to Bulgaria, assigning patriotic motives, although in so doing he had to part with his popular premier (March, 1915) and to ignore the mandate of a general election (June). When at length, late in August, Venizelos was reinstated in the premiership, the military situation was so universally unfavorable to the Entente that even he promised to maintain neutrality and to countenance no cession of Greek territory.

Rumania's position throughout this season was not a happy one. She longed for territorial expansion, but its achievement involved the solution of a difficult problem of tactics. If she joined the Entente, she might wrest Transylvania and Bukowina from Austria-Hungary. If, on the other hand, she should join the Central Empires, she might conquer Bessarabia from Russia. Obviously, she could not "eat the cake and keep it too." If she chose Bessarabia, she could not have Transylvania, and *vice versa* her appropriation of Transylvania would bar her from Bessarabia. Furthermore, her geographical situation was most embarrassing. Her irregular and unshapely boundaries exposed her to easy invasion from Russia, from Hungary, and especially from Bulgaria. On whatever side she chose to fight, she must be certain that the other sides were securely held by friends. The royal family in Rumania, though Hohenzollern by birth, were believed to be somewhat pro-Ally in sentiment; and probably a large majority of the Rumanian people hoped for and expected an eventual Allied victory. It was but natural, however, that the statesmen of the country should make Bulgaria's adherence to the Allied cause a prerequisite to Rumania's participation. Faced on the west by an unvanquished Austria and on the north by a retreating Russia, Rumania could not view with equanimity a hostile Bulgaria to the south. So, when neither Serbia nor Greece would make the concessions demanded by Bulgaria, Rumania prudently abstained from casting in her lot with the Entente. And her prudence seemed amply justified by the reverses and resulting miseries which beset great Russia in September, 1915.

The Anglo-French failures at the Dardanelles and on Gallipoli, the spectacular victories of the Austro-Germans in Russia, and the powerlessness of Great Britain, France, and Italy to render effectual assistance to their hard-pressed ally, made the task of Entente diplomacy in the Balkans difficult and painful. The prestige of the Allies had reached the vanishing point; they had failed to dominate the Near East — and had failed utterly. But by the same token the prestige of the Teutons had increased; their diplomatists found roses where the Allies had discovered thorns. Germany laid plans to master the Near East.

BULGARIA'S ENTRY INTO THE WAR AND THE CONQUEST OF SERBIA

Shifty King Ferdinand of Bulgaria and his faithful henchman, Premier Radoslavoff, were much-courted personages during the summer of 1915. Their active assistance was solicited alike by Central Empires and by Entente Powers. Knowing full well that Bulgaria held the balance of power in the Balkans, they were resolved to sell their country's aid to the highest bidder. As Radoslavoff said on August 9, "Bulgaria is fully prepared and waiting to enter the war the moment she receives absolute guarantees that by so doing she will obtain that for which other nations already engaged are striving, namely, the realization of her national ideals. . . . The bulk of these aspirations lie in Serbian Macedonia, which with its 1,500,000 Bulgar inhabitants was pledged and assigned to us at the close of the first Balkan war. It is still ours by right and principle of nationality. When the Triple Entente can assure us that this territory will be returned to Bulgaria and our minor claims in Greek Macedonia and elsewhere realized, the Allies will find us ready to fight with them. But these guarantees must be real and absolute. No mere paper ones can be accepted."

It was already apparent to the Bulgarian government that the offer of Macedonia, if made by the Entente, would not be concurred in by the parties most vitally concerned, Serbia and Greece, and could not be carried out by a France and Great Britain impotent to defeat the Turks, or by a Russia incapable of defending Warsaw. On the other hand, the Central Empires promised Bulgaria not only larger Serbian spoils than the Entente had ever contemplated but also a rectification of her Turkish boundary, a liberal financial loan, and immediate military aid by veterans of Mackensen's and Hindenburg's Drives. Ferdinand and Radoslavoff hesitated no longer. On September 6, 1915, they signed at Sofia a secret convention with representatives of the Dual Monarchy, providing for a joint attack upon Serbia and for the territorial rewards to Bulgaria.

Bulgaria, in accordance with the secret convention, speedily concluded arrangements with German bankers for an advance of fifty million dollars, of which about half was to be paid forthwith in cash and the remainder applied to outstanding obligations.[1] Likewise, in September, a treaty was signed with the Ottoman Empire, whereby Bulgaria was to receive the corner of European Turkey marked off by the line of the Maritza and Tunja rivers, including the railway station at Karagatch though not Adrianople, and in return was to maintain "armed neutrality."

At once the Bulgarian army was mobilized "for the maintenance of armed neutrality." Sir Edward Grey, manifestly unconvinced by the official announcement of the Bulgarian government that mobilization was not preliminary to war, declared in the British House of Commons on September 28, "If it should result in Bulgaria assuming an aggressive attitude on the side of our enemies we are prepared to give our friends in the Balkans all the support in our power." Early in October, Russia dispatched an ultimatum to Sofia, affirming that "The presence of German and Austrian officers at the Ministry of

[1] This was in addition to an advance of thirty millions made in February, 1915.

War and on the staff of the army, the concentration of troops
in the zone bordering Serbia, and the extensive financial support accepted from our enemies by the Sofia cabinet, no longer
leave any doubt as to the object of the military preparations
of Bulgaria." The ultimatum allowed the Bulgarian government twenty-four hours in which to dismiss the Teuton officers
and "openly break with the enemies of the Slav cause and of
Russia."

To the entreaties and threats of. the Entente Powers Bulgaria was deaf. On October 14, 1915, she declared war on
Serbia. On the next day Great Britain declared war against
her, and France followed suit on October 16, and Russia and
Italy on October 19. Sir Edward Grey admitted that the
Central Powers had successfully outbid the Entente in their
offers for Bulgarian support.

When Bulgaria finally entered the war and began an invasion
of Serbia from the east, the conquest of Serbia was already
under way from the north. It will be recalled that the Great
War had been precipitated by the purpose of Austria-Hungary
to "chastise" Serbia; yet for more than a year Serbia had remained unchastised. This fact was due not so much to Serbian
valor, of which, however, there were plentiful instances, as to
Austria's need of defending herself against Russia and her
desire not to alienate Italy. The entry of Italy into the war in
May, 1915, and the subsequent rapid retreat of Russia changed
the aspect of affairs. There was no longer any chance of keeping Italy neutral and the distant retirement and resulting exhaustion of the Russians made it practicable for Austria-
Hungary at the end of September, 1915, to transfer large forces
from the Russian to the Serbian Front. Moreover, the demonstrated ability of the German troops on the Western Front to
hold the main armies of the French and British rendered it
possible for Germany to send some of her victorious veterans
of the Russian campaign to coöperate with Austrians and Hun-
garians in a sensational, whirlwind drive, whose purpose would
be more than the mere chastisement of Serbia — it would be
Teutonic mastery of the Near East.

Serbia was no longer in a position to thwart the Teutonic
purpose. Her great losses in the battles of 1914 had been
succeeded by further depletions in 1915 from pestilence and
famine, until her total armed strength, allowing for the use of
every available man, amounted to less than 200,000. Thrice
she had been invaded and thrice in heroic battles she had flung

back the invader, but each time the enemy had been Austrian and in number had barely exceeded her own forces. Now, however, her northern border was threatened by at least 300,000 Austro-Germans, equipped with the most up-to-date guns and with unlimited stores of ammunition, flushed with recent victories over the Russians, and commanded by Field-Marshal von Mackensen, one of the ablest of German generals. Furthermore, unlike the campaigns of 1914, Serbia was now doomed to face an onset of Bulgarian troops, 350,000 strong, who would cross her extended eastern border and threaten at many points the capture of her one important line of railway up the Morava and down the Vardar rivers, her one dependable line of communication with Salonica and Western Europe. If no aid should come to her from Greece or from England and France, she would certainly be overborne by weight of numbers and quantity of munitions; her armies would be surrounded and probably annihilated.

Austro-German forces were thrown across the Danube and Save rivers on October 7. Belgrade fell two days later, and Semendria and Pojarevatz in quick succession. The main body of Mackensen's command were thus prepared to sweep southward up the Morava valley toward Nish, the Serbian war-capital, while the left flank possessed itself of the Danube valley in northeastern Serbia and the right flank crossed the Drina river and occupied northwestern Serbia. Then it was that Bulgaria declared war. King Ferdinand scented a corpse and proceeded to rifle dying Serbia.

The Serbians could barely cope with the Austro-Germans in the north; against the Bulgarians in the east and south they could only offer pitifully inadequate resistance and trust in the prompt arrival of foreign aid from Salonica. No aid arrived, however, and the Bulgarians enjoyed a triumphal procession into Macedonia. From Kustendil the main Bulgarian army, under General Teodorov, advanced by way of Egri Palanka. Rail connections between Nish and Salonica were cut first at Vrania. Veles, or Kuprulu, fell on October 20, and two days later the Bulgarians entered Uskub, the converging point of all the roads of southern Serbia.

On October 26, another Bulgarian army, under General Bojadiev, after crossing the Timok river and capturing Negotin and Prahovo, effected a junction with the Teutonic left wing in the northeastern corner of Serbia. Thereby the Teuto-Bulgarian forces were in contact with each other on a wide semi-

circular front extending from the Drina around north of Kragu-
jevatz, west of Negotin, east of Nish, to a point west of Uskub.
The Serbians now formed two forces, hopelessly isolated by the
Bulgarian advance from Uskub towards Prishtina, the one, the

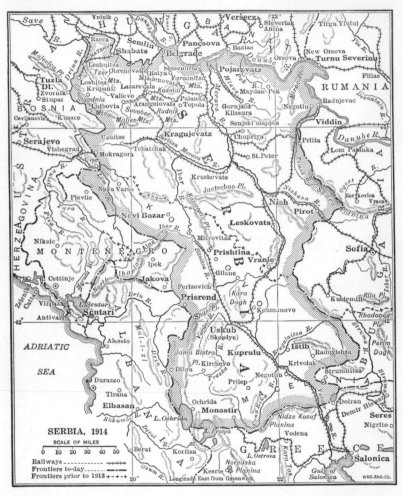

remnant of the armies of the North, lying from Kragujevatz
to east of Nish, the other and lesser in the hills north of Monastir.

The invaders pushed on relentlessly. Kragujevatz, the
principal Serbian arsenal, was captured on October 30. Nish,
after a stubborn defense, fell on November 6. In vain did the

Serbian armies of the north attempt to stand at the Ibar river; Novibazar was lost on November 20, and Mitrovitza and Prishtina three days later; the remnants were swept together in the plain of Kossovo by the converging Austrian, German, and Bulgarian columns. Thousands were taken prisoner, and only a band of refugees, including King Peter riding in a rude ox-cart, succeeded in reaching Montenegro.

The last action before the complete conquest of Serbia was fought by the small army in the south in a desperate effort to stem the Bulgarian advance from Uskub upon Prisrend and Monastir. At Babuna Pass, between Uskub and Prilep, the Serbians checked overwhelmingly superior forces of the enemy for a week and more. Eventually they had to abandon the Pass and Prilep as well. Prisrend was surrendered on the last day of November, and Monastir on December 5. The virtual completion of the conquest of Serbia was signalized by an announcement of Field Marshal von Mackensen on November 28, that "with the flight of the scanty remnants of the Serbian army into the Albanian mountains our main operations are closed."

FAILURE OF THE ALLIES TO RELIEVE SERBIA: THE SALONICA EXPEDITION

The only chance which the Serbians had of stemming invasion and preventing German mastery of the Near East lay in prompt and effective military aid from the Allies. That no such aid was forthcoming was due to several miscalculations on the part of the Allies: (1) it was fondly believed until too late that Bulgaria would not venture to ally herself with the Central Empires; (2) it was vainly expected that if peradventure Bulgaria should attack Serbia, Greece would feel constrained by the terms of her defensive treaty of 1913 with Serbia to go to the assistance of that country; and (3) it was foolishly imagined that an immediate transfer of Allied forces from Gallipoli to Salonica, from an offensive against the Turks to a defensive in support of Serbia, would be a confession of failure ruinous alike to domestic and to foreign prestige.

No doubt in the new crisis the Allies had good reason to count on Greek assistance. Back in March, 1915, Venizelos had been forced to resign the Greek premiership because of King Constantine's stubborn refusal to assent to the cession of Greek territory necessary to reconstitute the Balkan League and to draw Bulgaria, with Greece, into the war on the side of the

K

Entente. In August, however, when it was no longer a question of conciliating Bulgaria but rather of respecting treaty engagements with Serbia, Venizelos obtained from the king sufficient assurances to enable him conscientiously to resume the premiership. With Venizelos again in power, the Allies were encouraged.

Late in September, when the Allies first awoke to the gravity of the situation confronting Serbia, Great Britain and France promised Venizelos that they would send 150,000 men to Salonica to help Greece fulfill her treaty obligations. These obligations Venizelos acknowledged in a speech before the Greek Parliament on October 4. "The danger of conflict is great," he said, "but we shall none the less fulfill the obligations imposed on us by our treaty of alliance." He called for the complete mobilization of the Greek army. About the same time the first contingent of Allied troops arrived at Salonica. It was obvious that the Greek army of 350,000 men, in concert with an Anglo-French force, was preparing to strike the Bulgarians as soon as these should attack Serbia. Had matters worked out as thus planned, the success of Mackensen's Drive into Serbia would have been highly problematical.

Once more Venizelos had reckoned without his king. Constantine was thoroughly distrustful of the potency of Allied arms and filled with a craven fear of what the combined Teutons and Bulgarians would do to the Greek army; quite likely he had personal promises from the Kaiser of rich rewards for Greece if he would remain neutral. At any rate on October 5, Constantine for the second time forced the resignation of Venizelos, to the surprise of the Greeks and the consternation of the Allies. The new Greek ministry promptly declared that it would maintain "armed neutrality," but a neutrality, so far as concerned the British and French, "to be characterized by the most complete and sincere benevolence." If this assurance meant anything, it signified that the Allies might land troops of their own at Salonica and use Greek Macedonia as a base of operations against the Bulgarians, but they must not expect any armed assistance from Greece.

Under these circumstances the Allies fell to disputing as to what was best to do. Some of their officials urged that the defection of Greece had put a new burden upon them and that they should strain every nerve to gather quickly a very large army of their own at Salonica; the whole Anglo-French expeditionary force should be withdrawn immediately from Gallipoli for this purpose, and additional troops, if necessary, should be spared from the Western front.   Others felt that the burden put upon them by Greek defection was more than they could bear; these disputants protested against any weakening of the Western Front and against a wholesale withdrawal from Gallipoli; they advocated making a virtue of necessity and for the present leaving Serbia to her fate.

Between the extreme counsels of sending no aid to Serbia and of dispatching large forces thither, a curious compromise prevailed.   A few troops would be transported from Gallipoli, but not all.   General Sarrail would be brought from the Western Front to command the expedition at Salonica, but no troops would be spared from Marshal Joffre's command in France.   An Anglo-French force would gradually be assembled in Greek Macedonia, large enough to overawe neutral Greece but small enough to be of no striking assistance to friendly Serbia.[1]

Just as a mistaken faith in Bulgaria's good intentions had prevented the Allies in September from concerting measures for her coercion, so now in October the Allies grossly underestimated the stubbornness and pro-German sympathies of the Greek king.   They still seemed to imagine that they could get the Greek army to fight alongside of their Salonica expeditionary force.   Otherwise it is difficult to explain why Anglo-French forces at Salonica were as large — and as small — as they were. When, on October 14, 1915, Bulgaria finally entered the war, more than 200,000 Austro-Germans under Mackensen were pushing southward from the Save and the Danube against the Serbian front, a quarter of a million Bulgarians were moving westward against Serbia's exposed right flank, to the north Rumania was comfortably neutral, while far to the south 13,000 French and British troops in the vicinity of Salonica were preparing to march inland, and King Constantine was declaring that his treaty of alliance with Serbia had no binding force in the existing emergency.

Throughout October and November the Allies continued to dicker with King Constantine and his puppet ministers.   They begged and they implored.   They made offers and overtures. In November, the king dissolved his troublesome pro-Venizelist Parliament, and the ensuing general election, from which the Greek partisans of Venizelos absented themselves, appeared

---

[1] In this connection it should be noted that Sir Edward Carson, in Great Britain, and Théophile Delcassé, in France, resigned their ministerial posts rather than share in the responsibility of sending a pitifully weak expeditionary force to certain failure in Serbia.   Carson thought a much larger expedition should be sent.   Delcassé would send no expedition at all.

on the face of its returns to be a signal vindication of the royal policy. More obstinately than ever Constantine adhered to his policy of "armed neutrality," which by December had become to the Allies as much a threat as a promise.

Meanwhile the Teutons and the Bulgarians were overrunning Serbia, to the effective relief of which the Anglo-French forces at Salonica were too weak to proceed. General Sarrail's small army did manage to advance up the Vardar river and to intrench itself on a triangle of Serbian territory, the base of the triangle being the Serbo-Greek frontier, its apex the confluence of the Vardar and Tcherna rivers, its western leg the Tcherna, and its eastern leg a line to Lake Doiran near the angle of the Greek, Serbian, and Bulgarian frontiers. As soon as the Bulgarians had put an end to active Serbian resistance in the field and had occupied Prisrend and Monastir, they were free to turn their attention to the Allied positions in the south. The battle of the Vardar, from December 3 to 12, 1915, was simply a series of sledge-hammer blows delivered against the sides of the Anglo-French triangle. During the course of the battle the French line was withdrawn from the Tcherna to the eastern bank of the Vardar, the apex was drawn back to Demir-Kapu, the British line to the east was battered in, and the whole Anglo-French force was finally pushed back into Greek territory. The attempt of the Allies to relieve Serbia had ended in ignominious failure.

That the battle of the Vardar ended in defeat and not disaster was due to the ability of the Franco-British army, and the unwillingness of the Bulgarians, to cross the Serbo-Greek frontier. While the Bulgarians, doubtless in compliance with Germany's request, stopped short at the frontier, the Allies retreated through Greek territory and proceeded to strengthen the Greek city of Salonica in expectation of a Teutonic-Bulgarian attack. King Constantine, as might have been expected, caused his subservient premier, Skouloudis, to protest vociferously against this "abuse" of Greek neutrality, but the Entente Powers could reply that their troops had been sent to Salonica at the instance of Venizelos to assist Greece in fulfilling the terms of the secret Serbo-Greek defensive alliance against Bulgaria, and this interpretation was confirmed by the Greek ex-premier from his retirement.

Nevertheless the situation of the Allies at Salonica was precarious in the extreme. In front of them were a quarter of a million Bulgarian soldiers reënforced by Teutonic and Turkish units, awaiting only a word from the Kaiser's brother-in-law to cross into Greek territory. Behind them were a quarter of a million Greek soldiers held by King Constantine's orders under an "armed neutrality" that daily grew more menacing. It was now no longer a question of relieving Serbia; it was a question of relieving the Anglo-French expeditionary force at Salonica.

For this purpose the bulk of the Allied troops on the Gallipoli peninsula were still available. In October, when General Sarrail had loudly called for reënforcements to enable him to assume the offensive in the Vardar valley, Sir Ian Hamilton, the British commander on Gallipoli, had stoutly maintained that his troops could not be disembarked thence without incurring disastrous losses at the hands of the Turks and ruinous collapse of morale. Sir Ian had been recalled and Lord Kitchener himself had been sent to investigate the situation in Gallipoli. Withdrawal from the peninsula was openly advised by General Monro, Sir Ian's successor, frankly discussed by the press, and postponed, it seemed, only by the unwillingness of the British cabinet to admit a disheartening defeat at the very time when a supreme effort was being made at home to stir up popular enthusiasm for recruiting. Towards the end of December, however, when it appeared likely that disaster would overtake the expedition at Salonica, as well as that on Gallipoli, the long-deferred step was taken and the remaining British troops were withdrawn from the Suvla Bay and Anzac regions on the western shore. Shortly afterwards, early in January, 1916, the trenches on the tip of the peninsula were abandoned with slight losses.

The campaign against the Dardanelles, thus brought to an inglorious close, had cost the British alone from February to December, 1915, some 115,000 men, of whom 26,000 were dead. The most telling criticism of the management of the Dardanelles operations and at the same time the most vigorous apology for the higher strategy which had dictated the inauguration of the campaign, was expressed by Winston Spencer Churchill in a noteworthy speech before the House of Commons on November 15: "It has been proved in this war," he said, "that good troops properly supported by artillery can make a direct advance two or three miles in the face of any defense. The advance, for instance, which took Neuve Chapelle, or Loos, or Souchez, if made on the Gallipoli Peninusla, would have settled the fate of the Turkish army on the promontory, would probably have decided the whole operation, might have determined the attitude of the Balkans, might have cut off Germany from the East, and might have saved Serbia."

More bitter words could have been said. If Serbian entreaties had been hearkened to and the whole Allied force on Gallipoli had been withdrawn immediately after its August reverses and sent into Serbia, it might have deterred Bulgaria from entering the war, or, if Bulgaria had persisted, it might have saved Serbia from Bulgarian conquest and might have upheld the hands of Venizelos in his quarrel with a pro-German Greek king.

As it was, the Allies had two dismal failures to their debit in the Near East. They had failed to defeat the Turks and open the Dardanelles. They had also failed to resist the Bulgarians and relieve Serbia. One thing only was accomplished: with the arrival of the Gallipoli expeditionary force at Salonica in December, 1915, and January, 1916, they were enabled to prevent their Macedonian failure from becoming a disaster. They now had enough troops to intrench the territory about Salonica and temporarily to hold Constantine to the observance of "benevolent neutrality." As to the future, they simply must await developments. For the present, the developments elsewhere in the Near East appeared universally favorable to their enemies.

COMPLETION OF GERMAN MASTERY OF THE NEAR EAST

In October and November, 1915, Germany had taken two important steps toward the mastery of the Near East: the fairly powerful state of Bulgaria had become her ally, and troublesome Serbia had been "chastised" and conquered. Therefrom did many benefits accrue to the cause of the Central Empires. In the first place, Turkey was no longer isolated from her allies, for express trains could now be run from Berlin to Constantinople by way of Belgrade, Nish, and Sofia, and German domination of Turkey was strengthened. Secondly, there were significant economic benefits: not only were the copper mines of Serbia placed at Germany's disposal, but the resources of the Balkan peninsula and of the Ottoman Empire could be freely drawn upon to replenish the stock of foodstuffs and of minerals in the Central Empires, while on the other hand a large foreign market was at last procured, despite British mastery of the seas, for overstocked German manufacturers. Thirdly, the military advantages were obvious: Turkey and Bulgaria could now easily be supplied with guns and munitions and enabled to utilize their man-power to the full against the Allies; if unable actually to conquer Egypt and India, Turkey could at least so menace those rich outlying dominions of the British Crown as to frighten the English and lead perhaps to a weakening of British resistance on the Western Front.   Finally, the respect for Teutonic military prowess on the part of the two neutral states in the Near East, — Rumania and Greece, — had been enormously increased: Greece seemed quite dominated by her pro-German king; Rumania saw fit to open her grain-markets to German buyers.

To guarantee their conquest of Serbia, the Teutons and Bulgarians forthwith set about the conquest of Montenegro and of Albania, for otherwise these mountainous regions might become dangerous rallying points for Serb and Allied forces.   In fact, in December, 1915, Italian garrisons were occupying the Albanian ports of Avlona and Durazzo, and as many as 50,000 Serbian fugitives were being assembled on the Greek island of Corfu and there reorganized into a fighting force.

It was a fairly easy task to overwhelm Montenegro's little army of 30,000 men.   General von Koevess, with his Austrian army, in December quickly occupied the towns of Jakova, Ipek, and Plevlie, on the eastern border of Montenegro; then, penetrating into the interior, his converging columns defeated the Montenegrins in their last desperate stand in the Tara and Lim valleys, in January.   Meanwhile another Austrian detachment, attacking the western frontier, from the Austrian harbor of Cattaro, built military roads up the northern slopes of the supposedly impregnable but really ill-fortified mountain stronghold of Lovtchen, around which wound the steep road to the capital, Cettinje, five miles distant.   After three days' bombardment by the Austrian ships at Cattaro, Mount Lovtchen was stormed on January 10, 1916.   Lovtchen lost, the Montenegrins made no serious attempt to defend their capital, which fell three days later.   King Nicholas, after some rather questionable negotiations with the Austrians, made his way to Italy and thence to France, where at Lyons he established his "court." His fellow-Serb monarch, King Peter, found a more honorable refuge with the Allied army at Salonica.

Hardly had the Montenegrin capital fallen when General von Koevess with his Austrians turned southward into Albania. Scutari and the port of San Giovanni di Medua were captured in January, 1916, and early in February the Teutonic invaders reached the heights of Tirana, in central Albania, ten or fifteen miles from Durazzo.   In the meantime Bulgarian forces had crossed into Albania from southern Serbia and occupied El Bassan.   Essad

Pasha, the pro-Ally chief of the provisional Albanian government, could offer but feeble resistance to the dual invasion;
and on February 27, the Italians were obliged to evacuate
Durazzo, under fire of Austrian guns.   The larger Italian garrison
at Avlona, sixty miles south of Durazzo, was not dislodged,
however, so that from Avlona as a base the Italians were able to
dominate south-central Albania, while the northern and eastern
portions of the country remained in Austro-Bulgarian possession.

Thus was the new German rail connection with Constantinople
guaranteed against any hostile attack from the west.   Montenegro and the strategically important part of Albania, together
with Serbia, were Teutonic conquests.   True, an Allied army
was intrenched in the vicinity of Salonica and an Italian force
occupied Avlona, but these forces were too few to undertake a
successful counter-offensive : they were fearful of a possible
attack on their rear by the pro-German King Constantine of
Greece ; and in front they faced the stout Bulgarian army, now
flushed with victory and thoroughly loyal to the German alliance.
To the north, Rumania was isolated and wavering in her sympathy for the Entente ; from Rumania, at least for the present,
Germany had nothing to fear.   With the withdrawal of the
Anglo-French force from Gallipoli, moreover, no allied soldier
remained on the soil of European Turkey ; the Ottoman Empire
had proof positive of the worth and value of alliance with Germany, and news of rejoicing at Constantinople could be communicated uninterruptedly to Berlin by express-train or by
telegraph.   By force and by prestige Germany had mastered
the whole Balkan peninsula.   The "Drang nach Osten" and
"Mittel-Europa" were more than words and wishes ; they were
established facts.

It was now that Asiatic Turkey assumed an importance never
before recognized.   From Asia Minor Turkish sovereignty
reached out in two directions, — eastward over Armenia and
Mesopotamia to the Persian Gulf and the confines of Russian
and British spheres of influence in Persia, and southward across
Syria and Palestine to the Red Sea and the borders of British
Egypt.   Two great arteries traversed these reaches of Turkish
sovereignty, the German-owned Bagdad railway the one, and
the Mecca railway the other.   By either route powerful blows
might be struck against British colonial dominion.   And to
strike such blows the 200,000 Turkish soldiers who had been
engaged on the Gallipoli Peninsula for nearly a year, were now
available.   The "Drang nach Osten" suddenly assumed a

terrible significance. It meant not merely the attainment of German mastery over the Balkans and Constantinople; it meant also the threat of German mastery of Bagdad and Mecca and perhaps of Egypt and India.

It was not toward Egypt and the south, however, that the European Turkish army of 200,000 men was moved in January, 1916, but rather toward Persia and the east. It seemed preferable to employ the entire force for a single end; and complete mastery of the Berlin-to-Bagdad route appeared a more serviceable aim than control of the Suez Canal. The difficulties of campaigning in the desert region between Palestine and Egypt were much greater, as the Turkish defeats of 1914 had indicated, than in the mountains of Armenia and the fertile valleys of Mesopotamia. The stakes, too, were less significant: to strike at Egypt might merely interrupt or inconvenience British trade with the East Indies; on the other hand, to secure the Persian Gulf would certainly threaten British India itself. Besides, while no invasion of the Ottoman Empire had yet been attempted from Egypt, both British and Russian expeditions were already in possession of parts of the eastern marches; completely to rid the Ottoman Empire of Allied armies required an energetic campaign in Armenia and Mesopotamia.

It will be remembered that soon after Turkey entered the Great War a small expeditionary force of British regulars and Indian colonials had been landed at the head of the Persian Gulf as a sort of outpost of defense for British India. In the summer of 1915, without a very distinct purpose and with insignificant numbers, the expedition pushed on more than two hundred miles into Mesopotamia, until on September 29, it occupied the town of Kut-el-Amara on the Tigris. Bagdad, the terminus of the famous Turco-German railway,[1] only a hundred miles farther up the river, lured the British on, though what they would do with Bagdad once they occupied it none could say. Perhaps it was intended to offset in England the chagrin which concurrent defeats on Gallipoli and in Serbia were causing. At any rate, General Sir John Nixon, the commander of the expeditionary force, directed General Townshend to proceed to Bagdad. On November 22, 1915, Townshend attacked and carried a line of Turkish defenses at Ctesiphon, only eighteen miles from the fabled city of the caliphs. Then the tide turned. Townshend,

---

[1] The actual rail terminus of the Bagdad route was at Samara, seventy-five miles farther up the river. Bagdad was about 350 miles from the Persian Gulf by the shortest land route; by river, it was almost 600 miles distant.

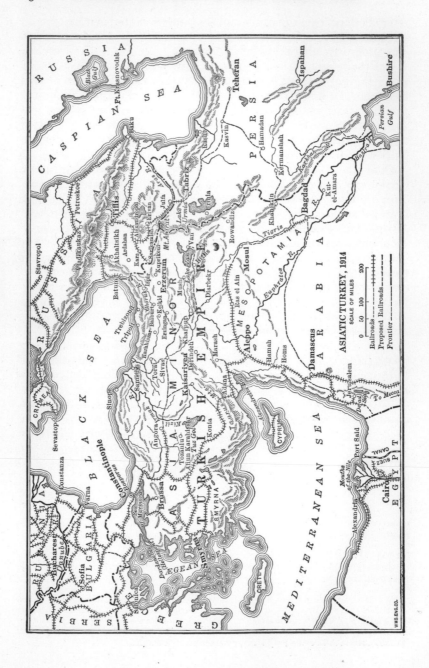

overwhelmed by superior numbers, was defeated with a loss of 4500 out of 20,000 men and driven back to Kut-el-Amara, which was promptly surrounded and invested.

For the relief of Townshend new British forces were dispatched from India. Likewise Russian columns were sent to his relief along the caravan route from Hamadan in Persia. Such was the situation when Teutonic-Bulgarian victories in Macedonia assured the security of Constantinople and when Anglo-French withdrawal from Gallipoli released almost a quarter of a million Turks for military use elsewhere.

Over the Bagdad railway were transported many of these Turkish troops, down into the valleys of the Tigris and Euphrates. There, under the able generalship of the German Marshal von der Goltz, they pressed the siege of Kut-el-Amara and fought off one relief expedition after another, whether British or Russian. Doubtless quicker results would have been achieved by the Turks and their German commander, had it not been for a great danger which simultaneously threatened them in Armenia and which might at any time nullify their immediate efforts in Mesopotamia.

The Grand Duke Nicholas, who, as a result of the Russian defeats in Poland, had been transferred to the Caucasus in September, 1915, had been marshaling an army of 180,000 men in preparation for a big offensive in Armenia [1] in the spring of 1916, but the plight of the British in Mesopotamia and the release of 200,000 Turks in January, 1916, for service in Asia, decided him to attack forthwith. The very unexpected character of the attack, in the dead of winter, with roads blocked by snow and the thermometer registering from twenty to forty degrees below zero, may account for the ease with which at the outset the unsuspecting Turks were routed. Under the actual

[1] Christian Armenia, throughout the first eight months of 1915, had been the scene of the most wholesale and cold-blooded massacres in the long history of the distracted country. At Angora, Bitlis, Mush, Diarbekr, at Trebizond and Van, even at distant Mosul, many thousands were butchered like sheep, partly by the gendarmerie, partly by the mob. Women were violated, and they and their children were shamelessly sold to Turkish harems and houses of ill-fame. Hundreds of wretched creatures were driven into the deserts and mountains to perish miserably of starvation. The protesting voices were few and ineffective: the sheikh-ul-Islam resigned; the pope remonstrated; the American ambassador at Constantinople did his best. The Turkish Government was obdurate: "I am taking the necessary steps," its premier told the American ambassador, "to make it impossible for the Armenians ever to utter the word autonomy during the next fifty years." And the Germans, quite used themselves to committing outrages in Belgium, shuddered not at the newest and gravest atrocities inflicted by their friends, the Mohammedan Turks, upon the hapless and helpless Christian Armenians.

command of General Yudenitch, who was intrusted with the execution of the Grand Duke's design, the Russian columns advanced southwestward from the Russo-Turkish Caucasian frontier, and about the middle of January, 1916, began their march through bleak mountain passes leading into Turkish Armenia. The northern column isolated one Turkish corps and drove it rapidly northward to the shores of the Black Sea; the southern column cut off two divisions from the main Turkish army; while the central column, following the highway from Sarikamish toward Erzerum, inflicted a crushing defeat on three Turkish divisions at Kuprikeui, January 16–18, and forced the crossing of the Araxes River in the midst of a blinding snowstorm. Ruthlessly pursued by Cossack cavalry, the Turkish infantry retired in disorder, strewing the road from Kuprikeui to Erzerum with discarded rifles, abandoned cannon, and half-frozen stragglers.

Against Erzerum, reputed to be the strongest fortified city in Asiatic Turkey, General Yudenitch now massed his heavy artillery. By a brilliant feat of arms a Siberian division planted its 8-inch guns on supposedly inaccessible peaks commanding the northernmost of Erzerum's many outlying forts. The fortified ridge just to the east of the city was thus outflanked and successfully stormed. Whereupon, without waiting to test the antiquated inner circle of redoubts and ramparts, the German staff officers and the Turkish garrison precipitately evacuated Erzerum, on February 16, 1916, leaving 323 guns and a huge stock of military supplies to fall into the hands of the victorious Russians. Only 13,000 prisoners were taken, but the total Turkish casualties in the whole campaign were estimated at 60,000. The capture of Erzerum was rightly recognized as a particularly brilliant piece of strategy.

Two days after the fall of Erzerum, the Turks lost the town of Mush to the southern column of the Grand Duke Nicholas's invading army, and on March 2, the important city of Bitlis, south of Erzerum and west of Lake Van. The northern column of the Russian forces, sweeping the Black Sea coast from Batum westwards, captured Trebizond on April 18 and pushed on as far as Platana. By April, 1916, the greater part of Turkish Armenia was in Russian hands, and Russia had demonstrated to the world that despite her sorry reverses of the preceding summer in Poland and Lithuania she was still in the war and was still a military power to be reckoned with. Optimists were not lacking among Entente publicists who perceived in the Grand

Duke Nicholas's Armenian offensive not only certain relief to the beleaguered British in Mesopotamia but a probable aid to Allied fortunes in the Balkans.

Again these Entente publicists were too optimistic. By April, 1916, the full force of Turkey's released Gallipoli army could be brought to bear in Mesopotamia and Armenia. Vigorously did Von der Goltz press the siege of Kut-el-Amara. A British relief detachment essayed in vain to break its way through the Turkish line at Sanna-i-yat, sixteen miles east of

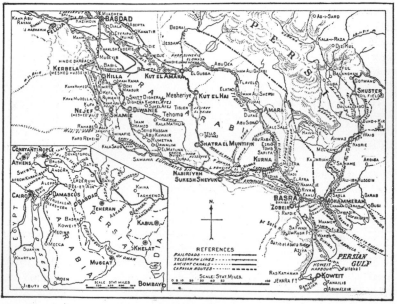

MESOPOTAMIA AND ITS STRATEGIC POSITION

Kut. So completely was Kut-el-Amara invested that no provisions could be sent to the famished garrison except by airplane. Nine tons of supplies reached General Townshend by this means in April, but they were not enough. At last the pressure of hunger constrained Townshend to surrender, on April 29, 1916, after enduring a siege of 143 days, — the only example of a protracted siege, except that of Przemysl, in the whole course of the Great War. Depleted by fighting and famine, Townshend's force at the time of surrender numbered only eight thousand men. Responsibility for the disastrous Bagdad venture of the British rested not so much on General

Townshend as on General Nixon and the military authorities in India.   Public opinion concurred in the verdict of a prominent British historian of the war that "on every ground of strategy and common sense" Townshend's expedition "was unjustifiable."

The fall of Kut-el-Amara enabled the Turks thenceforth to devote almost all their force and energy to staying further advance of the Russians in Armenia.   It is true that the Grand Duke Nicholas enjoyed a brief good fortune in July, 1916; he then advanced to, and captured, the city of Erzingian, 110 miles west of Erzerum.   But this marked the high tide of Russian success.   Thenceforth the Russians in Asiatic Turkey were strictly on the defensive, and in August, Bitlis was abandoned. In the meantime the Russian column which had gone to the relief of the British in Mesopotamia was routed by the Turks and pursued back into Persia, past Kerind, Kermanshah, and Hamadan.   If the Turks had lost part of Armenia, they had at least saved Bagdad and carried the war into Persia.

By the summer of 1916, Germany, with the aid of Austria-Hungary, Bulgaria, and Turkey, had transformed "Mittel-Europa" from a dream to a reality and had pushed far the "Drang nach Osten."   She now enjoyed uninterrupted and unmenaced communication and commerce with Constantinople not only, but far away, over the two great arteries of Asiatic Turkey, with Damascus, Jerusalem, and Mecca, and with Bagdad likewise.   Her vassal Ottomans were actually striking into Persia; they might yet irrupt into India.   With the exception of some Italians in inaccessible southern Albania, an Allied force at precarious Salonica, a Russian army in mountainous Armenia, and a handful of British at the head of the Persian Gulf, Germany was unopposed in her mastery of that whole vast region of southeastern Europe and southwestern Asia which goes by the name of the Near East.

To her spectacular defeat of Russia and conquest of Poland was thus added Germany's equally spectacular mastery of the Near East.   But was Germany thereby really winning the Great War?   Not so long as there was an unyielding Western Front.   To win the war, Germany simply must smash allied resistance in France.

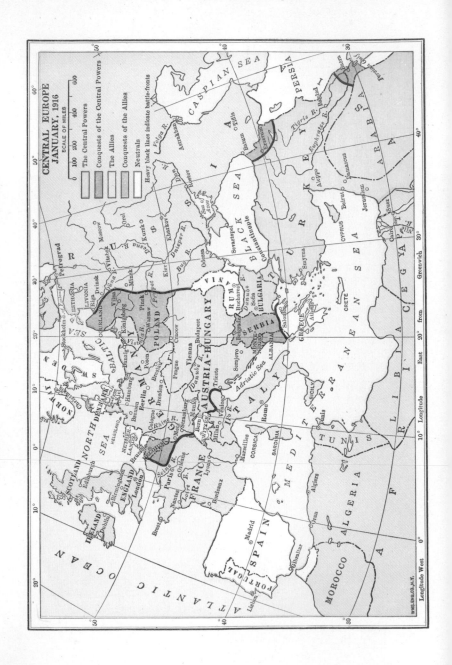

CENTRAL EUROPE
JANUARY, 1916

SCALE OF MILES

100 200 300 400 600

The Central Powers
Conquests of the Central Powers
The Allies
Conquests of the Allies
Neutrals

Heavy black lines indicate battle-fronts

CHAPTER VIII

GERMANY FAILS TO OBTAIN A DECISION IN 1916

TEUTONIC OPTIMISM AT THE BEGINNING OF 1916

IF military exploits had been as conclusive as they had been spectacular, Germany should have won the Great War in 1916 and imposed a *Pax Germanica* upon the world. Certainly the most spectacular achievements at arms from August, 1914, to January, 1916, had been Teutonic; and German statesmen and publicists expressed a puzzled inability to understand the stubborn refusal of the Entente Powers to sue for peace.

Spectacular had been the Teutonic "drives." In 1914 Belgium and the richest section of France had been overrun and occupied by German armies. In the summer of 1915 the Russian "steam roller" had been trundled back from Galicia and from Russian Poland to the Riga-Dvinsk-Tarnopol line in a badly battered condition. In the autumn of 1915 Bulgaria had been won over to the Turco-Teutonic coalition and had helped Field Marshal von Mackensen to conquer Serbia and master the Near East.

As a result of these spectacular "drives," the armed forces of the Central Empires not only had preserved their own lands practically inviolate, but had obtained extensive and valuable conquests at their opponents' expense. It was notable that whereas not a single Entente soldier stood on the soil of Germany or Austria-Hungary, except a few Frenchmen in one corner of upper Alsace and some Italians on a narrow strip near the Isonzo, the territory dominated by the Teutonic alliance had been expanded to embrace Belgium, northern France, Poland, parts of Lithuania and the Baltic Provinces, Serbia, Montenegro, and a portion of Albania. With the adherence of Turkey and Bulgaria to the Teutonic Alliance, and the triumphs of those states at the close of 1915, a Germanized *Mittel-Europa* could be said to stretch from the North Sea to the Persian Gulf, from the Baltic to the Red Sea, from Lithuania and Ukrainia to Picardy and Champagne. It was the greatest achievement in empire-building on the continent of Europe since the days of Napoleon Bonaparte.

Moreover, this Germanized *Mittel-Europa* appeared to possess certain qualities of strength and endurance lacking in whole or in part to the hostile coalition.   In the first place, it was a confederation of four states — Germany, Austria-Hungary, Bulgaria, and Turkey — of which the first was head and shoulders above the other three in prowess and prestige, with the result that there was relative unity of direction in the confederation's policies and actions.   Berlin completely overshadowed Vienna, Sofia, and Constantinople; and the chiefs of staff of Turkey, Bulgaria, and Austria-Hungary had their plans mapped out for them and much of their equipment supplied them by the German High Command.   At a time when Berlin could speak authoritatively for *Mittel-Europa*, the opposing Powers still acted in most respects independently of one another, and in Entente counsels something like equal weight had to be given to frequently diverse decisions of Paris, Petrograd, London, and Rome. Unity of plan was an important asset of the Central Powers as diversity was a liability of the Entente.

Secondly, Germanized *Mittel-Europa* occupied a geographical position of great strategic value.   It completely isolated Russia from her Western Allies, save for most faulty transportation from the White Sea or over the Siberian railway.   Its extent was sufficiently wide and continuous and its economic resources and industry sufficiently varied to give promise of enabling its civilian population to support life without suffering too severe hardship from British control of the seas.   Its inclusion of Belgium, northern France, and Poland provided it with a wealth of minerals useful alike to normal manufacturing and to abnormal production of munitions of war.   Moreover, its compactness and its possession of an enviable network of railways admitted of prompt and efficient transfer of troops from one frontier to another, and, therefore, of concentration against hostile Powers in turn.   If *Mittel-Europa* was a kind of beleagured empire, it had at any rate an advantage of interior lines of communication, which, taken in conjunction with its advantage of unified command, seemingly compensated it for its lesser number of potential soldiers.

To husband the supply of military man-power in *Mittel-Europa*, the German government was already planning to deport laborers from conquered districts, notably Belgium [1] and northern

---

[1] The deportation of Belgians was formally inaugurated by decree of the German military authorities on October 3, 1916. By the beginning of December, some hundred thousand had already been deported with great cruelty and amidst heartrending scenes.

France, and to compel them to work in German factories, thereby releasing many Teutonic laborers for active service with the colors.   And to add to the resources of man-power, the Central Empires sought to construct several dependent states out of "oppressed nationalities."   There was talk, for example, about this time of creating a South Slav state under the protection of Austria-Hungary and the nominal sovereignty of a Montenegrin prince who would ally himself with the Habsburg family. There was an attempt also to sow dissension in Belgium between Walloons and Flemings and to encourage the latter to establish a Flemish government under the protection of Germany.   There was an effort likewise to arouse a desire in the Russian Baltic Provinces either for outright annexation to Prussia or for the founding of an autonomous state under a German prince; and there were curious appeals to Polish patriots to perceive in Germany the staunch friend of Polish nationalism.   Little progress had so far been made in any of these directions, but the Pan-Germans and other fanatical advocates of *Mittel-Europa* entertained high hopes for the future.

Teutonic optimists at the beginning of 1916 pointed with pride and assurance not only to the construction of mighty *Mittel-Europa* during the preceding year and a half and to the military discomfiture in turn of Belgians, French, Russians, and Serbs, but also to what they imagined to be a resulting war-weariness or even political unrest in the chief Entente countries. Italy, it was thought, had entered the war haltingly, had fought lamely, and, in view of the fact that as yet she had not ventured to declare war against Germany, might be expected to limp off the battlefield if given half a chance.   Russia was cast down by defeat and by revelations of scandalous inefficiency and corruption, not to say treason, among her generals and her bureaucrats; she was honeycombed with popular disaffection and revolutionary doctrine.   France, still the very heart and soul of the coalition hostile to Mittel-Europa, was believed to be rapidly exhausting her never superfluous man-power; and the imminence of a complete break in French morale was the lesson drawn by Germans from the resignation of the Viviani Cabinet in October, 1915, and from the creation, seemingly "as a last resort," of a Ministry of All the Talents, including Aristide Briand as premier, representatives of all parties (even the Monarchist), and eight former prime ministers.   Apparently France had reached the end of her rope and would make but one more stand.

As for Great Britain the situation was somewhat different.

So far Germany had been unable to strike a direct blow at England and had had to witness, without power to prevent, the quick mastery of the seas by the British navy and the gradual occupation of her own distant colonies by Allied forces; and with the exception of a short-lived Boer insurrection in South Africa, no rebellion had as yet broken out in any part of the far-flung British Empire. Nevertheless, Germans at the beginning of 1916 professed greater optimism than ever as to the eventual defeat and humiliation of their great maritime rival. They insisted that the fate of colonial dominion would be settled on the battlefields of Continental Europe; and on these battlefields were the Teutons not winning victory after victory? They insisted, too, that British mastery of the seas was becoming a more serious obstacle to the welfare of neutral states than the success of the Teutonic Powers, and would surely prove in a brief while a veritable boomerang: quite probably it would cause the Scandinavian countries, the Netherlands, Spain, the United States, and the states of Latin America to unite in an Armed Neutrality which would recognize that "freedom of the seas" was dependent on British failure and German triumph. But even if such an auxiliary "Armed Neutrality" should not materialize, Germany might still confidently expect Britain's vanquishment. British prestige had recently suffered grievously from fiascoes at the Dardanelles, in Serbia, and in Mesopotamia; and millions in India, who only wanted a favorable opportunity, would presumably welcome with open arms the Turco-German deliverers now *en route* over the Bagdad Railway to Persia and the East. Besides, the glowing embers of Irish discontent would require only a little kindling from Germany to be fanned into consuming flame.

And there were signs, as interpreted by Teutonic optimists, which would betoken a war-weariness in England. The war was becoming a heavy charge on British wealth. Whereas the total public debt of Great Britain amounted in March, 1914, to three and a quarter billions of dollars, it had grown by war credits, including those of February, 1916, to nearly ten and a half billions, a sum which Premier Asquith characterized as not only beyond precedent, but actually beyond the imagination of the financiers of England or of any other country. Moreover, the war was taking an unexpectedly heavy toll of Britain's young manhood. British losses in battle up to January, 1916, numbered 550,000, of whom 128,000 were dead. Yet despite such heavy toll, little progress appeared to have been made. That the authorities themselves were dissatisfied was evidenced by the removal of Sir John French [1] from the supreme command of the British armies in France in December, 1915, and his supersession by Sir Douglas Haig.   That the British people were as dissatisfied as their government, and more apathetic, was gathered from the fact that although the rate of voluntary recruiting for military service had fallen very low by October, 1915, the country at large evinced much opposition to any departure from the traditional British policy of voluntary enlistment and stubbornly resisted any effort to substitute conscription.   It was only after Lord Derby had conducted a final three-months' campaign for soldier-volunteers throughout the length and breadth of the British Isles that the Parliament was induced, in January, 1916, to enact a conscription measure, and even this was to apply only to unmarried men in England, Scotland, and Wales.[2]   To the Germans it was obvious that the British armies had reached their maximum size, under the volunteer system, by the autumn of 1915, and that, inasmuch as the new conscripts could not properly be trained and rendered effective before the summer of 1916, the coming spring was most opportune for knock-out blows.

In fact, little more need be done.   While more or less subtle propagandists would be equipped with money and letters of introduction, with typewriters and stenographers, with secret inks and mysterious formulas for bomb-making, and turned loose in neutral countries to win converts to the precepts and practices of *Kultur*, the doughty armed hosts of the Teutonic coalition would be provided with an extra supply of howitzers and machine-guns, airplanes and Zeppelins, asphyxiating gases and poison for wells, and in one supreme effort on the chief European fronts would illustrate the irresistible might of *Kultur* in practical operation.   The Austro-Germans already in Lithuania would suffice to put the finishing touches on crumbling Russia.   The main armies of Austria-Hungary would be mobilized in the Trentino for a decisive drive into the vitals of desponding Italy. And the German legions, now disengaged elsewhere, could be consolidated into one mass that at last would break down the barriers to Paris and reduce France to her appropriate position as a tertiary power, as a lesser satellite to the full, glorious orb of *Mittel-Europa*.   With Russia, Italy, and France crushed, and with despair and rebellion at home, what could Great Britain do?

---

[1] Sir John French was created Viscount French of Ypres.

[2] Subsequently, in May, 1916, the Conscription Act was extended to married men, but Ireland remained exempted from its provisions.

Early in 1916 Teutonic optimism reached its zenith. There was no talk at Berlin of conciliation or compromise. It was to be a victory overwhelming and complete.

THE DIFFICULTY AT VERDUN: "THEY SHALL NOT PASS"

In planning war against combined Russia and France, the German General Staff had emphasized the necessity of crushing France first and then turning at leisure against slow-moving Russia. But France had not been crushed, in 1914. The ever memorable battle of the Marne had saved her field army, her capital, and her most important fortresses — Verdun, Toul, Épinal, and Belfort. And throughout 1915, while Germany was defeating Russia, France remained unconquered and undaunted.

At the beginning of 1916, therefore, the German General Staff, confronted with a new situation, adopted a new plan. The Russians were to be held at bay far from Germany's eastern frontier, while on the west a final irresistible blow would be dealt the French. If France could be convinced that further sacrifices for the recovery of Alsace-Lorraine would be futile, would not a victorious peace then be in sight for Germany? If this train of thought had not of itself been sufficiently cogent to the German General Staff, the preparations which General Joffre was making for a great Anglo-French Drive would have been reason enough for a German master-attack upon France. France was training her classes of 1916 and 1917, according to War Minister Galliéni's own statement, in readiness for "the moment when the intensive production of armaments and of munitions, together with the reënforcement of the battle-line with new masses of men, may permit new and decisive efforts." Great Britain, thanks to the Derby recruiting campaign and the January conscription bill, might be expected to throw another million of men into France in the spring, and her two thousand government-controlled factories were already producing tremendous and ever-increasing supplies of munitions. The anticipated Anglo-French offensive of 1916 would be of unprecedented power; and, if Russia and Italy should attack simultaneously, Falkenhayn, the German Chief of Staff, would then be unable to transfer troops to France without inviting disaster on the other fronts. Accordingly, it was imperative to forestall the Anglo-French offensive and if possible to compel Joffre to put his half-trained reserves into the battle-line prematurely.

Strategic and political considerations made Verdun the first objective of the new German offensive against France.   To be sure, the concrete-and-steel forts and the disappearing armored turrets, upon which French engineers had prided themselves before the war, were no longer considered of great military value, since 13-inch howitzers had demonstrated the frailty of Belgian fortifications.   But the strategic importance of Verdun lay less in its fortifications than in its position.   The army that possessed Verdun possessed the Heights of the Meuse, a plateau or ridge some five miles broad extending north and south like a natural palisade, just east of the Meuse river, on which Verdun is situated.   Their position on the Heights of the Meuse would be of incalculable advantage to the French when the time came for an attempt to reconquer Lorraine; impetuously descending the slopes to push the Germans back across the plain of the Woëvre, to the eastward, the French troops would be supported by heavy artillery mounted on hilltops five hundred feet or more above the plain, while the Germans would find it extremely difficult to emplace their heavy artillery on the clayey soil of the Woëvre. Should the French lose the Heights of the Meuse, not only would a French attack on Lorraine be out of the question, but for defensive purposes no new line could be found of such great natural strength.

The political considerations which recommended a German thrust at Verdun may be stated briefly: first, if France lost Verdun and the Heights of the Meuse, French patriots would lose hope of realizing their chief purpose in the war — the reconquest of Alsace-Lorraine — and might consent to make peace; secondly, inasmuch as the German Crown Prince commanded the Verdun sector, a victory there would enhance the prestige of the heir to the imperial throne; thirdly, certain influential elements in the Reichstag, notably the Conservative and National Liberal parties, who at the time were bitterly criticizing the Chancellor Bethmann-Hollweg for his tendency to yield to American remonstrances against ruthless submarine warfare, might be silenced by a great success like the capture of Verdun.

Every effort was made to disguise the German preparations for the intended move against Verdun.   During January and February, 1916, while corps after corps was quietly taking its place in the Crown Prince's lines, while hundreds of 4-inch, 7-inch, 13-inch, and even 17-inch guns were being massed in the forests of Verdun, feints were being made against a dozen other sectors of the Anglo-French front.   An attack against Nieuport on January 24, and rumors of troop movements through Belgium, seemed to forecast a new drive toward Calais; on the Somme, the village of Frise was captured by the Germans; in Artois, on the bitterly contested slopes of Vimy Ridge, Prince Rupprecht of Bavaria delivered a series of attacks with daily mine-explosions and infantry assaults; at the extreme southern end of the Western Front, the French lines southwest of Altkirch were assailed, and 15-inch shells began to drop into the French fortress of Belfort like heralds of an approaching storm. Meanwhile the Crown Prince had concentrated fourteen German divisions against the French trenches eight and a half miles north of Verdun. All was ready for the great effort.

A terrific bombardment preceded the first attack, on February 21, 1916. Never had artillery fire been of such withering intensity. High explosive shells fairly obliterated the French first-line trenches. Groves which might have afforded shelter to French artillery were wiped out of existence, trees being uprooted and shattered into splinters. Under the terrible hail of fire, the French soldiers with their machine-guns and "75s" — those that escaped destruction — waited with grim determination to make the German infantry pay heavily for its advance. But the Germans did not intend to sacrifice their men needlessly. No advance was attempted until scouts and sappers had cautiously stolen forward to make sure that the bombardment had accomplished its work of destruction. Then, while the German guns lengthened their range so as to place a "curtain of fire" in the rear of the French trenches, cutting off supplies and reënforcements, the German infantry with comparative safety occupied the ruined French first line. This was considered auspicious. Step by step the German howitzers would blast their way into Verdun; there would be no need of reckless infantry charges.

At first the German offensive against Verdun proceeded with the mechanical regularity of clockwork. In four days the Germans progressed over four miles, until at Douaumont they reached the first of the outlying permanent forts of Verdun. At this time eighteen divisions were massed on a front of four and one-half miles from the Côte du Poivre (Pepper Ridge) to Hardaumont. Throughout the day of February 25 the German infantry, wave upon wave, surged up the snow-covered slopes of the Douaumont Hill, only to recede under the murderous fire of French mitrailleuses and 75-millimeter guns. Towards evening a supreme assault, viewed from a distant hill by the Emperor himself, carried Fort Douaumont. The fort itself was a crumbling heap of ruins, but the hilltop (388 meters high) on which it was situated overlooked all the surrounding country and commanded a clear view of Verdun, less than five miles to the southwest. If the French could be hurled back from this their strongest natural position, before heavy reënforcements arrived and while the defense was still suffering from the initial shock of the German onslaught, Verdun's fate would be almost certain.

But French reënforcements, which had been withheld until General Joffre was sure the Verdun attack was not simply another feint, arrived in the nick of time, and with them arrived General Pétain, on the very day of Fort Douaumont's fall. Pétain infused new energy into the demoralized defense. He had already demonstrated his fighting temper in the battle of Artois (spring and summer of 1915) and in the Champagne offensive (September, 1915); before the war he had been an inconspicuous colonel, one of the many Catholic army officers who could scarce hope for promotion while anti-clerical politics held sway in the army; in actual warfare, however, his ability could not be ignored and he had speedily won the rank of general and the reputation of being one of Joffre's most brilliant subordinates.

On February 26, 1916, the morning after his arrival, Pétain ordered a counter-attack. By an impetuous charge the Germans were swept back down the hillside, and, although a German regiment remained ensconced in Fort Douaumont, possession of the fort was useless without command of the approaches and communicating trenches. For four days more the battle raged incessantly about the fort and village of Douaumont, until on March 1 the German attack slackened. That brief lull marked the passing of the crisis. The impact of the German drive had been broken before a real breach had been made in the vital defenses of Verdun; the French had recovered from their surprise, and now with heavy reënforcements and ample supplies, which an endless train of motor lorries was ceaselessly pouring into Verdun, they were ready to dispute every inch of ground.

During the first phase of the battle, from February 21 to 29, the brunt of the German drive had been borne by the French lines on the Heights of the Meuse, where the Germans had battered their way four miles southward to the Douaumont-Pepper Ridge position. Even more ground had been gained, though at smaller cost, in the Woëvre plain, directly east of Verdun, where the French had been pushed back some six miles. On March 1, however, the French were standing as firmly at Eix and Fresnes, east of Verdun, as at Pepper Hill and Douaumont, north of the city.

So long as there was hope of capturing Verdun with a moderate sacrifice of life, military as well as political wisdom justified the German offensive.   But when the French lines, instead of crumpling fatally, stiffened resolutely, the whole aspect of the offensive was altered.   Henceforth the Crown Prince would be hurling his men against carefully prepared, cunningly concealed, and adequately manned defenses.   As the French brought up their heavy guns, the German advantage in artillery would dwindle and disappear.   Victory could be won neither swiftly enough to terrify France nor cheaply enough to profit Germany.   Yet the German General Staff decided to purchase victory, cost what it might.   Discontinuance of the battle after the check at Douaumont would be a humiliating confession of defeat and a severe blow to the prestige of German arms; the name of the Crown Prince, already associated with failure in the battle of the Marne, would be brought into further disrepute; and the political situation of the German government would be extremely embarrassing as it attempted to face the scathing criticism of the Tirpitz party, which demanded ruthless submarine warfare, and the bitter complaints of an independent faction of the Socialists, who voiced the desire of a growing number of German civilians for food and for peace.   The battle of Verdun, therefore, must continue.

In the second phase of the struggle for Verdun, interest shifted to the west bank of the Meuse.   Prior to March 1, there had been little fighting except on the narrow front, six or seven miles in length, where the French line straddled the Heights of the Meuse, north of Verdun; the twelve-mile French sector east of the Heights, it is true, had been forced out of the Woëvre plain; but west of the Meuse only artillery had been active.   Owing to the fact that the hills west of the Meuse were much less imposing than those on the other bank — for example, Dead Man's Hill, the key of the situation on the western bank, was 280 feet lower than Douaumont — an advance there would be easier than east of the Meuse; furthermore, it seemed imperative to push the line west of the Meuse at least as far south as the line east of the river, since the French guns on the hills west of the Meuse were now in a position to rake the German line on the opposite bank from the flank and rear and by their fire to prevent an effective assault on Pepper Ridge.   If the Crown Prince was to turn the Douaumont position by capturing Pepper Ridge, the menace from across the Meuse must be removed.

So on March 2, 1916, the second phase of the battle of Verdun began with an attack upon the French positions west of the Meuse. By this time, however, the element of surprise contributed nothing to the German advance; the French were prepared to defend with dogged determination every inch of ground. For nearly two weeks the Germans struggled to master Goose Ridge, immediately west of the Meuse; for three weeks more they spent munitions and life recklessly in efforts to dominate Dead Man's Hill, farther west. From March 17 to April 8, the German advance amounted to one mile on a six-mile front. Still determined to conquer at any cost, the Crown Prince exhausted nine infantry divisions in a ferocious assault against the whole French line west of the Meuse, April 9–11. Yet in spite of the frightful carnage, Dead Man's Hill could not be conquered.

Not only west of the Meuse, but east of the river too, the Germans during March and April expended their strength in heroic efforts, but without decisive results. Ruined Douaumont changed hands several times, and the Germans got as far as the village of Vaux — but no farther. While both sides lay exhausted in the region of Vaux and Douaumont, the Germans with indefatigable energy prepared to launch a new attack upon Pepper Ridge. Their howitzers rained high-explosive shells on the ridge until it seemed that the French trenches must be annihilated; then confidently on April 18 twelve German regiments made the assault; but from the shattered French trenches the machine-guns spoke with so deadly an effect that the Germans recoiled in dismay.

The repulse at Pepper Ridge on April 18 and at Dead Man's Hill on April 9–11 concluded the second phase of the great battle for Verdun. French and British military critics already declared that "the battle of Verdun is won." True, throughout April and May each daily bulletin gave news of a mine exploded, a gas-attack resisted, a trench gained by the use of jets of liquid fire, a clash of grenadiers, or a duel of artillery. But having tested the French lines on both sides of the Meuse, the Germans at last knew that Verdun could not be gained by a few sledge-hammer blows, and henceforth they fought not with the confident expectation of victory, but rather with the fury of baffled but indomitable determination.

Towards the end of May, 1916, the third phase of the battle of Verdun was inaugurated by desperate and most sanguinary onslaughts on each side of the Meuse. The climax of the campaign on the western bank was reached on May 29, when sixty German batteries of heavy artillery poured a torrent of high-explosive shells, continuing twelve hours, on the whole French

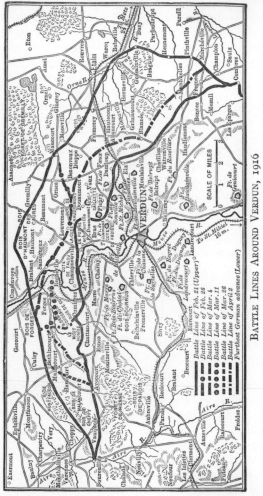

BATTLE LINES AROUND VERDUN, 1916

line from Cumières to Avocourt, and a new infantry charge was launched in which at least five fresh divisions participated. The French had been expelled from Cumières, and the summit of Dead Man's Hill had been gained, but the French still clung tenaciously to the southern slopes of the hill.

Simultaneously, on the east side of the Meuse, the Germans foiled an attempt of General Nivelle [1] to secure Douaumont and then moved in force against Fort Vaux. After a struggle of inconceivable fury the Germans captured Fort Vaux on June 7 and thus obtained, with Fort Douaumont, two positions in the outer ring of Verdun's permanent fortifications. Of the numerous remaining obstacles, the next would be Fort Souville or rather the hill (precisely the same altitude as Douaumont) upon which Fort Souville was situated, not quite two miles southwest of Fort Vaux and a little more than two miles directly south of Fort Douaumont. Fort Souville might be approached either from the north, by way of Thiaumont Redoubt and Fleury, or from the northwest, by way of Damloup Redoubt. The Germans during June tried both of these approaches. Thiaumont Redoubt and Fleury were gained on June 23–24, but were subsequently recaptured by the French; similarly, Damloup Redoubt was captured, recaptured, and captured again. Throughout July and August Fleury and the two redoubts repeatedly changed hands. Never did the Germans reach Fort Souville. Never were they able to drive the French from the southern slopes of Dead Man's Hill. Never was the hold of the French on Verdun relinquished.

From February to July, 1916, the Germans had gained about 130 square miles of battle-scarred French territory north and east of Verdun, with two demolished forts and desolate ruins of two-score villages. As the price of this gain, probably as many as three hundred thousand German soldiers had laid down their lives, or fallen wounded on the field of battle, or been captured by the French. The Crown Prince had played for high stakes and had lost. The great plan to take Verdun by surprise, to strike consternation into the heart of the French nation, to forestall an Anglo-French offensive, had obviously gone wrong; and Germany faced the discouraging fact that her tremendous sacrifices had failed of their chief purpose, while France, despite most serious losses, rejoiced in the consciousness that the battle-cry of her heroic sons at Verdun, "Passeront pas!" ("They shall not pass!") had been realized in truth. Pétain's holding battle at Verdun ranks with Joffre's holding battle at the Marne as one of the decisive conflicts of the Great War.

---

[1] Nivelle had succeeded Pétain in immediate command of the French defense at Verdun early in May, when Pétain was promoted to the command of the whole army-group on the Soissons-Verdun sector of the Anglo-French front.

THE DIFFICULTY IN THE TRENTINO: ITALY'S DEFENSE

While the Germans were still pounding at Verdun, the Austrians undertook an offensive against Italy. The Austrians elected to deliver their attack in the difficult mountain-country of the Trentino rather than in the Isonzo valley, for two reasons: first, the Italian line was less strongly held on the Trentino front; and, secondly, an offensive on the Isonzo, even if successful, would only drive the main Italian army back into Italian territory, whereas a quick thrust from the Trentino into the Venetian plain might cut the communications and possibly compel the capitulation of the Italian army of the Isonzo.

Up to May, 1916, there had been no large-scale fighting in the Trentino. Comparatively small detachments of the Italian Alpini had penetrated a little way into the inhospitable uplands of the western Trentino border through several mountain passes. In the south, the Italians had progressed fifteen miles up the Adige River to the outskirts of Rovereto, about half the distance from the frontier to Trent. In the east, the Italian line crossed the Val d'Astico not far from the border, and then cut more deeply into Austrian territory west of Borgo, in the Val Sugana.

The Italian line in the Trentino was hardly more than a broken series of detached outposts pushed unsystematically into the enemy's country. Even for defensive purposes it was dangerously weak. The exposed salient southeast of Rovereto might easily be crushed between attacks from the west and north: no good second-line position had been prepared; and some portions of the front were poorly munitioned and all parts were gravely short of artillery.

Against the ill-prepared Italian lines in the Trentino, on a front of less than thirty miles, the Austrians quietly concentrated 400,000 men and a mass of artillery, ready to overwhelm the Italians by sheer weight of number and metal. After a terrific bombardment on May 14, 1916, the Austrian infantry rushed forward all along the front from Rovereto to Borgo, the brunt of the attack being toward the center in the general direction of the Italian cities of Asiago and Arsiero. At first the Austrians were highly successful. The Italians retreated in such confusion that in several instances whole regiments lost their way and valuable strategic points were sacrificed without a struggle. Hurriedly General Cadorna rushed to the rescue and attempted to reform the line of the Trentino army. The Aus-

trians, relentlessly pursuing, descended the Posina valley to
Arsiero (seven miles inside the Italian border) and, to the east,
came down the Val d'Assa as far as Asiago (eight miles inside
the border), which fell on May 28. The Italian troops that
should have occupied the commanding height of Pria Forà (two
miles south of Arsiero) on the night of May 29 lost their way in
the dark and fell back farther south to the inferior height of
Monte Ciove. From Pria Forà, at an elevation of nearly 5000
feet, the victorious Austrians could look down upon Schio and
Thiene, less than ten miles to the southeast, where the foothills
of the Venetian Alps gave place to a gently sloping plain, nowhere
more than 500 feet above sea-level. Only twenty miles from
Arsiero lay the city of Vicenza; twenty miles farther, Padua;
and another twenty miles across the plain would bring the
invader to Venice and cut off the whole Italian army on the
Isonzo. Exultantly the Austrian order of the day, June 1,
announced that only one small mountain ridge (Ciove) remained
to be crossed before the army of invasion could swoop down into
the Venetian plain.

Fully conscious of the peril, General Cadorna ten days previously had ordered the concentration of every available reserve
at Vicenza, and now on June 3 he issued to the troops holding
the line south of Arsiero the famous order, "Remember that
here we defend the soil of our country and the honor of our army.
These positions are to be defended to the death." And they
were defended. On Monte Ciove, the key-position, one gallant
Italian brigade held fast though 4000 of its original 6000 men
were either killed or wounded. Likewise on Monte Pasubio,
which had halted the right wing of the advancing Austrians,
the Italians stood unflinchingly against odds of four to one under
a nerve-shattering bombardment. For three weeks Austrian
howitzers deluged Pasubio with high explosives; for three weeks
dense masses of Austrian infantry were hurled against the
Italian left flank; still the Italian defense stood firm. On
June 18 the Austrians made their final effort when they
flung twenty battalions against the Italian right flank, south
of Asiago, and failed. The Austrian offensive was definitely
checked.

As the result of a month's exertions, the Austrians had inflicted serious losses on the Italian army; they had captured a
large number of big guns, which the Italians could ill spare; they
had recovered 270 miles of Austrian territory; they had conquered 230 square miles of Italian territory; and they had

improved their strategic position.[1]   On the other hand, the Austrians had failed to achieve their main purpose; Vicenza and Venice were still in Italian hands and the Italian army of the Isonzo was still intact and ready to resume the offensive in Istria.   Nay more, the Austrians in putting forth their great effort against Italy had so seriously weakened their Eastern front that Russia was able to reorganize her army and invade Galicia and Bukowina.   German failure at Verdun and Austrian failure before Vicenza were synchronous blows at Teutonic optimism; [2] they were sure signs that the Central Powers were doomed not to win a victorious peace in 1916.

THE DIFFICULTY IN IRELAND: SUPPRESSION OF REBELLION

At the very time when the Austrians were preparing to invade Italy and when the Germans were making their supreme effort against Verdun, Teutonic hopes of rebellion within the British Empire promised to reach fruition.   In April, 1916, a republic was proclaimed in Ireland and fighting took place in Dublin.

The trouble in Ireland was traceable to the bitter five-hundred-year old feud between Englishmen and Irishmen, and particularly to British treatment of Ireland since 1910.   Between 1910 and the outbreak of the Great War in 1914 the Nationalist Party in the British House of Commons, representing three-fourths of the population of Ireland, had taken nice advantage of the exigencies of English politics to wring from the existing Liberal government a measure of limited home rule for Ireland.   But even before the enactment of the measure Irish Unionists (descendants of Scotch-English settlers in Ulster) had smuggled in arms from Germany and had prepared to resist Home Rule by force. The situation thus created might have been handled by the British Government in either of two ways, according to its judgment of Ulster : if Ulster was serious and sober in its opposition, then it might behoove the Government to withdraw the Home Rule Bill altogether and seek some other means of dealing with the Irish question; or, if Ulster was merely factious and unreasonable, then it would seem to be the Government's duty

---

[1] Premier Salandra, as the result of an adverse vote in the Italian Chamber of Deputies, resigned in June, 1916, and a new coalition ministry was formed under Paolo Boselli with Baron Sonnino still in charge of foreign affairs.

[2] It was a curious coincidence that just as the Crown Prince Frederick William of Germany commanded the offensive against Verdun, so the offensive in the Trentino was directed by the heir-apparent to the Austro-Hungarian crown — the Archduke Charles.

promptly to arrest Sir Edward Carson, the Ulster leader, and to crush the opposition.   Mr. Asquith's Government did neither. It allowed Ulster to raise and discipline a highly efficient army, and it went on with its Home Rule Bill.   The Nationalists very naturally claimed the same right to arm and drill their people, and the National Volunteers came into being.   The result was that in July, 1914, Ireland was split up into two armed camps, and the Government halted between two resolutions : on the one hand, the Home Rule Bill must be enacted ; on the other hand, "Ulster must not be coerced."

When the Great War actually came, the Home Rule Bill was placed on the statute-book, but its operation was suspended ; and temporarily Ulsterite and Nationalist leaders vied with one another in pledging Ireland's loyal support to the Allied cause. As time went on, however, the old distrust and misunderstanding reawoke.   The Ulsterites became more outspoken that the Home Rule Act must never be put in operation, while the Nationalists grew more impatient of delay.   When in May, 1915, Mr. Asquith admitted to his cabinet several Unionists, including Sir Edward Carson, it was apparent that the English Liberals were no longer dependent on Irish Nationalists and that Home Rule had been pushed into the limbo of forgotten dreams.   Henceforth the bulk of the Irish people began to lose interest in mere limited autonomy and faith in their Parliamentary party ; gradually they transferred their interest to demands for full independence and their faith to a hitherto unimportant faction — Sinn Fein.

Sinn Fein — which means "Ourselves"— was a body founded in 1905 for purposes not unlike those of the Gaelic League which preceded it by a few years.   The central idea of the society was that the Irish people should recover and assert their nationality in every possible way, in language, in dress, and in the development of Irish resources and industries.   But unlike the Gaelic League, whose program was exclusively educational, the scope of the Sinn Fein was political as well.   It opposed Irish representation in the British Parliament and attacked alike the Unionists and the Nationalists, accusing the latter of being tools of the English Liberal Party.   It had no patience with the Home Rule plan.   It held that Ireland should not wait for Home Rule as a gift from the British Parliament, but should start measures of republican independence on her own account.   Self-reliance was the Sinn Fein's motto.   At the outset it had been a harmless academic movement, much frowned upon by Nationalist leaders like Redmond and Devlin, and drawing its strength chiefly from the enthusiasts of Irish art and poetry, but its prestige had increased in 1913 through its activity in recruiting volunteers for defense against the Ulsterites, and the seeming collapse of the Home Rule project in 1915 furthered its popularity. As the Ulsterites obtained a preponderant voice in the councils of the British Government disappointment and disaffection flourished in other parts of Ireland; and as the Nationalists lost hope, Sinn Fein gained faith and followers.

Sinn Fein was frankly revolutionary, and, though not strictly pro-German, was quite as willing to make an alliance with Germany as with any other country if thereby an independent republic might be established in Ireland. Throughout 1915 negotiations of a somewhat obscure character were carried on between Germany and Sinn Fein agents, in Germany and also in the United States; funds were collected and military plans discussed. Sir Roger Casement, formerly a British consular agent and now a devoted disciple of the Sinn Fein, spent several months in Germany, visiting prisoners' camps in an attempt (for the most part unsuccessful) to form an Irish Brigade, and concerting measures with the German Government for abetting a revolt in Ireland. It was arranged that German submarines should transport Casement and a goodly store of arms and munitions to the Irish coast and that, simultaneously with their landing, the Sinn Fein leaders at Dublin should proclaim the republic and mobilize the Irish Volunteers; other German submarines would do their best to prevent England from reënforcing her garrison in Ireland, and German propagandists along the Western Front would strive to secure desertion of Irish soldiers from British regiments. It may have been a wild gambler's chance from the German standpoint, but in any event Germany had nothing to lose by Irish failure, and by Irish success Great Britain might lose heavily.

On the evening of April 20, 1916, a German vessel, disguised as a Dutch trader and laden with arms, together with a German submarine, arrived off the Kerry coast of Ireland, not far from Tralee. Detected by the British patrol, the vessel was sunk and its crew captured. Meanwhile Sir Roger Casement and two companions were put ashore from the submarine in a collapsible boat, but, without arms and unmet by the local Sinn Feiners, Casement was arrested early on Good Friday morning, April 21, and taken to England.[1]

[1] He was subsequently tried for high treason and condemned to death, and was executed on August 3.

The capture of Casement confused the Sinn Feiners. General MacNeill, their military chief, hastily canceled the projected Easter manœuvers of the Irish Volunteers, and the leaders at Dublin were thus deprived of immediate effective aid. Nevertheless the standard of revolt was raised. On Easter Monday, April 24, armed bands seized St. Stephen's Green, the post office, and other places in the center of Dublin. At the same time a proclamation was issued asserting the right of Ireland to national existence and announcing the establishment of a republic, based on adult suffrage and complete civil and religious liberty, equality, and fraternity. The flag of the new state — green and gold — was unfurled, and a provisional government was set up under Padraic Pearse as president and James Connolly as commandant.

After a sharp struggle in which many were killed and wounded, including a considerable number of civilians, the British forces, under General Sir John Maxwell, who had formerly commanded in Egypt, succeeded in overpowering the rebels, though not until artillery and machine-guns had been brought into action. On April 29, Provisional President Pearse ordered unconditional surrender, in order to prevent useless slaughter, and on the next day the rebels laid down their arms. In Dublin 300 Irish had been killed and 1800 made prisoners. The British troops suffered 521 casualties. The punishment inflicted by the British authorities was extremely severe. Pearse and fourteen others were tried by court-martial and shot; more were condemned to long terms in prison; several hundred were deported to England and gathered in detention-camps; and as many as 3000 were arrested.

Germany gained nothing by the abortive Irish rebellion, and Great Britain was not vitally handicapped in her prosecution of the war. The Irish Nationalists disavowed the Sinn Feiners as promptly and as fully as did the Ulsterites, and there was no serious disaffection among Irish troops in France. Subsequently, the severity meted out to the rebels by the British Government reacted in favor of the Sinn Fein, and the inability or unwillingness of the coalition ministry to govern Ireland except at the point of the bayonet deflected many British troops from France. But these developments were too late to alter in any respect the solemn fact that in 1916 Germany was failing to obtain a military decision.

M

DIFFICULTIES AT SEA: THE GRAND FLEET AND THE UNITED STATES GOVERNMENT

In addition to the military difficulties which the Teutons encountered in the spring of 1916 at Verdun and in the Trentino, there was the ever-present difficulty inherent in Allied mastery of the seas. Unable to foment serious rebellion within the British Empire or to meet the British fleet on equal terms, the Germans had to sit more or less idly by while Britain carried on her vast commerce and transported great numbers of men and huge quantities of munitions.

Such weapons as Germany might employ against British maritime supremacy were pitifully inadequate, and her naval exploits were largely of the spectacular sort. A few commerce-raiders still managed to elude the British blockade and to prey upon Allied shipping. Thus, the *Moewe* returned to Germany early in March, 1916, after capturing one French, one Belgian, and thirteen British merchantmen together with two hundred prisoners and one million marks in gold. But so long as the British Grand Fleet kept the German battleships in home waters, German raiders were pretty certain sooner or later to fall victims to the Allies.

There remained the submarine. But the submarine, while it had destroyed a considerable amount of Allied commerce during 1915 and might be depended upon to destroy a larger amount in 1916, had already raised most embarrassing points in international law and would be likely in the future, if pushed to extreme use, to alienate neutral Powers and force them to take common action with the Allies for mutual protection of trade. That this was no baseless apprehension was evidenced by the entry of Portugal into the Great War in March, 1916.

Portugal had long been in intimate trade-relationship with Great Britain, and an old treaty of alliance bound her to give military aid to Britain if requested. In accordance with this treaty, Portugal in 1914 signified her willingness to assist her ally, but she was not called upon to take action until the progress of the German submarine-campaign had caused hardship to the Portuguese people and had threatened a shortage of Allied shipping. Then it was, in February, 1916, that Sir Edward Grey, the British foreign secretary, requested the Portuguese Government to commandeer all German merchant vessels in Portuguese waters. As soon as the request was granted, Germany declared war against Portugal, March 9, and Austria-

Hungary followed suit on March 15. The intervention of Portugal was of small military advantage to the Entente, but it enabled the Allies to add to their common merchant marine some forty Austrian and German ships seized by Portugal.

Far more serious than the entry of Portugal into the war was the rising opposition of the United States to submarine warfare as conducted by Germany. Portugal was a small Power, and to declare war on her would cost Germany not very much more than the paper on which the declaration was written. But the United States was a Great Power whose enmity might be bought too dearly. It was worth while to think before one leaped into war with the United States.

There was undoubtedly a general feeling in Germany that the United States was naturally quite pacific; the Americans were reputed to be as adept at keeping out of European entanglements as at "chasing the almighty dollar," and the patience and forbearance of their government for almost a year after the sinking of the *Lusitania* were interpreted as signs of convinced pacifism if not of unmanly fear. At any rate, Admiral von Tirpitz, as director of Germany's maritime policies, was determined to utilize his submarines to the full, even if thereby the United States should be drawn into the hostile coalition. It was the one chance of breaking England's control of the seas, and the one chance must not be thrown away because of uncertainty as to what the United States might, or might not, do. All the jingoistic elements in Germany backed von Tirpitz and insisted vehemently upon an extension of submarine warfare as the only effective means of retaliation against Great Britain's effort to "starve" Germany.

Since by arming their merchantmen the Allies had endeavored to combat the growing submarine menace, the Central Powers announced on February 8, 1916, that beginning on March 1 their submarines would be instructed to attack without warning any enemy merchantman mounting cannon. Armed merchantmen were to be treated virtually as belligerent warships, and neutral Powers were to warn their subjects not to travel on armed merchantmen of belligerent nationality. Among the neutral Powers, Sweden complied with the Austro-German request, but the United States, after some hesitation, returned a flat refusal. Nevertheless, the Central Powers persisted in their intention, and in March a number of merchantmen were torpedoed without warning.

On March 24, 1916, the *Sussex*, an English Channel boat, was struck by a torpedo from a German submarine : about fifty persons lost their lives, and three American citizens were injured. A wave of indignation swept over the United States, which was soon swelled by lame attempts of the German Government to disclaim responsibility. The obvious anger of the American people and the now insistent demands of President Wilson tended to change the current of German opinion about the United States. Possibly the Americans were courageous after all; possibly they might join England in forceful manner; possibly, in this event, the situation created by unrestricted submarine warfare would be worse than the existing British blockade. It might pay to be conciliatory — at least for a time.

To a more discreet attitude in the matter Germany was turned by the retirement of Admiral von Tirpitz and by the succession, as secretary of state for the navy, of Vice-Admiral von Capelle. Von Capelle and Chancellor Bethmann-Hollweg worked together to quiet Tirpitz and other jingoistic Germans and to effect a settlement with the United States. At length, on May 4, 1916, the German Government promised that henceforth no merchantman would be sunk without warning and without due provision for the security of passengers' lives except when a merchantman attempted flight or resistance. Thereby Germany formally repudiated "ruthlessness" in submarine warfare and in so doing apparently abandoned the Tirpitz hope of bringing British mastery of the seas quickly to an end.

A more gradual ending of British naval dominance was the hope of Bethmann-Hollweg and the purpose of his seemingly conciliatory policy toward America. He intimated in his note of May 4 that in return for his concession he would expect the United States to aid Germany, at least diplomatically, in lightening the British blockade. But Bethmann-Hollweg was disappointed as well as Tirpitz, for on May 8 President Wilson declared in unequivocal words that the American Government "cannot for a moment entertain, much less discuss, the suggestion that respect by the German naval authorities for the right of citizens of the United States upon the high seas should in any way, or in the slightest degree, be made contingent upon the conduct of any other government as affecting the rights of neutrals and non-combatants. The responsibility in such matters is single not joint, absolute not relative." It was obvious that the United States would be no catspaw for Germany. It was a bit alarming, and Germany decided for the present to hold her submarines in leash.

Foiled in the effective use of commerce-raiders by the British Grand Fleet and in the ruthless use of submarines by the United States Government, the German naval authorities decided, as a last resort, to take as heavy toll as possible of the British blockading squadrons by risking their own high-seas fleet in a naval battle. The resulting battle, the only really important naval engagement of the Great War, was fought in the North Sea, off Jutland, on May 31, 1916. The German forces consisted of five battle-cruisers, three battle-squadrons (comprising seventeen dreadnoughts and eight pre-dreadnoughts), a number of fast light cruisers, and several destroyer flotillas; the battle-cruiser squadron was commanded by Vice-Admiral von Hipper, and the major part of the whole fleet by Vice-Admiral von Scheer. The British force, which at the time was making one of its periodical sweeps through the North Sea, consisted of: (a) a squadron of six swift battle-cruisers under Vice-Admiral Sir David Beatty, the "fifth" battle squadron of four fast battleships under Rear-Admiral Thomas, and several speedy light cruisers and flotillas of destroyers; (b) the main fleet under Admiral Sir John Jellicoe, composed of twenty-five dreadnoughts and a large number of subsidiary craft.

On the afternoon of May 31, Vice-Admiral Beatty with his command was scouting ahead of the main fleet and about fifty miles south of it, when suddenly the smoke of enemy ships was spied to the southeastward. Thinking he was in the vicinity of only a raiding squadron, he engaged von Hipper's fast battle-cruisers and was drawn on by them northeastwards until his squadron, now supported by that of Rear-Admiral Thomas, came into the range of the major portion of the German high-seas fleet. Being separated from the slower British forces under Jellicoe, the squadrons of Beatty and Thomas were severely punished and obliged to reverse their course, pursued by the whole German force. It was only when evening came, with a heavy mist, that the Germans were stayed by the arrival of the British Grand Fleet. During the night Jellicoe manœuvered to keep along the coast between the Germans and their base, but in the darkness the Germans managed to elude him, and in the afternoon of the following day the British squadrons left Jutland for their respective bases.

The battle of Jutland took a rather heavy toll of British seamen and ships. The British lost at least 113,000 tons, including the battle-cruisers *Queen Mary* (27,000 tons), *Indefatigable* (18,750 tons), and *Invincible* (17,250 tons). But the Germans lost proportionately more, and they had absolutely failed to shake Britain's mastery of the seas.

Shortly after the battle of Jutland, the British armored cruiser *Hampshire*, carrying Lord Kitchener on a secret mission to Russia, was sunk off the coast of Scotland (June 6), and England's war minister and foremost soldier lost his life.[1]   A month later the *Deutschland*, an unarmed German "merchant submarine," successfully eluded vigilant Allied warships and made a voyage across the Atlantic to the United States and back again.   These exploits were spectacular and sensational, but they were devoid of larger significance.   They served merely to emphasize the prosaic fact that Germany was being slowly strangled by the sea power of Great Britain.

At the beginning of 1916 Germany optimistically had expected to obtain a victorious peace before autumn.   By midsummer, however, very practical difficulties stood in Germany's way — the heroic French at Verdun, the gallant Italians above Vicenza, the dogged British off Jutland, the insistence of the President of neutral America — and these difficulties gave rise to a wave of domestic fault-finding which disturbed the serenity of German optimists.   The Social Democratic Party split into two factions in the spring of 1916, one faction — the Majority, under Scheidemann — still supporting the government, but the other — the Minority, under Haase and Ledebour — uniting their voices with the formerly lone voices of Karl Liebknecht and Rosa Luxemburg in bitter invective against the war and its German authors.   At the other extreme, certain Conservatives and National Liberals, forming the Fatherland Party, devoted their energies to vehement denunciation of the "conciliatory" policies and temperamental "softness" of Bethmann-Hollweg. Verily, it was no longer a perfectly united Germany on which the fortunes of *Mittel-Europa* would depend.   Henceforth the German Government must conduct the war not only with attention to strictly military strategy against the Entente but also with an eye to political strategy at home.

So in 1916 Bethmann-Hollweg began seriously to talk about "peace."   It must be a victorious peace — that was demanded by the Fatherland Party.   It must be a peace of conciliation — that was demanded by many Socialists.   And the patent in-

---

[1] Lord Kitchener was succeeded as British war minister by David Lloyd George. About the same time General Galliéni died; he had already been succeeded as French war minister by General Roques.

sincerity of the Chancellor's peace proposals in 1916 was not so much the outcome of weakness in his own character as the inevitable result of his efforts to reconcile irreconcilable popular demands. What he set out to do was to convince the Socialists that the Allies — and the Allies alone — were inimical to any peace of conciliation, and thereby to commit the Socialists to support the demands of the Pan-Germans. If seemingly honest endeavors at compromise were thwarted by the Entente, then Germany must fight on, cost what it might, to a victorious peace. On May 22, 1916, Bethmann-Hollweg declared that the Allies rather than the Central Powers were guilty of "militarism" and that they must "come down to a basis of real facts" and "take the war situation as every war map shows it to be." And early in June he announced that, if the Allies persisted in shutting their eyes to the war-map, "then we shall and must fight on to final victory." "We did what we could," the Chancellor asserted "to pave the way for peace, but our enemies repelled us with scorn ; consequently, all further talk of peace initiated by us becomes futile and evil."

As a matter of fact, the Allies in the first half of 1916 had re- pelled the Teutons with something more effective than scorn. They had repelled them with blood and iron. And in measure as the German hope of obtaining a military decision in 1916 receded, that of the Entente increased. In June, 1916, Lloyd George wrote that "only a crushing military victory will bring the peace for which the Allies are fighting," and Aristide Briand, the French premier, stated that peace "can come only out of our victory." German failure promised Allied success. The Allies set out in the summer of 1916 to obtain a military decision before the new year.

CHAPTER IX

THE ALLIES FAIL TO OBTAIN A DECISION IN 1916

ATTEMPTED COÖRDINATION OF ALLIED PLANS

By midsummer of 1916, it was apparent that Germany would not obtain an immediate military decision. It was less apparent, but quite as real, that Germany, though still tactically on the offensive, was already strategically on the defensive. *Mittel-Europa* was a vast fortress, but one besieged on all sides, and for its safety the territory held by it mattered far less than its relative man-power and economic resources.

It was generally recognized that what military superiority the Central Empires had demonstrated to date was due not to any absolute excess of man-power and economic resources, for in these respects the Entente Powers enjoyed remarkable superiority, but rather to greater efficiency and discretion in their use. What had most handicapped the Allies for two years was, first, a shortage of munitions, and secondly, a lack of unity in planning and conducting campaigns on all fronts.

For the Allies the situation was improved by the summer of 1916. The lessons of the unsuccessful drives on the Western Front in 1915 and of the Russian retreat had been taken to heart. In munitionment the change was amazing. France was now amply provided for, Russia had a supply at least four times greater than she had ever known, and Great Britain was manufacturing and issuing to the Western Front weekly as much as the whole pre-war stock of land-service ammunition in the country. Even more significant, the Allies were now seeking to coördinate their several military and economic efforts against the common foe.

Only by a long series of discouraging defeats were the Allies brought face to face with the stern necessity of coöperation. After Russia's field armies had been routed by Hindenburg; after the Anglo-French offensive of September-October, 1915, had proved to be merely another "nibble" at the German line; after Serbia had been conquered; after Gallipoli had been ingloriously evacuated; after Townshend had been surrounded at Kut-el-Amara; after the French lines north and east of Verdun had been battered back from village to village and from hill to hill by the German Crown Prince's terrific attacks; only then did the Allies clearly perceive their greatest need. Only then did the Allies lose faith in the precepts of the old international anarchy .and evince a willingness to abandon, at least temporarily, some of their individual sovereign rights for the sake of creating an effective league of nations against imperialistic Germany.

On March 27–28, 1916, the first general war council of the Entente Powers [1] was held in Paris. France, Great Britain, Italy, Belgium, Serbia, Russia, Japan, Montenegro, and Portugal were represented, the first five by their premiers and foreign ministers, and the others by diplomatic agents; Joffre, Castelnau, Kitchener, Robertson, Cadorna, and Gilinsky (aid-de-camp to the Tsar) attended in person to give authoritative military information; while Lloyd George and Albert Thomas, ministers of munitions respectively for Great Britain and France, reported on the vital subject of army *matériel*. Not only was the diplomatic unity of the Entente reaffirmed by the War Council, but military agreements were concluded among the general staffs of the various nations represented, and plans were laid for concerted attacks, during the summer of 1916, on the Western, the Eastern, the Italian, and the Balkan Fronts. As for economic coöperation, the War Council decided (a) to establish in Paris a permanent committee, representing all the Allies, to strengthen the blockade of the Central Powers, (b) to take common action through the Central Bureau of Freights in London for the reduction of exorbitant freight rates and for a more equitable apportionment of the burdens of maritime transport, and (c) to participate in an Economic Conference to be held shortly in Paris.

In April an Allied inter-parliamentary conference met in Paris, and in June the Economic Conference convened. The latter, during its brief three days' session, agreed upon a far-reaching scheme of economic solidarity, which not only would enhance the effect of the Allied blockade during the war, but would also prolong the commercial struggle after the war by enforcing a partial exclusion of German manufactures from Entente countries and by establishing within the Entente a uniform system of laws respecting patents, corporations, bankruptcy, *etc*. In fine, the Entente Powers were to consolidate themselves into a

[1] An Anglo-French War Council had been created in November, 1915.

huge economic coalition, a formidable engine of trade-war even in time of peace.[1]

In order that the war against German trade might be pushed with the utmost effect, it was urgently necessary that Italy be induced to abandon her absurd pretense of remaining at peace with Germany while being at war with Austria-Hungary. Italy's delay in declaring war against Germany had given rise in some quarters to a suspicion that her Government was playing false. In February, however, the Allies had persuaded the Italian Government to prohibit the exportation of German or Austrian merchandise through Italy as well as the transit through Italy of commodities for Germany or Austria-Hungary, and to requisition the thirty-four German merchant steamers interned in Italian ports. After the Allied War Council and the Economic Conference, Italy finally, on August 28, 1916, declared war against the German Empire, on the ground that Germany was aiding Italy's enemies, Austria-Hungary and Turkey.

Already economic conditions within the Central Empires were causing grave concern to the Teutonic authorities. Due to the pressure of the Allied blockade, the food situation was becoming alarming in Austria-Hungary and in Germany, and naturally it was the civilian population which in both countries suffered most. As early as May, 1916, what amounted to a food dictatorship had been established in Germany under Herr von Batocki, who received wide discretionary powers to regulate the supply, consumption, and sale of foodstuffs.

In June and July there were frequent reports of food difficulties. Riots occurred in Munich and in Essen. It appeared as though *Mittel-Europa* was on the verge of starvation and perhaps of revolution.

Time seemed to be ripe for the Allies to strike powerful blows on all fronts, in France, in Russia, on the Isonzo, in Macedonia, in Mesopotamia. The Central Empires, weakened by the economic blockade and by famine, would be unable to withstand concerted military pressure against their frontiers. Defeat on battlefields must surely be followed by revolution at home, and in that event Teutonic collapse would be inevitable and speedy — perhaps before the end of 1916.

---

[1] Shortly after the Economic Conference of June, 1916, the Entente Powers proceeded formally to repudiate the Declaration of London as a code of international law for maritime warfare, and Great Britain even went so far as to draw up an official "blacklist" of neutral firms with German affiliations. American protests against this action of Great Britain were fruitless.

SIMULTANEOUS ALLIED DRIVES: THE SOMME, THE ISONZO, AND THE SERETH

The first of the series of great offensives planned by the Allies for the summer of 1916 was the Russian drive, which began on June 4 and continued for about ten weeks. Though Russia had suffered grievously in 1915 and had been compelled to evacuate Galicia, Bukowina, Poland, and considerable parts of Lithuania and Courland, she had utilized the respite afforded her by Teutonic concentrations on other fronts — in the Balkans, against Verdun, and in the Trentino — in order to reform her lines, replenish her stores of ammunition, and reorganize her command. In the winter of 1915–1916 she had gallantly and brilliantly defended Riga against German attacks by land and sea; in March, 1916, she had contested enemy positions north and south of Dvinsk and had thereby prevented the Germans from sending additional reënforcements to Verdun from the East; and by June, she held in unexpected strength a long line from west of Riga past Dvinsk, Smorgon, the Pripet marshes, Rovno, and Tarnapol, to the northern border of Rumania.

The Russians elected to deliver their attack on the southern third of the Eastern Front. In the middle sector, which extended north from the Pripet marshes across the Lithuanian plain to the lake region northeast of Vilna, the opposing line was held too strongly by hardened German veterans for the Russian commander, General Ewarts, to attempt an offensive there with his raw recruits. Nor was an offensive practicable along the northern third of the Russian front; even if General Kuropatkin, commander of the Russian armies of the north, had the courage and genius to try conclusions with the master-strategist of Germany, Field Marshal von Hindenburg, the network of lakes and rivers and the broad stream of the Düna would impede a Russian drive just as effectively as they had blocked Hindenburg's advance toward Riga and Dvinsk. On the southern sector, however, between the Pripet marshes and the Russo-Rumanian border, a Russian offensive would be both more feasible from a military point of view and more desirable from a political standpoint, since that portion of the hostile line was manned mainly by a miscellaneous assortment of Austro-Hungarian nationalities, rather than by the invincible Prussians, and since a successful drive against Austria-Hungary would certainly relieve pressure on Italy and perhaps induce Rumania to enter the war on the side of the Entente.

General Brussilov, the commander of the Russian southern
sector, was by all odds the best man who could have been selected
for the conduct of a great offensive. Energetic, aggressive,
indefatigable, Brussilov had splendidly led one of the Russian
armies in the first invasion of Galicia, in 1914; in April, 1916,
he had been selected to succeed General Ivanov in supreme

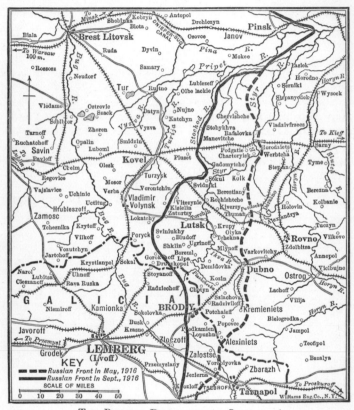

THE RUSSIAN DRIVE ON THE STYR, 1916

command of the southern army-group. Against the scant
700,000 men with whom the Austrian Archduke Frederick opposed him, Brussilov could muster more than a million, with
another million of half-trained recruits to draw upon for later
reënforcements.

Brussilov's drive began most auspiciously. Military critics
were no less surprised than the Austro-Hungarian trenchmen

were dismayed at the immense quantities of high explosive shells with which the Russian artillery accurately and thoroughly bombarded the Austrian defenses. Following the artillery preparation, Brussilov on June 4 launched simultaneous infantry attacks at innumerable points all along the 250-mile front from

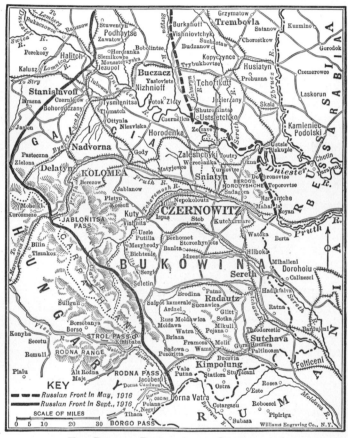

THE RUSSIAN DRIVE ON THE SERETH, 1916

the Pripet to the Pruth, rudely interrupting the festivities with which at that very moment the Archduke Frederick's sixtieth birthday was being celebrated behind the Austrian lines. In Volhynia the Russians advancing from Rovno speedily captured the fortresses of Dubno and Lutsk and occupied an important stretch of territory west of the Styr River. At the same time in eastern Galicia they crossed the Sereth River and captured Buczacz on the Strypa. Still farther south, they forced the crossing of the Pruth on June 16 and on the following day entered Czernowitz, the capital of Bukowina.

After the first fortnight, the Teutonic lines in Volhynia and Galicia began to stiffen, as German reënforcements arrived. At least four divisions were brought from France; others came from Hindenburg's northern armies; the Austrians, also, with frantic haste, recalled several divisions from Italy. Nevertheless, by the end of June the greater part of Bukowina was in Russian hands and Russian cavalry were "approaching the Transylvanian passes"; and during July Brussilov made some further gains west of the Dniester and west of the Styr. The drive expired about the middle of August simply because the Russians had then exhausted their supply of shells and worn out their howitzers and field guns.

The results of the Russian drive were appreciable. The supposedly impregnable Austro-German lines along the Styr and the Sereth had been carried on the whole front of 250 miles to a depth varying from twenty to fifty miles, north of the Dniester, and over sixty miles south of the Dniester. The entire province of Bukowina had been conquered. Altogether, between June 4 and August 12, some 350,000 men, 400 guns, and 1300 machine-guns had been captured. Most important of all, Russia had demonstrated to the world that she was still in the war and still capable of contributing her share to the grinding of Germany between upper and nether millstones. Her sudden rise, phœnix-like, from the disastrous fire and flame of the preceding autumn reassured all the Allies and incidentally conferred on her Balkan neighbor, Rumania, a new faith in the cause and the prowess of the Entente.

Brussilov's Drive on the Eastern Front was closely articulated with efforts of General Cadorna on the Italian Front. It was mainly the Russian offensive which enabled the Italians to check the Austrian invasion from the Trentino and to inaugurate a vindictive counter-offensive not only in the Trentino but along the Isonzo.

In the face of Cadorna's assaults, the Austrians about June 25 began a retreat on the Trentino front, evacuating in turn Asiago, Arsiero, and Posina. The Austrian retirement was planned and executed with such skill that very few prisoners and almost no guns were lost; nevertheless, it removed any immediate danger from northern Italy, and in this way amounted

to an important Italian victory.   Throughout July, Cadorna
exerted pressure against the Trentino front, but his principal
blow was reserved for the Isonzo.

Heavy mortars and howitzers, transferred from the Trentino,
opened fire along the Isonzo front on August 4, just before the
conclusion of the Russian drive.   The first day's attack, directed

THE ITALIAN CAMPAIGN AGAINST GORIZIA

against hills east of Monfalcone, was really a feint to draw the
Austrian reserves toward the southern wing.   The frontal
attack delivered two days later along an eight-mile line opposite
Gorizia was in deadly earnest.   The Austrian trenches were
pulverized by nine-hours' continuous bombardment.   The Italian infantry, believing that the hour of victory had at last arrived,
charged with unexampled impetuosity.   The heights on the

western bank of the Isonzo, overlooking Gorizia across the stream, were carried the first day, as were also the heights farther north. South of Gorizia, on the left bank of the Isonzo, the Italians stormed the summit of Monte San Michele, the key of the Gorizia position, for which they had striven for fourteen months. The Austrians resisted with stubborn courage. Isolated groups held out to the bitter end, in grottoes, in dugouts, or on inaccessible hilltops. General Boroevic, the Croatian commander of the Austrian army of the Isonzo, urged his troops to "repulse the attack in such a way that none of the enemy shall escape." Nevertheless, after two days' battle, all the heights west of the Isonzo were carried; and on August 9, 1916, Italian infantry escorted King Victor Emmanuel into Gorizia.

After the conquest of Gorizia, formidable obstacles had to be surmounted before the Italians could hope to "emancipate" Trieste. East of Gorizia were frowning hills, bristling with Austrian guns. South of Gorizia, directly barring the way to Trieste, lay the Carso plateau, the surface of which, naturally scarred by innumerable caverns and crater-like depressions, had been covered by the Austrians with a veritable labyrinth of entrenchments, blasted in the solid rock and connected by subterranean tunnels. In a region such as this, no offensive could make rapid progress; and the slight Italian advance beyond Gorizia was achieved only by dint of the hardest kind of fighting. But at least Gorizia was won and with it a foothold on the Carso. The loss inflicted on the Austrians by the whole Italian offensive in the first two weeks of August was estimated at 65,000; the Italians announced that 18,750 prisoners, 30 guns, 62 trench mortars, 92 machine-guns, 60,000 grenades, and other booty, had fallen into their hands.

Cadorna's drive on the Isonzo and Brussilov's on the Styr and the Sereth were hardly expected by the Allies to be decisive. They were intended primarily to divert the energies and forces of the Central Empires from the Anglo-French line on the Somme, where the Allies willed to make their major effort. A month after the Russians inaugurated their offensive on the Eastern Front and a month before the Italian offensive reached its height, the French and British struck furiously against the Germans on the Western Front.

The Anglo-French attack of July, 1916, was delivered on a front of thirty miles from Gommécourt to Estrées, on both flanks of the Somme River. The Somme, as a glance at the map will show, cut the Western Front at a point about eighty miles north of Paris and the same distance south of the Belgian coast.   It was significant that the theater selected for the major 1916 offensive was thirty-five miles south of the Loos-Vimy sector, which had been attacked in September, 1915, and forty-five miles south of Neuve Chapelle, the scene of the first British drive, in March, 1915.   The southward gravitation of successive Anglo-French offensives proved that the Allies, temporarily at least, had abandoned hope of reconquering the rich coal and iron fields of Flanders and Artois.   The new drive was launched, not among mines and slagheaps, but among the smiling agricultural villages of Picardy.

The obvious objective for the British, who fought on the northern side of the Somme, was the town of Bapaume, nine miles northeast of the front; for the French, who held a mile of the front on the northern bank and four (later, ten) miles south of the river, Péronne, seven miles east of the French line and twelve miles southeast of Bapaume, was the natural goal. Midway between Péronne and Bapaume, the less important town of Combles, three miles from the front, might constitute a preliminary objective.   Sanguine "military experts" declared that once the British took Bapaume they would speedily advance to Cambrai and Douai, two of the most important strategic centers behind the German lines, and that the French, by pressing on beyond Péronne to St. Quentin, would make the German position at Noyon so dangerous a salient that it would have to be evacuated.

In the technique of attack the Allies this time had many surprises in store for the Germans.   Hundreds of airmen in battle-planes of an improved type, darting back and forth across the German lines just before the attack, drove the German air-scouts to cover, dropped "fire-balls" on the German observation-balloons, and carried back wonderfully clear photographs of the German trenches, so that the Anglo-French artillery could accurately place its high-explosive shells precisely where they would do the most damage.   The British, on Sir Douglas Haig's own admission, had learned a lesson from the enemy and had "developed and perfected" the art of using poisonous gas and liquid fire.   An original British contribution to the science of trench-warfare was the "tank,"[1] a heavy motor-truck encased in invulnerable steel armor-plate and cumbrously moved on caterpillar treads.   With machine-guns spitting murderously

[1] The "tank" was first used in the second phase of the Somme drive, in September, 1916.

N

from apertures on either side, a "tank" could lumber across "no man's land" to the enemy's trenches, unscathed by ordinary rifle or machine-gun fire; it could brush aside barbed-wire entanglements as though they were cobwebs; it could even crawl across trenches and shell-craters and spread confusion and panic behind the enemy's lines.

Most promising of all was the improvement of British and French artillery. France now had a very large number of heavy guns, including some 16-inch mortars; and many military critics regarded the French howitzers, as well as the 3-inch field gun (the famous "75"), as distinctly superior to their German counterparts. British arsenals, likewise, were now turning out howitzers of the largest caliber, and the weekly production of high explosives was 11,000 times as great as the total output in the whole month of September, 1914. It was upon their tremendously powerful artillery that the Allies chiefly relied to blast a way through the wire entanglements, to plow up the intricate German entrenchments, to silence the German machine-guns before the infantry charge, and to cut off German counter-attacks by a "curtain of fire."

When on the night of June 30–July 1, 1916, the artillery "preparation" of the Somme drive reached its climax, "parapets crumbled beneath the impact of the shells, cover hitherto thought bomb-proof was crushed and destroyed, and the garrisons of the enemy's works, sorely shattered in morale, were driven down into the deepest dugouts to seek shelter from the pitiless hail of projectiles." Early in the morning of July 1 there came a lull in the thunder of the howitzers, as the gunners lengthened the range, and the infantry leaped forward from Allied trenches, with cheers, to charge the German lines.

Every inch of Allied advance was stubbornly contested by the Germans, and it soon became apparent that the Somme drive would not immediately menace Cambrai, Douai, or St. Quentin. In the first fortnight of the battle, July 1–14, the French took 12,200 prisoners, pushed forward their line on a front of eleven miles to a maximum depth of six miles and conquered thirty square miles of territory. In the same period the British advanced on a ten-mile front to a maximum depth of three miles and made 10,000 prisoners.

Badly battered, but not broken, the German line stiffened perceptibly after the first fortnight. The French were brought to an abrupt halt a mile from Péronne; and furious German counter-attacks stayed the British. After a month of the great drive, the British found themselves in possession of twenty-four square miles of conquered territory, but blocked by strong German positions along the hilly ridge north of the Somme from Thiepval to Saillisel.   Until this ridge could be carried, it would be impossible to take Bapaume.

During the long pause, lasting through the entire month of August, in which the Anglo-French drive came practically to

BATTLE OF THE SOMME

a standstill, gaining at the most a few hundred yards here and there, the French and British guns were being moved forward to new positions, to blast open the path for a new advance. A terrific bombardment on the night of September 2, 1916, gave notice that the second phase of the battle of the Somme had begun.   At noon on September 3 the infantry charged, with renewed confidence and dash.   The decisive struggle for the town of Combles and for the ridge, between Thiepval and Saillisel, now ensued.

Gallant Irish troops, bearing the brunt of the battle on the heights northwest of Combles, expelled the enemy at the point of the bayonet and repelled ferocious counter-attacks. British "tanks" appearing for the first time, smashed their way through the German trenches and were followed by infantry with hand-grenades. The artillery thundered with "unheard-of violence." By September 25 the whole German line between Thiepval and Combles was pushed over the ridge; only Thiepval, at the north-western end, and Combles, on the southeast, held out. But Combles was already enveloped from the south and east by the army of the French General Fayolle. At the very last moment, on September 26, the German garrison evacuated Combles, fighting as it went, and retired through a ravine to the north-east under cross-fire from both sides. On the same day, at the opposite end of the ridge, Thiepval was stormed and captured, and in the center the British line was pushed more than a mile north of the crest. The prisoners taken at Combles and Thiepval swelled the total, for the French, to 35,000; for the British, to 26,000.

Torrential rains and weeks of cloudy weather hindered the further progress of the Anglo-French drive, by making it almost impossible to move the heavy guns forward, over muddy roads, or to direct artillery fire by airplane observations. The French infantry, to be sure, in October fought its way into Sailly and Saillisel, but was repeatedly thrown back and did not completely occupy Saillisel until November 12. On their right wing, the French got close to Chaulnes; and during the same period the British extended their successes at some points north of the Thiepval-Combles ridge to within four miles of Bapaume.

Measured in terms of territory, the results of the Anglo-French drive on the Somme were small. Nowhere had the advance been more than seven miles. The total area conquered was approximately 120 square miles, only slightly greater than the area won by the Germans at Verdun. Neither Bapaume nor Péronne had been attained, and neither Cambrai nor the German salient at Noyon had been threatened. Nevertheless the drive had achieved three purposes: (1) it had relieved Verdun and transferred the offensive in France from the Germans to the Allies; (2) by holding the bulk of the German army on the Western Front, it had condemned Austria-Hungary to stand pretty much alone and therefore unsuccessful against the Russians on the Styr and the Sereth and against the Italians on the Isonzo; and (3) it had worn down the German forces.

By way of comment on the third point it may be noted that the German casualty list as added up by the British War Office showed a grand total of 3,920,000 (since the beginning of the war) on December 1, 1916, as compared with about 3,130,000 on July 1 ; the difference, 790,000, represented the total German losses in killed, disabled, and captured, on all fronts during the five months from July to November, 1916. Allowing 90,000 for losses in the East, the German loss in the battle of the Somme could not have been less than 700,000. The British loss was announced as approximately 450,000, and that of the French was estimated at 225,000. But the Allies could afford higher losses than the Central Empires. In the very year when Great Britain instituted compulsory military service and prepared to double her armed strength, the forces of Germany and Austria-Hungary, already passing their numerical maximum, were wasting rapidly — the Austro-Hungarians on the Russian and Italian fronts, the Germans at Verdun and on the Somme. In an endurance test such as the Great War was proving itself to be, relative wastage of man-power and economic resources was destined to become the decisive factor.

If none of the Allied drives in 1916 — Russian, Italian, or Anglo-French — had succeeded in obtaining an immediate military decision, all of them together had demonstrated the great advantage of simultaneous efforts on all fronts in wearing down Teutonic defense and wasting Teutonic strength. However, they had been too exhausting to the Allies themselves to enable the democratic nations at that time to perceive in them an augury of ultimate triumph for the Allied cause. Allied discouragement was not immediately remedied. Allied gloom was not immediately dispelled.

But the simultaneous drives did produce one immediate result. They brought Rumania into the war on the side of the Entente, and little Rumania, in the circumstances, might suffice to tip the balance of armed power and to bring Austria-Hungary and perhaps Germany to terms.

THE PARTICIPATION AND DEFEAT OF RUMANIA

Before the war Rumania had been associated with the Triple Alliance, on the basis of commercial and defensive agreements, but since the Balkan Wars of 1912–1913 she had shown a marked leaning toward Serbia and the Triple Entente, and since the outbreak of the Great War the Entente diplomatists had strained every nerve to enlist Rumania's support. During the first two years of the struggle, however, Rumania had remained neutral, whether because King Ferdinand [1] was a Hohenzollern, or because Russia refused to offer Bessarabia as part of the price of Rumania's aid, or because the Rumanian War Office feared to try conclusions with the conquerors of Poland and Serbia, or because Rumanian landlords found it too profitable to sell their grain to the Central Empires. At any rate, Rumania wavered and hesitated.

In April, 1916, when Teutonic fortunes appeared most favorable, the Rumanian minister at Berlin signed a convention with Germany, providing for free interchange of domestic products, and for a time the Allies feared lest Rumania should follow Bulgaria into the embrace of *Mittel-Europa*. But subsequent military events changed the aspect of affairs fundamentally. By August, 1916, Russia had displayed unexpected signs of renewed strength and power by conquering Bukowina and threatening Transylvania — provinces ardently coveted by Rumanian irredentists; and the Italian conquest of Gorizia on August 9, together with the German failure at Verdun and the Anglo-French victories on the Somme in July, seemed to indicate that the Teutonic armies were no longer able to hold their own.

Furthermore, the situation in the Balkans was less disturbing to Rumania in August, 1916, than it had been in the preceding winter. So long as Rumania was to be assailed not only by determined Hungarian armies on the west but also by numerous Teutonic-Bulgarian-Turkish forces along her extended southern frontier, she prudently refrained from espousing the Allied cause and from thereby inviting certain disaster. But by August, 1916, her Danubian boundary did not seem to be directly endangered. Exigencies on other fronts had led to the withdrawal of the greater part of Mackensen's Teutonic army from the Balkans. The Turks were beginning to find their freed Gallipoli army inadequate for the defense of Asiatic Turkey against Russian attacks in Armenia and British pressure in Mesopotamia and against uprisings of Arab chieftains. In fact, the Russians under the Grand Duke Nicholas on July 25 captured the important city of Erzingian, over a hundred miles west of Erzerum, and in August General Sir Stanley Maude took command of the British forces in Mesopotamia, reorganized and reënforced

---

[1] Ferdinand had succeeded his uncle, Charles I, in October, 1914, and was thought to be less devoted to his Hohenzollern relatives in Germany than his predecessor had been.

them, and prepared to retrieve Townshend's reverses.   Bagdad
was again menaced.   To add to the uneasiness and alarm of the
Turks, the British began the construction, across the Sinai
desert, of a railway over which an expeditionary force might
readily be transported from Egypt for an invasion of Palestine,
and already on June 9 the Sherif of Hedjaz, the most powerful
Turkish vassal of western and central Arabia, had proclaimed
from sacred Mecca his independence of the Ottoman Empire.
Obviously Rumania now had little or nothing to fear from Turkey.   Turkey had need of all of her available forces for the
defense of her own lands; she could ill afford to spare troops
from her hard-pressed Asiatic fronts to back Bulgaria's imperialistic ambitions in Europe.

Turkish and Teutonic military necessities seemingly left
Bulgaria almost alone to bear the burden of *Mittel-Europa* in
the Balkans.   And a growing burden it was.   Not only was
the Allied expeditionary force at Salonica steadily augmented
by British and French reënforcements, but there came also a
detachment from Russia, contingents from Albania and Italy,
and a force of some 120,000 Serbians who had been assembled
and organized on the island of Corfu.   Altogether by August,
1916, General Sarrail, the Allied commander at Salonica, had
at his disposal a formidable army-group of 700,000 men.   These
troops were flung out on a fan-shaped front in Greek Macedonia
north of Salonica: the left flank was close to the Serbian frontier
in the mountains south of Monastir;   the center was pushed
up the Vardar valley to the border towns of Gievgheli and Doiran,
forty miles north of Salonica;   and the right wing rested on the
Struma River and Lake Tahynos, with outposts even farther
to the northeast.   On August 21, 1916, the French War Office announced that General Sarrail's forces " were taking the offensive
on the entire Macedonian front."   In that event, the Bulgarians
would be obliged to devote all their efforts to the defense of their
recent conquests in southern Serbia; they would be in no position to cross the Danube and assail Rumania.   Rumania hesitated no longer.

Negotiations between Rumania and the Entente had already
reached fruition in a secret treaty signed on August 17, 1916.
By this treaty Rumania agreed to break off all economic relations with *Mittel-Europa* and to declare war and begin offensive
operations in ten days; in return, France, Great Britain, Italy,
and Russia assured Rumania of the special assistance both of
Russian armies and of General Sarrail's army at Salonica, and

promised to reward her with Bukowina, Transylvania, and the Banat of Temesvar.   On August 27, true to its word, the Government of King Ferdinand declared war against Austria-Hungary. To the press the Government explained that, although Rumania had formerly been in defensive alliance with the Dual Monarchy, altered circumstances constrained her to resume full liberty of action and to join the Entente Powers in order to safeguard her national interests and to emancipate the three million Rumans resident in Austria-Hungary.   Germany, Turkey, and Bulgaria, as allies of Austria-Hungary, promptly declared war against Rumania.

For the Central Powers, the participation of Rumania in the war on the side of their adversaries was the culminating point in a period of bitter disappointment.   The tremendous German effort at Verdun (February–July, 1916) had won a few ruined forts and desolated villages, but not victory; after July 1, when the Anglo-French drive on the Somme began, the Germans seemed unable even to hold their own on the Western Front; the Austrians, likewise, after attempting an offensive (May) against Italy, had been thrown back on the defensive and had been driven out of Gorizia (August 9); the Eastern Front, weakened to supply men for the Teutonic thrusts against Italy and France, had been seriously dented by the Russians (June–August); and now at the close of August the intervention of Rumania added 600,000 bayonets to the "ring of steel" surrounding the Central Powers and 900 miles to the front which the Central Powers had to defend.   It was natural, if not wholly fair, that these disasters should popularly be ascribed to the strategy pursued during the first half of the year 1916 by General Erich von Falkenhayn, chief of the German General Staff.

The dismissal of Falkenhayn on August 29 — two days after Rumania's declaration of war — betokened a desperate resolve on the part of the German Government to stem the tide of reverses.   The most popular of German field commanders, Field Marshal Paul von Hindenburg, hero of Tannenberg, conqueror of Russian Poland, and commander-in-chief of the German armies on the Eastern Front, was chosen to succeed Falkenhayn as chief of the general staff.   Ludendorff, who had formerly been Hindenburg's chief of staff on the Russian front, now became quartermaster-general and was recognized as Hindenburg's " right-hand man."

The effects of Hindenburg's appointment were soon apparent. The command of the armies on the Western Front was reorganized, with Field Marshal Duke Albrecht of Württemberg as commander of the northern army group, Crown Prince Rupprecht of Bavaria as commander of the central group (including the region of the Somme), and the Prussian Crown Prince Frederick William in charge of the Verdun army group. On the Russian Front, Prince Leopold of Bavaria and the Austrian Archduke Charles Francis were the titular commanders of army groups, but operations were really directed by trusted German staff officers. In conferences held at German Headquarters behind the Eastern Front in September, 1916, it was decided to concentrate the energies of *Mittel-Europa* for the present upon a great offensive against Rumania. The crushing of Rumania would be not only a highly spectacular achievement but an object-lesson to neutral Powers such as Greece and the United States and a source of renewed morale to the citizens of the Central Empires.

To crush Rumania, Hindenburg collected a composite Bulgar-Turco-Teutonic army. Teutons were brought from the Eastern and Western Fronts. Hindenburg, knowing that the Russians had already exhausted their surplus of munitions, believed that his eastern lines could be securely held by somewhat diminished numbers. Feeling, moreover, that the protracted battle of the Somme was gradually exhausting Anglo-French reserves of men and *matériel*, he was willing to run the risk of drawing off a few German defenders from that area, even if thereby he must forego in the near future another Teutonic offensive on the Western Front. The Austro-Hungarians could rely on the rocky heights east of Gorizia and the naturally impregnable Carso plateau to halt the Italian offensive; they, too, could now spare men for a campaign against Rumania. Besides, Hindenburg prevailed upon Turkey to overlook her own needs in Asia and upon Bulgaria to weaken the Macedonian front. If the latter should be obliged to yield some ground to General Sarrail's Salonica army, she was assured of Teutonic aid in recovering it as soon as Rumania should be crushed. Incidentally, Bulgaria had not forgotten Rumania's hostility to her in the second Balkan War; she had a territorial dispute of her own with Rumania.

Meanwhile, the Rumanian General Staff, counting upon General Sarrail in Macedonia to engage the attention of Bulgaria and upon Russia's formal promise to inaugurate a violent offensive in Bukowina and thereby prevent the shifting of Austro-German troops from Poland and Galicia, threw the bulk of its available forces into Transylvania, with little regard to the possibility of counter-attacks. The Ruman-speaking principality of Transylvania, for many years an integral part of the

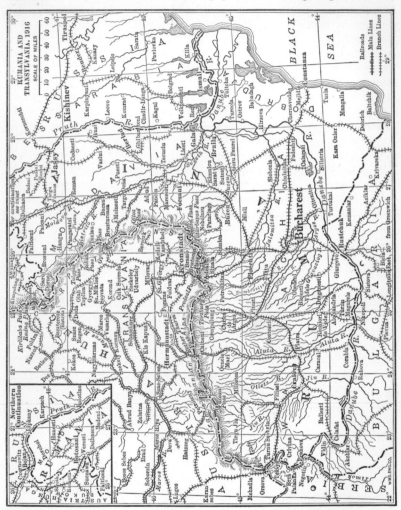

Kingdom of Hungary, lay in the acute angle between the Carpathians and the Transylvanian Alps, half surrounded to the east and west by Rumania. In fact, Rumania bore some resemblance to the open jaws of a pair of gigantic pincers — Moldavia forming the upper jaw, Wallachia the lower — with

Transylvania caught in between them. It was the purpose of the Rumanian General Staff that Transylvania should be wrested from Hungary by the simultaneous pressure of both jaws. Accordingly, the Rumanians pressed heavily on both the Wallachian and the Moldavian fronts. From Moldavia they swiftly penetrated the chief passes leading through the Carpathians into eastern Transylvania, and within a fortnight they had reached the valley of the upper Maros and the upper Aluta about twenty miles inside the frontier. At the same time they advanced from Wallachia, passed the "Iron Gates" of the Danube, took Orsova, and marched northward along the railway to Mehadia. Other forces penetrated the mountain passes between these extreme flanks of the Rumanian front and descended into the valleys of Transylvania.

Within three weeks of Rumania's declaration of war, one-fourth of Transylvania was "delivered" from Magyar rule, and some 7000 prisoners were captured. But while the Rumanians, flushed with victory, were still deep in Transylvania, signs were at hand of an impending counter-stroke. Germany had sent two of her ablest strategists, Mackensen and Falkenhayn, to the Rumanian front, and had the Rumanian air-scouts ventured far behind the Austrian lines they would have seen, at Temesvar and other Hungarian railway centers, grim howitzers and immense stores of munitions accumulating ominously. Or, could the same air-scouts have perceived the deadly preparations going forward simultaneously in Bulgaria, they would have wondered at the temerity and rashness of Rumania's participation in the Great War.

Field Marshal von Mackensen, who had coöperated with Hindenburg in the great German invasion of Russia in 1915 and had subsequently superintended the conquest of Serbia in October and November, 1915, unexpectedly appeared in the second week of September, 1916, as commander of a formidable Bulgar-Teutonic army ready to pounce upon the exposed and poorly defended southern border of Rumania, while General von Falkenhayn took command of a powerful Austro-German army in Transylvania. The German General Staff had evolved a masterful plan of strategy. Falkenhayn would press the main Rumanian armies so hard that no considerable portion of them could be dispatched from Transylvania to the Dobrudja; and Mackensen, encountering little armed opposition, would invade the Dobrudja and cut off the retreat of the Rumanians from Transylvania. In this fashion, Rumania would be ground to bits between the jaws of Falkenhayn and Mackensen; her army would be destroyed and her complete conquest assured.

Mackensen's army advanced in the Dobrudja so quickly that in a few days it was fifty miles north of the Bulgarian frontier and within ten miles of the very important Constanza-Chernavoda railway which connects Bucharest with Constanza, the chief Rumanian port on the Black Sea. While Russian troops were being rushed to the assistance of the hard-pressed Rumanians in the Dobrudja, General von Falkenhayn dealt the Rumanian invaders of Transylvania a series of hard blows. The cities of Hermannstadt, Schässburg, and Kronstadt were in turn relieved, and the Rumanian columns in eastern Transylvania were soon in headlong flight toward the Rumanian frontier. By the middle of October the Rumanians had been driven back all along the line; Transylvania had been cleared, and the Austro-German armies were gaining footholds on Rumanian soil.

By this time Mackensen had brought up a sufficient number of big guns to break through the Russo-Rumanian lines south of the Chernavoda-Constanza railway; Constanza fell on October 22 — just eight weeks after Rumania's entry into the war. In vain Russia sent one of her ablest generals, Vladimir Sakharov, with reënforcements to stiffen the Dobrudja line; the Constanza-Chernavoda railway was irretrievably lost, and the best Sakharov could do was to reorganize the shattered Russo-Rumanian army in northern Dobrudja.

No aid was forthcoming to the Rumanians in the west. There Falkenhayn captured Vulcan Pass on October 25, defeated the Rumanians in a bloody battle, and on November 21 captured Craiova, seventy-five miles south of the frontier. By this bold stroke Falkenhayn won the western third of Wallachia. The Rumanian force operating in the extreme west, finding itself completely cut off from the other Rumanian armies, hastily evacuated Orsova and Turnu-Severin and retired into near-by mountains, but was soon compelled to surrender.

With frantic haste General Averescu, the Rumanian commander-in-chief, endeavored to marshal his demoralized army behind the Aluta River, ninety miles west of Bucharest. But the line of the Aluta was turned on both flanks. From the north, Austro-German troops advanced down the slopes of the Transylvanian Alps into the Wallachian plain, behind the Aluta. On the south, Mackensen flung strong forces across the Danube and by November 27 reached Alexandria. With both flanks crumpling, the Aluta line was no longer tenable, and General

Averescu fell back to his last line of defense, the Arges River, less than ten miles west of Bucharest. Again Mackensen and Falkenhayn resorted to their flanking tactics, from the south and from the north respectively; and the Arges line too had to be abandoned.

With its supposedly invulnerable cincture of nineteen armored forts and redoubts, constructed by the famous Belgian engineer, Brialmont, Bucharest was one of the most formidable fortresses in Europe, but the Rumanians made no serious attempt to defend their capital against Mackensen's heavy howitzers. On December 6, — his birthday, — Mackensen entered Bucharest in triumph. On the same day the city of Ploechti, thirty miles north of Bucharest, and the whole line of the Bucharest-Kron-stadt railway fell into the invader's hand. In three weeks' campaign, November 15–December 6, Falkenhayn and Mackensen had routed the Rumanian army, taken over 80,000 prisoners, and conquered the greater part of Wallachia, including the capital city of Bucharest.

Violent Russian counter-attacks in the Carpathians failed to stay the enemy. By the middle of January, 1917, the Rumanians had lost all Wallachia, all the Dobrudja, and a portion of southern Moldavia; their king was at Jassy and their armed remnants, supported by Russians, were standing at bay along the Sereth River from Galatz westwards.

The collapse of Rumania was due in large part to the failure of General Sarrail to exert sufficient pressure on the Macedonian front. General Sarrail, it will be recalled, had announced on August 20 that he was taking the offensive, with his 700,000 Allied troops, against the Bulgarians. But this "offensive" was either a sham or a fiasco. Instead of driving northward into Serbia and Bulgaria, Sarrail actually lost ground. His left wing was beaten back from Florina, and the Bulgarians in this sector occupied Koritza and Kastoria. At the same time, on Sarrail's right wing, Bulgarian troops seized the railway between Drama, Seres, and Demir-Hissar, and on September 12 occupied the Greek port of Kavala.

The months of October, November, and December, — so disastrous for Rumania, — witnessed no significant operations either on the right wing or in the center of Sarrail's line; only on the left wing was anything achieved. Here the reorganized Serbian army of 120,000 men unrelentingly fought its way, mile by mile, northward toward Monastir. After two months' plodding and pushing over bleak hills and across dreary ravines the Serbians at length on November 19, 1916, reëntered Monastir. It was exactly four years since Monastir had been captured from Turkey by the Serbs, and almost one year since it had been occupied by the Bulgarians.

Despite this Serbian achievement, the fact remained that the Bulgarians not only had been able to transfer troops and guns from Macedonia to Dobrudja in order to assist in the Austro-German conquest of Rumania, but also had prevented the Allied force at Salonica from inflicting any grave injury on their weakened Macedonian front; if they had lost Monastir, they had gained Kavala. Of General Sarrail's seeming inactivity in this crisis there were two explanations. In the first place, his army was heterogeneous, and as yet badly disciplined and poorly equipped and munitioned. In the second place, he did not dare move his forces far forward so long as a hostile Greek army might assail him from the rear.

It was the Greek King Constantine again who paralyzed Allied plans to relieve a Balkan state hard-pressed by Teutonic-Bulgarian invaders. When Rumania entered the war in August, 1916, confident of an easy triumph, Constantine exultingly predicted that she would speedily be conquered by German arms. The event confirmed the Greek king's prophecy and strengthened at once his devotion to Germany and his contempt for the Allies. Even the seizure of the Greek port of Kavala by the Bulgarians in September — the very port whose peaceful cession to Bulgaria had been advocated by Venizelos and vehemently resisted by the king only the year before — was now viewed most complacently by Constantine. It appeared as if Constantine had some sort of formal agreement with the Central Empires and only awaited a favorable opportunity to assail the Allies as suddenly and as theatrically as King Ferdinand of Bulgaria had done.

Until Rumania entered the war, the Allies had labored chiefly by diplomacy to enlist the support, or at least the benevolent neutrality, of King Constantine and his succession of puppet premiers. Thereafter they resorted to coercion. In September Greece was compelled to surrender her telegraphs and postal system to Anglo-French authorities. In October the French Admiral du Fournet seized the Greek navy; all German, Austro-Hungarian, Turkish, and Bulgarian diplomatic representatives were unceremoniously expelled from Greece; Athenian newspapers were subjected to French censorship; Anglo-French marines were landed at Piræus and on Greek islands in the

Ægean; an Anglo-French fleet trained its guns on Athens; the coast of Greece was blockaded; and in December Constantine was forced not only to transfer his troops to the southernmost districts of Greece but also to turn over to the Allies a considerable part of the munitions and artillery of the Greek army.

These measures, necessary as they were from the Allied point of view, served to render King Constantine still more truculent and to divide the Greek people into two hostile camps. On the one hand, Venizelos applauded the drastic measures of the Allies and formally repudiated the king; he established a provisional government in Crete and Macedonia and on his own account issued a declaration of war against Bulgaria (November 28, 1916). On the other hand, the Greek army chiefs, with a sizable popular following, espoused the cause of the king and denounced the "treason" of Venizelos and the "hypocrisy" of the Allies; they were intent on aiding the Germans and embarrassing General Sarrail at Salonica. Early in December there were riotous demonstrations in Athens against the Allies, and hundreds of Venizelists were clubbed or imprisoned. Only the landing of Anglo-French marines restored order.

Because of the disquieting situation in Greece and because of the disorganized condition of Sarrail's motley forces in Macedonia, no Anglo-French aid was forthcoming to Rumania. Russia, it is true, sent troops into Moldavia and the Dobrudja, but they were too few in number and too ill munitioned to stay the oncoming rush of Teutonic-Bulgarian invaders. Besides, it was subsequently disclosed that the Tsar's government at the time of Rumania's direst need was playing a double game. Russia, for the sake of retaining Bessarabia and making Rumania an object of her own imperialistic ambition, did not desire her southern neighbor to acquire too great prestige by a decisive victory over Austria-Hungary, and therefore neglected to assist her until too late. Struck in the face by Germany and in the side by Bulgaria, and stabbed in the back by Russia, Rumania collapsed barely three months after her participation in the Great War.

STALEMATE AND THE TEUTONIC PEACE DRIVE

The Allies, hopeful in midsummer of 1916 that their fortunes were at last in the ascendant, had counted upon Rumania's intervention as the last straw which would break the back of Germanized *Mittel-Europa*. At the close of 1916, however, it was obvious that the net result of Rumania's participation in the Great War had been favorable to the Central Empires. German prestige and Austro-Hungarian confidence, shaken by the failures at Verdun, on the Somme, in Volhynia, in Galicia, in Bukowina, and on the Isonzo, were restored by the spectacular campaign in Rumania. To be sure, the battle-front was now approximately two hundred miles longer than before Rumania's intervention, but actually fewer men would be required to oppose, or to pursue, the shattered fragments of the Rumanian field army, which had lost at least two-thirds of its effectives, than had previously been required to guard nine hundred miles of frontier with Rumania's long-delayed intervention a standing menace. Moreover, a large quantity of Rumanian wheat, which British agents had purchased to prevent its exportation to the Central Powers, was now in possession of the Teutons; and the fertile grain-fields of Wallachia, scientifically cultivated under the supervision of German agricultural experts, might relieve the shortage of foodstuffs in Austria-Hungary and Germany, in case the war should be prolonged over another harvest season. Nor should it be forgotten that in capturing the Rumanian city of Ploechti, in the Prahova valley, the Germans won the center of Europe's richest oil-fields, although the oil-wells were found in flames and the oil-tanks destroyed. The economic results of the campaign of Mackensen and Falkenhayn were as important as its strategy was brilliant.

The only Allied success in the autumn of 1916, which in any way could offset the Teutonic conquest of Rumania, was a French counter-stroke at Verdun. In late October and early November, General Nivelle launched a furious attack on the east bank of the Meuse,[1] north of Verdun, broke through the German line on a four-mile front to a depth of two miles, and recovered Forts Douaumont and Vaux and the village of Damloup. In mid-December, a second French assault carried German trenches on a front of six miles and took several other villages, with 11,000 prisoners. Although the territory regained by these two French counter-strokes represented only a small part of what had been lost in the vicinity of Verdun between February and July, nevertheless the significance of the French exploit was very real. With trifling sacrifice of men, the French had easily regained the most important strategic positions on the east bank of the Meuse — positions which the Prussian Crown Prince had cap-

[1] The French operations, under the general command of Nivelle, were actually conducted by General Mangin.

tured only after desperate, protracted, and frightfully sanguinary battles.   The moral of which was that while the Germans might still win sensational victories on other fronts — for example, over little Rumania — the Allies were gradually gaining military superiority on the substantial and all-important Western Front.

Nevertheless, for the moment, Mackensen's spectacular exploits in Rumania loomed larger in popular imagination than Nivelle's counter-attack at Verdun.   If the Germans had failed to obtain a final military decision in 1916, it was equally true that the Allies had failed too.   And the result was bitter disappointment and depression within each of the Entente Powers.

In Great Britain, Lord Northcliffe, the proprietor of the London *Times* and of several other influential newspapers, assailed Mr. Asquith's Government and sowed serious dissension between the premier and David Lloyd George.   Early in December, 1916, Lord Northcliffe's journalistic campaign received sufficient approbation throughout the country and in parliament to lead to the resignation of the Asquith cabinet.   After the refusal of Andrew Bonar Law, the Unionist leader, to become prime minister, David Lloyd George was invited to form a ministry and his acceptance was announced on December 6.   The Lloyd George cabinet, like the most recent Asquith cabinet, was a coalition affair, representing the Liberal, Unionist, and Labor parties, but with the exception of the premiership itself the most important posts in the new ministry were assigned to Unionists rather than to Liberals; Arthur J. Balfour succeeded Sir Edward Grey [1] as foreign secretary; Bonar Law became chancellor of the exchequer and leader of the House of Commons; and the "war cabinet," a steering committee of five members newly created from within the ministry, comprised the premier, Bonar Law, Lord Milner, Earl Curzon, and Arthur Henderson, — one Liberal, three Unionists, and one Laborite.

In France, Premier Briand managed to retain office and the confidence of a majority of his countrymen by constituting, like Lloyd George, a special centralizing "war committee" within his cabinet.   The French war committee, as announced on December 12, comprised, in addition to the premier, Alexandre Ribot, General Lyautey,[2] Admiral Lacaze, and Albert Thomas, ministers respectively of finance, war, marine, and munitions.   Shortly afterwards, General Joffre was made a

---

[1] Viscount Grey of Falloden.

[2] General Hubert Lyautey, who had made a name for himself in Morocco, was just succeeding General Roques as minister of war.

o

Marshal of France and retired from active command of the French forces, his successor being General Robert Nivelle, the leader of the recently successful counter-attack at Verdun.

In Russia, affairs were going from bad to worse. At the very time when the army was recovering from its defeats and demoralization of 1915 and becoming once more a potential weapon of offense against the Teutons, the Tsar and his entourage were willfully blinding their eyes to the signs of economic distress throughout the empire and persistently closing their ears to popular demands for political reform. Boris Stürmer, who served as premier during the greater part of the critical year 1916, was a confirmed reactionary and was suspected of pro-German leanings. He muzzled the press, forced the able and loyally pro-Entente Sazonov out of the ministry of foreign affairs (August, 1916), appointed ultra-conservatives to office, suspended the Duma from July to November, executed obnoxious autocratic decrees, and endeavored to repress altogether popular organizations, such as the All-Russian Union of Zemstvos, the Union of Municipalities, and the War Industries Committee, formed for the twofold purpose of advocating democratic reform and supporting the government in the vigorous prosecution of the war. In October, Stürmer placed all meetings of these popular organizations under police supervision; and, to cap the climax, he appointed as minister of the interior M. Protopopov, who was the most zealous prosecutor of liberals in all Russia and who was known to cherish German sympathies.

These and other causes of complaint united nearly all Russian factions against the government. But when at length, in November, 1916, Stürmer resigned, the Tsar apparently had still learned no lesson, for he promptly raised to the premiership Alexander Trepov, a reactionary of the same faith and outlook as Stürmer and Protopopov. The year 1916 closed in Russia with a stormy session of the Duma in which Professor Paul Milyukov, leader of the Constitutional Democrats, indicted the government and was followed by several speakers who reported sensational instances of criminal negligence in the prosecution of the war. The Duma passed a resolution affirming that certain "dark forces" were tending to paralyze the nation's energies and to cause disorganization in all departments. Russia was rapidly becoming volcanic, but the weak Tsar, the "little father," was hopelessly deaf and blind.

As for the Central Empires, the common people were temporarily reassured by the surprisingly speedy conquest of Rumania and were therefore less critical of their civil and military authorities. In Austria-Hungary, the death of the aged Emperor-King Francis Joseph on November 21, 1916, which should have been, according to Allied forecasts, the signal for the dissolution of the Dual Monarchy, was succeeded quietly, and apparently with cordial popular acquiescence, by the coronation of the Archduke Charles, Francis Joseph's grand-nephew, as emperor of Austria and king of Hungary. In Germany, a "Patriotic Auxiliary Service Act," passed by the Reichstag on December 2, subjected all males between sixteen and sixty years of age not yet called to the colors to auxiliary war work, such as service in war industries, agriculture, and nursing the sick; it was a kind of *levée en masse* and represented the closest sort of coöperation between the German government and the German people in a supreme endeavor to win the war.

Meanwhile, the Teutons were doing everything in their power to strengthen and consolidate *Mittel-Europa*. Laborers were being deported in large numbers from Belgium and from the conquered districts of France and Rumania for work in German factories and fields. Encouragement was being given to the "national aspirations" of the Belgian Flemings and more especially of the Russian Poles.

In glaring contrast to the failure of Russia to establish and maintain autonomy in Poland, the Teutons after driving the Russians out of the country set about elaborating measures of self-government for the Poles. On November 5, 1916, the German and Austrian emperors conjointly published a proclamation promising to create an "independent" Kingdom of Poland, "a national state with an hereditary monarch and a constitutional government," in "intimate relations" with Austria-Hungary and Germany. This proclamation was read publicly at Lublin and at Warsaw, in the Polish language, and was followed by the hoisting of Polish flags while Teutonic military bands played the Polish national anthem. A Regency was set up, and elections were instituted for the State Council, or upper house, of the future Polish Parliament. The Polish Jews, moreover, were conciliated by the grant of special religious and social privileges.

It soon became apparent that the "independent kingdom of Poland in intimate relations with Austria-Hungary and Germany" was not intended to be a national state for all Polish people; the Polish provinces of Prussia were to remain Prussian as before, and Polish Galicia, while securing a larger measure of autonomy within the Dual Monarchy, was not to be united with independent Poland. Austro-German magnanimity was to be displayed only in Russian Poland, and even there it was most properly suspected when proclamations were issued by the German Governor-General von Beseler at Warsaw exhorting the Poles to volunteer for service in the Polish army which "would join in the struggle against Russia."

Russia then did grudgingly in defeat what she might have done with better grace during the preceding year. She issued a counter-proclamation, denouncing the Austro-German manifesto as illegal and insincere, threatening to treat as traitors rather than as prisoners of war any Russian Poles captured from the new Polish army, and promising to create a unified and autonomous Poland on an ethnographical basis (which would mean the inclusion of Prussian Poland and Austrian Galicia as well as Russian Poland), under the sovereignty of the Tsar, after the war. The French and British premiers congratulated Russia upon her "generous initiative" and associated themselves with Russia's plans.

The Poles had no cause to be pro-German; they were, in fact, almost to a man anti-German. But many of them were also, quite naturally, anti-Russian, and these Poles perceived in Russia's promises as much hypocrisy as in the Teutons'. On the assumption that "a bird in the hand is worth two in the bush," they were willing to accept the German pronouncement at face-value and to help the Teutons put Russia out of the way. Their day of reckoning with the Germans would come later. Such was the reasoning of the leaders of an important political party among the Poles, — the Committee of National Defense (popularly called, from the initials of its Polish name, the K. O. N.), — whose most conspicuous representative, General Pilsudski, a truly national hero, at once raised a Polish army and put it at the disposal of the Austrians. Pilsudski's course was all the more popular with his compatriots since a proposal of the United States, in the spring of 1916, to organize relief for the battle-scarred and famished country of Russian Poland had been brought to naught, so Germany made it appear, by the malice and meanness of Russia and her allies.[1]

---

[1] The United States, on February 21, 1916, asked Great Britain for permission to send some 40,000 tons of foodstuffs to be distributed by an American Commission among the civilian inhabitants of certain districts of Russian Poland and Lithuania, on condition that the remainder be cared for by Germany and that imported foodstuffs be used solely for the need of civilians. Russia would agree to the proposal only on the further condition that the Central Empires provide relief for

Yet despite the seeming attachment of Poland to *Mittel-Europa* and the sensational conquest of Rumania, the military authorities of Germany must have recognized in the winter of 1916–1917 that they were still far from winning the war. Temporarily Allied offensives had come to a standstill — the Anglo-French on the Somme and at Verdun, the Italian at Gorizia and on the Carso, the Russian in Volhynia and Bukowina, — but it was only a question of time when they would be renewed and when, with waxing man-power and increased unity and efficiency, they would be pressed more decisively against Germany already utilizing her resources to the full. No longer, apparently, could the Central Empires conduct a sustained and overpowering drive against any one of their great enemies, such as they had conducted in France in 1914 or in Russia in 1915. Perhaps, after all, the winning of the Great War would require astute appeals from civilians as well as sledge-hammer blows from the military. A drive for peace, at the psychological moment, might bring its victory no less renowned than the war-drive of a Hindenburg or a Mackensen. To forward the new policy, Gottlieb von Jagow, who had been foreign secretary of Germany since 1912, was succeeded in December, 1916, by Alfred Zimmermann.

It was the "psychological moment" for a Teutonic peace drive. The collapse of Rumania meant little to the strictly military fortunes of the rival armed coalitions, but it signified much to civilian morale among the belligerents. A curiously unjustified optimism possessed the Teutons, while an oddly unwarranted pessimism seized the Allied nations. It was remarkable, on the one hand, how loyally the subjects of the Dual Monarchy acclaimed their new Emperor-King Charles and how universally the Germans supported the *levée en masse*, and, on the other hand, how bitterly the influential Northcliffe journals assailed Asquith's British government, how irritably the Socialists and Radicals in France grumbled at the governmental authorities, and how profoundly Russia was stirred by unrest and rumblings of revolution. Undoubtedly there was a growing war-weariness everywhere. "We behold," said Pope Benedict XV in an allocution to his cardinals on December 4, 1916, "in one place the vile treatment inflicted on sacred things and on

Serbia, Montenegro, and Albania; and Great Britain indorsed the Russian demand on May 10. Ten days later Germany rejected the Russo-British stipulations. To subsequent humanitarian appeals of the United States, Germany constantly affirmed that "owing to the cruel British blockade policy" nothing could be done.

ministers of religion, even of high dignity, although both should
be inviolable by divine law and the law of nations; in another,
numerous peaceful citizens taken away from their homes amid
tears of mothers, wives, and children; in another, open cities
and undefended populations made victims especially of aërial
raids; everywhere on land and on sea such misdeeds perpetrated
as fill the soul with horror and anguish."

On December 12, 1916, Germany, Austria-Hungary, Bulgaria, and Turkey simultaneously submitted almost identical
notes to the diplomatic representatives of Spain, Switzerland,
and the United States, as well as to other neutral Powers and to
the Vatican, proposing "to enter forthwith into peace negotiations." No concrete terms were offered by the Central Powers,
but the Allies were invited to discuss "an appropriate basis for
the establishment of a lasting peace," and apparently the intention was to hold *pourparlers* at The Hague during the winter,
while hostilities continued. The notes were forwarded to the
Entente Powers without comment by the neutral intermediaries.

Immediately the Russian foreign minister, with the emphatic
approval of the Duma, denounced the Teutonic peace offer and
declared Russia's unwillingness to enter into any peace negotiations whatsoever. The Tsar, in a proclamation to his armies,
stated that "the time has not yet arrived. The enemy has not
yet been driven out of the provinces he has occupied. Russia's
attainment of the tasks created by the war — regarding Constantinople and the Dardanelles, and the establishment of a free
Poland embracing all three of her racial districts — has not yet
been guaranteed." Foreign Minister Sonnino of Italy and
Premier Briand of France likewise disclaimed any intention of
concluding a premature peace. In behalf of Great Britain,
Lloyd George declared that while the Allies would wait to hear
what terms Germany had to offer, little could be expected of
peace negotiations at the moment; "the very appeal for peace,"
he said, "was delivered ostentatiously from the triumphal
chariot of Prussian militarism." It would be a "cruel folly"
not to stop Germany from "swashbuckling through the streets
of Europe."

On December 30, a formal answer to the peace-note of *Mittel-
Europa* was returned signed by Russia, France, Great Britain,
Japan, Italy, Belgium, Montenegro, Portugal, and Rumania.
It declared that "no peace is possible so long as the Allies have
not secured reparation for violated rights and liberties, recogni-
tion of the principle of nationality and of the free existence of

small states; so long as they have not brought about a settlement calculated to end, once and for all, causes which have constituted a perpetual menace to the nations, and to afford the only effective guarantees for the future security of the world."

Beyond these references to "reparation" and "guarantees," the Allied governments did not indicate the terms on which they would consent to make peace. Evidently they were convinced of their own ultimate power to dictate peace, or they were determined to elicit a clear statement of the war aims of the Central Powers. They certainly knew, with the war map as it was and with the people of the Central Powers confident of success, that the responsible authorities of *Mittel-Europa* would hardly hazard a frank, public confession of war aims. For if, contrary to expectations, these authorities should suggest terms of peace conciliatory enough to merit serious discussion by the Allies, the German people would be most painfully disillusioned as to the invincible prowess of Teutonic arms, and their morale would be destroyed; and if, more naturally, these same authorities should announce specific terms in keeping with the spirit of braggadocio with which the populace of Central Europe had been inspired, the Allied nations would then understand perfectly what the Allied governments had repeatedly declared — that peace with militarized victorious Germany would mean a Germanized Europe and a Germanized world. In the latter case, Allied morale would be enormously strengthened, and the Allied nations would put forth military efforts such as they had never put forth before.

The governments of *Mittel-Europa* escaped the dilemma by maintaining a terrible silence as to the precise terms of peace which they would offer. They pretended to be sad and grieved that the wicked Allies would not discuss "peace" with them, and they actually duped the bulk of their subjects into believing that it was the Allies alone who persisted in war and bloodshed. This effect, at least, the Teutonic peace drive of December, 1916, had, that it temporarily consolidated public opinion in *Mittel-Europa* in support of any measures, no matter how drastic or ruthless, which the military authorities might take.

For the time being, too, the Teutonic peace drive served to reawaken pacifist agitation in Entente countries. In radical circles the Allied governments were criticized for not making clear their own war aims; and from this criticism sprang up the curious movement known as defeatism, a movement which reached its greatest growth in 1917 and which will require our attention in a subsequent chapter.[1]

The Teutonic peace drive had succeeded in 1916 scarcely better than the year's military exploits. Neither Germany nor the Allies had obtained a decision in the Great War. In negotiations for peace as well as in military campaigns the year 1916 closed with an apparent stalemate between the gamesters of the hostile coalitions.

In certain respects the failure of the peace drive in December, 1916, marked the end of a period of the Great War. For two years and a half, Germany had tried by force of arms to master the Continent of Europe — in vain. For two years and a half, France, Russia, and Great Britain had attempted to smash German imperialism — in vain. Now, however, Russia was on the brink of revolution, and the United States was on the point of intervention. There would be something of a new alignment and of a new emphasis, and the Great War would enter upon a new period.

[1] See below, pp. 287–298.

CHAPTER X

THE UNITED STATES INTERVENES

THE STAKES: ISOLATION OR A LEAGUE OF NATIONS?

By January, 1917, the Great War had been in progress two years and a half. In this respect it was in marked contrast to the international conflicts of the preceding century. The war of 1859 between France and Austria had lasted less than three months; the war of 1866 between Prussia and Austria, only seven weeks; the war of 1870–1871 between France and Germany, scarcely seven months; the Balkans Wars together, only a few months; and the Russo-Japanese War, less than eighteen months. In each of these conflicts, one side or the other had obtained almost at the outset a distinct military advantage which had been pressed to a speedy, favorable decision. In the Great War, on the other hand, Germany with all her preparedness and her efficiency had failed to obtain a military decision, and the Allies likewise, despite their superior man power and economic resources, had failed to win a decisive victory. The Great War was protracted and indecisive; it was becoming obviously an endurance test.

The Great War had been occasioned by pretty strictly European disputes — disputes between Austria-Hungary and Serbia, and the long-standing feud between France and Germany over Alsace-Lorraine. It had been undertaken by Germany in the spirit of international anarchy — in the spirit which would sacrifice the small to the great, the weak to the strong, right to might. It represented an attempt on the part of a single Great Power — Germany — to impose its will and its *Kultur* by force upon the European state-system and upon European peoples. If Germany should win the war, it would mean a Germanized Europe and perhaps a Germanized world; nay more, it would mean the signal exaltation of one state and one nation and thereby the submergence of the idea that the world's progress depends upon friendly and respectful coöperation between independent and sovereign communities. A German triumph would menace the whole world.

That the world menace of German victory was not clearly perceived in neutral countries in 1916 should occasion no surprise. The Great War, as yet, was viewed essentially as a European war. And to many neutrals it was doubtful whether Allied victory would not, almost equally with German victory, furnish a grave menace to world peace and world security. Englishmen and Frenchmen and Italians were suspected of imperialistic ambitions, and in this particular the Tsar's government was more than suspect. So long as autocratic Russia and oligarchical Japan were influential allies of democratic France, Italy, and Britain, it was difficult to interpret the struggle as one for liberty and democracy or as one for setting limits to imperialism.

Nor was there as yet any well-defined alternative to the international anarchy which Germany championed and which, if she were victorious, she would fasten more or less permanently upon the world. Each of the Allies had entered the war primarily to serve its own ends, and for long the chief weakness of the Allies had lain in their inability to coöperate effectually with one another and in their unwillingness to subordinate any individual interests to the good of their common cause. Beyond defeating Germany they appeared to have no common cause. And if they were unwilling or unable, in the stress of the Great War, to depart from theories and practices of international anarchy and adopt some sort of enduring covenant among themselves, what guarantee would there be against an endless succession of Great Wars? Perhaps on the morrow of German defeat, Russia would arise and, with a band of confederates, essay to re-play the rôle of Germany. Or it might be Japan, or some other proud sovereign state. In this fashion even Allied triumph might be but a prelude to still vaster wars in which European civilization would be utterly annihilated. History taught only too well that mere alliances were quite kaleidoscopic, and that a "balance of power" was perpetually getting out of equilibrium.

Germany stood for international anarchy, for isolation from the needs and interests of other states and other peoples; she relied upon her sword to gain what she desired of this world's glory and this world's goods. For what did the Allies stand? Simply to break the German sword, meanwhile sharpening the sword of a Russia or a Japan? It was a question asked in that reflective winter of 1916–1917 in France and Great Britain as well as in neutral countries. And out of the searching of Allied conscience emerged a new conviction — a new purpose — that the Great War must be ended by the crushing not alone of Germany but of that spirit of international anarchy which Germany incarnated. Isolation and self-sufficiency of sovereign states had had their day; tried in the balance, they had been found wanting.

As the Great War progressed, its stakes were becoming clearer. On the one hand were isolation, international anarchy, and domination of the world by a militaristic and autocratic Great Power; on the other hand were coöperation, a league of free nations, and a partnership among democratic and peace-loving governments in assuming the responsibilities as well as the profits of world management. The two most fateful factors in clarifying the stakes of the Great War early in 1917 were the Russian revolution and the intervention of the United States. These two events, transpiring simultaneously, are treated in the present and next following chapters.

Six of the Great Powers — Germany, Austria-Hungary, Russia, France, Great Britain, and Japan — had entered the war in 1914, and from such a supreme test of strength the remaining European Great Power, Italy, could not long hold aloof. Only one Great Power — the United States of America — preserved neutrality throughout 1915 and 1916. The unique position of the United States during those years was due less to lack of interest in world-affairs than to geographical situation and historical traditions.

The United States was separated from the chief centers of military operations by two or three thousand miles of ocean. Because of her vast territorial extent on the American continent and the abundance of her natural resources, she was not dependent, as were certain European countries, upon foreign trade for adequate supplies of food, fuel, and clothing. Rendered economically self-sufficing by her geographical situation, she adhered by tradition to political isolation.

Once upon a time, almost a century and a half ago, the United States had been in formal alliance with France, but this alliance had been made for the definite purpose of assuring American independence, and once the purpose was achieved the alliance lapsed. To be sure, Americans still had a lively sympathy — in the abstract — for the land which had given them a Lafayette and a Rochambeau in their hour of direst need; but there was an all-too prevalent notion in the United States, on the eve of the Great War, that modern Frenchmen were unworthy and degenerate descendants of illustrious sires.

For more than a century Americans had almost superstitiously heeded the letter of Washington's admonitions against "entangling alliances," and their insistent aloofness from world-responsibilities had fostered among them a notable provinciality. It was natural that many of them should maintain a traditional dislike and hatred of England; George III meant more to them than George V, and the "patriotic" school-book accounts of the Revolutionary War and the War of 1812 tended to obscure the cultural bonds which united all the English-speaking peoples and to keep Americans in ignorance of the amazing democratic developments in England during the nineteenth and twentieth centuries. To the traditional American opinion of Great Britain, the host of Irish immigrants gave confirmation.

Moreover, on the eve of the Great War, Germany was held in high esteem in the United States. The sudden rise of imperial Germany, with her marvelous achievements in science and industry, was likened to the mighty progress of republican America. Americans praised the splendid qualities of sobriety and thrift and domesticity which seemed to characterize their numerous fellow-citizens of German origin. And between New World America and the Germany of the Old World, conspicuous citizens of the United States — public officials, college-presidents, and philanthropical capitalists — sought to forge intellectual and spiritual chains. German literature was taught and admired in the United States as was no other foreign literature. German music was rendered and appreciated as was no other. German scholarship was prized and patterned as was no other.

America's political isolation served to confirm popular misapprehensions about foreign peoples and at the same time to strengthen popular devotion to the traditional foreign policies of the United States Government. These policies may be stated as three. In the first place, there was the "Monroe Doctrine," the constant refusal of the United States to interfere in European disputes or to be entangled in any foreign alliance, her chief external interest being to keep the New World free from European aggression. Secondly, there was "arbitration," the repeated attempts of the United States to substitute a judicial for a military settlement of international differences. Thirdly, there was the "freedom of the seas," for which the United States Government had persistently contended; save during the Civil War, America had espoused the doctrine of the inviolability of private property at sea, a generous free list, and a narrow definition of contraband, and in urging the acceptance of this doctrine by European governments she had been led into frequent diplomatic clashes with Great Britain.

Under these circumstances none of the belligerents in 1914 expected the United States actively to intervene in the Great War. And in America there was no considerable movement at the outset in behalf of intervention on either side. In fact, as the war progressed, the American Government and the bulk of the American people seemed to think that if the United States adhered loyally to the Monroe Doctrine, she must hold aloof from the conflict in Europe, and, if she held aloof, she would be in a better position impartially to advocate arbitration and freedom of the seas, and eventually to assume leadership in rebuilding a ruined world and healing the wounds of the nations. America's part in the Great War should be curative, not punitive.

But those persons who thought the United States, in the long run, could hold aloof from the Great War were quite mistaken. Despite traditional political isolation and apparent economic self-sufficiency, the United States was drawn irresistibly, willy-nilly, into the world maelstrom. For the world of the twentieth century was very different from that world of the eighteenth century in which American independence and American traditions were implanted. Between the eighteenth and twentieth centuries had occurred a series of events in the common, workaday life of mankind so amazing and epochal as to justify its description as an "Industrial Revolution." It was this Industrial Revolution which girdled the globe with railways, steamship lines, telegraph and telephone wires, and drew all sorts of men together. It was this Industrial Revolution which brought the chief nations of the world in closer contact with one another than were the original thirteen English-speaking American colonies. It was this Industrial Revolution which created a world-market for capital, raw materials, finished products, labor, and ideas, and which, by breaking down the real barriers of local isolation and self-sufficiency, laid deep and broad, if imperceptibly, the economic foundations for a political superstructure of internationalism.

No longer could there be exclusively European questions or narrowly American problems. The cultures and the interests of America and Europe were now so inextricably intertangled that any important armed conflict on either hemisphere would certainly affect seriously all neutrals the world over. If signs of the times were read aright, the Great War would be a war not only in Europe but on all the seas, and in all dominions beyond the seas, and passing strange would that state be which could preserve an undisturbed neutrality in such a cataclysm.

How the United States underwent a transformation in thought and policy from aloofness and strict neutrality and fancied security, in August, 1914, to belligerency and juncture with the Allies in Europe, in April, 1917, is a long story, only a few of whose episodes can be mentioned here.   Early in the war, the splendid stand of the French armies at the Marne and the flocking to Britain's standard of Canadians and Australians and East Indians gave America new ideas about French character and British loyalty and a notable respect for the Allied cause, just as the initial atrocities of the Germans in Belgium and France opened American eyes to the fact that the much-vaunted Teuton had other and less desirable assets than literature, music, and scholarship.   Gradually the notion grew prevalent in America that imperial and militaristic Germany was a horrible menace to civilization, and that France and Great Britain were fighting for something vastly more significant than Alsace-Lorraine and German colonies : they were fighting in defense of civilization itself.   For this reason the majority of Americans became sympathizers with the Allies, but between sympathy and active participation there was still a wide gulf.

It was not long before the United States as a neutral was drawn into diplomatic conflicts with the belligerents over rights at sea. American pride was especially wounded by insistent representations of the German Government that the United States had no right to trade in munitions with the Allies.   And American feelings were outraged by the sinking of the *Lusitania* in May, 1915, and by the preposterous German demands that American citizens should surrender their right of free travel by sea.   The protracted diplomatic negotiations on the subject of ruthless submarine warfare sorely tried the patience of the American people.   And the loud-mouthed expressions of sympathy for the German cause on the part of many German-Americans, as well as the manifest insincerity and procrastination of the German diplomatists, only stimulated fresh outbursts of popular anger in the United States. It was not until May 4, 1916, — a year after the sinking of the *Lusitania*, — that the German Government promised henceforth not to sink merchant vessels without warning and without due provision for the safety of passengers, but even then the promise was faltering and conditional.

That Germany's protestations of friendship for the United States were essentially insincere, was proved by a continuous campaign of German espionage and outrage in the New World. Throughout 1915 and 1916 diplomatic agents of the Central Empires organized and supported a staff of conspirators against the laws of the United States; they stirred up strikes in munition plants; they manufactured bombs for the destruction of factories and ships; they perpetrated passport frauds. In September, 1915, the United States had to request the recall of the Austro-Hungarian ambassador, Dr. Constantine Dumba, because of his systematic instigation of labor difficulties. In November, 1915, the German ambassador, Count Bernstorff, was informed that his military and naval attachés, Captains von Papen and Boy-Ed, were "no longer acceptable or *personae gratae* to this Government," and their recall was demanded because "of what this Government considers improper activities in military and naval matters."

But Germany, after the recall of Dumba, Papen, and Boy-Ed, continued her machinations in America. As the Committee on Public Information of the United States Government subsequently said: "In this country official agents of the Central Powers — protected from criminal prosecution by diplomatic immunity — conspired against our internal peace, placed spies and *agents provocateurs* throughout the length and breadth of our land, and even in high positions of trust in departments of our Government. While expressing a cordial friendship for the people of the United States, the Government of Germany had its agents at work both in Latin America and in Japan. They bought and subsidized papers and supported speakers there to arouse feelings of bitterness and distrust against us in those friendly nations in order to embroil us in war. They were inciting insurrection in Cuba, in Haiti, and in San Domingo; their hostile hand was stretched out to take the Danish Islands; and everywhere they were abroad sowing the seeds of dissension, trying to stir up one nation against another, and all against the United States. In their sum these various operations amounted to direct assault of the Monroe Doctrine."

There were persons, of course, who were only too anxious to utilize the sinister activities of German *provocateurs* in order to inflame the Americans against Germany and to secure for the Allies the active aid of the United States. The Entente Powers countenanced and encouraged widespread propaganda in their own behalf; with one hand they cut off German postal and telegraphic communications, while with the other they poured into America a flood of books, pamphlets, and newspapers, favorable to their own cause. Distinguished Frenchmen made lecture-tours throughout the country. And the British resorted to every known device of propaganda from employing secret-service agents in New York to maintaining at Washington the great journalist, Lord Northcliffe, with a host of assistants, as a publicity director. With these official or semi-official propagandists of the Entente coöperated, whether for economic or for sentimental motives, a considerable number of influential Americans, such as bankers who made loans to the Allied Governments or acted as purchasing agents for the Allies, manufacturers of munitions and other war *matériel* who sold their goods to the Allies, and college professors who had been educated in France or England or who from their studies and researches had developed a special admiration for the literature and learning of one or another of the Allied countries.   Entente propaganda in the United States was even more general than that of the Teutons; it was also more adroit, more sympathetic, and more conformable to American prejudices and American wishes.

During 1916 two currents of opinion were steadily growing in the United States.   On the one hand was the conviction of such men as Ex-President Roosevelt and Elihu Root that the Great War was in very truth America's war, that the Allies were fighting for America's interests, the greatest of which was the maintenance of the public right.   On the other hand was the desire, cherished by such leaders as President Wilson and Ex-President Taft, that the Great War should be the last war fought under the old bad conditions of international isolation and that America should take an important part at the right moment in the establishment of a League to Enforce Peace.   President Wilson, in accepting renomination in 1916, declared: "No nation can any longer remain neutral as against any willful destruction of the peace of the world. . . .   The nations of the world must unite in joint guarantee that whatever is done to disturb the whole world's life must be tested in the court of the whole world's opinion before it is attempted."

For a time in the autumn of 1916 American interest was absorbed in the electoral campaign for the presidency.   In the ranks of both the Democratic and the Republican parties were German sympathizers and also strong advocates of the Allies.   Mr. Hughes, the Republican candidate, contented himself with general criticism of Wilson's policy towards Mexico and Germany, and took no clear stand on the question of intervention.   The slogan that "Wilson kept us out of the war" undoubtedly drew votes from American pacifists and traditionalists for the Democratic candidate; and President Wilson was reëlected by a small majority.

Woodrow Wilson could properly interpret his reëlection in November, 1916, as a warrant from the American people to keep the United States at peace and to endeavor to secure international reform. At any rate he speedily urged on the belligerents the formation of a League of Nations, the while giving no indication that he would take sides with either coalition. On December 18, 1916, he addressed to each of the militant Powers a remarkable note which had been prepared quite independently of the Teutonic Peace Drive then in full swing.

The American note of December 18 called attention to striking similarities in the generally professed war aims of the Allies and of the Central Powers. "Each side desires to make the rights and privileges of weak peoples and small states as secure against aggression and denial in the future as the rights and privileges of the great and powerful states now at war. Each wishes itself to be made secure in the future, along with all other nations and peoples, against the recurrence of wars like this, and against oppression and selfish interference of any kind. Each would be jealous of the formation of any more rival leagues to preserve an uncertain balance of power against multiplying suspicions; but each is ready to consider the formation of a League of Nations to insure peace and justice throughout the world." The note then went on to beg the belligerents to state their special war-aims more explicitly, and ended with the significant words : "The President is not proposing peace ; he is not even offering mediation. He is merely proposing that soundings be taken in order that we may learn, the neutral nations with the belligerents, how near the haven of peace may be for which all mankind longs with an intense and increasing longing."

The replies of Germany and Austria-Hungary, on December 26, 1916, were essentially the same and equally vague and unsatisfactory. Germany, for example, suggested "the speedy assembly, on neutral ground, of delegates of the warring states" and a direct exchange of views, but declared that plans for the prevention of future wars could not be taken up until the end "of the present conflict of exhaustion"; only then would Germany be ready "to coöperate with the United States in this sublime task."

The Allies, replying to President Wilson on January 10, 1917, explained that they could not formulate their war-aims in detail until the hour for negotiations arrived, but they associated themselves with the projects of a League of Nations and stated some of their objects quite specifically. "The civilized world knows

P

that they imply, necessarily and first of all, the restoration of Belgium, Serbia, and Montenegro, with the compensation due to them; the evacuation of the invaded territories in France, in Russia, in Rumania, with just reparation; the reorganization of Europe, guaranteed by a stable régime and based at once on respect for nationalities and on the right to full security and liberty of economic development possessed by all peoples, small and great, and at the same time upon territorial conventions and international settlements such as to guarantee land and sea frontiers against unjustified attack; the restoration of provinces formerly torn from the Allies by force and against the wish of their inhabitants; the liberation of the Italians, as also of the Slavs, Rumanians, and Czechoslovaks from foreign domination; the setting free of populations subject to the bloody tyranny of the Turks; and the turning out of Europe of the Ottoman Empire as decidedly foreign to Western civilization."

The obvious contrast between the candid answer of the Allies and the ambiguous replies of the Central Powers served to deepen those currents of public opinion which had been gathering headway in America throughout 1916. It now seemed as though the Allies could be counted upon to coöperate with the United States in abolishing international isolation and in fashioning a League of Nations, and, whether such a league should prove permanently effective or not, it now became patent to a majority of Americans that the Allies were fighting at least indirectly for the United States, that a Germany emerging triumphant from the Great War could not long be restrained from forcing her *Kultur* on the New World.

Utilizing the replies to his note of December 18, and the state of public opinion throughout the country, President Wilson appeared before the United States Senate on January 22, 1917, and delivered a remarkable discourse. The peace that would end the war, he said, must be followed by a "definite concert of Powers" which would "make it virtually impossible that any such catastrophe should ever overwhelm us again." In that the United States must play a part. It was right before such a settlement was reached that the American Government should frankly state conditions on which it would feel justified in asking the American people "to approve its formal and solemn adherence to a League of Peace." He had come to state those conditions:

"No peace can last, or ought to last, which does not (1) recognize and accept the principle that governments derive all their just powers from the consent of the governed, and that no right anywhere exists to hand people about from sovereignty to sovereignty as if they were property. . . .

"I am proposing, as it were, that the nations should with one accord adopt the doctrine of President Monroe as the doctrine of the world : that no nation should seek to extend its policy over any other nation or people but that every people should be left free to determine its own policy, its own way of development, unhindered, unthreatened, unafraid, the little along with the great and powerful.

"I am proposing (2) that all nations henceforth avoid entangling alliances which would draw them into competitions of power, catch them in a net of intrigue and selfish rivalry, and disturb their own affairs with influences intruded from without. There is no entangling alliance in a concert of power. When all unite to act in the same sense and with the same purpose, all act in the common interest and are free to live their own lives under a common protection.

"I am proposing . . . (3) that freedom of the seas which in international conference after conference representatives of the United States have urged with the eloquence of those who are the convinced disciples of liberty; and (4) that moderation of armaments which make of armies and navies a power for order merely, not an instrument of aggression or of selfish violence.

"(5) Mere agreements may not make peace secure. It will be absolutely necessary that a force be created as a guarantee of the permanency of the settlement so much greater than the force of any nation now engaged or any alliance hitherto formed or projected that no nation, no probable combination of nations, could face or withstand it. If the peace presently to be made is to endure, it must be a peace made secure by the organized major force of mankind."

Thus President Wilson cleared the ground for the building of a League of Nations to supplant the international anarchy which, according to him, was the prime cause of the Great War and the chief danger to the future peace of the world. That the President still thought it possible and desirable for the United States to preserve neutrality was evinced by his declaration in the same discourse of January 22, that the peace about to be negotiated must be a "peace without victory," that is, a peace not dictated by a victor to a loser, leaving a heritage of resentment. By implication it meant that the Allies must not seek to destroy and dismember Germany, and, on the other hand, that Germany must abandon any project of mastering other European countries or of dominating the world.

Though many citizens of the Entente states misunderstood the phrase "peace without victory" and grumbled at its utterance by the president of a prosperous neutral which was supposed to know nothing of the sacrifice and hardships of the belligerents, the Allied Governments promptly repudiated the suggestion that they might be seeking the annihilation or enslavement of Germany. On the whole, the President's proposals met with an unexpectedly favorable reception in the Entente countries.

Promptly the Allies redoubled their efforts to draw America actively into the war. The second half of the year 1916, as we have seen,[1] had not been particularly advantageous to them: Rumania had collapsed; Russia was faltering; and neither on the Italian nor on the Western Front, nor in Macedonia, had any brilliant success been achieved. Pacifism and defeatism[2] were appearing in France and Italy; war-weariness was growing throughout all the Entente countries. If the energetic assistance of the one remaining neutral Great Power could not immediately be secured, Allied morale might completely disappear and Germany might win a speedy victory. It was a dark hour in the history of the Entente and of the world. Only the United States could dispel the darkness, and to this end English and French and Italian propagandists brought all sorts of pressure to bear upon the American Government and the American people. They pressed the argument that America's welfare and safety all along had depended upon their success and that now their success depended upon America's direct aid. They called loudly to the United States.

Germany herself was responsible for the suddenness and ease with which the United States heard and heeded the Allied call. The German Government had failed to respond frankly and sincerely to the President's note of December 18, or to his address of January 22. While it was endeavoring to create a pacifist sentiment in the Entente countries, it was girding itself and encouraging its own people to undertake another campaign for the mastery of Europe and the domination of the world. This time Germany would not drive furiously with her armies against France or Russia or Italy or against a Serbia or a Rumania; rather, she would hit at Great Britain, the brain and sinew of the hostile coalition; she would challenge the mistress of the seas ruthlessly by a campaign of unrestricted submarine warfare.

[1] See above, p. 193.   [2] See below, pp. 287–298.

THE OCCASION: UNRESTRICTED SUBMARINE WARFARE

It has already been explained that the chief weapon of any German counter-offensive against Great Britain was the submarine, but that this weapon would be ineffectual unless its use were unrestricted. Unrestricted use of the submarine, though absolutely at variance with recognized rules of international conduct, had always been advocated by Tirpitz, Reventlow, and other Pan-Germans who viewed England as the main stumbling-block to Teutonic victory; it had actually been attempted in the spring of 1915 and had been abandoned definitely in May, 1916, only because of the threatening expostulations of the United States and other neutral Powers and because of a conviction in the minds of more moderate German statesmen, such as the Chancellor Bethmann-Hollweg, that there were other and less perilous means of bringing Britain to terms.

From May, 1916, to January, 1917, Bethmann-Hollweg, holding the German submarines in leading strings, pursued in turn two policies which were calculated to disrupt the Entente and bring a German peace. The one was the smashing of the Allied fronts on the continent of Europe — the military drives against Verdun, against Vicenza, and into Rumania. The other was the diplomatic peace drive, culminating in the Teutonic peace-note of December, 1916. But both policies miscarried. The Teutons failed to obtain a military decision; they failed likewise to make the Allies sue for peace. And meanwhile the Allies were tightening their economic strangle-hold on *Mittel-Europa*.

Tirpitz had been forced out of the German naval office in the spring of 1916, but from his retirement he had never ceased to berate Bethmann-Hollweg for what he deemed a cowardly surrender of the best German weapons to the susceptibilities of "mercenary" America; and as Bethmann-Hollweg's alternative policies went wrong, the popular following of Tirpitz in Germany grew noisier and more numerous. Eventually there was a veritable clamor for the resumption of unrestricted submarine warfare, cost what it might. Even the more moderate elements in German public life were won over, by the failure of their peace-drive, to espouse a campaign of ruthlessness. Germany had already risked much in pursuit of world dominion; Bethmann-Hollweg was now willing to risk everything.

On January 31, 1917, the German Government officially notified the United States that inasmuch as the Allies had rejected Germany's peace offer, and inasmuch as the Entente Powers, led by England, had sought for two and a half years to starve Germany into submission, " a new situation has thus been created which forces Germany to new decisions," and that therefore Germany would exercise the freedom of action which she reserved to herself in her note of May 4, 1916.   Accordingly, announcement was made that from February 1, 1917, all sea traffic within certain zones adjoining Great Britain, France, and Italy, and in the eastern Mediterranean, would, "without further notice, be prevented by all weapons."   This meant that German submarines

GERMAN "WAR ZONE" OF FEBRUARY 1, 1917

proposed to sink at sight within these areas all vessels whether neutral or belligerent.

The German note of January 31, 1917, reopened the whole submarine question not only, but further outraged American pride (and, it must be said, touched at an ironical point the American sense of humor) by laying down hard and fast rules for United States shipping.   "Sailing of regular American passenger steamships," stated a condescending memorandum which accompanied the German note, "may continue undisturbed after February 1, 1917, if — (a) the port of destination is Falmouth; (b) sailing to, or coming from, that port, course is taken *via* the Scilly Islands

and a point 50° N., 20° W.; (c) the steamships are marked in
the following way, which must not be allowed to other vessels in
American ports — on ship's hull and superstructure three ver-
tical stripes, one meter wide each, to be painted alternately white
and red; each mast should show a large flag checkered white
and red, and the stern the American national flag; care should
be taken that, during dark, national flag and painted marks are
easily recognizable from a distance, and that the boats are well
lighted throughout; (d) one steamship a week sails in each direction, with arrival at Falmouth on Sunday and departure from
Falmouth on Wednesday; (e) the United States Government
guarantees that no contraband (according to German contraband list) is carried by those steamships."

Every right to the freedom of the seas for which the United
States had ever contended was violated by the brusque German
declaration of January 31, and all those emotions of dislike, fear,
and hatred of Germany, which had been steadily heightened in
the United States by adroit Allied propaganda, were instanta-
neously welded into resolute hostility. On February 3, the German ambassador at Washington, Count Bernstorff, was handed
his passports, and the American ambassador at Berlin, James
Gerard, was summoned home. On the same day President Wilson told Congress that he still could not believe the German
Government meant "to do in fact what they have warned us they
feel at liberty to do," and that only "actual overt acts" would
convince him of their hostile purpose. But he ended with the
solemn announcement that if American ships were sunk and
American lives were lost, he would come again to Congress and
ask for power to take the necessary steps for the protection of
American rights.

The rupture of diplomatic relations between the United States
and Germany did not necessarily mean war, though it pointed in
that direction. Undoubtedly a majority of the American people
still cherished the idea expressed by the President that Germany
would not venture to put her threats into effect. Nevertheless
the mere threats of Germany sufficed to deter American ships
from sailing for Europe, with the result that powerful economic
interests in America increased the clamor against Germany, the
excitement being particularly acute in New England and in the
Middle Atlantic States.

On February 26, 1917, President Wilson again addressed Congress, pointing out that Germany had placed a practical embargo
on American shipping, and urging that the United States resort

to "armed neutrality," a measure just short of war.   On March 1 the House of Representatives voted "armed neutrality" by 403 to 13, but in the Senate the measure was defeated by a "filibuster" of a handful of "willful men," who prolonged the debate until the expiration of the congressional session, on March 4.

In the meantime, on February 28, the Associated Press published an order which had been issued on January 16 by Herr Zimmermann, German Under-Secretary for Foreign Affairs, to the German minister in Mexico, and which had fallen into the hands of the United States Government.   The "Zimmermann Note" instructed the German minister to form an alliance with Mexico in the event of war between Germany and the United States, and to offer as a bribe the states of Texas, New Mexico, and Arizona; it also suggested that efforts might be made to seduce Japan from the Allies and bring her into partnership with Mexico and Germany.   From the date of the note — January 16 — it was obvious that the German Government had been planning the resumption of ruthless submarine warfare at the very time when it was pretending to be most friendly to the United States, and from the contents it was apparent that Germany would go to any length in opposing American rights.   The result of the disclosure was increased resentment against Germany, especially in the southwestern states and on the Pacific coast. The whole United States was being rapidly galvanized into war-activity.

Woodrow Wilson, in his inaugural address, on March 5, said: "We stand firm in armed neutrality, since it seems that in no other way we can demonstrate what it is we insist upon and cannot forego.   We may be drawn on by circumstances, not by our own purpose or desire, to a more active assertion of our rights as we see them and a more immediate association with the great struggle itself."   One week later he issued formal orders to arm American merchant vessels against submarines.   And within another week the "actual overt acts" of which he had warned in his speech before Congress on February 3 were committed. On March 16–17 three homeward-bound ships,[1] — American-built, American-owned, and American-manned, — were sunk by German submarines.   German defiance of the United States was now flagrant and unmistakable.

Not only was the case against Germany perfectly plain, but an event had just occurred which now made it easier for the United States to intervene in the Great War on the side of the

[1] The *Vigilancia*, the *City of Memphis*, and the *Illinois*.

Allies. It was in March, 1917, that the Russian Revolution broke out; the Tsar abdicated; a provisional democratic government was proclaimed; and on March 21, the United States led all the nations of the world in according recognition to the new régime at Petrograd. The destruction of autocracy in Russia signified that the lines were now drawn quite distinctly between isolated, militaristic, oligarchical *Mittel-Europa*, on the one hand, and a league of peace-loving, democratic nations, on the other. So long as Russia retained a reactionary absolutism, the United States might well adhere to a policy of "armed neutrality," but as soon as Russia patterned her political institutions after those of democratic France, Britain, and Italy, then the United States saw the way clear to a juncture with the Allies and to a fight to the finish with Germany. The Great War would no longer be in any respect a conflict between dynasties; it would be "the eternal war of liberty and despotism."

On April 2, 1917, President Wilson came before Congress and asked for a declaration of war against Germany. His address on that occasion, one of the greatest of America's famous documents, was in part as follows: "With a profound sense of the solemn and even tragical character of the step I am taking and of the grave responsibilities which it involves, but in unhesitating obedience to what I deem my constitutional duty, I advise that the Congress declare the recent course of the Imperial German Government to be in fact nothing less than war against the Government and people of the United States; that it formally accept the status of belligerent which has thus been thrust upon it; and that it take immediate steps not only to put the country in a more thorough state of defense but also to exert all its power and employ all its resources to bring the Government of the German Empire to terms and end the war. . . . It will involve the utmost practicable coöperation in counsel and action with the Governments now at war with Germany. . . .

"A steadfast concert of peace can never be maintained except by a partnership of democratic nations. No autocratic Government could be trusted to keep faith within it or to observe its covenants. It must be a league of honor, a partnership of opinion . . . . Only free peoples can hold their purpose and their honor steady to a common end and prefer the interests of mankind to any narrow interest of their own. . . .

"The world must be made safe for democracy. Its peace must be planted upon the tested foundations of political liberty. We have no selfish ends to serve. We desire no conquest, no dominion. We seek no indemnities for ourselves, no material compensation for the sacrifices we shall freely make. We are but one of the champions of the rights of mankind. We shall be satisfied when those rights have been made as secure as the faith and the freedom of nations can make them. . . .

"It is a fearful thing to lead this great, peaceful people into war, into the most terrible and disastrous of all wars, civilization itself seeming to be in the balance. But the right is more precious than peace, and we shall fight for the things which we have always carried nearest our hearts — for democracy, for the right of those who submit to authority to have a voice in their own Governments, for the rights and liberties of small nations, for a universal dominion of right by such a concert of free peoples as shall bring peace and safety to all nations and make the world itself at last free.

"To such a task we can dedicate our lives and our fortunes, everything that we are and everything that we have, with the pride of those who know that the day has come when America is privileged to spend her blood and her might for the principles that gave her birth and happiness and the peace which she has treasured. God helping her, she can do no other."

On April 4, the Senate adopted a declaration of war by 82 votes to 6, and on the next day the House, by 373 votes to 50. And on April 6, 1917, the President issued a proclamation declaring that "a state of war exists between the United States and the Imperial German Government." Two days later the United States broke off diplomatic relations with Austria-Hungary, although a declaration of war against the Dual Monarchy was delayed until December 7.

Thus by April, 1917, the resumption of unrestricted submarine warfare by Germany had brought the United States, the last of the world's Great Powers, into the war on the side of the Allies. Furthermore, German ruthlessness now stirred up a wave of pro-Ally sentiment among the remaining neutrals, and protests against submarine warfare and barred zones were speedily filed at Berlin by Spain, Holland, Norway, Sweden, Denmark, China, and the republics of Latin America. Within a week of America's declaration of war, Brazil and Bolivia severed diplomatic relations with Germany, and Cuba and Panama formally joined the Allies.

The intervention of the United States was a godsend to the Entente, for at the time, as subsequently was generally admitted, the Entente was on its "last legs." Russia was soon to quit the war altogether, and France and Italy were alike suffering from bad cases of "nerves." Now, however, the United States could put at the disposal of the Entente her rich metals, her copious foodstuffs, her numerous shipyards, her powerful fleet, her vast man power, and, most significant of all, her fresh enthusiasm and her unselfish idealism. The character of the Great War in popular imagination was changed for the better, and the chances of victory for the public right were enormously increased. Germany, already inferior to the Allies in natural resources and staying power, would soon be rendered hopelessly inferior. For this dénouement Germany had only her own ruthlessness to blame.

THE PROBLEM: PREPAREDNESS

Germany had staked everything on the success of her submarine warfare, and the intervention of the United States did not swerve her from her purpose. She realized that the United States was ill prepared for immediate active participation in the struggle in Europe. No matter how energetic the American Government might be, it would certainly take the whole year 1917 for the United States to raise, train, equip, and transport to Europe an army large enough to have any appreciable effect upon the fortunes of the war. Food, munitions, and shipping, in addition to men, would have to be supplied in enormous quantities not only for an American Expeditionary Force but for the Allies also, and as yet America was not ready to fulfill these obligations. It would be the spring of 1918, at the earliest, before Germany need reckon seriously with the United States.

In the meantime Germany would vigorously prosecute her submarine warfare against Great Britain. Ruthlessly would she seek to destroy every merchant vessel endeavoring to enter or leave a British port, and in this way she would destroy Allied shipping, put a practical embargo on British industry and trade, deprive the Allied armies of munitions and supplies, and starve out the civilian population of the United Kingdom. If all went well for the Germans, Great Britain would be brought to terms; and once Great Britain submitted, France and Italy and Russia would have to sue for peace. And with Allied shipping destroyed and with the Allies submitting to the inevitable, there would be neither means nor purpose of transporting an American Expeditionary Force to Europe. American intervention, Germany thought, could not be effective before the spring of 1918, and then it would be too late. Perhaps Germany was again over-optimistic, but at any rate the Allies themselves were worried. They trembled when they tried to face the question.   Could the United States complete preparedness before Germany had succeeded in her unrestricted submarine warfare?

No sooner had the United States declared war against Germany than special missions visited America from England and France — the British mission headed by Foreign Secretary Balfour, and the French by Ex-Premier Viviani and Marshal Joffre.   These missions explained the dire situation confronting the Allies and the urgent need for the United States not only to dispatch supplies of all sorts to their countries and to assist in averting the submarine danger but to rush large armies to France, if not immediately to engage in the actual fighting, at least to reassure the Allied troops that the United States was really in the war and thus to strengthen their morale.   The response was sympathetic and enthusiastic.

It is perhaps regrettable that the American Government did not take advantage of the exigencies of the Allies and the visit of the foreign missions to make full participation of the United States in the war conditional upon the formal repudiation by the Entente of all existing "secret treaties."   If this had been done, most probably the "secret treaties" would have been thrown overboard, the Great War in its subsequent phases would have been waged more distinctly in harmony with the spirit that impelled American intervention, and certain very troublesome problems which later confronted the Peace Congress would never have arisen or would have been solved more equitably.   As it was, however, the visiting missions carefully concealed from President Wilson the existence of numerous secret international engagements by which they were bound, notably the pledges made Japan in February, 1917, in respect of the German rights in the Chinese province of Shantung and the German Pacific islands north of the equator.   That the United States made no such conditions or reservations was a tribute to American unselfishness and likewise to the naïve faith of the American Government that all other Powers arrayed against Germany were equally unselfish.   At any rate America was resolved to show the faith that was in her not alone by words but also by deeds.

It was none too soon.   Even before the formal resumption of unrestricted submarine warfare on February 1, 1917, Germany had made noteworthy progress in destroying Allied shipping and in hampering Allied commerce.   Since August, 1914, every month had witnessed the sinking of hundreds of thousands of tons of belligerent and neutral merchant vessels.   In 1914 nearly 700,000 tons of British and Allied and neutral shipping had been destroyed; in 1915 the amount increased to 1,700,000 tons; and in 1916 it soared to 2,800,000 tons. Apparently, as time went on, the German submarines were becoming more numerous, more daring, and more experienced. By February, 1917, submarine warfare had passed its trial stage and was to be put to the supreme test. And just as the German navy yards completed a host of new submarines and German factories equipped them with powerful torpedoes for their deadly work, the German Government laid aside all pretense of observing international law in their use and proclaimed the ruthless orders of February 1.

The German campaign of sea-ruthlessness started off with spirit and dash. From January to June, 1917, German submarines sank 2,275,000 tons of British shipping and 1,580,000 tons of allied and neutral shipping, — an aggregate loss to the Entente of nearly four million tons in six months. If this huge total could be doubled in the second half of 1917, German hopes and Allied fears might be justified.

As a matter of fact, however, the spirit and dash which characterized the submarine campaign of Germany in the first half of 1917 were not sustained in the second half of the year, for the Allies were finding means of lessening the menace. Merchant vessels began to sail under convoy, guarded above by dirigible balloons and hydroplanes, and on the surface by a fleet of patrol boats. Close watch was kept of the movements of submarines, either by means of lookouts on patrol boats or by means of wireless operators who detected messages passing between the submarines and the German naval bases. The camouflaging of Allied ships, moreover, proved a useful deception; "the war brought no stranger spectacle than that of a convoy of steamships plowing along through the middle of the ocean streaked and bespotted indiscriminately with every color of the rainbow in a way more bizarre than the wildest dreams of a sailor's first night ashore." Gradually, Allied naval commanders were enabled to trap and destroy, or capture, German submarines; and the German authorities found it increasingly difficult to repair and replenish their submarines and to make their sailors undertake joyfully the new hazards of life in a periscope. Though the losses to Allied shipping continued heavy throughout 1917 and far into 1918, the turn of the tide was reached in the midsummer of 1917. In the second half of 1917 the destruction of Allied and neutral shipping amounted in the aggregate to two and three-fourths million tons, as against nearly four millions in the first half of the year. It was obvious that Germany had miscalculated the success of unrestricted submarine warfare and that Great Britain would not be brought to terms by the spring of 1918.

It became obvious, too, that Germany had miscalculated the time required for the United States to intervene actively in the war. For the United States, after declaring war on April 6, 1917, lost no time in collecting vast sums of money, in gathering and training a large army, and in mobilizing industries and resources. Immediately German ships in American harbors were seized, and the navy and the small standing army were mobilized. A Council of National Defense was formed, comprising the secretaries of war, navy, interior, agriculture, commerce, and labor, with an advisory commission of seven men drawn from civil life, and with a host of affiliated local boards and committees throughout the country to assist in coördinating America's war efforts. To arouse an intelligent popular enthusiasm for the war, a Committee on Public Information was created under the chairmanship of George Creel. There was some natural and inevitable "muddling" in transforming America suddenly from a peace footing to a war basis, but, considering the manifold difficulties and handicaps, the task as a whole was achieved with surprising efficiency and dispatch.

A Selective Service Act, passed in May, authorized the President to increase the regular army, by voluntary enlistment, to 287,000 men, the maximum strength provided by existing law; to draft into service all members of the National Guard; and to raise by selective draft an additional force of 500,000 men, and another 500,000 at his discretion. The age limits for drafted men were twenty-one and thirty years, and all male persons between these ages were required to register "in accordance with regulations to be prescribed by the President." On June 5, "registration day," some nine and one-half million young Americans enrolled, and the drawing of the 625,000 men to form the first selective army took place at Washington on July 15. In July the National Guard was mobilized, and in September the mobilization of the new national army began.

Meanwhile Congress was enacting a series of important war measures: two liberty loan acts (April and September); an espionage act, in June; an aviation act, in July; food control and shipping acts, in August; and in September, a revenue act imposing war taxes on income and excess profits, a trading-with-the-enemy act, and a soldiers' and sailors' insurance act. During the congressional session which closed in October, 1917, appropriations were made totaling nearly nineteen billion dollars, of which seven billions were to cover loans to the Allies. In July Mr. Herbert Hoover became "food dictator," and in August Mr. Garfield was appointed "fuel administrator." In December the Government took over the management and operation of the railways. Every possible step was taken to expedite the production of munitions and other war supplies, including foodstuffs, and to transport all these commodities to American seaports on the Atlantic coast and thence to Europe for the relief alike of the armed forces and of the civilian population, of the nations now associated with the United States in the Great War. To place American grain, meat, munitions, and money so promptly and so effectively at the disposal of the Allies was of itself no mean contribution of the United States to the eventual defeat of Germany.

But the United States Government was resolved to go much farther and to put American troops in front-line trenches alongside those Allied troops who for two years and a half had borne the heat and burden of the greatest war in history. On June 13, General John J. Pershing, who had been designated to command the projected American Expeditionary Force abroad, arrived in Paris, and the first contingent of American troops reached France on June 25. The first American shots from European trenches were fired on October 27, and the first trench fighting of Americans occurred a week later. By December, 1917, about 250,000 American troops had been safely landed in France; and towards the end of January, 1918, the War Department at Washington let it be known that United States soldiers were occupying front-line trenches "in a certain sector."

Against American preparations the German submarine warfare made little headway. It is true that during the first year of unrestricted submarine warfare, ending January 31, 1918, some sixty-nine American vessels, representing a gross tonnage of 170,000, were sunk by submarines, mines, or raiders. On the other hand, it should be remembered that enemy merchant ships were seized by the United States to the number of 107, with an aggregate tonnage of nearly 700,000, and that many of these former German and Austrian liners were promptly repaired and used to carry American troops and supplies to France. Besides, the United States Government inaugurated a shipbuilding program of huge dimensions, so that by the first anniversary of America's participation in the war the United States had put in commission 1275 vessels of every sort of service — mine-sweeping, mine-laying, transport, patrol, and submarine-chasing. By the same date the personnel of the American navy had grown from its original number of 4800 officers and 102,000 men to 20,600 officers and 330,000 men, and the navy itself with great speed and small loss was conducting the most amazing ferrying business on record.

Before the spring of 1918 had rolled around, the problem of American preparedness was solved, and it was solved in manner wholly disconcerting to the Teutons.   At the beginning of 1917 Germany had, with mad imprecations, unloosed the ruthless submarines in order to bring Great Britain to terms.   At the close of 1917, despite the submarines and the fierce invectives of Germany, Great Britain was still resolutely hostile.   Nay, more, at the close of 1917, because of those same submarines and invectives, the United States was an active associate of the Entente, pouring out to Britain and France and Italy vast streams of food and minerals and treasures and, most startling of all, her own man power.   Verily it was a new stage of the Great War which the intervention of the United States marked, and one ominous to Germany's vaulting ambitions and likewise to any perpetuation of international anarchy.

CHAPTER XI

RUSSIA REVOLTS AND MAKES "PEACE"

DESTRUCTION OF RUSSIAN AUTOCRACY: THE MARCH (1917) REVOLUTION

AUTOCRACY of the Russian variety proved itself absolutely unfit to meet the supreme test of the Great War. Such was its corruption and inefficiency that rather early in the struggle Russia had lost to the foreign foe more men and more territory than any other Great Power. And such was the obtuseness of the Russian autocracy that it would learn no lesson from military defeat and would brook no honest criticism of its own conduct. In fact, as time went on, the court and the bureaucracy appeared to think less and less of how to defeat Germany and more and more of how to ward off domestic revolution.

Throughout the winter of 1916–1917 popular disaffection overspread Russia. Army officers complained of the lack of governmental energy in prosecuting the war. The middle classes complained of absurd governmental restrictions on trade and industry. Landlords complained of silly governmental restrictions on the export of grain from one district to another. Peasants groaned under an intolerable system of economic and political abuses. Workingmen in the towns suffered from a shortage of food and a general paralysis of business. Against the bureaucracy were arrayed all popular bodies — the Union of Zemstvos, the Union of Municipalities, the War Industries Committee, the Imperial Duma, and even the conservative Council of the Empire. In Petrograd and Moscow, strike followed strike.

Yet the autocracy adhered to its traditions of secrecy, suspicion, repression, and intrigue. The Tsar Nicholas II himself was naturally clement and well-meaning, but he was hopelessly dominated by his wife, the Tsarina Alexandra Feodorovna; and this ambitious and neurotic woman surrounded herself with fools and hypocrites and charlatans, chief among whom was the notorious Gregory Rasputin. Rasputin, a curious compound of shrewd peasant, avaricious politician, erotic maniac, and religious fanatic, acted as official "medicine man" to a superstitious court and gave tone and character to the blind, perverse autocracy. Rasputin was said, on good authority, to have been responsible for the dismissal of the Grand Duke Nicholas from supreme command of the Russian armies in 1915; certainly Rasputin was a friend of the reactionary premiers Goremýkin and Stürmer, of the traitorous War Secretary Soukhomlinov, and especially of Protopopov, the generally hated and feared minister of the interior.

In November, 1916, the Duma had held a stormy session, but its attacks on the administration had produced no important results. Boris Stürmer, it is true, had been replaced in the premiership by Alexander Trepov, but Trepov was either unwilling or unable to persuade the Tsar to dismiss Protopopov or to break the spell of Rasputin. To the popular Russian mind it was becoming ever more patent that court circles were controlled by "dark influences" and that any premier acceptable to the court, whether a Stürmer or a Trepov, was capable of betraying the country to the Germans if thereby autocracy might be strengthened in Russia. To the confirmed bureaucrats the Romanov dynasty seemed to have much more in common with the dynasties of the Hohenzollerns and Habsburgs than with the democracies of France and Great Britain. Treason to the Allied cause was becoming the highest object of statesmanship on the part of the Russian Government. At the same time the Russian Government was pursuing such an unpopular course that its domestic enemies openly charged it with aiming to provoke a futile rebellion, to suppress the rebellion by force, to quell by terrorism any agitation for reform, and to intrench Russian autocracy anew in power for another century.

Under these circumstances a conspiracy was formed by several prominent Russian liberals against Rasputin, and at the end of December, 1916, the sinister monk was assassinated. The popular rejoicing which greeted the news of this bloody deed was unmistakable proof of the wide divergence of the sentiments and feelings of the nation from those of the court. But still the court was deaf, dumb, and blind to popular feelings. Rasputin dead exercised upon the mind of the Tsàrina — and, through her, upon the Tsar — even a greater influence than when he was alive. Though Trepov was dismissed from the premiership he was replaced by Prince Golitzin, a typical bureaucrat of compressed brains and elastic conscience. And while Prince Golitzin kept postponing the assembling of the Duma throughout January and February, 1917, the fanatical Protopopov, with a superabundance of misplaced energy, was suppressing newspapers, breaking up meetings, and filling the prisons with political offenders and suspects.

In the meantime many Russian people were hungry. The winter of 1916–1917 was bitterly cold, with heavy snowfalls; and, although there was enough grain in Russia, if properly distributed, to satisfy all, nevertheless the enormous demands of the army strained the transport machinery to its utmost, and a situation naturally bad was rendered incalculably worse by the mismanagement and corruption of the Government. At the very time when bread lines were becoming a daily occurrence in the larger cities and when the Government appeared to have no remedy for the food shortage, the Duma at last reassembled in Petrograd on February 27, 1917, — amid bodyguards of Protopopov's police.

Thus it happened that early in March the national representatives in the Duma assailed the Government more vehemently than ever, while in Petrograd the workers went on a strike and participated in street demonstrations and riots. No concession, however, was forthcoming. The Government was plainly determined to overawe workers and parliamentarians alike. On Sunday, March 11, Prince Golitzin formally prorogued the Duma, and the military governor of Petrograd solemnly ordered the strikers to keep the peace and return to work. But the workers simply refused to obey, and the Duma declined to be prorogued, declaring that it was now the sole constitutional authority in Russia. The supreme test of Russian autocracy had come. Could the Government enforce its will?

To enforce its will the Government must command the loyalty and obedience, not only of the police, but also of the soldiers, and it was a disquieting symptom that some soldiers in Petrograd when directed on March 11 to fire on the crowd had mutinied. On that evening a Committee of Workmen set itself up in the city with the twofold purpose of organizing the lower classes for revolutionary purposes and of winning the soldiers to their cause; it was intent upon destroying autocracy, root and branch, and building some sort of radical republic. At once it obtained a great influence over the troops pouring into Petrograd.

The activities and threats of the Petrograd workingmen alarmed the more moderate Duma and made the parliamentary leaders all the more anxious to wring speedy and sweeping concessions from the Government. On the evening of March 11,

Rodzianko, the conservative president of the Duma, telegraphed the Tsar: "The situation is grave. Anarchy reigns in the capital. The transport of provisions and fuel is completely disorganized. General dissatisfaction is growing. Irregular rifle-firing is occurring in the streets. It is necessary to charge immediately some persons enjoying the confidence of the people to form a new government. It is impossible to linger. Any delay means death. Let us pray to God that the responsibility in this hour will not fall upon a crowned head."

The next day — March 12 — was decisive. The bulk of the troops, both the Petrograd garrison and the reënforcements brought into the city, responded to the appeals of the Council of Workmen's Deputies and engaged in free-for-all fights with their officers and with the police. In the afternoon the great prison fortress of Saint Peter and Saint Paul surrendered to the revolutionaries; and with the fall of the Bastille of the old régime, the organs of autocracy ceased to function. Some of the old bureaucrats were arrested; others made their escape.

So far the revolution was confined to Petrograd, and there was much uncertainty both in the Duma and in the Council of Workmen's Deputies as to whether the Tsar could or would turn his huge field armies against the capital. Attempts of the Tsar and of General Ivanov to reach Petrograd were frustrated by revolutionary railway-employees, who for two critical days wilfully sidetracked or blocked their trains. Meanwhile the armies of Brussilov and Ruzsky declared their adherence to the Revolution, and at Moscow and other important places in the interior of the empire similar declarations were made. The Russian autocracy of the Romanovs and of the bureaucrats collapsed universally and suddenly.

As a result of negotiations between leaders of the Duma and the Council of Workmen's Deputies at Petrograd — now styled the Council of Workmen's and Soldiers' Deputies, or Soviet — Professor Milyukov, the chief of the Constitutional Democratic party in the Duma, was able to announce on the afternoon of March 15 that an agreement had been reached: that it had been decided to depose the Tsar, to constitute immediately a provisional government composed of representatives of all parties and groups, and to arrange for the convocation of a Constituent Assembly at an early date to determine the form of a permanent democratic government for Russia. Earlier on the same day, the Tsar had been waited upon in his railway train at Pskov and his abdication had been counseled by Rodzianko, Alexeiev, Brussilov, Ruzsky, and the Grand Duke Nicholas. There was only one thing for the well-meaning, weak-kneed Nicholas II to do and that was to abdicate. Abdicate he did in graceful language and in deep emotion; and, hoping against hope that at least the dynasty might be saved, he abdicated in favor of his brother, the Grand Duke Michael.

The Grand Duke Michael dared not essay to play the imperial rôle. On March 16, the day after his brother's abdication, he issued a statement in which he said:

"This heavy responsibility has come to me at the voluntary request of my brother, who has transferred the imperial throne to me during a period of warfare which is accompanied by unprecedented popular disturbances. Moved by the thought, which is in the minds of the entire people, that the good of the country is paramount, I have adopted the firm resolution to accept the supreme power only if this be the will of our great people, who, by a plebiscite organized by their representatives in a Constituent Assembly, shall establish a form of government and new fundamental laws for the Russian state.

"Consequently, invoking the benediction of our Lord, I urge all citizens of Russia to submit to the Provisional Government, established upon the initiative of the Duma and invested with full plenary powers, until such time which will follow with as little delay as possible, as the Constituent Assembly, on a basis of universal, direct, equal, and secret suffrage, shall, by its decision as to the new form of government, express the will of the people."

It is not likely that the Grand Duke Michael entertained any idea that he would ever become the Tsar of All the Russias by vote of a Constituent Assembly or otherwise. He must have known, what the revolutionaries now thoroughly understood, that the Romanov dynasty was permanently retired to private life and that the autocracy which it had enshrined for three centuries and the bureaucracy with which it had been served were henceforth forever doomed.

The Provisional Government, as organized on March 15, 1917, consisted of a ministry selected from, and responsible to, the Duma. It represented a coalition of the parties and groups of the Center and Left Center, and was essentially bourgeois and respectable. The popular elements throughout the country, on which it counted most, were the professional classes, business men, and country gentlemen. Its head, at once premier and minister of the interior, was Prince George Lvov, president of the Union of Zemztvos, member of the Constitutional Democratic Party, a specialist in local government, and an eminently practical man. The important ministry of war and marine was assigned to Guchkov, a moderate conservative of the Octobrist faction; that of finance, to Terestchenko, a wealthy employer and a sort of Tory democrat; that of justice, to Alexander Kerensky, a leader of the radical peasant party — the so-called Socialist Revolutionaries, — easily the most radical member of the new government; and the ministries of foreign affairs and agriculture, respectively to Professor Milyukov and to Shingarev, both doctrinaire liberals belonging to the Constitutional Democratic Party. Altogether in the Provisional Government there were eight Constitutional Democrats, three Octobrists, and one Socialist Revolutionary.

By the end of March, 1917, the Russian Revolution was an accomplished fact. The autocracy had fallen. The Tsar had been deposed. The bureaucrats were in prison or in exile. The Provisional Government, representing a coalition of the liberal groups of the Duma and championing a thoroughly democratic régime for revolutionized Russia, had been accorded formal recognition by the United States, Great Britain, France, Italy, and Japan, and had apparently obtained the support of the vast majority of Russian people. Already thousands of political prisoners had been liberated and brought back from Siberia. Freedom of association, of the press, and of religion had been proclaimed. Finland had been given back her constitution (March 20). And on March 30 the Provisional Government declared: "The Polish nation, liberated and unified, will settle for itself the nature of its own government, expressing its will by means of a Constituent Assembly convoked on the basis of universal suffrage in the capital of Poland." Not only was the autocracy dead, but its policies were being reversed as rapidly as possible.

What promised to assure the permanence of democratic Russia was the speedy acceptance of the Revolution by the principal army generals. Alexeiev, as generalissimo; Ruzsky, commander of the northern army group; Brussilov, commander of the southern army group; Kornilov, in command of the Petrograd garrison, — all swore loyalty to the Provisional Government. Only General Ewarts, commander of the central army group, opposed the new régime; and there was no difficulty in replacing him with General Gourko, an able soldier and a friend of the Revolution. The attitude of these generals promised even more than the permanence of democratic Russia; it promised the continued participation of Russia in the Great War and the heartiest and most effective coöperation of Russia with her sister democracies of France, Great Britain, Italy, and the United States, against the menace of Teuton imperialism. There was gayety in Russia. There was rejoicing and there was fêting of the Russian Revolution in Rome, in Paris, in London, in New York, and in San Francisco. There was despair in old Russian court circles, as temporarily there was gloom in Vienna and in Berlin.

DISINTEGRATION OF DEMOCRACY: POLITICAL AND MILITARY EXPERIMENTS

To expect the transformation of Russia, within a month, from autocracy to democracy was to believe in miracles and magic. Russia was a huge, heterogeneous empire, in which national ambitions of Finns, Poles, Letts, Lithuanians, Ukrainians, Jews, and Georgians were bound to interfere with the successful operation of democratic institutions, if not to constitute disruptive forces. Russia, moreover, was politically and economically the most backward country in Europe; unlike the peoples of France and Great Britain, the population of the Russian Empire had had no thorough training or long experience in political democracy; unlike the democracies of western Europe, the Russian revolutionary government would have to base itself less upon an electorate of educated bourgeois and prosperous inedependent farmers than upon a mass of illiterate, poverty-stricken peasants and upon noisy groups of ill-disciplined urban workers. For a democratic harvest in Russia, neither the field was favorable nor the seed fertile.

For many years "government" in the abstract had meant to the bulk of the Russian people the concrete government of the tsars; and the protracted popular protests and agitations against the tsars' autocracy and bureaucracy had bred in the Russian masses a natural repugnance to government in general rather than any particular devotion to untried democracy. Consequently, when the Revolution occurred in March, 1917, and the government of the Tsar ceased to function, Russia became "democratic" only in the minds of the Duma leaders and other Russian doctrinaires and of foreigners. What Russia really became was anarchical. Extreme individualism supplanted despotism. The collective duties and responsibilities of freedom were quite lost sight of in the frenzied joy of individual

emancipation. Enthusiasm was centered in blind destruction
of the old rather than in farsighted construction of the new.
Liberty was truly license.

Like children the Russian people utilized their newly won
freedom. In large numbers they stopped work and took holi-
days. They talked and harangued. In the country districts
they withheld rents and taxes. In the towns they destroyed
machinery and drove out employers and inspectors. In the
army the common soldiers proceeded to choose their own officers
and to debate plans of campaign. The police were gone, and
the armies were rapidly degenerating into chaos.

No single authority gained the assent of the Russian people
at large. The Provisional Government of Prince Lvov claimed
sole authority, but it really represented only certain middle-
class groups in a Duma which had been elected by a very restricted suffrage under the auspices of the discredited and fallen
autocracy. More representative of the bulk of the Russian
people than the bourgeois Provisional Government were the
extra-legal Soviets of Workmen's, Soldiers', and Peasants'
Deputies, which, following the example of the Petrograd workers,
hastily sprang up throughout the length and breadth of the
country and even in the army. The Soviets were organized
locally, on something like a town-meeting basis, and they undoubtedly performed very important services in satisfying vital
local needs and in spreading and applying the principles of the
revolution locally. But the Soviets were too numerous, too
diverse, and too irresponsible to admit of unification and of
effective direction of constructive policies for all Russia. Besides, the Soviets, being dominated largely by Socialist Revolutionaries and Social Democrats, were out of sympathy with
the more moderate parties of Constitutional Democrats and
Octobrists which controlled the Provisional Government. The
latter were seemingly content to interpret the March Revolution
merely as a political change from autocracy to middle-class
political democracy, while the former were intent upon pushing
it further so that all the institutions of the old régime — social
as well as political — would be utterly annihilated. The Soviets
acted on the supposition that the overthrowing of the Romanovs
should be the signal for economic and social changes so radical
as to make the political program of the Provisional Government
appear paltry and ridiculous. The Soviets distrusted the Provisional Government, and the Provisional Government feared
the Soviets.

It was on the question of war aims that the first significant cleavage appeared between the Provisional Government and the Soviets. Milyukov, the minister of foreign affairs, and Guchkov, the war minister, were particularly zealous imperialists; they prevailed upon the Provisional Government to champion most of the traditional foreign policies of the old autocracy — a strongly unified Russian state, a close secret alliance with France, ambitious designs on Constantinople and Armenia, and an unyielding attitude toward Rumania and the Balkan states. On the other hand, the Soviets reflected the war weariness of the Russian masses. Russia had already suffered more serious losses than any other Great Power; and the Russian people were sick and tired of a struggle into which they had blindly been led by the Tsar and whose stakes had been less the preservation of Russia from German dominion than the extension of Russian imperialism and the aggrandizement of the autocratic régime. Now that the Tsar was deposed, the majority of the Russian people felt instinctively that all his policies — foreign as well as domestic — were discredited, and that the political revolution should carry with it a revolution in war aims. "Self-determination" was now the all-important objective of the Russians; it should be the common objective of all the belligerent nations. Hitherto the Great War had been a struggle between governing classes of different countries for imperialistic purposes; henceforth it must be a popular contest for the assurance of self-determination, and of that kind of self-determination expressed in the simple formula "no annexations and no indemnities."

Such was the purport of resolutions adopted by the first All-Russian Congress of Soviets, which met in Moscow on April 13, 1917. The delegates, it is true, declared themselves in favor of the continuation of the war, provided it was waged on their terms, and expressed themselves as willing to exclude from the formula of "no annexations and no indemnities" the questions of Belgium, Poland, Serbia, and Armenia. But in all other respects they insisted upon their principles and demanded the assent of the Allies to their formula.

There was little likelihood of Allied acceptance of the demands of the Russian Soviets. For if peradventure they should be accepted, Italy and Japan would gain absolutely nothing from the war; France would have to renounce Alsace-Lorraine forever; and Great Britain would still be confronted by a German Empire mighty in resources, in colonies, in industry, and in shipping. Nor were the Soviets' demands attractive to the Russian Foreign Minister Milyukov, who had set his heart on strict adherence to the secret treaties negotiated by the Tsar's Government with the several Entente Powers and who hoped thereby to win for democratic Russia the rich prize of Constantinople, which for centuries had been fondly contended for by autocratic Russia. Accordingly, early in May, 1917, Milyukov addressed a joint note to the Allied Governments, proclaiming the firm resolution of Russia to conclude no separate peace with the Central Empires, but to carry the war to a victorious conclusion in conformity with Russia's past engagements.

Milyukov's note was as distasteful to the Soviets as it was pleasing to the Allies. The Soviets were plainly annoyed. There were open demonstrations against the Foreign Minister. There were mutinous outbreaks in the army. On May 13, Guchkov resigned as minister of war and navy, and Milyukov soon followed him into retirement. The Provisional Government of Prince Lvov was breaking down. Real power was passing rapidly from the middle classes to the workers and peasants, from the Duma to the Soviets.

The swing of the revolutionary pendulum toward social radicalism was registered in the reconstruction of Prince Lvov's Provisional Government, on May 16, 1917. This reconstruction was largely the work of Tcheidze, a Social Democrat and the commanding figure in the Petrograd Soviet, and Alexander Kerensky, the only member of the first Provisional Government who sympathized fully with the aims of the Soviets. In the new ministry, Kerensky himself became minister of war and navy; Tchernov, the leader of the Socialist Revolutionaries, took the portfolio of agriculture; another Socialist Revolutionary succeeded Kerensky as minister of justice; Social Democrats, Skobelev and Tseretelli, became ministers respectively of labor and of posts and telegraphs. Although the moderate Constitutional Democratic Party was allowed to retain the portfolio of foreign affairs, the new incumbent, Terestchenko, was not such a zealous imperialist as Milyukov. Altogether, in the reconstructed Provisional Government, there were seven Constitutional Democrats, two Octobrists, three Socialist Revolutionaries, and three Social Democrats. The Soviets now had several able representatives in the Provisional Government.

On the crucial question of war aims, a manifesto, drafted in conference between the ministry and the Soviets, was issued three days after the reconstruction of the Provisional Govern-

ment: "The Provisional Government, reorganized and re-
enforced by representatives of the Revolutionary Democracy,
declares that it will energetically carry into effect the ideas of
liberty, equality, and fraternity, beneath the standards of which
the great Russian Revolution came to birth. . . . In its foreign
policy the Provisional Government, rejecting, in concert with
the entire people, all thought of a separate peace, adopts openly
as its aim the reëstablishment of a general peace which shall
not tend towards domination over other nations or the seizure
of their national possessions or the violent usurpation of their
territories — a peace without annexations or indemnities and
based on the right of nations to decide their own affairs. In
the firm conviction that the fall of the régime of Tsardom in
Russia and the consolidation of democratic principles in our
internal and external policy will create in the Allied democracies
new aspirations towards a stable peace and the brotherhood of
nations, the Provisional Government will take steps towards
bringing about a new agreement with the Allies. . . ."

The new Government grappled with the prodigious problems
of reconstructing and regenerating Russia with determination
and pluck. Energetic efforts were made to put manufacturing
plants again in operation, to get the peasants to augment their
crops, and to improve the transport system. To secure the
assistance of foreign capital and of foreign technical advisers,
as well as to enlighten the Russian people about the theories
and practices of political democracy, especially its duties and
responsibilities, foreign missions were welcomed and afforded
every opportunity to travel and to lecture throughout the
country; and eloquent were the appeals addressed to the Russian
people by the American mission under Elihu Root, the French
under Albert Thomas, the Belgian under Émile Vandervelde,
and the British under Arthur Henderson.

Meanwhile the Government was negotiating with the Entente
Powers for the summoning of an Inter-Allied Conference which
should revise the past secret treaties in harmony with the Russian
manifesto of May 19; and at the same time, Kerensky, with
fiery enthusiasm, was exerting himself to the utmost to restore
some discipline in the army and to prepare Russia for a resumption of the offensive against Germany and Austria-Hungary.

It was an impossible task. The Allied Governments certainly applauded the deposition of the Tsar and wished the
revolutionaries well, but for the present they were naturally
far more concerned that Russia should give full military assistance

to their war aims than that Russia should set her own house in order. The Allies, intent upon winning the war, feared lest the Russians should become so absorbed in developing their revolution and in effecting radical social readjustments at home as to lose interest in the war abroad. The Russian people, on the other hand, felt quite as naturally that for the present the completion of their own domestic revolution was infinitely more important than the prosecution of the foreign war along lines determined by bourgeois statesmen in Paris, London, and Rome; they could not comprehend why, if the Allies were sincere in their good wishes for the Russian Revolution, favorable response was not immediately forthcoming to the request for a radical revision of war aims; they began to distrust the political democracies of western Europe, and to imagine that France, Italy, and Great Britain were addicted, almost as much as Germany and Austria-Hungary, to the vice of greedy imperialism. A fissure was appearing in the rock of Entente solidarity. The Russian people were perceptibly separating from the other Allied nations.

Anxiously the Government of Prince Lvov sought to prevent the fissure from becoming a chasm. They tried to explain to the Russian people that so long as Germany was undefeated the Revolution was not safe. They attempted to make clear to the Allies that until the Revolution was assured Russia could not give her chief attention to the defeat of Germany. The more they urged the Allies to adopt a conciliatory peace program the more fearful grew the Allies of radical socialistic tendencies in Russia. The more the Provisional Government begged the Russian people to continue the war at any cost, the more unpopular they became in Russia and the more susceptible were the Russians to radical socialistic and pacifistic propaganda.

The relation of revolutionized Russia to the Entente was only one aspect of the insoluble problem before the Provisional Government. The Provisional Government itself was essentially unstable; it comprised representatives of a shadowy Duma which had ceased to function and of informal and irregular Soviets which were in state of constant flux; it embraced leaders of such diverse and naturally quarrelsome parties as the bourgeois Octobrist and Constitutional Democratic, the peasants' Socialist Revolutionary, and the proletarian Social Democratic; it was a compromise, and as a compromise it pleased no strict partisans. By virtue of its composite personnel, the Provisional Government could not hope to carry out any consistent policy of political or social reconstruction. Yet thoroughgoing reconstruction was what Russia most needed.

Reconstruction of the vast Russian Empire, with its divergent nationalities, its illiterate masses, its extremes of poverty and affluence, and its long record of political corruption and tyranny under the scepter of the tsars, would have been enormously difficult in normal times of peace. It was rendered well-nigh impossible in 1917 by reason of the fact that Russia was a party to the greatest war in human annals and was peculiarly open to five forms of insidious propaganda.

In the first place, there was the propaganda of reactionary elements in Russia. At first these elements were confined pretty much to the bureaucrats of the old régime and to certain disgruntled landlords and manufacturers; and their propaganda, beginning under Stürmer and Protopopov, was directed toward peace with the Central Empires, to the end that the autocracy might be restored and likewise the social distinctions and privileges of the old régime. These elements were not numerous or outspoken, but they had wealth and a talent for intrigue.

Secondly, there was the propaganda of those Russians who, while supporting the Revolution in its earliest stages, denounced subsequent developments as evil or inexpedient. The more radical the Provisional Government became and the more it catered to the social demands of the Soviets, the noisier and more numerous grew these conservative revolutionaries, until by June, 1917, they included not only the Nationalists but important groups of Octobrists and Constitutional Democrats. They were still too few to dominate the country or any considerable part of it, but they were sufficiently brilliant and eloquent to embarrass the Provisional Government. They insisted upon war at any price and denounced the attempts of the Government to obtain a restatement of Allied war-aims. They misled the Allies into thinking that they represented the Russian people; and their propaganda did much to give the Allies false hopes and the masses in Russia groundless alarms. Unconsciously and indirectly they contributed potently to widening the breach between Russia and the Allied democracies.

Thirdly, there was a movement of various lesser nationalities within the Russian Empire toward political independence or autonomy. Poles and Finns were determined to utilize the destruction of the tsardom in order to free themselves entirely from union with Russia. In April, 1917, a congress of Little Russians (Ruthenians) met at Kiev and demanded complete autonomy for a Ukrainia which should reach from the Pripet River on the north to the Black Sea and Kuban River on the south and from the Don on the east to the Dniester and Bug on the west. In July a national assembly of Esthonians met at Reval and formed a provisional government. In August a conference of the Letts of Courland and Livonia, convened in Riga, demanded "a united, politically autonomous Lettland (Latvia) within the Russian Republic." Similar demands were made by Lithuanians and by Georgians of the Caucasus. And all these national committees and "provisional governments" engaged actively in propaganda which threatened to disrupt the Russian Empire not only, but to stimulate the counter-agitation of Russian conservatives and to serve the cause of Germany.

Fourthly, there was out-and-out German propaganda. Before the Revolution a goodly number of German agents had been at work in Russia intriguing with old-régime bureaucrats for a separate peace. After the Revolution the unsettled political and social conditions in Russia enabled the Teutons to widen and deepen their efforts to secure by intrigue what they had failed to obtain by force of arms. The German agents were now all things to all Russians. To reactionaries, they were apostles of a counter-revolution which could be achieved only by the cessation of war. To extreme revolutionaries, they were devotees of the doctrine that the revolution could be completed only if the existing Provisional Government, which sought to continue the war, were overthrown. The separatist propaganda among the lesser nationalities within Russia they aided and abetted. But principally they devoted their energies to undermining the morale of the Russian field-armies. With the fall of autocracy, discipline in the Russian armies rapidly declined; privates left the ranks and went home without leave; officers who tried to do their duty were arrested by the men; fighting ceased; and Russian and German soldiers began to fraternize. Taking advantage of this situation, German agents went about in the Russian lines trying to persuade the troops to demand a separate peace or at least an armistice. The French and British were accused of the grossest imperialism and of a desire needlessly to prolong the carnage and bloodshed in order to further their own selfish ambitions; and the Teutons were represented as angelic victims of the jealousy and greed of others and as confirmed friends of a just and durable peace. The German agents insisted that the Central Empires were willing and anxious to conclude peace but that the Entente was not.

Finally, most directly menacing to the unity and permanence of the Provisional Government was the propaganda of the Russian revolutionaries of the extreme Left. These ultra-revolutionaries assailed the members of the Socialist Revolutionary and Social Democratic parties who had accepted portfolios in a "bourgeois" government, charging them with sacrificing the social revolution to the political exigencies of war. Gradually, by means of this kind of propaganda, a considerable number of revolutionary peasants were weaned away from the leadership of Tchernov and Kerensky, and a large proportion of urban workers transferred their loyalty from Tseretelli and Tcheidze to still more radical Social Democrats. Gradually many Soviets passed from moderate Socialism to extreme Socialism. And the leaders of extreme Socialism in Russia stood quite outside of organized government; they were as anxious to rid Russia of Prince Lvov's provisional middle-class democracy as they were to have done once and for all with the Tsar Nicholas's divine-right autocracy.

Russian Socialism in the twentieth century comprised two major movements. The one, essentially indigenous, extolled Russian national customs and aimed at expropriating great landowners and establishing a kind of peasant proprietorship with coöperative features; it appealed to the agricultural lower classes and was crystallized into the Socialist Revolutionary Party. The other, an imported product, took its faith and works from Karl Marx and his doctrinaire disciples in western Europe; it emphasized the "class-struggle," the eventually inevitable rout of capitalism by a class-conscious proletariat, and all the other tenets of international Socialism; it spread among urban workers and found expression in the Social Democratic Party.

But the Social Democratic Party, since its second congress, in 1903, had been divided into two wings, the Bolsheviki, or "majority," and the Mensheviki, or "minority." At first the two wings differed merely on matters of party organization, but in course of time their separation and mutual antagonism were increased by divergent views as to party tactics. The Bolsheviki cherished the strict Marxist precepts, including the idea that the Socialist state of the future would be ushered in by an overwhelming cataclysm, sudden, proletarian, and international. The Mensheviki, on the other hand, were "reformist," in the sense in which that word was used in Germany and France; they believed that Russia could be Socialized only through the coöperation of Social Democrats with other radicals, through gradual political and economic reforms, and through the slow education of the masses. In practice the Mensheviki were the moderates, and the Bolsheviki the extremists. Despite the fact that the extremists constituted a minority of Russian Socialists, the appellation of Bolsheviki, or "majority," still stuck to them.

In the reconstructed Provisional Government of Prince Lvov, the Socialist Revolutionaries had three representatives including Tchernov and Kerensky, and the Mensheviki had three. The Bolsheviki, alone of the Socialist groups, were not represented; they were too extreme for the comfort and safety of the moderate revolutionaries, and besides, their strict principles forbade them to accept office in a "bourgeois" government even if they were invited. Relieved of all responsibility of dealing with the actual problems then confronting the Provisional Government, the Bolsheviki were free to make the most bitter attacks upon the government and at the same time to make the most extravagant promises to ignorant workers and peasants concerning the millennium which they would inaugurate if they had the chance. For conducting this highly subversive and destructive propaganda the Bolsheviki had two remarkable leaders and agitators in Lenin and Trotsky.

Vladimir Ulyanov, better known under his pen-name of Nikolai Lenin, belonged by birth and training to the Russian nobility, but as a young man he had become a revolutionary and in 1899 had published an important book on "The Development of Capitalism in Russia." A doctrinaire Socialist of the most dogmatic type, he had lived in exile in Switzerland almost continuously from 1900 until the Revolution of March, 1917, when the German Government permitted him to return to Russia. He accepted German assistance and German gold, but he had as little love for the Hohenzollerns as for the Romanovs.

Leon Trotsky, a Moscow Jew whose name was really Bronstein, belonged to the middle class. Becoming a radical socialist, he had been imprisoned for political offenses and transported to Siberia. Escaping thence, he had lived several years in Vienna and in Paris. Expelled from France in 1916, he arrived in New York in the following January, but in May managed to reach Russia.

The Bolshevist program of Lenin and Trotsky in the spring of 1917 was as follows: (1) the Soviets of Workmen, Soldiers, and Peasants, to constitute themselves the actual revolutionary government and exercise the dictatorship of the proletariat; (2) immediate confiscation of landed estates without compensation and without waiting for legal forms, the peasants organizing into Soviets; (3) control of production and distribution by the revolutionary government, nationalization of monopolies, and repudiation of the national debt; (4) the workmen to take possession of factories and operate them in conjunction with technical experts; (5) refusal by the Soviets to recognize any treaties made by the governments either of the Tsar or of the bourgeoisie, and the immediate publication of all such treaties; (6) the workers to propose at once and publicly an immediate armistice, and negotiations for peace to be carried out by the proletariat and not by the bourgeoisie; and (7) bourgeois war debts to be paid exclusively by the capitalists. Lenin himself proposed further "that universal, equal, direct, and secret suffrage be frankly abandoned, and that only the industrial proletariat and the poorest section of the peasantry be permitted to vote at all."

In repudiating political democracy and in demanding immediate peace, the Bolsheviki arrayed themselves squarely against the Mensheviki and Socialist Revolutionaries as well as against the bourgeois parties. Manifestly the whole Provisional Government was menaced by Bolshevist propaganda.

In June, the All-Russia Congress of Soviets assembled in Petrograd under the presidency of the Menshevist leader Tcheidze. A furious attack by Lenin on the Coalition Government, especially on Kerensky, was successfully answered by Tseretelli and other Mensheviki, and for the time being the moderates, the friends of law and order, triumphed. Late in June an attempted uprising of Bolsheviki in Petrograd fell flat. Apparently there was still a large measure of popular faith in the Provisional Government.

The Provisional Government was staking everything on the outcome of the military measures which at that very time it was taking. Kerensky, the war minister, had reached the conclusion that an advance of the Russian armies against the Teutons, even if trifling in itself, would do incalculable good to the Provisional Government by offsetting subversive propaganda alike of the Germans and of the Bolsheviki, by reënforcing the faith of the Allies in the Revolution, and by reinvigorating the morale of Russia both military and civilian.

Supreme efforts were put forth by Kerensky in June to prepare the Russian field-armies for a resumption of the offensive. With his burning eyes and hoarse voice and with restless energy the war-minister visited the several commands at the front and went

R

among the common soldiers, urging upon all the paramount duty of acting loyally together and of fighting the Teutons to the last ditch. Supplies and reënforcements were rushed up, and important changes were made in the General Staff. Generals Alexeiev and Gourko were dismissed because of their increasingly unsympathetic attitude toward Kerensky, and were succeeded respectively as generalissimo and commander of the central army group by Generals Brussilov and Denikin.

At this time the Teutonic armies on the Eastern Front embraced three groups: (1) the northern group, under Prince Leopold of Bavaria, extending from the Baltic to a point just south of Brzezany; (2) the central group, under Archduke Joseph Frederick, extending thence to the Rumanian frontier; and (3) the southern group, under Field Marshal von Mackensen, arrayed against the Russo-Rumanians along the Sereth. It was against the right wing of the northern group, under Boehm-Ermolli, and the left wing of the central group, under Count Bothmer, that General Brussilov, the new Russian Chief of Staff, decided to launch the offensive. He would seize Brzezany, Halicz, and Stryj, and thence advance on Lemberg.

Russian artillery preparations began in the early morning of June 29, 1917, and on July 1, the infantry leaped from their trenches and charged the Teutons. To the southeast of Lemberg unexpected success crowned the Russian offensive. The Lomnica River, the last natural defense in front of Stryj, was gallantly crossed; and simultaneously with this attack south of the Dniester, the Russians started a drive on the Dniester itself, capturing Halicz on July 10. Within ten days the Russians had taken 50,000 prisoners and vast quantities of war material and had driven a wedge twenty miles long and ten miles deep into the Austro-German lines. But this was the high tide of Russian success.

Sudden, heavy rainfall swelled the Galician streams and rendered them difficult to ford; Teutonic reserves were hurried to threatened positions on the Eastern Front; and in the Russian ranks the revolutionary lack of discipline soon received most painful illustration. Russian regiments in the vicinity of Brzezany, under General Erdelli, abandoned their posts and threw down their arms, and during the last week of July their mutinous spirit was communicated to other commands, with most disastrous results. The tragic facts were recorded in a telegram sent to Kerensky by General Erdelli:

"A fatal crisis has occurred in the morale of the troops recently

sent forward against the enemy.   Most of the military are in a
state of complete disorganization.   Their spirit for an offensive
has utterly disappeared; they no longer listen to the orders of
their leaders, and they neglect all the exhortations of their comrades, even replying to them by threats and shots.   Some elements voluntarily evacuate their positions without even waiting
for the approach of the enemy.   Cases are on record in which
an order to proceed with all haste to such and such a spot to
assist hard-pressed comrades has been discussed for several
hours at meetings, and the reënforcements consequently delayed for several hours. . . .   For a distance of several hundred
versts long files of deserters, both armed and unarmed men, who
are in good health and robust, but who have utterly lost all
shame, are proceeding to the rear of the army.   Frequently
entire units desert in this manner. . . .   Orders have been
given to-day to fire upon deserters and runaways.   Let the
Government find courage to shoot those who by their cowardice
are selling Russia and the Revolution."

Appeals from officers at the front and appeals from the Provisional Government could not stay the rout.   The whole
Russian line in Galicia was now in flight, and all the gains of
1916 were wiped out in a day.   The Germans, with their Austrian
allies, occupïed Halicz, Tarnopol, Stanislau, Czernowitz, and
Kolomea, and drove the fugitive Russians across their own border
and entirely out of Galicia and Bukowina.   General Erdelli was
assassinated, and on August 2, 1917, Kornilov succeeded Brussilov
in nominal command of the disorganized Russian armies.

To the south, the Rumanians assailed Mackensen's army-
group in order to save the Russian retreat from becoming a
final disaster.   Though unable to make much headway against
the Austro-Germans, the Rumanians acquitted themselves
most admirably and at least prevented Mackensen from inflicting serious counter-attacks upon them.   The last effort of
the Teutons to cross the Sereth met with decisive failure on
August 19.

While the southern army-group of the Teutons was held in
check at the Sereth and the central army-group rested near the
Russo-Galician frontier, the northern group in August utilized
Russian demoralization in order to carry German invasion
further into the Baltic Provinces.   Late in August, German
forces under General von Hutier, reached the River Aa and
attacked at Keckau, ten miles south of Riga.   On September 2,
they cut the Dvinsk railway five miles east of the Düna River.

On the following day the Russians evacuated Riga and the Germans entered in triumph. On September 23, Hutier captured Jacobstadt, seventy miles up the Düna from Riga. In October, following some naval fighting, the Germans occupied the islands at the mouth of the Gulf of Riga, and threatened the chief Russian naval-base at Reval.

Meanwhile the fate of the Provisional Government was sealed. Having risked everything on a military offensive, the moderate Revolutionaries, in the turn of the war-tide, had lost everything. On one hand, the militarists and patriots redoubled their attacks upon the Government, blaming it for the destruction of military discipline. On the other hand, the Bolsheviki put all the blame upon the "militaristic" policies and ambitions of a Government dominated by the bourgeoisie.

On July 17, 1917, Prince Lvov and other Constitutional Democratic members of the Provisional Government resigned, and on the same day the Bolsheviki in Petrograd, led by Lenin and Trotsky, attempted to seize the reins of government. The Bolsheviki were supported by Kronstadt sailors and by various disaffected elements in the garrison. But Kerensky threw himself with ardor into the struggle against them, and, with the assistance of the Petrograd Soviet, which was still under Menshevist influence, he succeeded in putting down the insurrection. Kerensky, however, in his moment of victory, declined to disarm the workmen and dared not punish the Bolshevist leaders. On July 20, the war minister became head of the Provisional Government and assumed a practical dictatorship.

It was Kerensky's hope that by arranging for an early assembling of the Inter-Allied Conference, at which the war-aims would be restated in terms similar to those which President Wilson had employed, and by definitely fixing the date for elections to a Constituent Assembly, September 30, and at the same time by sternly repressing the Bolsheviki, it might be possible to save Russia. Alexander Kerensky doubtless knew that his was a forlorn hope. At any rate, despite his almost superhuman efforts, and the loyal support of the great majority of the Soviets, his eventual defeat was only a question of time. Day after day conditions grew worse. The military situation went rapidly from bad to worse. Finances were in chaos. Reactionaries, at one extreme, and Bolsheviki, at the other, waxed more wroth and violent. The Allies kept postponing their conference and obscuring their war-aims. The separatist tendencies of lesser nationalities within Russia became more pronounced. And above all, German propaganda everywhere took root and flourished and bore fruit in increasing abundance. The Great Russian Revolution was not leading immediately to orderly democratic government and to more effective participation in the war; rather, it was now heading straight toward anarchy and full confession of national defeat and disgrace.

Late in August, an Extraordinary National Conference met in Moscow, representing all classes and all parties. For three days the great assembly debated and listened to speeches from leading revolutionaries: Kerensky, Tseretelli, Tcheidze, Kropotkin, and Madame Breshkovskaya spoke for the workers; Generals Kornilov and Kaledine, for the army; and Milyukov, Guchkov, and others, for the bourgeoisie. Strangely enough, there was an apparent agreement among the great majority of the delegates on three vital points — (1) the reform of the army and the restoration of its discipline, (2) the continuance of the war, and (3) the reconciliation of party quarrels. But with most the first two were merely pious wishes, and the third was irony. The breaches had not been closed. The Radicals insisted upon the ultimate control of the Government by the Soviets, which the Moderates bitterly opposed. Three-fourths of Russia outside of the Conference had no inclination for the sacrifice and discipline which a continuance of the war demanded. "The gulf between the soldiers and the dreamers had been made visible to all, and across it straddled Kerensky, a hopeless Colossus, who must soon make his election and leap to one side, or fall into the chasm."

At first Kerensky leaned toward the soldiers. He postponed the elections to the National Constituent Assembly from September 30 to November 25. He strengthened military discipline by decreeing the restoration of the death-penalty. And early in September he seems to have concerted plans with General Kornilov for the establishment of a military dictatorship. At any rate, Kornilov drew up a scheme for a Council of National Defense, with himself as president and with Kerensky as vice-president.

Then suddenly Kerensky veered toward the radicals. Fearful of the effect of a military dictatorship, he ordered Kornilov's removal. Kornilov, on his side, dispatched a division of troops, drawn from the front, against Petrograd. This revolt was crushed without much trouble and with very little bloodshed, Kornilov being arrested and Kerensky assuming the supreme command of the Russian armies.

But the Russian armies were already in process of rapid dissolution. Without loyal troops no military dictator, whether a Kornilov or a Kerensky, could long maintain himself. In vain Kerensky leaned further toward the extremists. A National Democratic Conference convened on September 27 and contented itself with summoning a "Preliminary Parliament," which met on October 8 and wasted time in idle debate. Neither of these consultative bodies had any cohesion or dignity. All political groups and all social classes which had at any time supported the Provisional Government or Kerensky, were, like the Russian armies, in process of disintegration. Moderate political democracy had failed in Russia. Military dictatorship had likewise failed.

What was left was one extreme political faction — the Bolsheviki. And the Bolsheviki were resolutely determined to create a class-dictatorship. They were already well organized and now they were in a position to make capital out of the manifest failures of Lvov, Milyukov, Kornilov, and Kerensky. The overthrow of the political tsardom in March, 1917, was to be supplemented in November by the destruction of Russian society.

DICTATORSHIP OF THE BOLSHEVIKI: THE NOVEMBER (1917) REVOLUTION

One of the chief reasons why Kerensky lost the support of the army and of the Russian people was the failure on the part of his Government to persuade the Allies to restate their war-aims in accordance with the peace formula of the Soviets. Time and again Kerensky had assured the Soviets that the Allies were about to hold a conference to revise their war-aims, but time and again the date of the conference had been postponed. At last, on November 1, Kerensky in despair served notice on the Allies that Russia was exhausted and that the other members of the Entente would thereafter have to shoulder the burden. Although on this occasion be added that his warning did not imply the withdrawal of Russia from the war, nevertheless the Allies took fright and announced that their long-deferred conference would be held in Paris late in November.

But the hope that the Paris Conference would satisfy the longing in Russia for an early peace was not realized. Mr. Bonar Law, speaking in the House of Commons in behalf of the British Government, declared that the conference would not deal with "political" matters, that is, with the revision of war-aims, but would concern itself simply with the discussion of more effective means of prosecuting the war.

This statement caused bitter disappointment in Russia and furnished the Bolsheviki with a potent means of completing the undermining of Kerensky's Government. Under Kerensky, they pointed out, Russia could not wage war or make peace; under a dictatorship of their own, Russia could and immediately would make peace. And the masses of war-weary Russian peasants and workmen were now quite willing to acquiesce in any dictatorship, provided only that it would bring peace. To the ignorant masses the Bolsheviki promised peace not only, but the millennium besides.

The drift of popular opinion in Russia was clearly observable in the new elections to the Congress of Soviets, which had been called to convene on November 7. Of nearly seven hundred delegates elected, a large majority adhered to Bolshevism. To be sure, certain Soviets refused to send delegates and others were intimidated by Bolshevist partisans. But the fact remained that for the first time, in November, 1917, the Bolsheviki apparently had a majority in a working-class convention.

Already the Bolshevist Trotsky had succeeded the Menshevist Tcheidze in the presidency of the Petrograd Soviet. With this support Trotsky and his associates now set to work to prepare a kind of General Staff, called the Military Revolutionary Committee, which should coördinate the Bolshevist elements in the army and navy and in the industrial communities and organize bands of "Red Guards." Time seemed ripe for a Bolshevist Revolution and for the establishment of the dictatorship of the proletariat.

On the night of November 6, a few hours before the convocation of the Congress of Soviets, the Bolsheviki struck the decisive blow. Red Guards occupied the principal government buildings in Petrograd; part of the local garrison joined them, the other part simply refusing to do anything. On the morning of November 7, the members of the Provisional Government were placed under arrest in the Winter Palace, Kerensky alone managing to escape.

On November 8, the All-Russian Congress of Soviets ratified the Bolshevist *coup d'état* and formally entrusted the conduct of affairs to a body styled the Council of People's Commissioners, with Lenin as premier, Trotsky as people's commissioner for foreign affairs, and General Krylenko as commander-in-chief of the armies.

Of the Bolshevist régime, two or three aspects are worthy of emphasis at the present time. In the first place, it was based on force and violence rather than upon the mandate of a popular majority. It originated in a *coup d'état*, and it was maintained by methods which savored of the old Tsardom. Its enemies — whether reactionaries, or moderates such as Octobrists and Constitutional Democrats, or radicals such as Socialist Revolutionaries and Mensheviki — were put under surveillance. Opposition newspapers were suppressed. Terrorism was invoked and increasingly practiced.

Secondly, the new régime was essentially a dictatorship in the interest of certain classes in the community. Its internal policy was directed toward effecting a complete social revolution. Aristocracy and bourgeoisie must go; the rights of property were no longer to be respected. One of the first decrees of the Bolshevist Government empowered municipal authorities to seize any houses whether inhabited or not and to allow citizens who possessed no adequate dwelling to occupy them. Another decreed the transfer of all factories into the hands of the workmen. But the chief of these early measures was the decree which undertook to solve the land problem: private ownership being abolished, the land was to be nationalized and to be turned over to the people who cultivated it; local committees were to dispose of all large holdings and all lands belonging to state and church; mines, waterways, and forests of national importance, were to be expropriated by the state; and smaller forests and waterways were to become the property of the village communities.[1]

Thirdly, the Bolshevist régime was not a step forward in the direction of political democracy, at least of "political democracy" as that phrase had been interpreted in western Europe, in the United States, and by the preceding Provisional Government of Russia. The Bolsheviki themselves constituted a minority — a very small minority — of the Russian people; and when the elections to the National Constituent Assembly, which was conducted in November, 1917, on the democratic basis of equal, direct, universal, and secret suffrage, returned a large majority of Socialist Revolutionaries stanchly opposed to the Bolsheviki, the Council of People's Commissioners became convinced that the only way in which it could maintain itself in power was to

---

[1] Subsequent decrees disestablished the Russian Church, repudiated most of the national debt, and transferred the seat of government from Petrograd to Moscow (February, 1918).

repudiate political democracy.   At first, it merely postponed the opening of the National Assembly from December 12, 1917, to January 18, 1918.   Subsequently, it charged the Assembly with being a counter-revolutionary body, and the Socialist Revolutionary Party with being a traitorous party "directing the fight of the bourgeoisie against the workers' revolution."   Not only was the National Constituent Assembly suppressed, but local soviets which could not be controlled by the Bolsheviki were likewise dissolved and many of their leaders were imprisoned or exiled.   Proletarian dictatorship — not political democracy — was the end and aim of the Bolshevist régime.   In this respect their government, strictly speaking, was not a champion of either Anarchism or Marxian Socialism—it represented rather an attempt to achieve communism by methods essentially tsar-like.

To secure "popular" support for the "proletarian dictatorship," care was taken by the Council of People's Commissioners to purge the Soviets of non-Bolshevists and then to federate the "purified" Soviets into a Congress which would faithfully ratify the decrees of the Council.   By provision of the Constitution of the "Russian Socialist Federated Soviet Republic" the following categories were expressly denied the right to vote or to hold office: "(1) Persons who employ hired labor in order to obtain an increase of profits; (2) Persons who have an income without doing any work, such as interest from capital, receipts from property, etc.; (3) Private merchants and commercial brokers; (4) Monks and clergy of all denominations; (5) Employees and agents of the former police, the gendarme corps, and the Tsar's secret service, also members of the former reigning dynasty; (6) Persons who have legally been declared insane or mentally deficient, and also persons under guardianship; and (7) Persons who have been deprived by a Soviet of their rights of citizenship because of selfish or dishonorable offenses, for the period fixed by the sentence."

Furthermore the Bolshevist Government created an All-Russian Extraordinary Commission, which in turn created Provincial and District Extraordinary Commissions.   These bodies — the local not less than the national — were empowered to make arrests and even to decree and carry out capital sentences.   There was no appeal from their decisions; they were merely required to "report afterward."   From this systematic terrorism only professed Bolsheviki were immune.

Whither the Bolshevist régime in Russia was tending, what was its goal and what were its policies, may perhaps be best indicated by reproducing in full the "Declaration of the Rights of the Toiling and Exploited People," a document which Lenin and Trotsky had prepared and which was presented to the National Constituent Assembly in January, 1918:[1]

I

"1. Russia is to be declared a Republic of the Workmen's, Soldiers', and Peasants' Soviets. All power in the cities and in the country belongs to the Soviets.

"2. The Russian Soviet Republic is based on the free federation of free peoples, on the federation of national Soviet republics.

II

"Assuming as its duty the destruction of all exploitation of the workers, the complete abolition of the class system of society, and the placing of society upon a socialistic basis, and the ultimate bringing about of victory for Socialism in every country, the Constituent Assembly further decides:

"1. That the socialization of land be realized, private ownership of land be abolished, all the land be proclaimed common property of the people and turned over to the toiling masses, without compensation; on the basis of equal right to the use of land;

"(All forests, and waters which are of social importance, as well as all living, and other forms of property, and all agricultural enterprises, are declared national property);

"2. To confirm the decree of the Soviets concerning the inspection of working conditions, the highest department of national economy, which is the first step in achieving the ownership, by the Soviets, of the factories, mines, and means of production and transportation;

"3. To confirm the decree of the Soviets transferring all banks to the ownership of the Soviet Republic, as one of the steps in the freeing of the toiling masses from the yoke of capitalism;

"4. To enforce general compulsory labor, in order to destroy the class parasites, and to reorganize the economic life.

"In order to make the power of the toiling masses secure and to prevent the restoration of the rule of the exploiters, the toiling masses will be armed and a Red Guard formed of workers and peasants, and the exploiting classes shall be disarmed.

[1] The "Declaration" was rejected by the Assembly by a large majority, but it was subsequently utilized as the basis of the Constitution of Bolshevist Russia. The document is in John Spargo, *Bolshevism* (1919), pp. 242 *sqq.*

III

"1. Declaring its firm determination to make society free from the chaos of capitalism and imperialism, which has drenched the country in blood in the most criminal war of all wars, the Constituent Assembly accepts completely the policy of the Soviets, whose duty it is to publish all secret treaties, to organize the most extensive fraternization between the workers and peasants of warring armies, and by revolutionary methods to bring about a democratic peace among the belligerent nations without annexations and indemnities, on the basis of the free self-determination of nations — at any price.

"2. For this purpose the Constituent Assembly declares its complete separation from the brutal policy of the bourgeoisie, which furthers the well-being of the exploiters in a few selected nations by enslaving hundreds of millions of the toiling peoples of the colonies and the small nations generally.

"The Constituent Assembly accepts the policy of the Council of People's Commissioners in giving complete independence to Finland, in beginning the withdrawal of troops from Persia, and in declaring for Armenia the right of self-determination.

"A blow at international financial capital is the Soviet decree which annuls foreign loans made by the governments of the Tsar, the landowners, and the bourgeoisie. The Soviet government is to continue firmly on this road until final victory from the yoke of capitalism is won through international workers' revolt.

"As the Constituent Assembly was elected on the basis of lists of candidates nominated before the November Revolution, when the people as a whole could not yet rise against their exploiters, and did not know how powerful would be the strength of the exploiters in defending their privileges, and had not yet begun to create a Socialist society, the Constituent Assembly considers it, even from a formal point of view, unjust to oppose the Soviet power. The Constituent Assembly is of the opinion that at this moment, in the decisive hour of the struggle of the people against their exploiters, the exploiters must not have a seat in any government organization or institution. The power completely and without exception belongs to the people and their authorized representatives — the Workmen's, Soldiers', and Peasants' Soviets.

"Supporting the Soviet rule and accepting the orders of the Council of People's Commissioners, the Constituent Assembly acknowledges its duty to outline a form for the reorganization of society.

"Striving at the same time to organize a free and voluntary, and thereby also a complete and strong, union among the toiling classes of all Russian nations, the Constituent Assembly limits itself to outlining the basis of the federation of Russian Soviet Republics, leaving to the people, to the workers and soldiers, to decide for themselves, in their own Soviet meetings, if they are willing, and on what conditions they prefer, to join the federated government and other federations of Soviet enterprise.

"These general principles are to be published without delay, and the official representatives of the Soviets are required to read them at the opening of the Constituent Assembly."

DEFECTION OF RUSSIA: THE TREATY OF BREST-LITOVSK

One of the chief reasons why the Tsar was deposed and divine-right autocracy came to an end in Russia in March, 1917, was the inability of the old-régime government, on account of its corruption and inefficiency, to obtain a military victory over Germany. A major reason why the Provisional Government was overthrown and Russian political democracy was transformed into a proletarian dictatorship of the Bolsheviki, in November, 1917, was the inability of the moderate revolutionaries — Lvov and Kerensky — to terminate the war with a favorable peace. Behind both the March and the November phases of the Great Russian Revolution was the war weariness of vast masses of the Russian people. Ever since the disastrous defeats and re-treats of 1915, Russian morale had steadily been declining. In the chaotic social and political conditions of 1917, already sketched, it was destroyed utterly.

What the Bolsheviki would do in the internal affairs of the Russian Empire, once they were in power, was largely con-jectural. What they would do in foreign policy admitted of no doubt whatsoever. On the first day following his advent to the premiership, Lenin telegraphed to all the belligerent Powers, proposing a three months' armistice for the discussion of peace-terms. Receiving no formal responses from the Allies, Trotsky, the Bolshevist foreign minister, then published the "secret treaties" which had been made among the members of the Entente in earlier periods of the war. According to the "secret treaties" Russia was to acquire the Dardanelles, Constantinople, the west shore of the Bosphorus, and certain defined areas in Asia

Minor; Arabia was to be placed under an independent Mussulman government; Russia agreed to permit France and Great Britain to draw the western boundaries of Germany, and Russia was given a free hand to delimit the eastern frontiers of Germany; Italy, in return for joining the Entente, was to receive the Trentino, southern Tyrol, Trieste, Istria, and Dalmatia, to exercise a protectorate over Albania, to obtain certain concessions in Asia Minor, and to acquire additional holdings in Africa if France and Great Britain should increase their territorial possessions there; and Greece, if she should join the Allies, was to take part of Albania and some Turkish territory in Asia Minor. Trotsky stated that his purpose in publishing these documents was to disclose to the people of all nations the arrangements effected by "financiers and traders through their parliamentary and diplomatic agents." At the same time he warned Germany that "when the German proletariat by means of revolution secures access to their chancelleries they will find documents which will appear in no better light."

The publication of the secret treaties produced a deep impression on the Russian public and made it easier for the Bolshevist Government to open separate peace-negotiations with the Teutons. Early in December, Trotsky demanded of the Allies that they restate their war-aims within seven days. But the Allies, who had not recognized the Bolshevist Government and who were now doubly incensed at it because it had published the secret treaties and because it had already suspended hostilities along the Eastern front and encouraged the fraternization of Russian and German troops, paid no heed to Trotsky's ultimatum. Whereupon, the Bolshevist Government informed the Russian people that the Allies would not restate their aims because their aims were really "imperialistic" and that therefore Russia was fully justified in breaking with the Allies and in making immediately a separate peace with *Mittel-Europa*.

Following a conference at the army headquarters of Prince Leopold of Bavaria, at Brest-Litovsk, attended by representatives of Russia, Germany, Austria-Hungary, Turkey, and Bulgaria, an armistice between these Powers was signed on December 15, 1917, providing for a truce. The Germans bound themselves not to transfer troops from the Eastern to the Western Front.[1]

---

[1] This engagement was not observed by the Germans. It should be noted that Rumania, left in the lurch by the impending Russian defection, had agreed to a truce with the Central Powers, at Focsani, on December 9.

The Peace Conference itself was formally opened at Brest-Litovsk on Saturday, December 22, 1917. The Central Empires were represented by their respective foreign secretaries, Richard von Kühlmann of Germany, and Count Czernin of Austria-Hungary. Both these men were personally inclined to be ingratiating and even magnanimous, but Kühlmann was hopelessly dominated by von Ludendorff, the brusque military master of the Teutons, and Czernin dared not break with Kühlmann. In sharp contrast to the titled and pompous dignitaries who represented the might of *Mittel-Europa* were the obscure envoys of revolutionary Bolshevist Russia. The latter did everything they could to ruffle the dignity of the august assembly. They frankly disdained diplomacy and utilized the occasion for spreading Socialist propaganda.

At the opening session of the Peace Conference, the Russians made fifteen proposals as the bases of permanent peace : (1) evacuation of all Russian territory occupied by Germany, with autonomy for Poland and for the Lithuanian and Lettish provinces; (2) autonomy for Turkish Armenia; (3) settlement of the Alsace-Lorraine question by a free plebiscite; (4) restoration of Belgium and indemnity through an international fund for damages; (5) restoration of Serbia and Montenegro, with similar indemnities, Serbia gaining access to the Adriatic, and Bosnia-Herzegovina securing complete autonomy; (6) other contested Balkan territory to be temporarily autonomous, pending plebiscites; (7) restoration of Rumania, with autonomy for the Dobrudja, and with enforcement of the Berlin Convention of 1878 concerning equality of the Jews; (8) autonomy for the Italian population of Trent and Trieste, pending a plebiscite; (9) restoration of the German colonies; (10) restoration of Persia and Greece; (11) neutralization of all maritime straits leading to inland seas, including the canals of Suez and Panama, and prohibition of the torpedoing of merchant vessels in time of war; (12) no indemnities to be paid, and war requisitions to be returned; (13) economic boycotts after the war to be forbidden; (14) final, general peace to be negotiated at a congress composed of delegates chosen by the representative bodies of the several nations, all secret treaties being declared null and void; and (15) gradual disarmament on land and sea, and the substitution of militia for standing armies.

With many of these proposals the delegates of *Mittel-Europa* expressed their sympathy; but on the first they immediately made a significant reservation. They were willing, they said, to evacuate strictly Russian territory, but they must insist on their right to deal separately with Poland, Lithuania, Courland, and parts of Esthonia and Livonia.   In other words, they were resolved to make such disposition of conquered portions of the Russian Empire as was pleasing to themselves alone.

It soon became obvious that Teutonic policy aimed at detaching various lesser nationalities from Russian allegiance and constituting them semi-autonomous states dependent upon *Mittel-Europa*.   In this way, the federation of *Mittel-Europa* would be enormously extended eastward, and most valuable new resources of men, metals, and foodstuffs would be available to Germany for an indefinite prolongation of the Great War against the Powers of Western Europe and against the United States.   In this way, too, what remained of Russia could speedily be brought politically and economically into the orbit of Teutonic ambition.   It was a menace to the future independence of the whole Russian Empire; it was a most serious threat, moreover, against the Entente.

The disintegration of the Russian Empire into small republics was already making notable progress, thanks to the national chaos which accompanied and followed the Bolshevist revolution of November, 1917, and thanks also to constant German propaganda which adroitly abetted the separatist tendencies of the smaller nationalities within the Russian Empire.   The Rada, or parliament, of the Little Russians at Kiev proclaimed the independence of the "Ukrainian People's Republic" on November 20, and sent representatives to Brest-Litovsk.   The same important step was taken by Finland, which formally declared its independence as a republic on December 4, and was recognized by Denmark, Sweden, and Norway, as well as by the Central Empires.   Lithuanian freedom from Russia was proclaimed on December 11.   The Don Cossacks, representing a reactionary movement against the Bolsheviki, declared a separate republic with Rostov as its capital and with General Paul Kaledine as first president and prime-minister.   Separatist movements also developed in the Baltic Provinces of Courland, Livonia, and Esthonia, in the Caucasus, in Turkestan, among the Mussulmans and the Tartars, and in Siberia.

Taking advantage of a suspension of the Peace Conference, which had been voted in order to enable the Allies to participate if they should so desire, the Bolshevist Government conducted propaganda on its own account, with a view especially to inciting the German people against the "imperialistic aims" of the

Teutonic diplomatists at Brest-Litovsk. In an official statement, made public on January 2, the Executive Committee of the Soviets declared "that the Russian Revolution remains faithful to the policy of internationalism. We defend the right of Poland, Lithuania, and Courland (Latvia) to dispose of their own destiny actually and freely. Never will we recognize the justice of imposing the will of a foreign nation on any other nations whatsoever. . . . We say to the people of Germany, Austria-Hungary, Turkey, and Bulgaria : 'Under your pressure your Governments have been obliged to accept the motto of no annexations and no indemnities, but recently they have been trying to carry on their old policy of evasions. Remember, that the conclusion of an immediate democratic peace will depend actually and above all on you. All the people of Europe, exhausted and bled by such a war as there never was before, look to you and expect that you will *not permit the Austro-German imperialists to make war against revolutionary Russia for the subjection of Poland, Lithuania, Courland, and Armenia.'"

The Bolsheviki were doomed to double disappointment. On one hand they could not prevail upon the Allies to join them in peace-negotiations, the Entente statesmen contenting themselves with renewals of their solemn protests to Russia against a separate peace. On the other hand, far more significant, the German people seemed peculiarly impervious to Bolshevist propaganda; the only occasions on which the German people ever appeared to doubt the all-wise and all-good character of their Government were when their armies met sharp reverses, and now, with Russia crumbling into chaos, no amount of Russian propaganda could shake the faith of the German masses in the providential guidance of Kühlmann and Czernin. "Kamerad!" was shouted by the Teuton only when he was beaten; when he was successful, his motto was "Woe to the vanquished!"

Consequently when the Peace Conference was resumed at Brest-Litovsk on January 10, 1918, the Teutonic envoys categorically refused to accede to the Russian suggestion to transfer the negotiations to Stockholm or to agree to the evacuation of occupied Russian territories. At the same time they protested vehemently against the efforts of the Bolshevist leaders to appeal to the German people over the heads of the Government's accredited representatives. The result was an *impasse*. And on January 14, the parleys at Brest-Litovsk broke up, the armistice having been extended to February 12, but the conference itself adjourning without fixing a day for reassembling.

Fighting had already occurred in Ukrainia between partisans of the Bolsheviki and those of the so-called Ukrainian People's Republic. To the latter the Austro-Germans now gave their moral support. Despite the protests of Trotsky and Lenin, negotiations were continued throughout January between Germany, Austria-Hungary, Bulgaria, and Turkey, on one side, and Ukrainia, on the other, leading finally to the signature of a treaty on February 9, 1918, whereby southeastern Russia was constituted the free and independent republic of Ukrainia, comprising a territory of about 195,000 square miles and a population of about forty-five millions.

On the following day, Trotsky, the Bolshevist foreign minister, served notice on all the Powers that Russia, though unable to sign a treaty of peace with Germany, was henceforth definitively out of the war. Not at peace — not at war — such was the remarkable import of the Russian declaration of February 10, 1918:

"The peace negotiations are at an end. The German capitalists, bankers, and landlords, supported by the silent coöperation of the English and French bourgeoisie, submitted to our comrades, members of the peace delegations at Brest-Litovsk, conditions such as could not be subscribed to by the Russian Revolution.

"The Governments of Germany and Austria are in possession of countries and peoples vanquished by force of arms. To this authority the Russian people, workmen and peasants, could not give its acquiescence. We could not sign a peace which would bring with it sadness, oppression, and suffering to millions of workmen and peasants.

"But we also cannot, will not, and must not continue a war begun by tsars and capitalists in alliance with tsars and capitalists. We will not and we must not continue to be at war with the Germans and Austrians — workmen and peasants like ourselves.

"We are not signing a peace of landlords and capitalists. Let the German and Austrian soldiers know who are placing them in the field of battle and let them know for what they are struggling. Let them know also that we refuse to fight against them.

"Our delegation, fully conscious of its responsibility before the Russian people and the oppressed workers and peasants of other countries, declared on February 10, in the name of the Council of the People's Commissioners of the Government of the Federal Russian Republic to the Governments of the peoples

s

involved in the war with us and of the neutral countries, that it refused to sign an annexationist treaty. Russia, for its part, declares the present war with Germany and Austria-Hungary, Turkey, and Bulgaria, at an end.

"Simultaneously, the Russian troops received an order for complete demobilization on all fronts."

This "no war, no peace" declaration of the Petrograd Government was received in Germany with jeers. Obviously the armistice was ended, but not the war. What the Teuton envoys had failed to achieve at Brest-Litovsk, could certainly be achieved by a spectacular military thrust against disorganized and demobilized Russia. So on February 18, the German armies on the Eastern Front were again set in motion. Rapidly they advanced, capturing within a fortnight 7000 Russian officers, 57,000 men, 5000 machine guns, and enormous quantities of munitions and supplies. Reval, Dorpat, and Narva were occupied; also Pskov, Polotzk, and Borissoff; Kiev, the capital of Ukrainia, was in German possession, as was almost all of Russia lying west of a line drawn from Narva on the Gulf of Finland, seventy miles west of Petrograd, to south of Kiev. There were now under German domination the provinces of Russian Poland, Lithuania, Courland, Esthonia, and Livonia, and a large part of Ukrainia; the islands in the Gulf of Finland were later occupied.

On February 24, the Germans, through Foreign Secretary Kühlmann, announced their readiness to make a new offer of peace, involving new and more drastic terms than the previous offer, and added the condition that this offer must be accepted within forty-eight hours. Premier Lenin, in urging the Executive Committee of the Soviets to accept the new peace terms, said, "Their knees are on our chest, and our position is hopeless. . . . This peace must be accepted as a respite enabling us to prepare a decisive resistance to the bourgeoisie and imperialists. The proletariat of the whole world will come to our aid. Then we shall renew the fight." The Soviet Committee accepted the German terms on the following day, by a vote of 112 to 84, with 22 abstentions, and peace negotiations were resumed at Brest-Litovsk. All the Russian envoys could do was to protest against Teutonic injustice — and this they did solemnly and vigorously.

The Treaty of Brest-Litovsk, signed on March 3, 1918, reduced the huge Russian Empire practically to the size of the medieval Grand Duchy of Muscovy. The Bolsheviki promised to evacuate Ukrainia, Esthonia, Livonia, Finland, and the Åland islands, and to surrender the districts of Erivan, Kars, and Batum to the Turks. All Bolshevist propaganda was to be discontinued in *Mittel-Europa* and in the newly ceded territories. The unfavorable Russo-German commercial treaty of 1904 was revived. By these terms Russia lost a fourth of her population, of her arable land, and of her railway system, a third of her manufacturing industries, and three-fourths of her total iron production and of her coal-fields. Russia was humbled in the dust, but she was at "peace."

Rumania, completely isolated by the collapse and defection of Russia, felt obliged to sign a peace-treaty with the four Powers of *Mittel-Europa*, at Bucharest, on March 7. By this humiliating Treaty of Bucharest,[1] Rumania agreed to give up all Dobrudja, the Petroseny coal basin, and the Carpathian passes, and to promote Austro-German trade through Moldavia and Bessarabia to Odessa on the Black Sea. Subsequently the Central Empires consented to the incorporation of Bessarabia into Rumania, which had been voted by a Bessarabian council on March 27.

On March 7, a peace-treaty was concluded between Finland and Germany, whereby the latter recognized the independence of the former.[2] A week later the German landlords of Courland, meeting at Mittau, were inspired to petition for a union of the "freed" Baltic Provinces under the crown of the "House of Hohenzollern"; and the emotional William II, stirred to his very heart-depths, wired "God's blessing on your land, upon which German fidelity, German courage, and German perseverance have made their impress." Everything seemed to be progressing as auspiciously for Germany as unhappily for Russia. Intrigues were being steadily prosecuted to secure scions of princely German families as popular candidates for the new thrones which had been rendered desirable and needful by Teutonic military prowess in the East — in Finland, in the Baltic Provinces, in Lithuania, in Ukrainia, and in Poland. What a mighty *Mittel-Europa* was in process of construction! Against the treaties of Brest-Litovsk and Bucharest, the Governments of Great Britain, France, and Italy formally protested on March 18, 1918.

The defection of Russia from the cause of the democratic

---

[1] This treaty was ratified by the German *Bundesrat* on June 4, by the Rumanian Chamber on June 28, and by the Rumanian Senate on July 4.

[2] A treaty of amity between the "Finnish Social Republic of Workmen" and the "Russian Federal Soviet Republic" had been signed on March 1, 1918. Peace between Finland and Austria-Hungary was concluded at Vienna on May 29.

Entente Allies should not be blamed upon the Revolution or even upon the mischievous and short-sighted Bolsheviki so much as upon the old tsardom whose tyranny and corruption had made revolution necessary and temporary excessive radicalism natural. For the time being, the defection of Russia was certainly a source of bitter disappointment to France, Great Britain, Italy, and the United States; and the formal repudiation of the Russian foreign debt in February, 1918, served to accentuate the bitterness felt in Allied countries. Yet the Russians themselves were doomed to suffer more and worse from the Bolshevist régime than were any foreign peoples. And, as events were to prove, entry of the United States into the Great War in 1917 was ample compensation to the Allies for the disintegration and defection of Russia.

CHAPTER XII

THE ALLIES PAVE THE WAY FOR ULTIMATE VICTORY

ALLIED PLANS AND PROSPECTS IN 1917

THE Great War entered a peculiarly critical stage in 1917. In the preceding year the Teutons and the Allies had failed in turn to obtain military decisions. On the one hand, the Allies had been unable to recover any appreciable portion of territories formerly lost to them or to prevent the humiliation and subjugation of Rumania. On the other hand, the Teutons had failed to capture Verdun or Vicenza, or to weaken the hostile resolution of any of the Great Powers arrayed against them. It was obvious that the Great War was a tremendous endurance-test; and, as had been pointed out repeatedly, such an endurance-test was less promising, in the long run, to the Teutons than to the Allies.

Early in 1917, however, the resumption of unrestricted submarine warfare by Germany and the resulting entrance of the United States into the war on the side of the Allies served to emphasize one aspect of the endurance-test to the exclusion of others. The question then was whether the United States Government, in the face of the threat of the wholesale destruction and paralysis of Allied shipping by German submarines, would and could transport sufficient troops and supplies to Europe to tip the balance of military power in favor of the Entente. As we have already seen, this question was in a fair way toward an answer by the second half of 1917: ruthless submarine warfare, though terribly destructive in the first half of the year and still menacing, was now distinctly on the decline; American foodstuffs, munitions, and other *matériel* were flowing in streams to Britain, France, and Italy; and it was apparent that a large American Expeditionary Force, well trained and well equipped, would be ready to take the field in 1918 alongside the seasoned veterans of the Allies. The unrestricted submarine warfare of the Germans was not accomplishing its purpose, and this aspect of the great endurance-test between the Allies and the Central Empires was becoming monthly more favorable to the former and less advantageous to the latter. If only Russia could continue to press against the extended Austro-German lines from the Sereth to the Baltic, while the French and British forced offensives on the Western Front, and the Italians on the Isonzo and the Carso, and General Sarrail's motley hosts in Macedonia, it would be but a question of time when *Mittel-Europa* must break and crumble.

But the situation in 1917 was not so simple. For at the very time when the Great War appeared to assume the character of a speed-contest between German preparations for ruthless warfare on the high seas and American preparations for large-scale campaigning on the Continent of Europe, one of the Great Entente Powers — Russia — began to revolt and to upset many Allied calculations. The Russian Revolution introduced a new and important element of uncertainty into the endurance-test which the Great War had become.

In its earliest phases the Russian Revolution seemed to be an asset to the Allied cause. The destruction of autocracy in Russia was acclaimed in Paris, in London, in Rome, and in Washington, as putting an end once for all to dangerous intrigues between the courts of Petrograd and Berlin, as removing a too well-merited reproach of Teutonic sympathizers and apologists, and as completing the alignment of democratic nations against the oligarchial and militaristic states of *Mittel-Europa*. Thereby the political stakes of the Great War were clarified and point was given to President Wilson's celebrated phrase that the aim of the Allies was "to make the world safe for democracy."

If any confirmation were needed of the new democratic enthusiasm which overspread all the Entente Powers, it was provided by a radical electoral reform in Great Britain, the bill for which, introduced in the House of Commons on May 15, 1917, and passed in December, provided for the equal, direct suffrage of all adult males and of most adult females. Great Britain not only was adopting thoroughgoing democracy in the old sense but was playing the rôle of pioneer among the Great Powers of the world in the grant of the parliamentary franchise to women. Moreover, Lloyd George, the British premier, announced in May, 1917, that his Government was prepared to recognize the national aspirations of Ireland by offering to the Irish people a choice between the acceptance of immediate home rule for all parts of the island, except the six counties of Ulster, and the convocation of a constituent assembly which should represent all factions and all faiths. The Irish Nationalists chose the latter; and from July to December, 1917, an Irish Convention was in session endeavoring to draft a constitution for the country.[1]

High hopes were aroused in the Entente countries that the Russian Revolution would occasion serious internal disorders in the Central Empires. And events in the spring and summer of 1917 did not altogether belie these hopes. Austria-Hungary was already in ferment, and the democratic and nationalistic revolutions elsewhere brought into bold relief the glaring political inequalities in the Dual Monarchy. In Austria itself, it should be remembered, some ten million Germans dominated some eighteen million Slavs — Czechs, Poles, Ruthenians (Ukrainians), and Jugoslavs (Slovenes, Croats, and Serbs), — while in Hungary some ten million Magyars tyrannized over some ten million Rumans, Slovaks, and Jugoslavs. Only the Germans of Austria and the Magyars of Hungary accepted loyally the Prussian hegemony in *Mittel-Europa*, and these dominant minority elements encountered ever greater difficulties in dealing with the majority nationalities subject to them. There were frequent conspiracies and executions of civilians, and mutinies of troops. The Czechs of Austria and the Slovaks of Hungary — constituting in reality the single Czechoslovak nationality — were on the verge of armed rebellion. The Slovenes, Croats, and Serbs were becoming more conscious of their community of race and interest with the peoples of Serbia and Montenegro and were agitating in favor of separation from Austria and Hungary and creation of an autonomous Jugoslavia. The Rumans of Hungarian Transylvania were advocating union with the kingdom of Rumania, and the Poles of Austrian Galicia were demanding union with a free and independent Poland. The Ruthenians of eastern Galicia, affected by the establishment of an autonomous Ukrainia by their kinsfolk in Russia, were hostile alike to the Poles and to the German Austrians. The hodge-podge of nationalities within the Dual Monarchy raised problems perplexing enough at any time, but now, in the face of the Russian Revolution, doubly perplexing.

The Emperor Charles, who had succeeded the aged Francis Joseph in November, 1916, was reputed to be sincerely desirous of undertaking a radical reformation of his ramshackle dominions. It was gossiped that he planned to transform the Dual

---

[1] The Report of the Irish Convention was published in April, 1918, but was not acted upon by the British Government. See below, pp. 310-312.

Monarchy into a Quintuple Monarchy of which the constituent states would be Austria, Hungary, Jugoslavia, Czechoslovakia, and Poland. At any rate he had intrusted the important posts of Austrian premier [1] and minister of foreign affairs in December, 1916, respectively to Count Clam-Martinitz and to Count Ottokar Czernin, two Germanized Czechs, who intrigued delicately and spoke many fair words. But the task was too arduous for Czernin, Clam-Martinitz, or Charles. Any concession to Czechs or Poles angered the Germans, and any strengthening of the dominant position of the Germans exasperated the subject nationalities.

So long as an overwhelming majority of Austrian subjects were bitterly hostile to the existing political régime, democracy could exist in Austria only in name; and it was a notorious fact that the Austrian parliament — the *Reichsrat* — had not been convoked since the outbreak of the Great War in July, 1914. Now, however, after the Russian Revolution, the Emperor and his ministers had to prove at home and abroad that Austria was democratic in fact as well as in theory; and thus it happened that the *Reichsrat*, after a vacation of three years, was convened in Vienna in May, 1917. No sooner had the *Reichsrat* met than the Czech and the Jugoslav deputies demanded the abolition of the dual system and the grant of independence and unity to their respective nations. Unable to coerce or cajole these deputies, Clam-Martinitz turned his attention to the Poles. If the Polish deputies could be prevailed upon to support him, they with the German Austrians would constitute a majority of the *Reichsrat* capable of demonstrating the regularity and orderliness of democratic government in Austria. But the Poles claimed more favors than Clam-Martinitz could grant and still retain the confidence of the German Austrians. To the Polish demand for a united, independent Poland, including Galicia and access to the Baltic, Clam-Martinitz ventured to give only rambling and non-committal answers; and on June 16, 1917, the Polish deputies resolved to join the Czechs and Jugoslavs in voting against the budget. At the same time the National Council of the Czechs prepared and issued a formal indictment of the Habsburg Monarchy, accusing it of having brought on the war without the consent of the Czech deputies

---

[1] The Austrian premier since 1911, Count Karl Stürgkh, had been assassinated on October 21, 1916, by a Socialist editor. From October to December, a stop-gap ministry had been presided over by Ernst von Koerber, a zealous Pan-German, who had been finance minister of the Dual Monarchy since February, 1915.

or of the Czech nation, of having shot Czech soldiers in masses, interned hundreds of Czech civilians, and condemned Czech deputies to death or imprisonment, of having suppressed or gagged the Czech press, of having involved the Czech communities in ruin, and of having "spent more than sixty billions on a criminal war." Furthermore, on July 20, 1917, the head of the Jugoslav party, Dr. Anton Trumbitch, signed with Nikola Pashitch, the premier of Serbia, the famous Declaration of Corfu, whereby it was agreed to constitute an independent, unified state of the five million Serbs of Serbia and Montenegro and the seven million Jugoslav (Serb, Croat, and Slovene) subjects of Austria-Hungary; in the proposed state all religions would be on an equal footing, the Gregorian calendar would be adopted, and suffrage would be universal, secret, equal, and direct.

Uncomfortably oppressed by the sensation of an ominous rumbling that might betoken the nearness of earthquake and volcanic eruptions, Count Clam-Martinitz retired from the Austrian premiership late in June as gracefully as the circumstances would warrant. Dr. von Seidler, a typical bureaucrat, then formed a stop-gap ministry, dissolved the *Reichsrat*, and awaited developments.

Superficially the situation in Hungary was less critical. Count Tisza, who had been in office since 1913 and had had a hand in precipitating the Great War, was forced out of the premiership, it is true, in May, 1917, but he was forced out by fellow-Magyar aristocrats rather than by non-Magyar nationalists. And so accustomed to domination were the titled Magyars that they experienced no serious difficulty in refusing popular demands for much-needed constitutional reform and in exalting one of their own number, Count Julius Andrassy, to succeed Count Tisza.

Nevertheless, below the surface, there was seething discontent in Hungary. And Austria, as we have seen, was on the verge of revolution. Instinctively the Emperor Charles and Count Czernin, his suave foreign minister, felt that the Dual Monarchy could be saved and its complicated nationalistic problems safely dealt with, not by indefinite prolongation of the war, but by speedy conclusion of peace. The result was that throughout the spring and summer of 1917 Czernin and Charles were intriguing with the Allies, especially with France, for the termination of the war. Charles went so far as to state to the French Government through a confidential intermediary, — his cousin,

Prince Sixtus of Bourbon, — that Austria-Hungary would support "France's just claim relative to Alsace-Lorraine." [1]

That Austria-Hungary was longing ardently for peace and was weakening in her attachment to Germany was no secret in the midsummer of 1917. And so long as there was open to the Allies the prospect of detaching the Dual Monarchy from *Mittel-Europa*, British and French diplomatists evinced a remarkable charity and kindliness toward the Habsburg Estate. The United States, though at war with Germany since April, 1917, did not declare war against Austria-Hungary until the following December.

The Russian Revolution occasioned political crises not only in Austria-Hungary, but also in Germany; and any event which divided German counsels and weakened German morale was of obvious advantage to the Allies, for Germany was the brain and sinew of *Mittel-Europa*. In January, 1917, before the upheaval in Russia, the German Chancellor, Bethmann-Hollweg, had seemingly won the enthusiastic approbation of the bulk of the German people in espousing the Pan-German policy of ruthless submarine warfare. But as time went on and the Russian Colossus was perceived to have feet of clay and the submarine warfare did not bring a speedy suit for peace from the Allies, a growing reaction against Bethmann-Hollweg and his Government was observable in Germany. With the Great War about to enter upon its fourth year, even the most militaristic nation could not wholly escape the general war weariness which affected all the other belligerents. In particular, there were political groups in Germany, such as the Socialists, the Catholic Centrists, the Radicals (Progressives), and the Poles, which had always been by tradition and circumstance hostile to the imperial régime, and which, though supporting the Emperor and his Chancellor so long as autocratic Russia made common cause with democratic France in arms against the integrity of the Fatherland, were now prepared to qualify their support.

These Moderates in Germany were affected not only by the Russian Revolution directly, which removed an important part of the "Slavic Peril," but also by the papal appeals for peace, by the troubles and tribulations then brewing in Austria-Hungary, by the eloquent appeals of President Wilson to the German people against the German autocracy, and by the plain talking

[1] The exposure of this Austrian duplicity in April, 1918, led to the resignation of Count Czernin, and to the restoration of Baron Burian to the Austro-Hungarian ministry of foreign affairs, which had been held by him from January, 1915, to December, 1916.

of foreign Socialists to Scheidemann and other German Socialist leaders at an international conference in Stockholm in June. In vain did Bethmann-Hollweg endeavor to conciliate the Centrists and Poles by securing the repeal of the law against the Jesuits and of the law forbidding the use of any language other than German at public meetings. Such liberal sops did not satisfy the real hunger of German liberals.

On July 6, 1917, a serious crisis was precipitated in Germany by Mathias Erzberger, a conspicuous leader of the left wing of the Catholic Center Party, who in a speech before the Main Committee of the Reichstag assailed the Government with the utmost candor and vehemence, criticising the conduct of the war, especially the use of the submarines, and demanding radical reforms in both domestic and foreign policy and a declaration in favor of peace according to the formula of revolutionary Russia — without annexations or indemnities. Straightway the Centrists, Socialists, Radicals, and a sprinkling of National Liberals formed an anti-Government *bloc*, comprising a large majority of the total membership of the Reichstag and pledged to uphold democratic amendment of the Prussian Constitution, introduction of parliamentary government in the Empire, and a declaration of war aims on lines laid down by Erzberger.

To accept the demands of the new *bloc* meant the alienation of all the Conservatives and of a majority of the National Liberals from the Government, and this meant a signal reverse for the war party and perhaps an open confession of national defeat. Bethmann-Hollweg, who had been chancellor continuously since 1909 and as such had played a most significant part in preparing for the present war, in precipitating it, and in assuming responsibility for its conduct, could not bring himself to coöperate with the *bloc;* after a week's disorder in the Reichstag, Emperor William II received and accepted, on July 14, 1917, the resignation of Bethmann-Hollweg.

Five days later the unruly Reichstag, against the strenuous protests of Tirpitz, Reventlow, and all other fiery pan-Germans, passed by a majority of more than one hundred a remarkable peace resolution, that the object of the war was solely to defend the liberty, independence, and territorial integrity of Germany, that the Reichstag championed peace and understanding between the belligerents, and that annexations and political and economic oppression were contrary to such a peace. Thereby did a large majority of the duly elected representatives of the German nation put themselves squarely on record as opposed to the war aims of the Kaiser, the militarists, the Junkers, and the industrial magnates.

So used was the Reichstag, however, to limiting itself to words, that in this crisis it had no single opinion as to what legal methods it should employ to give effect to its resolution and no courage to transcend the constitution and proclaim a revolution.   Fearful of their own vocal audacity, the leaders of the *bloc* hesitated to invoke violence, and in hesitating they were lost.   The Emperor took no notice of the peace resolution and calmly ignored the Reichstag in appointing Dr. George Michaelis as successor to Bethmann-Hollweg.

Michaelis was a typical Prussian bureaucrat, sixty years old, docile, and safe, of Conservative sentiments and sympathies, who was known to the public almost exclusively by his recent record as a fairly competent Food Administrator.   Under Chancellor Michaelis, Helfferich became vice chancellor and minister of the interior, and Kühlmann succeeded Zimmermann as foreign minister.   Michaelis was no intellectual giant, but he was clever enough to befool the credulous *bloc* leaders in the Reichstag. He declared himself ready to accept the peace resolution of July 19, "as he understood it," announced that he would take matters of political reform "under consideration," and sent the Reichstag home with a benediction.

Throughout August and September, Michaelis with the aid of the more adroit Kühlmann continued openly to profess his love for peace while stealthily he abetted the propaganda actively conducted by Pan-Germans in favor of the repudiation of the Reichstag's peace resolution.   It was hard for Michaelis, bungler as he was, to labor for a German victory through peace, when the simpler and more straightforward Conservatives could only think of peace through a German victory.   When, in October, the Reichstag reassembled, it was in an electrical atmosphere. The submarine warfare was failing.   There were grave disorders, even mutinies, in the fleet.   The Independent Socialists were growing more troublesome.   The Conservatives and National Liberals were annoyed that the Chancellor did not break completely with the Reichstag.   The Centrists, Socialists, and Radicals were furious that the Chancellor should give only lip-service to their program of reform and their declaration of war aims.

Delay on the part of the Reichstag in voting war credits and attacks of the *bloc* leaders upon the Chancellor for his blunders and shiftiness were sufficient to precipitate a second political crisis in Germany. On October 21, 1917, Michaelis resigned; and ten days later — the four hundredth anniversary of the posting of Luther's theses upon the church-door at Wittenberg — the Emperor designated as chancellor and minister-president of Prussia the Catholic leader Count Hertling. Count Hertling, a Bavarian by birth and latterly premier of his native state, had spent most of his seventy-four years as professor at Bonn; he was a prominent member of the Center Party, a devout Catholic, a profound student of philosophy, and a skillful parliamentarian. His advent to the highest civil office in the Empire and in Prussia was hailed at first as a signal triumph for the Reichstag *bloc* and as a happy augury of a democratic reaction in Germany against militaristic autocracy. Hertling's program, elaborated in conference with the party leaders in the Reichstag, included promises to carry out sweeping electoral reforms in Prussia, to abolish or relax the political censorship and the state of siege, and to direct peace negotiations in harmony with the resolution of July.

Only a week after Hertling's elevation to a leading position in Germany occurred the Bolshevist Revolution in Russia (November 7, 1917), which definitely deprived the Entente of one of its most important members and at the same time put a stop, at least temporarily, to the popular unrest and disquiet in Germany and in Austria-Hungary. The Allies soon received full confirmation of their fears that the Russian Revolution, as it progressed, was becoming a liability, rather than an asset, to their cause. Bolshevist Russia was concluding first an armistice and then a separate peace with the Central Empires. Rumania, left isolated and defenseless, was obliged to surrender. The Teutons were organizing a series of dependent states out of the wreckage in eastern Europe — a Finland, a Lettland (Latvia), a Lithuania, a Poland, and a Ukrainia. On all of these states as well as on what remained of Russia, *Mittel-Europa* was strengthening her political and economic hold. She was preparing to draw from them vast stores of foodstuffs and war *matériel*. She would be able before long to do away entirely with her Eastern Front and to bring all her fighting strength to bear on France, on Italy, and on Salonica. No wonder that Dr. Seidler, the Austrian premier who had taken office in June in fear and trembling, breathed quite easily in December. No wonder that Count Hertling, the German Chancellor who had appeared in October as a harbinger of democracy and early peace, was transformed by the rapid course of events into an exponent of domestic conservation and foreign annexation. The immediate prospects of *Mittel-Europa* were too alluring to a Seidler and a Hertling. They were compelling to a Czernin and a Kühlmann. They were satisfying even to the Teutonic military chieftains — to Hindenburg, Ludendorff, and Mackensen. The sceptical Emperor Charles was silenced, and the grandiloquent Emperor William burst forth in hysterical pæans to the Almighty.

Still the Allies had no reason to despair of ultimate victory. With the Russian autocracy gone, their cause was now unquestionably the cause of democracy and civilization, and as such it had a popular appeal infinitely more enthusiastic than that of *Mittel-Europa*. Even with the defection of all Russia from the alliance of free nations, the Entente was superior to the Central Empires in man-power and in munitions and supplies Besides, the political and economic conditions in Bolshevist Russia were so chaotic that the Teutons could not hope to organize and utilize its natural resources in the near future; and in the meantime the full strength of the United States would be available to the Allies. Moreover, the dependent states on which the Teutons had counted for grateful and timely assistance soon displayed signs of putting their own welfare above that of *Mittel-Europa*, and some of them, notably Poland and Ukrainia, fell to quarreling violently with each other, to the scandal and chagrin of Vienna and Berlin. At the worst for the Allies, the Russian Revolution merely injected a new element into the endurance-test which the Great War had become; it simply postponed the ultimate victory of the Allies.

Less and less throughout the year 1917 did the purpose of the Allies appear to be merely the chastisement of Germany and the parceling out of conquered territories; more and more it became the fashioning of a league of free nations which should preserve a peace of justice and put an end to anarchy — to the rule of force — in international relations. More and more the whole world awoke to an understanding of the real stakes of the Great War, and nation after nation entered the struggle on the side of the Allies. The four Powers of *Mittel-Europa* — Germany, Austria-Hungary, Turkey, and Bulgaria — remained alone in 1917 as they had in 1915. On the other hand, the Entente, though suffering the defection of Russia and of Rumania in 1917, could now count not only upon the former members — France, Great Britain, Italy, Japan, Belgium, Serbia, Montenegro, and Portugal, — but also upon a considerable number of fresh associates. The United States joined the Allies in April, speedily followed by Cuba and Panama. China severed diplomatic relations with Germany on March 14; and then after the suppression of a royalist uprising, the reconstructed republican government under President Feng Kwo-Cheng declared war on the Central Empires on August 14. Brazil, after severing diplomatic relations in April, formally went to war with Germany on October 26. Siam declared war on the Central Empires on July 22. Liberia declared war on Germany on August 4. Greece, as we shall see in a subsequent section of this chapter, united with the Allies on July 2.

Several states showed clearly their sympathies in the struggle by severing diplomatic relations with Germany, though they did not formally declare war. Such were Bolivia, Costa Rica, Ecuador, Guatemala, Haiti, Honduras, Nicaragua, Peru, Santo Domingo, and Uruguay.[1] Feeling ran high in Argentina against the German submarine ruthlessness, especially when it became known that Count Luxburg, the German chargé at Buenos Aires, had telegraphed his government in May that if Argentine vessels were destroyed, it should be done "without a trace being left" ("spurlos versenkt"); and only a profuse apology from Germany and a formal promise not to sink any more Argentine ships, together with an unpopular insistence on the part of the Argentine president, kept Argentina out of the war. Altogether, at the close of 1918, approximately half the sovereign states of the world (and these by far the richest and most populous) were banded together in a sort of league against the four Powers of Germanized *Mittel-Europa*.

The better to coördinate their military operations, the prime ministers and chiefs of staff of France, Great Britain, and Italy conferred at Rapallo on November 9, 1917, and agreed to create a Supreme War Council, the organization and functions of which were set forth as follows: "The Supreme War Council is composed of the prime minister and one other member of the government of each of the Great Powers whose armies are fighting on the Western Front; it is to supervise the general conduct of the war; it prepares recommendations for the consideration of the governments and keeps itself informed of their execution and reports thereon to the several governments." The first act of the Supreme War Council was the appointment of an Inter-

---

[1] Subsequently, in 1918, Costa Rica (May 23), Guatemala (April 22), Haiti (July 15), Honduras (July 19), and Nicaragua (May 24) declared war against Germany.

Allied General Staff, consisting of Generals Foch (France), Wilson (Great Britain), and Cadorna (Italy). Early in December an Inter-Allied Naval Board was created by the Supreme War Council. It was obvious that at last the Allies were becoming convinced of the imperative need of unity of counsel and unity of action.

At the end of November, 1917, the long deferred Allied Conference met at Paris. Delegates were present from France, Great Britain, Italy, the United States, and all the other allied and associated states, except Russia, which was then in the midst of negotiations with Germany for an armistice. No detailed statement was made of the plans formulated, but it was indicated that satisfactory agreements had been reached whereby a unified and vigorous prosecution of the war was made possible.

Allied prospects should have seemed bright. Russia, it is true, was deserting the Allies, but the United States was coming to take Russia's place. The ruthless submarine warfare was weakening. There were signs of unrest and discomfort within the Central Empires. The Allies were clarifying their war-aims, husbanding their resources, and effecting a unity of purposes and methods. As we shall discover in the next two sections of this chapter, the Allies in 1917 were likewise gaining noteworthy advantages in the fighting on the Western Front and were recovering much of their prestige in the Near East.

THE LESSON OF THE HINDENBURG LINE

On the Western Front the year 1917 marked the first significant retirement of the Germans since the battle of the Marne in 1914, and it also marked noteworthy progress in the war of attrition. The Anglo-French offensive on the Somme in the autumn of 1916 had failed to reach its chief objectives, — the towns of Bapaume and Péronne, — but it had caused the enemy many casualties and had badly dented his line; it had created an awkward salient for him between Arras and Saillisel and an even greater salient hardly less difficult between Arras and the Aisne. Continued pressure of the British in the valley of the Ancre throughout January and February of 1917, increased the awkwardness of the smaller German salient and endangered Bapaume.

Early in March, 1917, it became apparent that the German General Staff was planning to evacuate not only the salient between Arras and Saillisel but the larger salient between Arras and the Aisne. For some time Field Marshal von Hindenburg, the German Chief of Staff, had been directing the preparation of an exceptionally strong defense system of trenches, officially styled the "Siegfried Line" but subsequently called by the Allies the "Hindenburg Line," branching off from the old position near Arras and thence running in a relatively straight line southeastward through Quéant and west of Cambrai, St. Quentin, and La Fère, to the heights of the Aisne. Hindenburg employed the same methods of defense during his general withdrawal to the Siegfried Line as had been developed in the smaller retirement from the Ancre valley. Machine-gun units were placed

THE WESTERN FRONT NEAR ARRAS AND ON THE AISNE

in selected strategic positions to delay the advance of the British and French, while the bulk of the German soldiers, stealthily quitting their former trenches, transported guns and ammunition to the rear and systematically devastated the territory covered by their retreat.

When the British discovered on March 15 that a general withdrawal was being carried out by the Germans, General Sir Douglas Haig gave orders for an immediate advance of his forces along the whole line from Arras to Roye. Simultaneously, the French under General Nivelle began to advance on the front from Roye to Rheims. Chaulnes and Bapaume fell to the British on March 17, and Péronne and Mont St. Quentin were occupied the next day. At the same time the French entered Noyon, and speedily reached Tergnier, a town less than two miles from La Fère.

The reasons given for this German withdrawal in March, 1917, were many and varied. Reports from Berlin represented it as a strategical retreat intended to shorten the German line, to

T

draw the Allies out into the open so that they could be defeated in pitched battles, and to nullify the vast preparations which the French and British had been making for a smashing offensive in the summer of 1917. On the other hand, Allied authorities insisted that the withdrawal had been forced upon the Germans and was in no way voluntary; they pointed out that previous Anglo-French gains in the valleys of the Somme and Ancre had threatened the entire Noyon salient to such an extent that further gains would have caused a gigantic German disaster. At any rate the outstanding undisputed effects of the German retirement were, first, that the Germans now stood on a shortened line of great, perhaps impregnable, strength, and secondly, that the Allies had recovered more than a thousand square miles of French territory, including nearly four hundred towns with a population, before the war, of approximately 200,000.

The territory abandoned by the Germans was a scene of horrible desolation. Wanton destruction was visible everywhere. Of the acts of barbarism and devastation committed by the retreating Teutons with calculated cunning, only a faint notion can be given. As the official note of the French Government on the subject stated: "No motive of military necessity can justify the systematic ruin of public monuments, artistic and historical, and of public property, accompanied as it is by violence against civilians. Cities and villages in their entirety have been pillaged, burned, and destroyed utterly; private homes have been stripped of all furniture, which the enemy has carried off; fruit trees have been torn up or blasted; streams and wells have been polluted. The inhabitants, comparatively few in number, who have not been removed, have been left with a minimum of rations, while the enemy has seized stocks supplied by the neutral food commission for the sustenance of the civil population. . . . This concerns not acts designed to hinder the operations of our armies but sheer devastation having for its sole purpose the ruin for years to come of one of the most fertile regions of France. The civilized world can only revolt against this conduct on the part of a nation which wished to impose its *Kultur* on all mankind, but which now reveals itself once again as very close to barbarism and which, in a rage of disappointed ambition, tramples on the most sacred rights of humanity."

By April, 1917, the Germans were standing on the famous Hindenburg Line. They were certain that they could ward off frontal attacks against it, so splendid were both its natural and its artificial defenses, but they were not so sure of the pivots upon which it rested. These pivots were the positions about Arras in the north, and those in the south around Laon. It was near Arras and Laon that Generals Haig and Nivelle were already aiming offensives respectively of the British and of the French.

The Battle of Arras was opened Easter Monday (April 9) on a front approximately forty-five miles long with Lens, the coal city, as the British objective at one end, and with Quéant, an important point in the Hindenburg Line, as their objective at the other end. If these immediate objectives were taken, the way might then be open to the important cities of Douai and Cambrai. At first the British offensive went like clock-work. Aircraft, artillery, infantry, and tanks worked in perfect combination. Within three days Vimy Ridge and some two miles of the northern end of the Hindenburg Line had been carried and 12,000 prisoners and 150 guns had been captured. Quéant was not yet reached, but Lens was inclosed in a dangerous "pocket."

On April 16, exactly a week after the beginning of the British offensive in the vicinity of Arras, the French under General Nivelle inaugurated the second battle of the Aisne by assailing the southern pivot of the Hindenburg Line near Laon. Nivelle's rapid rise in the French army from the rank of colonel in September, 1914, to that of generalissimo, succeeding Marshal Joffre,

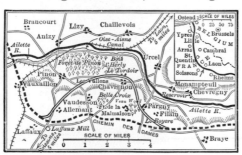

THE HEIGHTS OF THE AISNE

in December, 1916, had gone to his head. He had scant patience with the tactics which the Allies had developed during the past year on the Western Front — the advance by steady stages to limited objectives and the gradual defeat of the Germans through wastage of their man-power rather than by means of decisive engagements. Nivelle's aim was the "decisive blow" — not to weaken but to crush, not to "wear down" but to "break through." With superb self-confidence he gathered his armies for a supreme effort. He would force the heights of the Aisne in one bold assault from west, south, and southeast; he would simultaneously carry the Rheims heights from the north; and at the same moment he would launch his main offensive through the gap between the two into the plain of Laon. It was by far the most ambitious attack planned in the West since the battle of the Marne, and the divisions employed were three times those used by Haig at Arras.

Valorously the French fought, and some progress they made. They won all the banks of the Aisne from Soissons to Berry-au-Bac and all the spurs of the Aisne heights, and they captured 21,000 prisoners and 175 guns. But the main German positions were too strong and too stubbornly defended to be taken by open, spectacular assault; they firmly barred the way to Laon. The major strategy of Nivelle failed completely.

The result was a pronounced popular reaction in France against the audacious methods of Nivelle in favor of the more cautious tactics previously exemplified by Pétain and Foch. On April 28, the premier, Alexandre Ribot, and Paul Painlevé, who had recently succeeded General Lyautey as war minister, conferred with Nivelle; and two days later it was announced that the post of Chief of the General Staff at the Ministry of War had been revived, and that Pétain had been appointed to fill it. This announcement proved to be only a precursor to a more drastic change, for on May 15 Pétain formally succeeded Nivelle as commander-in-chief of the French armies in France while General Foch became Chief of Staff in Paris.

Thus the French Government logically applied a fundamental lesson learned in the battle of the Aisne. Foch and Pétain were just the men to comprehend that the Hindenburg Line could not be "broken through" or turned on its pivots and that their function was less to recover square miles of desolated territory than to wear down the man-power of the Germans by cautious but incessant offensives. With Pétain and Foch the Allied strategy on the Western Front returned to the patient, laborious, and deadly methods which had been practiced on the Somme in the autumn of 1916 and which had compelled the German withdrawal in March, 1917, to the Hindenburg Line. This was, in fact, the great lesson of the Hindenburg Line, and one which, when taken to heart through the bitter experiences of the battles of Arras and the Aisne, augured best for the ultimate victory of the Allies.

Throughout the remainder of 1917 both the French and the British adhered to the policy of attrition, that is, wearing the Germans down in man power, morale, and *matériel*. In sector after sector along the Western Front they launched local offensives against limited objectives, and every little gain they made was an irrefusable invitation to the Germans to undertake wasteful and costly counter-attacks. For the Allies it was the way to ultimate victory, and the only way.

In May the British made a few further gains in the vicinity of Arras, strengthening their hold on Vimy Ridge and increasing their toll of prisoners for the entire battle of Arras to 20,000. In the same month, the French took the village of Craonne, ten miles southwest of Laon, and captured both ends of the Chemin des Dames, a celebrated shaded road constructed by Louis XV along the heights north of the Aisne. During the summer months the German Crown Prince is estimated to have lost more than 100,000 men in unsuccessful efforts to regain the eastern and western ends of the Chemin des Dames. Altogether the German losses along the Hindenburg Line and at the pivots from April to September were not less than 350,000.

After a lull of several months, a renewal of the offensive on the Aisne occurred in October. The French struck on a six-mile front northeast of Soissons and in one of the most brilliant operations of the war advanced to an average depth of a mile and a half. The perfect coöperation between the artillery, tanks, aircraft, and infantry was a tribute to General Pétain's foresight, energy, and organizing ability. The Germans soon found their remaining positions on the Chemin des Dames untenable, and consequently, by the end of the month, they fell back across the Ailette river upon Laon. In this last thrust the French regained nearly forty square miles of territory and captured 12,000 prisoners and 200 guns; they now dominated the valleys of the Ailette and the Aisne.

Meanwhile the French executed a significant movement, far to the east of the Hindenburg Line, at Verdun. On August 20 they made a quick thrust, after a brief artillery preparation, against the German positions on either side of the Meuse; they captured Avocourt Wood, Le Mort Homme (Dead Man's Hill), Corbeaux, and Cumières Woods, and 4000 prisoners. In the next four days smashing blows were delivered which resulted in the capture of Regnéville, Samogneux, Côte de l'Oie (Goose Ridge), and more than 15,000 prisoners. By the middle of September, the French had recovered more than one hundred of the

120 square miles of territory which the the Germans, under Crown Prince Frederick William, had seized in their mighty and protracted offensive of 1916.

The same tactics employed by the French at Verdun and on the Aisne were used by the British in Flanders. Following the cessation of the battle of Arras in May, 1917, Sir Douglas Haig turned his attention northward. His first care was to straighten the British lines between Ypres and Lens by driving the Germans from their commanding salient on the Messines-Wytschaete ridge. Under the principal German fortifications on this ridge, British and colonial sappers had been digging for over fifteen months until now they had placed nineteen mines containing nearly five hundred tons of ammonite. Early in the morning of June 7, 1917, the mines were exploded by electricity, and a veritable man-made earthquake occurred. The tops of the hills were blown off and the earth rocked like a ship rolling at sea. The detonation could be heard within a radius of 150 miles. Simultaneously with the explosion of the mines, the artillery fire, which had been growing in intensity for two weeks, reached its culmination. Then the infantry, composed of English, Irish, Australian, and New Zealand units, swept forward on a front extending from Observation Ridge, south of Ypres, to Ploegsteert Wood, north of Armentières, and within a brief time captured German positions on a ten-mile front including the villages of Messines and Wytschaete, and wiped out the menacing German salient. Seven thousand prisoners fell into British hands, and the estimated German casualties were 30,000. The total British losses were under 10,000.[1]

With the Messines-Wytschaete Ridge in British possession, it was now safe for the Allies to inaugurate an offensive from Ypres. Of this offensive the immediate object was to gain the high ground in front of Ypres, called Passchendaele Ridge; the ultimate objects were to compel the Germans to withdraw from the Belgian coast and thus to surrender their submarine bases at Ostend and Zeebrugge, and also to envelop the industrial city of Lille and the railway-center at Roulers. From July to November the conflict raged. British on the right and French on the left pressed forward yard by yard. Frequent torrential downpours of rain which repeatedly turned the low flat terrain into a sea of mud, made progress slow and halting. Yet the Allies, with the aid of vastly improved artillery, with

---

[1] Conspicuous among the British dead on this occasion was Major William Redmond, a member of Parliament and brother of the Irish Nationalist leader.

an apparently inexhaustible supply of ammunition, and with grim determination, plodded on. The Germans, heavily reën-forced from the Eastern Front, soon found that ordinary trenches could not withstand either the rains or the enemy-guns; they began to take refuge behind bags of sand and in what the British soldiers called "pillboxes." These were concrete redoubts. They were oftentimes some distance apart and were just about level with the ground, making them in many cases invisible

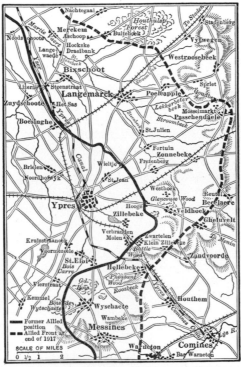

BATTLES OF MESSINES RIDGE AND YPRES

to aviators. They fairly bristled with machine guns, and unless they were destroyed by artillery fire, they were peculiarly fatal to attacking infantry.

Preliminary attacks were made by the Allies at the end of July and in August, each resulting in expensive German counter-attacks. Between the middle of September and the middle of October the Allies delivered five extremely heavy blows, which won them an area of nearly twenty-three square miles and carried them to the Ypres-Roulers road on the northwest as well as advancing them a mile astride of the Ypres-Menin road. British artillery now commanded the Flanders plain, and guns of the largest caliber could effectively shell Roulers, about five miles distant. On October 30 the British entered Passchendaele, but were almost immediately driven out by vigorous counter-assaults. After a week of heavy bombardment, Canadian troops retook the town and German positions 800 yards beyond and held their gains in face of furious counter-attacks. Throughout November the Allies fought successfully to consolidate their new positions and to clear the sides of Passchendaele Ridge.

The political and economic results of the Battle of Flanders were not advantageous to the Allies; no sensational victory had been achieved; the Germans were still profiting by their control of the Belgian coast and by their occupation of the important industrial center of Lille. From a strictly military point of view, however, the protracted conflict was advantageous. The Allies had enormously strengthened their hold on Ypres and had secured important new positions from which they might direct a more decisive offensive in 1918; vastly more important, they had inflicted upon Germany such serious losses as no party to an endurance test could comfortably sustain.

On November 20 the British started a drive toward Cambrai, which for a time threatened to smash the Hindenburg Line and possibly put an end to the deadlock on the Western Front. With scarcely any artillery preparation, the infantry, aided by a large number of huge tanks, plunged forward on the Bapaume-Cambrai road and toward the Scheldt Canal, capturing several villages, securing a part of Bourlon Wood, and rendering German occupation of Quéant and Cambrai for a time most precarious. On the last day of November, however, before the British had been able to complete the consolidation of their newly won positions, the Germans launched a counter-offensive on a sixteen-mile front north, south, and east of the British wedge. On the north and east they failed to gain, but on the south they made such headway that the British were compelled to evacuate Bourlon Wood and to retire to their original positions. The battle of Cambrai ended on December 7, with honors — and losses — about evenly divided. In one respect this battle was enormously significant: it heralded the break-through and the open warfare of the succeeding spring.

Over against all the numerous and varied offensives conducted by the British and French during the year 1917, — at Arras, on the Aisne, at Verdun, and in Flanders, — only two offensives were attempted by the Germans on the whole extended Western Front. One of these was the counter-attack in the vicinity of Cambrai, just described; and the other was a little offensive on the Yser, close to the Belgian coast, late in July. Here the British were surprised and driven back across the river, with a total loss of 3000 men. The very pettiness of the German success on the Yser and of the German recovery at Cambrai, when considered in conjunction with the large-scale German

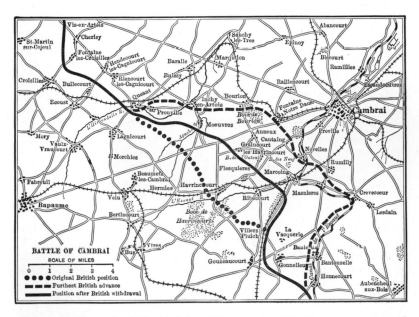

withdrawal to the Hindenburg Line and with the constant and effective Anglo-French thrusts along the whole Front, indicated to the world that the Allies not only were fully holding their own, but could take the offensive whenever and wherever they wished. The endurance test was beginning to tell heavily against Germany.

RECOVERY OF ALLIED PRESTIGE IN THE NEAR EAST

Until 1917 the most uniformly inglorious scene of Allied operations had been the Near East. Beginning with the failure of the naval attack upon the Dardanelles in March, 1915, one disaster after another had attended Allied arms and Allied diplomacy. There were the failures in 1915 to wrest the Gallipoli peninsula from the Turks, to reconstruct the Balkan League, to prevent Bulgaria from joining *Mittel-Europa*, and to save Serbia and Montenegro from conquest.   In 1916 a large Allied army in Macedonia, frightened by the Bulgarians and flouted by a Greek king, had been helpless to succor Rumania; and in far-away Mesopotamia a British expedition for the capture of Bagdad had ended in disaster.   The Russians, it is true, had wrested Old Armenia (just south of the Black Sea) from the Turks, but their success was slight compensation for the over-whelming advantages which Germany had gained and still retained in the Near East.   To Berlin and Vienna were tied fast by steel rails the cities of Belgrade, Sofia, and Constantinople; and from the Bosphorus ran those Germanized trade-routes across Asia Minor and thence, either through Mesopotamia to Bagdad and the Persian Gulf, in the general direction of India, or through Syria and Palestine to the Red Sea, in the general direction of Egypt.   The Near East had become an aggregation of German satrapies.   *Mittel-Europa* from the Baltic to Bagdad was a fact and not a fiction, and as a fact it would remain so long as Allied prestige was lacking in Turkey and in the Balkans.   The Allies might undertake many offensives in France and in Flanders; they would not shake the confidence of the peoples of the Near East or of the German people them-selves in the proud imperial destiny of the Hohenzollerns until they had won significant military successes in the Near East and recovered some of their own prestige.

In the latter half of 1916 the British Government matured plans to assure the security of India and Egypt against the *Mittel-Europa* menace of the Turks.   The expeditionary force in Egypt was augmented and its commander, Sir Archibald Murray, from his headquarters at Cairo, directed the building of a railway eastward from Kantara across the Sinai desert, whence a British invasion of Palestine might later be attempted. This project was aided by an open revolt of the Arabs against the Turks.   Already predisposed to rebellion by the "liberalism" and scarcely concealed agnosticism of Enver Pasha and the other Young Turks, and by the deliberate abrogation of pro-visions of the Sacred Mohammedan Law laid down in the Koran itself, the Arabs of Hedjaz, east of the Red Sea, now felt them-selves provoked beyond endurance by the execution of some of their leaders.   On November 16, 1916, Husein, sherif of Mecca, solemnly proclaimed the independence of Hedjaz with himself as Sultan, and was promptly recognized by the Entente Powers.

The revolting Arabs, by their operations north of the Red Sea and east of the Dead Sea, did much to render futile the Turco-German advance against Egypt, thus enabling the British to protect the Suez Canal and to construct the railway across the Sinai desert. And meanwhile, as special protection to India, the small expeditionary force at the head of the Persian Gulf was strengthened by reënforcements from India and from Great Britain and put under the command of Sir Stanley Maude (August, 1916).

By February, 1917, General Maude was ready to attempt to retrieve General Townshend's disaster at Kut-el-Amara. The transport system was working well; several river monitors had arrived to aid the projected offensive; and the weather conditions were favorable to a renewal of fighting. As a result of a series of local engagements and of manœuvering for position, the British, by the middle of February, established their lines on both banks of the Tigris, where it formed a bend west of Kut-el-Amara. On February 24 Sanna-i-yat and part of the Shumran peninsula, the keys to Kut, were taken. The Turks believed these positions to be impregnable, and made gallant though costly efforts to defend them. Their fall compelled the Turks to abandon Kut-el-Amara and retreat up the river.

In the pursuit the British gunboats on the Tigris wrought considerable havoc among the Turks by getting ahead of them and firing upon them as they approached. The Turkish boats on the river were destroyed, and the monitors which had been lost with the surrender of General Townshend's army were recaptured. The British reached Aziziyeh, halfway to Bagdad, on February 28, and early in March they forced the crossing of the Diala. Then, attacking the Turks from both sides of the Tigris, they drove them into Bagdad. In the night of March 10, 1917, the Turks evacuated the city, leaving in the hands of the British their own artillery, seized a year before at Kut-el-Amara, and a large number of Turkish guns. The capture of Bagdad was not of great strategic importance, but it had a remarkable effect upon morale. It appealed to jaded imaginations in England, France, and America; it alarmed the Central Empires; and in the Near East it gave shape and substance to Allied prestige.

To secure Bagdad against counter-attacks, General Maude pursued the fleeing Turks in three directions: his right wing cleared the caravan route leading into Persia; his left wing moved twenty-five miles up the Euphrates to the prepared

Turkish position of Ramadie; and his center, advancing up the Tigris, took Samara on April 23 and thus gained control of the Bagdad-Samara railway, which facilitated the bringing up of supplies.   Had it not been for the intense heat which began to prevail at that season of the year in Mesopotamia and for the Russian Revolution which simultaneously demoralized the Russian forces in Armenia, the Turkish armies might have been caught between upper and nether millstones and ground to bits on their nodal points at Mosul and Aleppo.   As it was, the better part of Mesopotamia was in Allied hands, and the Turks had received a blow from which they could not recover.

Meanwhile, there were significant developments in the Greek peninsula.   For four months after the capture of Monastir by the Serbs, in November, 1916, the motley Allied Front in Macedonia, under General Sarrail, had remained comparatively inactive.   In April, 1917, a slight forward movement was attempted near Doiran and a few local gains were registered. But Sarrail's force was not yet strong enough to crush the Bulgarian and Austro-German armies facing it, especially since behind it lurked, in the person of King Constantine of Greece, a pro-German commander of a fairly large army which at any moment might be thrown into the balance against the Allies. The weakening of Russia and Rumania in 1917 and their ultimate defection left the forces of *Mittel-Europa* in Macedonia quite unhampered and thereby postponed indefinitely any decisive offensive on the part of Sarrail.   This was obviously of immediate disadvantage to the Allies.   On the other hand, the Allies recovered enough prestige in the Near East as a result of General Maude's successes in Mesopotamia to enable them fearlessly and drastically to interfere in the internal affairs of Greece and to deprive the dangerous, treacherous King Constantine of his occupation as trouble-maker.   And this promised, in the long run, to be of the utmost advantage to the Allies.

During May the Allied authorities at Salonica did everything they could to encourage Greeks to flock to the standard of revolt which Venizelos had already raised.   By the end of that month Venizelos was estimated to have furnished nearly 60,000 Greek soldiers to the Allied army in Macedonia.   Then, on June 10, 1917, French and British troops, entering Thessaly, occupied Volo and Larissa, and on the following day a French force seized the isthmus of Corinth.

On June 11, Charles Jonnart, formerly French governor of Algeria and now named high commissioner of Greece, arrived in Athens and demanded of the royalist premier, M. Zaimis,[1] the immediate abdication of King Constantine and the renunciation of the Crown Prince's right of succession. The king was not in a position to fight, and Jonnart was peremptory. There was only one thing to do. And so on June 12, 1917, Constantine abdicated the throne of Greece in favor of his second son, Prince Alexander; and on the next day the late sovereign and his Hohenzollern wife sailed away from Hellas under escort of two French destroyers. Under Jonnart's supervision, King Alexander was duly proclaimed, several notoriously pro-German Greek leaders were expelled from the country, and an accord was reached between the partisans of Venizelos and those of Zaimis. On June 25 Zaimis resigned and Venizelos became prime minister of a united, pro-Ally Greece. On July 2 all diplomatic relations between Greece and the Central Powers were ruptured and the state of war which had hitherto existed in Venizelos's jurisdiction was now extended to the whole country. On July 7 the Government convoked the Chamber which had been elected in May, 1915, but which had been dissolved illegally by Constantine. At the end of July the Allied troops of occupation were withdrawn. Greece was finally in the Great War on the side of the Allies, and the entire Greek army, instead of constituting a hostile threat in the rear of General Sarrail's force, was now available in full strength for an Allied offensive in the Balkans. Throughout the remainder of 1917 much attention was given to strengthening and reorganizing the Macedonian Front; and General Sarrail, whose reputation had been fatally clouded for two years by a most unfortunate series of untoward circumstances, was succeeded in the supreme command in December by the energetic and resourceful General Guillaumat.

Even more helpful to the recovery of Allied prestige in the Near East than the revolution in Greece and the capture of Bagdad was the success which attended in 1917 the British offensive in Palestine. Under Sir Archibald Murray, British troops, advancing from northern Egypt, had driven the Turkish forces before them across the Sinai Desert [2] and had constructed a railway from Kantara to Rafa on the southwestern edge of Palestine. Thence they had moved northward along the coast, but had been checked in two successive battles, in March and

[1] Zaimis had succeeded Lambros as King Constantine's prime minister on May 4, 1917.

[2] The Turkish forces, it should be remembered, were here engaged on two fronts: the one, against the British advancing from Egypt; the other, against the Arabs of Hedjaz.

in April, and prevented from occupying Gaza. It was then that General Murray was recalled and succeeded by General Edmund Allenby, a particularly brilliant British cavalry leader, who devoted the hot summer months to improving the morale and equipment of the expeditionary force.

In October the offensive was renewed. While the Arabs of Hedjaz under their sultan kept large Turkish forces desperately engaged east of the Dead Sea, Allenby took Beersheba in a surprise attack and on November 6 captured Gaza. Continuing his advance northward, with comparatively little opposition, General Allenby cut the Jaffa-Jerusalem railway at Ludd

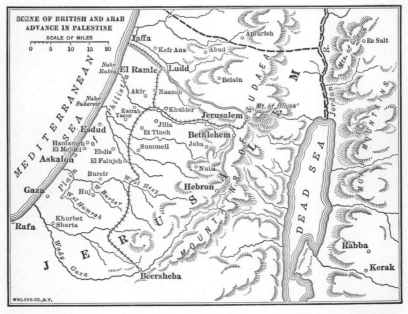

and El Ramle and on November 16 occupied Jaffa. The British then began a movement to encircle the city of Jerusalem, drawing towards it from the northwest, west, and south. All the Turkish positions around the Holy City were taken by storm; and, as the British closed in, it became apparent that the Turks would not risk a siege. On December 10, 1917, Jerusalem was surrendered to the British army of General Allenby, and the Turkish rule which had there endured for seven centuries came to an end.

The success of British arms in Palestine was loudly acclaimed by the Christian populations of the Entente Powers as the final

achievement of the goal of the medieval Crusaders. It likewise
stimulated the aspirations of the Zionists for the reëstablishment
of a Jewish state in Palestine and of the Mohammedan Arabs
for the construction of a "Greater Arabia."

SEEMING OBSTACLES TO ALLIED VICTORY

From the preceding sections of this chapter one would be
justified in concluding that the Allies in 1917 were clearly on
the way to ultimate certain victory. They were recovering
their prestige in the Near East. They were proving their superiority on the Western Front. And if they were temporarily
weakened by the defection of Russia, they were strengthened
by the adherence of the United States to their cause. Of their
enemies, one after another was experiencing discomfort and
humiliation: Turkey was losing Mesopotamia and Palestine;
Bulgaria was becoming cynical and indifferent; Austria-Hungary was on the verge of revolution and disruption; and in
Germany there was ominous fault-finding. The submarine
warfare, on which the Teutons now chiefly relied, fell far short
in December of what in January had been expected; and the
governments of the Central Empires devoted less attention to
military campaigns than to "peace drives."

Yet, curiously enough, the peoples of France, Italy, and Great
Britain did not perceive the signs of the time or did not read
them aright. Instead of realizing that the chances of their
ultimate victory were immeasurably improved by the events
of 1917, they fell into a strange mood of poignant pessimism.
Like wanderers in a wilderness who, without knowing it, were
almost in sight of the promised land, they were more terrified
by the dangers and shadows through which they had passed
than elated by the prospect of sunshine and refreshment beyond.
Month after month, and year after year, the Great War had
dragged on; and the Entente nations, who had borne its heat
and burden almost from the beginning, would not have been
human if they had not in their hearts grown sick and tired of
it by 1917. In their natural war-weariness these peoples viewed
daily developments out of proper perspective. They magnified
the assistance which the defection of Russia would bestow upon
their enemies, and they mimimized the aid which they themselves
would obtain from the United States. It seemed as though
all the resources of Russia would be instantly at the command of
Germany, and as though American troops could never be trained

and equipped and transported to France and rendered really serviceable. Barred by governmental censorship from exact knowledge of the progress of the submarine warfare, they tended to discount the official statements that it was failing of its purpose. The battles along the Hindenburg Line, at Arras, on the Aisne, at Verdun, and in Flanders, were too protracted, too bitterly contested, too sanguinary, to establish Allied military superiority as a demonstrated fact. And the deposition of a Greek king and the capture of Bagdad and of Jerusalem, though noisily acclaimed, were popularly deemed too insignificant in themselves materially to affect the fortunes of the Great War.

Under these circumstances a movement gathered headway in Allied countries in 1917 in favor of a "negotiated peace," that is, in favor of a "peace without victory" as opposed to a "peace through victory." This so-called defeatist movement drew its strength from quite diverse, even incompatible, elements. In the first place, there were groups of Socialist and other ultra-radical workingmen who, influenced largely by their Russian brethren, accused their own governments of pursuing "imperialistic" aims and themselves championed the principle of "no annexations, no indemnities." Secondly, there were certain bankers and industrial magnates who feared lest protraction of the war might destroy national credit, drive all governments into bankruptcy, and pave the way for the spread of socialistic revolution throughout the world and for the demoralization of the whole capitalistic structure of civilized society. Thirdly, there were ecclesiastical groups who viewed with pity and chagrin this most terrible war between professed Christian nations and who felt instinctively that the Church should reassert its moral leadership in the affairs of mankind. Fourthly, there were groups of pacifists who, though pretty effectually silenced by their warlike compatriots during the earlier years of the war, now found expression for their conviction that war in general is immoral and inexpedient and that peaceful negotiation and arbitration are always preferable to organized slaughter. Finally, there were a few old-time diplomatists who, long deprived of the exercise of their vocation, yearned to supplant the soldiers in the limelight and to obtain if possible by intrigue what had not been secured by force of arms.

Defeatism in Allied countries was naturally encouraged by Germany. The three successive chancellors — Bethmann-Hollweg, Michaelis, and Hertling — constantly prated about their desire for a negotiated peace and about the demoniacal victory-lust of the Allied governments. At the same time they intrigued more or less adroitly with every disaffected or discontented element in Allied countries. For example, the German Government was doubtless privy to the secret, informal conferences which were held in Switzerland in the summer of 1917 among certain bankers of France, Great Britain, and Germany. There were signs, moreover, that Bethmann-Hollweg backed the efforts of the Socialists to hold an international conference at Stockholm. And it was evident that Michaelis and Hertling, as well as Count Czernin of Austria, welcomed the papal proposals for peace. Each of these intrigues promised to embarrass the Allies and to weaken their morale.

It was natural that many Socialists should seek the early ending of the Great War. The war was not of their making, they insisted, and it was working havoc among them. Karl Marx, the master mind of Socialism, had pointed seventy years ago to the international solidarity of all the world's workingmen as the goal of his movement; yet most of the progress made in this direction in the sixty-seven years from 1848 to 1914 appeared to have been lost in the three years from 1914 to 1917. In every belligerent country there was a cleavage in the national Socialist Party on the question of supporting, and coöperating with, the bourgeois government, the Majority Socialists usually sharing the popular enthusiasm for national victory, and the Minority Socialists, or Independents, normally indulging in carping criticism. Besides, as a general rule, the Socialists of *Mittel-Europa* were on most unfriendly terms with the Socialists of the Entente Powers. The international organization was moribund: conspicuous figures in it, like Scheidemann of Germany, Guesde of France, and Vandervelde of Belgium, were now whole-hearted champions of their respective national causes; and what remained was a disjointed and dispirited remnant in Holland and in the Scandinavian countries.

With the advent of the Russian Revolution, the Socialists took heart. In May, 1917, a group of Russian Socialists published an appeal for the reassembling of the International and for the calling of a peace congress, and a Dutch-Scandinavian Committee, under the presidency of Branting, the leader of the Swedish Socialists, invited Socialist representatives of all nations to meet at Stockholm. Almost simultaneously, Austrian and German Socialists drew up a peace program, of which the main points were: (1) no annexations; (2) no indemnities; (3) autonomy for the subject nationalities of the Dual Mon-

U

archy; (4) independence for Finland and Russian Poland; (5) restoration of commerce on land and sea, modification of the productive system, completion of an international administration for all sea routes and interoceanic canals, and construction and administration of railways under international auspices; and (6) prohibition of the capture and of the arming of merchant vessels. In Germany, the Majority Socialists set forth a supplementary program including limitation of armaments, compulsory arbitration, the "open door" for colonies, free trade, and democratic control of diplomacy; while the Minority Socialists included in their special peace-aims the restoration of Belgium and Serbia, an independent Poland, and a plebiscite for Alsace-Lorraine. In June Socialist leaders arrived at Stockholm from Germany, Austria-Hungary, and Bulgaria; and discussions began between them and Socialists of neutral states.

In most Allied countries the proposed Stockholm Conference was viewed at first with disfavor and suspicion as a bit of subtle German propaganda. But the Russian Government of Kerensky endorsed the project so enthusiastically that gradually a majority of the French Socialists and of the British Labor Party were won over to its support. Nevertheless, the Governments of France, Great Britain, and the United States withheld passports from Socialist delegates and prevented their countries from being represented at Stockholm. One result was the complete failure of the Stockholm Conference. Another result was acrimonious discussion of the subject in Allied countries and increased opposition to the vigorous prosecution of the war. In Great Britain, Arthur Henderson, the leader of the Labor Party, resigned from the war cabinet on August 11. In France, the Socialists withdrew from the cabinet in September. Altogether, the opposition of the Allied Governments to the Stockholm Conference opened a new and rich field for insidious German propaganda.

From the Catholic Church, as well as from the Socialists, came in 1917 a special plea for peace. In a note dated August 1, Pope Benedict XV called upon all the belligerent Powers to consider the possibilities of the cessation of war. The pope outlined the general terms which he thought would assure "a just and lasting peace": (1) the replacing of material force by "the moral force of right"; (2) a "simultaneous and reciprocal decrease of armaments"; (3) settlement of international disputes by arbitration; (4) a guarantee of "true freedom and community of the seas"; (5) mutual renunciation of indemnities, although allowing for exceptions which "certain particular reasons" would seem to justify; (6) evacuation and restoration of all occupied territories; (7) an examination "in a conciliatory spirit" of rival territorial claims such as those of Alsace-Lorraine and the Trentino, taking into account "the aspirations of the population." To this note President Wilson replied on August 27. He pointed out that the actions of the existing German Government rendered fruitless any negotiations with it, and called upon the German people to repudiate their "irresponsible" government. At the same time the President indicated that it was no part of the plan of the United States to join in a movement to crush the German people. He repudiated the idea of "punitive damages, the dismemberment of empires, the establishment of selfish and exclusive economic leagues" as "inexpedient and in the end worse than futile." The Entente Powers generally accepted President Wilson's statement as embodying their own views, and made no detailed replies to the Pope. On the other hand, the Central Empires, though preserving a marvelous silence upon the vital questions of restoration of conquered territory and the payment of indemnities, were quite punctilious in flattering Pope Benedict and in assuring him that they approved the limitation of armaments, the guarantee of the freedom of the seas, and the substitution of the "moral power of right" for the "material power of arms." The pope could hardly have been deceived by the Teutonic diplomatists, so wide was the gulf between their theory and their practice, and certainly the great bulk of Catholics in Allied countries continued, as before, to give the most loyal support to their respective governments; yet among the more ignorant classes of Catholics, the papal peace effort was doubtless utilized for purposes of German propaganda.

Enough has been said perhaps to indicate the bases of the defeatist movement. There were echoes of it in Great Britain [1] and even in the United States, but it was in France that it reached truly alarming proportions. In France, the scene of the most heartrending combats of three years, there was naturally a greater war-weariness than elsewhere, in measure as the sacrifices and sufferings of France had been greater. There was in France, moreover, an instinctive popular fear lest out of the war might arise a military dictator, — and France had had in the past too

[1] British pacifists applauded the resignation of Arthur Henderson, the Labor Party leader, from the War Cabinet and welcomed a plea put forward by Lord Lansdowne, a distinguished Conservative diplomatist, in behalf of a "peace by compromise."

many military dictators. These feelings led to the downfall of the Briand cabinet in March, 1917, and to the creation of a more "moderate" ministry under Alexandre Ribot. Ribot was an estimable gentleman, seventy-five years of age, who had had much experience in public and private finance, but whose firmness consisted in obstinacy and whom sluggishness led to repose confidence in unworthy or inefficient subordinates. He angered the French Socialists by refusing to allow their delegates to proceed to Stockholm; yet he clung tenaciously to his minister of the interior, Louis Malvy, who actually encouraged Socialists and pacifists to air their grievances and to agitate for a "negotiated peace." The weakness, if not corruption, of Malvy combined with the depression which overspread France as the result of General Nivelle's costly failure in the battle of the Aisne to pave the way for the campaign of defeatism, championed and in part financed by Germany.

Among the active agents of the defeatist movement in France were a certain Duval, the manager of the newspaper *Bonnet Rouge;* M. Humbert, a member of the Senate and the owner of the Paris *Journal;* Bolo Pasha, a former French official of the Egyptian khedive, a financier and an adventurer; and several members of the Chamber of Deputies. These men accepted large sums of German money, which they devoted to the creation of a sentiment within France in behalf of an early peace with the Central Empires. But the real head of the defeatist movement was Joseph Caillaux, a wealthy banker, acknowledged head of the anti-clerical Radical Party in France, and formerly prime minister. Ever since the beginning of the war this distinguished "grandmaster of the backstairs" had led a strange, peripatetic life, and wherever he went mischief seemed to seed and flourish. He was at heart a friend of Germany and an enemy of England; he believed that Germany was certain to win the war and that France should make terms with the inevitable victor before it was too late. He was determined to safeguard his own banking interests. He was thoroughly selfish and absolutely unscrupulous. He associated with pro-German pacifists, adventurers, and traitors. He conducted mysterious intrigues in Spain, in Switzerland, and in Italy. Formerly a professed pope-baiter, he now condescended to visit the Vatican and endeavored to ensnare bishops and cardinals in the meshes of his conspiracy. Formerly a stout proponent of capitalism, he now hobnobbed with extreme Socialists and praised their revolutionary aims.

Neither Malvy nor Ribot took any steps to counteract or destroy the propaganda of defeatism, which grew steadily throughout the summer of 1917. But gradually voices were raised by true French patriots alike against the defeatists for their temerity and against the Government for its supineness. Particularly strident rose the voice of that old war-horse of French politics and patriotism, Georges Clemenceau. In his Parisian newspaper he fairly lashed the Government and the intriguers. He recognized that the hour was supremely critical in French history and he was ready to dare anything to save his beloved France from treason and dishonor.

So great was the patriotic outcry of Clemenceau and his friends that Malvy resigned as minister of the interior on the last day of August. In September the whole cabinet was reconstructed, Painlevé becoming premier, Ribot assuming the portfolio of foreign affairs, and the Socialists dropping out. But Painlevé's ministry lasted only two months; an adverse vote in the Chamber on the subject of the defeatist scandals occasioned its resignation; and on November 16, 1917, Clemenceau himself, the "Tiger" and the "breaker of cabinets," as he was variously styled, became prime minister and minister of war.

Clemenceau, though seventy-six years of age, threw himself with the zest and zeal of a young man into the task of destroying defeatism and assuring "peace through victory." Stephen Pichon became minister of foreign affairs; Jules Pams, of the interior; Louis Klotz, of finance; Louis Loucheur, of munitions; and Charles Jonnart, of blockade and invaded regions. The small fry of defeatist intrigue, such as Bolo and his associates, were promptly arrested, tried, and punished. Malvy was exiled. And in January, 1918, Clemenceau dared to order the arrest of the formidable Caillaux on the charge of having endangered the security of the state. "It was probably the most courageous political act of the war."

Clemenceau's brusque dealing with French defeatists came none too early, for at that very moment the poison of defeatism was bringing Italy to the point of national disaster. Taking advantage of the spread of pacifism and of the spirit of unrest and sedition in Italy,[1] the Austro-Germans in October and No-

[1] A secret campaign was conducted for months by German and Bolshevist agents in Italy. Insidious appeals were addressed to ignorant Catholic peasants as well as to the extreme Socialists of the cities. In August there were serious riots at Turin and even more serious mutinies among troops sent to suppress the riots. Yet despite the multiplication of signs of the weakening of popular morale, the Government of Premier Boselli remained strangely indifferent and unmoved.

vember, 1917, hurled large armies against General Cadorna's forces and succeeded in occupying four thousand square miles of Italian territory and in capturing nearly 300,000 prisoners and 2700 guns.   Just as Serbia had been overcome in the autumn of 1915 and Rumania in the autumn of 1916, so in the autumn of 1917 it was planned by Germany to put Italy out of the war. Having prepared the ground by means of sinister defeatist propaganda, Germany sought to complete the work of destruction by resort to a crushing military blow.

At the beginning of October, 1917, the main Italian armies, composed of seasoned veterans, were fighting the Austrians on comparatively narrow fronts in the difficult country east of the Isonzo river: one army was struggling for the mastery of the Carso Plateau and the route to Trieste; the other, based on Gorizia and Cividale, was concentrating its attacks upon the Bainsizza Plateau, farther north.   Still farther north, on the upper Isonzo east of Caporetto, was yet another Italian force; but it, like the Italian armies along the peaks of the Carnic Alps and on the Trentino Front, consisted chiefly of "territorials," that is, of older men who in peace time were held in reserve, with only a sprinkling of soldiers who had seen long and active service.

Meanwhile Ludendorff, the actual director of *Mittel-Europa's* General Staff, was preparing a great Austro-German offensive. The growth of the pacifistic Bolshevist agitation in Russia enabled him to transfer about 100,000 men and great quantities of heavy artillery from the Eastern to the Italian Front.   The simultaneous development of defeatism in Italy led to an astonishing fraternization of Austrian and Italian troops at certain points on the Italian Front and resulted in a serious impairment of the morale of various Italian military units.   The stage was set for another spectacular Teutonic offensive; and for it Ludendorff's strategy was excellent.   He planned to strike the chief blow at the unseasoned and corrupted Italian troops on the upper Isonzo, to break through, and then to cut the lines of communication of the Bainsizza and Carso armies, thereby causing their retirement, and perhaps their surrender, by outflanking them.   Italian disaster would relieve Austria-Hungary of fear for her western frontiers, just as the Bolshevist revolution in Russia was ridding her of enemies on her eastern borders.   Austria-Hungary could then breathe again quite freely, and *Mittel-Europa* would be able to bring all its resources and all its energies to bear upon the French Front.

On October 21 Austro-German batteries of heavy artillery bombarded the Plezzo-Tolmino front and the northern edge of the Bainsizza Plateau. As the Italian guns were greatly outranged and outnumbered, the Teutons with little difficulty broke through the defensive positions and crossed to the western bank of the upper Isonzo. Two Italian corps threw down their rifles and treasonably ran away or surrendered, thus uncovering Caporetto and permitting the enemy promptly to outflank the Italian armies to the south. The rapid advance of the Teutons from Caporetto made the hasty retreat from the Bainsizza and Carso plateaus westward across the Isonzo almost a rout. On October 27 Berlin announced the capture in five days of 60,000 men and 500 guns. For a time it seemed as though General Cadorna would be unable to extricate his menaced armies. On

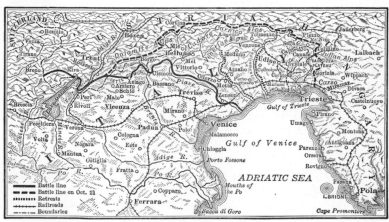

THE AUSTRO-GERMAN INVASION OF ITALY

October 28 Cividale was taken, and on the same day Gorizia was reoccupied by the Austrians. On October 30 Udine, the seat of Italian general headquarters, fell; and by November 1 the Austro-Germans were on the Tagliamento river, well within Italian territory, and in possession of 180,000 prisoners and 1500 captured guns. The forced withdrawal of the main Italian armies from the Isonzo jeopardized the Italian troops guarding the frontier in the Carnic Alps. These troops were consequently obliged to abandon the mountain passes and to beat a precipitate retreat down the streams running into the upper reaches of the Piave and Tagliamento rivers.

The Tagliamento did not suffice to hold the victorious

Teutons, who threw pontoon bridges across it in scores of places and drove the Italians back to the Livenza, the next river flowing into the Gulf of Venice parallel to the Tagliamento. The Livenza, too, proved inadequate for serious defense and was frantically clung to merely to allow the completion of intrenchments along the line of the Piave River, ten to twenty miles farther west.

At this juncture French and British infantry and artillery, hurriedly dispatched from the Western Front, began to arrive. General Diaz supplanted General Cadorna as commander-in-chief of the Italian armies. And resistance to the Teutonic offensive commenced to stiffen. The line of the lower Piave held, despite a few temporary successes of the Austrians, notably the capture of Zenson. Allied monitors were employed to shell the southern extremity of the enemy line and thus, in a measure, to protect Venice. A large area between Venice and the mouth of the Piave was flooded to prevent a direct attack upon the famous old city.

Finding all efforts to force a crossing of the lower Piave futile, the Austro-Germans sought to outflank the new Italian lines by striking at the Asiago Plateau and the range of mountains between the upper courses of the Brenta and Piave rivers. Masses of Austrians and Germans were hurled at the Italian rock positions, but in vain. Their assaults were comparable to those made by the Crown Prince during the great drive on Verdun in 1916. Although the Italians were forced to yield some ground, the Austro-German attempt to reach the Venetian plains from the north was foiled as effectually as was their attempt to cross the lower Piave. In December, however, new anxiety was caused the Allies by desperate assaults on the Asiago Plateau and the upper reaches of the Brenta; Monte Asolone was captured by the Teutons, and likewise the lower of the two summits of Monte Tomba.

With the coming of the new year, Italian prospects brightened perceptibly. On December 30 Monte Tomba was recovered, and in January the Teutons were compelled to relinquish Monte Asolone and the bridgehead on the Piave at Zenson. The Austro-Germans rested from their labors and the Italians firmly established themselves in their new lines from the Asiago Plateau to the mouth of the Piave. The retreat from the Isonzo had reached its end; it had taken heavy toll of Italy's strength, but it had failed to eventuate in that decisive disaster which for some weeks had seemed inevitable.

The retreat to the Piave, though not a disaster, was enough of a misfortune to shock the Italian people profoundly. It welded them into a closer union, and roused among them a more fiercely patriotic spirit. It forced reforms in the army, and compelled the Government to give special attention to the "civil front," which had been weakened from neglect and treason. In the midst of the reverses on the Isonzo, the Boselli ministry had resigned, and a new and more energetic one had been formed with Vittorio Orlando as premier and minister of the interior, and Francesco Nitti as minister of the treasury, Baron Sidney Sonnino retaining the portfolio of foreign affairs. Under Orlando's leadership, defeatism was stamped out of Italy.

The defeatist movement (with all which defeatism implied in Italy and in France) was seemingly in 1917 a very grave obstacle to Allied victory. It was due, as has been pointed out, to general war weariness and to specific discouragement resulting from the revolutionary defection of Russia and the unavoidable delay in America. Abetted and exploited by the Central Empires, it might have proved fatal to the Allied cause had not the Teutons overreached themselves. The military drive of the Austro-Germans into Italy in the autumn of 1917 and the peace which they forced upon Russia at Brest-Litovsk and upon Rumania at Bucharest, sufficed to convince the bulk of the Allied free nations, even many former pacifists and "defeatists" among them, that the Central Empires were thoroughly dishonest in pretending to champion "peace without victory." Germany was obviously intent upon "victory through peace." And in this circumstance the only safe and sane motto for the Allies was "peace through victory." It took a long time and bitter experience to commit the Allied peoples to this view of affairs, but it was a happy augury of the future that early in 1918 they were so committed. It was a happy augury, too, that by that time the Allies were coöperating with one another loyally and unselfishly and that presiding over the destinies of the chief associated Powers were such resolute men as Clemenccau, Orlando, Lloyd George, and Woodrow Wilson.

It was also a happy augury of the future that at this very time, when the patience of many persons had been exhausted in fruitless efforts to obtain any clear and concise statement of war aims from the professional diplomatists of *Mittel-Europa*, President Wilson should set forth succinctly and eloquently a code of Allied war aims. Speaking before the American Congress on January 8, 1918, the President presented his views in fourteen points: (1) open covenants of peace, openly arrived at, and no secret diplomacy in the future; (2) absolute freedom of navigation in peace and war outside territorial waters, except where seas may be closed by international action; (3) removal as far as possible of all economic barriers; (4) adequate guarantees for the reduction of national armaments; (5) an absolutely impartial adjustment of all colonial claims, the interests of the peoples concerned having equal weight with the equitable claim of the Government whose title is to be determined; (6) all Russian territory to be evacuated, and Russia given full opportunity for self-development, the Powers aiding; (7) complete evacuation and restoration of Belgium, without any limit to her sovereignty; (8) all French territory to be freed, invaded portions restored, and the wrong done by Prussia in 1871 in the matter of Alsace-Lorraine righted; (9) readjustment of Italian frontiers on lines of nationality; (10) peoples of Austria-Hungary accorded an opportunity of autonomous development; (11) Rumania, Serbia, and Montenegro evacuated, Serbia given access to the sea, and relations of Balkan States determined on lines of allegiance and nationality under international guarantees; (12) Non-Turkish nationalities in the Ottoman Empire assured of autonomous development, and the Dardanelles to be permanently free to all ships; (13) an independent Polish state, including territories inhabited by indisputably Polish populations and having access to the sea; and (14) a general association of nations must be formed under specific covenants for the purpose of affording mutual guarantees of political independence and territorial integrity to great and small states alike.

The celebrated "Fourteen Points" speedily became the charter of Allied war aims. They constituted the goal throughout 1918 of that way which the Allies, despite obstacles, had been paving during 1917 for ultimate victory.

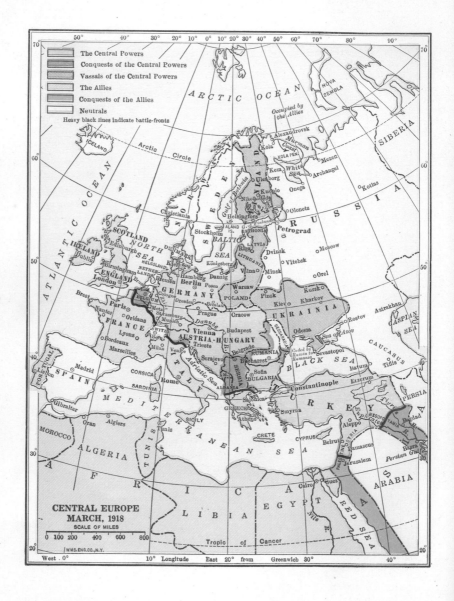

CENTRAL EUROPE
MARCH, 1918
SCALE OF MILES
0 100 200   400   600   800

The Central Powers
Conquests of the Central Powers
Vassals of the Central Powers
The Allies
Conquests of the Allies
Neutrals
Heavy black lines indicate battle-fronts

CHAPTER XIII

GERMANY MAKES THE SUPREME EFFORT

"WHOM THE GODS WOULD DESTROY"

GERMANY was possessed of madness. It was her delusions of persecution and grandeur which had been the immediate cause of the Great War in 1914, and throughout its subsequent course she had harbored in her disordered mind recurring hallucinations of victory. As a rule, striking feats such as the Drives of Mackensen and Hindenburg into Russia and the conquest of Serbia in 1915 and of Rumania in 1916 signified more to her than the uprising of the whole world against her, more than the mighty holding battles of the Marne, of Verdun, of the Somme, and of Flanders, more than the very real loss of sea power, more even than the increasingly frightful attrition and wastage of her stores of men and munitions.

For a time in 1917 Germany's madness took the form of melancholia. She grew depressed and morose. To foreigners it appeared as though she were about to put on sackcloth and ashes. And in fact, had it not been for certain external stimuli which recalled her earlier madness, she might conceivably have passed from mania through temporary melancholia into a state of mind approaching healthy sanity. There was a time in 1917, it should be remembered, when the majority of the German people felt stirrings of reform and aspirations for peace, and when the Government itself was coquetting with diplomacy and making eyes at democracy. Late in 1917, however, the Austro-Germans won a great military victory on the Isonzo and drove the Italians far back to the Piave, and at the same time Russia's descent to chaos became rapidly accelerated. German melancholia speedily disappeared, and Germany lapsed once more into acute megalomania. Every section of the country, except the Minority Socialists, became converted to a "German" peace, and the journalists and the politicians shrieked as loudly for conquest as they had done in 1914.

Domestic discontents of the summer of 1917 were quelled by

March, 1918. By this time German eyes were blinded to the steadily disruptive tendencies in Austria-Hungary, to the cynical indifference of Bulgaria, and to the actual dismemberment of the Ottoman Empire; they still saw, or thought they saw, *Mittel-Europa* stretching in majesty from the Baltic and North Seas to the Ægean and on to Mesopotamia and Syria, united in aims, rich in resources, and indomitable in arms. They perceived on all sides vanquished and vassal states — Belgium, Luxemburg, Poland, Serbia, Montenegro, Rumania, Finland, Lettland (Latvia), Lithuania, and Ukrainia. They had just beheld the signing of the treaties of Brest-Litovsk and Bucharest, which formally acknowledged the subjugation of the whole Russian Empire and abolished the entire Eastern Front. They reflected that the submarine warfare was doing its work rapidly and effectively, that the United States was despatching few troops to Europe, and that England, starved and bleeding, would soon sue for peace. They knew that Italy was defeated and on the defensive. Only the Western Front remained an eyesore to the Germans, and surely this one little spot on Europe's surface could now be quickly cleaned up by those Teutonic demigods who had conquered the rest of the world.

In February, 1918, Ludendorff and Hindenburg, the Thors of modern German mythology, met the Reichstag in secret session and explained their supreme plan. They would concentrate all available forces immediately on the Western Front and inaugurate a colossal drive against the French and British. Simultaneously the Bulgarians would press the Allied troops in Macedonia, and the Austrians would launch another offensive against the Italians; but the Western Front would become the scene of the final, decisive combat. Confession had to be made, in confidence, that the submarine campaign during 1917 had not done all that had been expected of it and that American troops could and would land in Europe in large numbers. But American troops must come slowly, and once across the Atlantic they must undergo thorough training before they would be fit to serve in front-line trenches. During the next six months, therefore, the French and British would have to fight their own battle. But the British could add no new recruitment of any appreciable size to their forces already in the field, — they were kept too busy supplying *matériel* and circumventing submarines and coping with Irish difficulties; while the French were absolutely at the end of their rope, so far as man power was concerned, and their *morale* was thought to be at a very low ebb. On the other hand,

Germany could at once materially strengthen her armies on the Western Front, she could add to them not only new recruits from home and some divisions withdrawn from Italy and from the Balkans, but also at least half a million seasoned veterans no longer needed in the East. Furthermore, she could now effect an enormous concentration of guns, what with captures from Italy and Russia, and those either released from the defunct Eastern Front, or loaned from Austria.

In view of these circumstances Ludendorff and Hindenburg promised certain and complete victory before the autumn of 1918. Now, if ever, was the hour to strike. Matters should be pushed. All the German armies should be set in motion to overwhelm the Franco-British forces in the West, to capture the channel ports and Paris, to put France out of the war, and, in a word, to complete the task begun in 1914, but interrupted at the Battle of the Marne. It must be done in four months, — in six months at the outside, — and it would be done. Hindenburg and Ludendorff gave their word for it. To be sure, for such a triumph a price must be paid. The army chiefs put it at a million German casualties; on reconsideration, they increased their estimate to a million and a half.

To a nation gone mad with megalomania, losses of a million and a half seemed cheap stakes for a peculiarly grand and glorious gamble. The Reichstag applauded the plan. And when news of the enterprise spread among the German people, a wave of delirious enthusiasm surged across the Fatherland. Editorials in the patriotic press and speeches of Junkers and bureaucrats, of chancellor and Emperor, assumed a new and fateful truculence.

So far as Ludendorff and Hindenburg were concerned, their madness did not lack method. Assured of enthusiastic popular sympathy with their purpose of making a supreme effort to obtain a speedy military decision on the Western Front, they proceeded to devise strategic plans with rare judgment and discernment. Their main plan was simplicity itself. They would strike with all their might at what was assumed to be the weakest spot in the Allied line, the valley of the Somme, where the British forces under Field Marshal Haig joined the French forces under General Pétain. Breaking through at this pivotal point, they would isolate the British army by rolling it up from its right and pinning it to an intrenched camp between the Somme and the Channel. This done, they would hold it with few troops, swing round on the French, and put them out of action. If all went well and fast, the Americans, by the time they were really ready to assist the French and British, would find no British or French to assist; they would not fight Germany alone; and they would promptly come to terms.

In carrying out this major plan of strategy, the Germans in March, 1918, possessed four advantages over the Allies. In the first place, they enjoyed numerical superiority, thanks to the transfer of divisions from Russia, from Italy, and from the Balkans. Secondly, since they occupied interior lines and since the most intricate railway network of France was inside their own front, they were in a better geographical position; they could concentrate at will in almost any angle of the huge salient running from the sea to La Fère and from La Fère to Verdun, and until they actually attacked they could keep the enemy in ignorance as to which side of the salient they proposed to strike; simultaneously with the same force they could threaten the French in Champagne and the British in Picardy. Thirdly, in conducting the offensive the Germans were subject to a single supreme authority, which could treat the whole front as a unit and subordinate the needs of one sector to those of another, whereas the Allies were still capable of that unfortunate fumbling which must be a characteristic of the division of the supreme command between equal and independent generals of different nationality. Finally, the Germans had developed more perfectly than the Allies the new tactics of surprise attack and "infiltration," by means of which open warfare might be restored and chances increased of winning an early decision.

Just what these new tactics were upon which Ludendorff relied for the success of Germany's supreme effort, may best be gathered from the interesting description of them by an acknowledged expert and critic: "The first point was the absence of any preliminary massing of troops near the front of attack. Troops were brought up by night marches only just before zero hour, and secrecy was thus obtained for the assembly. In the second place, there was no long artillery 'preparation' to alarm the enemy. The attack was preceded by a sharp and intense bombardment, and the enemy's back areas and support lines were confused by a deluge of gas shells. The assault was made by picked troops (*Sturmtruppen*), in open order, or rather in small clusters, carrying light trench mortars and many machine guns, with the field batteries close behind them in support. The actual method of attack which the French called 'infiltrations' may best be set forth by the analogy of a hand whose finger tips are shod with steel, pushing its way into a soft substance. The picked troops at the fingers' ends made gaps through which others poured, till each section of the defense found itself out-flanked and encircled. A system of flares and rockets enabled the following troops to learn where the picked troops had made the breach, and the artillery came close behind the infantry. The troops had unlimited objectives, and carried iron rations for several days. When one division had reached the end of its strength another took its place, so that the advance resembled an endless wheel or a continuous game of leap-frog.

"This method, it will be seen, was the very opposite of the old German massed attack, or a series of hammer blows on the one section of the front. It was strictly the filtering of a great army into a hostile position, so that each part was turned and the whole front was first dislocated and then crumbled. The crumbling might be achieved by inferior numbers; the value of the German numerical superiority was to insure a complete victory by pushing far behind into unprotected areas. . . . Ludendorff's confidence was not ill-founded, for to support his strategical plan he had tactics which must come with deadly effect upon an enemy prepared only to meet the old methods. Their one drawback was that they involved the highest possible training and discipline.   Every detail — the preliminary as-sembly, the attack, the supply and relief system during battle — presupposed the most perfect mechanism, and great initiative and resource in subordinate commanders. The German army had now been definitely grouped into special troops of the best quality, and a rank and file of very little. Unless decisive success came at once, the tactics might remain, but men to use them would have gone. A protracted battle would destroy the *corps d'élite*, and without that the tactics were futile." [1]

Having worked out these new tactics and hit upon that stragetic plan which admitted of the fullest utilization of Ger-man advantages and Allied weaknesses, Ludendorff massed seven powerful armies on the front from the North Sea to Rheims. These armies were commanded and disposed as follows: (1) Gen-eral Sixt von Arnim, from the Sea to the Lys; (2) General von Quast, from the Lys to Arras; (3) General Otto von Below, from Arras to Cambrai; (4) General von der Marwitz, from Cambrai to St. Quentin; (5) General Oskar von Hutier, from St. Quentin to the Oise; (6) General von Boehn, from the Oise to Craonne; and (7) General Fritz von Below, from Craonne to Rheims. The first four were under the superior control of Prince

[1] John Buchan, *Nelson's History of the War*, vol. xxii, p. 19.

Rupprecht of Bavaria and the last three under that of the Crown Prince Frederick William.

Everything was in readiness for Germany's supreme effort. It was to be the mightiest trial by battle that the world had ever witnessed, the final test of the Religion of Valor. And so as not to be entirely off stage in a modern production that promised to surpass and consummate the epics and sagas of primitive Teutonic folk-lore, the War Lord himself, the Emperor William II, prepared to betake his own anointed person to General Headquarters at Spa and thence to communicate to the obsequiously faithful staff of journalists who attended him, for the edification of his subjects and of posterity, his own inspired and ecstatic interpretations of the Apotheosis of Might.

But the histrionic Emperor appealed to popular imagination in Germany far less than the burly Field Marshal von Hindenburg. It was Hindenburg's presence on the Western Front which silenced civilian critics and keyed up the morale of the soldiers. Throughout the Fatherland there was everywhere expectancy of big events. "Where is Hindenburg?" asked Vice-Chancellor Helfferich in an address on March 16, 1918; "he stands in the West with our whole German manhood for the first time united in a single theater of war, ready to strike with the strongest army that the world has ever known."

THE DRIVE AGAINST THE BRITISH: THE BATTLE OF PICARDY

On March 21, 1918, the Germans began the great battle which military experts of both sides believed would decide the Great War. They struck from points where the British lines, owing to the uncompleted battles of Flanders and Cambrai and the Allied failures at Lens, St. Quentin, and La Fère in 1917, were relatively weak or could be out-manœuvered with superior force of men and munitions. And while they struck directly at the British, they opened fire at long range on Paris.[1]

The Germans took the Allies by surprise. Some attack in force was of course expected; but General Pétain imagined it would be directed against the French armies in Champagne,

---

[1] In heavy artillery the Germans now surpassed themselves. Three guns, each weighing 400,000 pounds and capable of hurling 330-pound shells some seventy-five miles, they emplaced twelve miles northeast of St. Gobain, and with these they opened fire on Paris on March 23 and subsequently at fairly frequent intervals they bombarded the French capital. The gigantic guns amazed the Allies but did actual damage incommensurate with the expense incurred, the total casualties in Paris, after an expenditure of about four hundred shells, numbering only 196.

while Field Marshal Haig judged from the preliminary artillery preparations that it would be delivered in the vicinity of Ypres. The result was that neither Haig nor Pétain felt it possible to

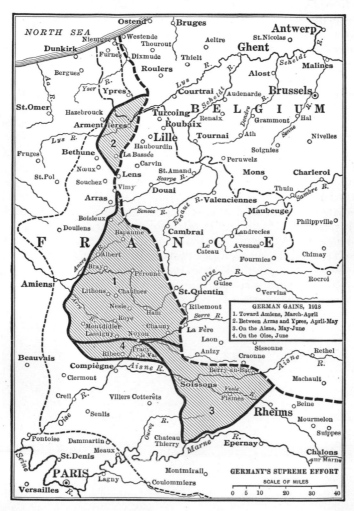

spare troops from the northern and eastern sectors to strengthen the central sector from Arras to the Oise.   This sector was held from Arras to St. Quentin by the Third British Army under Sir Julian Byng, and from St. Quentin to the Oise by the Fifth Army under Sir Hubert Gough.   Yet it was against this sector, particu-

x

larly between Cambrai and the Oise, that the Germans inaugurated their herculean offensive.

The weather favored the Germans and their new "infiltration" tactics to a very high degree. The attack was launched by the troops of Generals Otto von Below, von der Marwitz, and von Hutier, a little before five o'clock on the morning of March 21 under cover of such a heavy mist and fog that it was impossible to see more than a hundred feet ahead. The outpost line was taken before the British were cognizant of the fact that the attack had begun. The Germans with their carefully trained *Sturmtruppen* and with their tremendous superiority of numbers soon forced the British second line and rushed on to the third and last line of defense. Here again the inequality of numbers ultimately told.

By the second day of the battle Gough's army, outnumbered four to one, lost contact with the French on its right and gave way at several vital points. Retreat soon became rout and what had been a disciplined army was rapidly transformed into a struggling mass of disorganized humanity. The Germans were advancing from St. Quentin along direct routes west toward Amiens and southwest toward Noyon; it seemed almost certain that they would succeed in driving a permanent wedge between the French and the British armies. They took Péronne, Ham, and Chauny on March 24, and crossed the Somme; and on the next day they occupied Barleux, Nesle, and Noyon. Meanwhile, farther north, the army of Sir Julian Byng had been heavily engaged; it had managed to hold its lines intact before Arras, but its right wing, embarrassed by the rout of Gough's forces, had been obliged to yield Bapaume and to uncover the road to Albert.

March 26 was the decisive day of the German effort to isolate the British, for this day witnessed the closing of the gap between the British and the French. A French army under General Fayolle came up and established itself along the Oise and the Avre, joining the British at Moreuil, southeast of Amiens. At the same time a new British army was improvised from sappers, laborers, engineers, in fact anybody that could be found, and with this curious array General Sandeman Carey faced the Germans before Amiens for six days, fighting over unknown ground, and with officers in charge of men whom they had never seen before. Try as they might, the Germans could not capture Amiens.

Failure to capture Amiens left the Germans in a rather difficult position. They had pushed a thirty-five-mile salient into the Allied lines, but the salient, bounded roughly by the Ancre river on the north and by the Avre on the south, was too narrow for comfort. It was with the hope of broadening the salient that the Germans repeatedly assailed the armies of General Byng and General Fayolle. Byng lost Albert on March 27, and on the next day Fayolle lost Montdidier. And during the first week of April tremendous assaults were made from Albert against the Ancre line on the north, and from Montdidier against the Avre line on the south.

Although local successes were won by the Germans, they were unable to achieve their immediate purpose of widening the salient materially. The chief reason for this was the time element which had permitted the British and French to bring up men and guns and thus to stabilize their new lines. A contributory reason was the fact that heavy rains turned the Somme battlefield into a hopeless sea of mud and interfered seriously with the Germans' transport system.

In the first phase of the battle of Picardy, the Germans had regained nearly all the ground they held at the beginning of the battle of the Somme in 1916 and besides had gained approximately 1500 square miles. They had also taken 90,000 prisoners, 1300 guns, and 100 tanks. Though they had suffered grievously themselves, they had probably inflicted even heavier losses upon the British. But the main German plan was frustrated, at least temporarily: the French and British were not separated and both still held strong defensive positions.

The Germans, as soon as they were checked before Amiens, launched a second gigantic offensive against the British farther north, between Arras and the high ground north of Ypres. Instead of trying to separate the French from the British, the plan here was to separate the British army at Ypres, commanded by Sir Herbert Plumer, from that at Arras, under Sir Henry Horne. A successful thrust by the opposing armies of Generals von Arnim and von Quast would throw back Horne's forces upon the British armies which had retreated to the Ancre and would isolate Plumer's army. Apparently the Germans hoped to create a gap in Horne's command, as they had recently done in Gough's army, and then pour through it and advance to the Channel. An advance similar to that before Amiens would result in the capture of Calais, one of the chief bases of supply of the British armies. Should only half this distance be covered, the town of Hazebrouck would fall, and with its fall Ypres would become untenable and the entire railway system behind the British and Belgian armies would be dislocated.

On April 9 the Germans attacked a small sector, held by a Portuguese division, between Armentières and La Bassée, smashed it completely, and occupied Richebourg St. Vaast and Laventie. A gap of about three miles was thus created in the British lines, and through it poured German troops in ever-increasing numbers. On the next day they crossed the river Lys and occupied Armentières and Estaires. On April 12 they took Merville, only five miles from Hazebrouck. The serious-ness of the British position was reflected by Sir Douglas Haig's order of the day: ". . . Many among us are now tired. To those I would say that victory will belong to the side which holds out the longest. . . . Every position must be held to the last man; there must be no retirement. With our backs to the wall, and believing in the justice of our cause, each one of us must fight on to the end. The safety of our homes and the freedom of mankind depend alike upon the conduct of each one of us at this critical moment."

The next few days witnessed the stabilizing of the British lines southeast of Hazebrouck and the shifting of the chief German efforts to points northeast of Hazebrouck. On April 14 the Germans took Neuve Église, close to Mont Kemmel, and two days later they completed the conquest of Messines Ridge by capturing Wytschaete.

German occupation of Messines Ridge and assaults on Mont Kemmel placed the British at Ypres in a precarious position. In order to prevent a serious catastrophe, Sir Douglas Haig directed a withdrawal from Passchendaele Ridge, which had been captured by the British at a tremendously heavy cost in 1917,[1] and which constituted an exposed salient northeast of Ypres. The surrender of Passchendaele Ridge was a terrible blow to British pride, but subsequent events proved that the resultant shortening of the British lines strengthened their general position. On April 18–19 French reserves arrived, and the British lines, both new and old, held against repeated German onsets.

Mont Kemmel was the scene of extremely bitter fighting for three days, April 24–27. The Germans, prodigal of men as at Verdun, made frontal and flank attacks on the position, until by sheer weight of men and metal they compelled the British and French to relinquish the height. Nevertheless the losses suffered by General von Arnim's army were so great that he was unable to reap the fruits of his victory: he could not secure other hills that belonged to the same range as Mont Kemmel;

---

[1] See above, pp. 278–280.

he was unable further to endanger Ypres.   In the meantime renewed German assaults southeast of Hazebrouck, in the

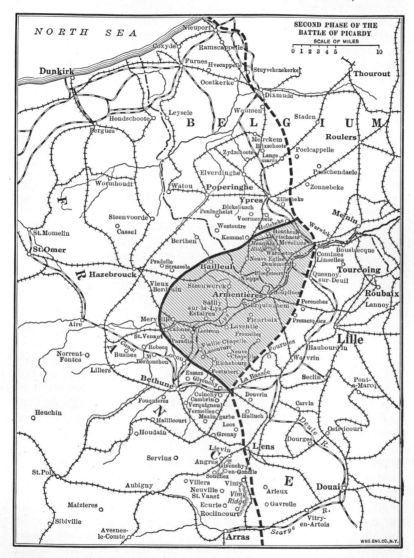

vicinity of Béthune, not only failed, but were followed by Allied counter-attacks which won back some ground.   The struggle on this front died down by the middle of May, 1918.

Thus ended the second great German thrust. The British again had suffered grievously; they had lost Armentières, Merville, and the ridges of Messines and Passchendaele; they were now back to positions which they had held after the first battle of Ypres in 1914; of their holdings at the close of 1917 the Germans now occupied approximately 800 square miles. Yet the Germans, as in their first thrust toward Amiens, had failed to achieve their real ends: they had not isolated any British army, or plowed their way to the Channel Ports; the Allies still dominated the strategic railway lines centering in Ypres, Hazebrouck, Béthune, Arras, and Amiens. Not even the Belgian ports were longer available as bases for German submarines, for, in the midst of Ludendorff's military efforts, a British squadron in daring fashion had sunk ships at the entrance to the harbors of Zeebrugge (April 23) and Ostend (May 10) and had thus partially closed them.

In the midst of the great German drive against the British, the Government at London took steps to make good its heavy losses in men and to bolster up weakening English morale. On April 8, a new military service bill was introduced in Parliament; and its third reading was quickly carried by a majority of 198. Thereby military service was imposed on every British subject who had been in Great Britain since 1915 and who was between the ages of eighteen and fifty-five; immunity for ministers of religion was withdrawn; and, unlike the service act of 1916, this measure was specifically extended to Ireland.

Thus the German drive served to make British determination more dogged than ever. But at the same time it served to render more difficult than ever the solution of the already highly perplexing problem of Ireland. For Irishmen objected to conscription — and with cause. It will be recalled that with the sanction of the British Government an Irish Convention, representing all factions of the unhappy island except the Sinn Fein, had met at Dublin in July, 1917, under the chairmanship of Sir Horace Plunkett, in an endeavor to reach an agreement on the home-rule question.[1] The report of the Convention's recommendations was made public in April, 1918, in three separate documents: the proposals for a scheme of Irish self-government, adopted by 44 to 29; a vehement dissenting statement by nineteen Ulster Unionists; and a minority report of twenty-two Nationalists, who were unable to indorse the majority's fiscal recommendations. The general scheme of

[1] See above, pp. 262–263.

proposed home rule was accepted by practically all the Nationalists, all the Southern Unionists, and five out of seven Labor
delegates; only the Ulster Unionists were *intransigeant*. Because of the attitude of the latter, however, the British Government at once rejected the Convention's recommendations and
declared that it itself would proceed to fashion a new home-rule
instrument, in the meantime applying the service act to Ireland.
Immediately there was a hue and cry. The vast majority of
Irishmen felt that again they had been duped by the British
Government, that again they were at the mercy of English
Unionists and Sir Edward Carson's Ulster garrison, and that
again they were to be forced to fight for a Britain which persisted in denying them rights enjoyed by Canadians and Australians and Boers. Nationalist members of the House of Commons
ostentatiously quit Parliament, and at a meeting in Dublin on
April 20 adopted a resolution affirming that the enforcement of
compulsory military service on a nation without its assent constituted "one of the most brutal acts of tyranny and oppression
of which any Government can be guilty." On the same day
fifteen hundred Labor representatives met in Dublin and pledged
their resistance to conscription. Two days earlier the Catholic
bishops at a meeting in Maynooth had condemned the injustice
of forcing conscription upon a people without that people's
sanction and, while warning against rebellion or violence, had
directed their priests to administer an anti-conscription oath to
the laity on Sunday, April 21. This oath was duly taken by all
classes of Catholic Ireland, including lawyers, bankers, and
merchants, as well as farmers and workmen. Thus it transpired
that all factions of Irishmen except the group of Ulster Unionists
were united on a common platform and that Catholic bishops,
Laborites, and Nationalists, — most of whom had been whole-
heartedly loyal to the cause of the Allies, — now stood shoulder
to shoulder with Sinn Feiners in opposing the increase, at Ireland's expense, of British armies on the Continent. John Dillon,
the new Nationalist leader, joined hands with Eamonn de
Valera, the leader of the Sinn Fein.

Faced by the imminence of rebellion, the British Government
by an order-in-council suspended indefinitely the application
of the Service Act to Ireland and at the same time postponed
the formulation of any scheme of home rule. The results were
painful and unfortunate in the extreme. Premier Lloyd George
stated on May 2 that "the difficulties have not been rendered
easier of settlement by the challenge to the supremacy of the

United Kingdom Parliament which recently was issued by the Nationalist Party and the Roman Catholic Hierarchy in concert with the leaders of the Sinn Fein"; and throughout England the Irish were accused of base ingratitude and of treason to the Allied cause. Taking their cue from the attitude of English officials, the Ulster Unionists, under the guidance of Sir Edward Carson, became more truculent than ever toward the grant of home rule in any form. On the other hand, the bulk of Irishmen were not mollified by the appointment, on May 5, of Field Marshal Viscount French, a notorious Unionist and "strongarm" man, as Lord Lieutenant of their country, nor by the military and police coercion under which their administration was now conducted; from support of the moderate, pro-war Nationalists and a program of autonomy, they rapidly veered toward support of the radical, anti-war Sinn Feiners and a program of complete independence. Between England and Ireland, and between Ulsterites and other Irishmen, the breach had been widened and deepened.

The great German drive of March and April against the British led, however, not only to an unhappy resuscitation of Irish troubles, not only to courageous efforts on the part of Englishmen, Scotchmen, and Welshmen to increase their own man power at the front, but also to the taking of a step of the utmost practical significance to all the Allies. It was the unification of the Allied command in France. That such a step had long been highly desirable admitted of no doubt, but it was difficult so long as British and French commanders — to say nothing of Italian generals — were jealous of each other. Ever since the United States had entered the war, President Wilson had urged upon the Allies unity of command as well as the pooling of resources, but beyond a meeting of the Inter-Allied Conference and the creation in November, 1917, of a Supreme War Council, with strictly advisory functions, little in this direction had been accomplished.

When the Germans launched their huge offensive in March, 1918, General Pershing promptly offered the American troops then in France to the Allies for use in any way they saw fit, either to be used as an independent unit, or to be broken up and brigaded with the British or the French, or both. This self-effacement of the American commander, coupled with the defeat of General Gough's army and the resultant grave danger to the whole Allied Front, finally overruled the last objection of the British General Staff and the British public. On March 25,

1918, Lord Milner and M. Clemenceau and Sir Henry Wilson met Sir Douglas Haig and General Pétain at Doullens, midway between Amiens and Arras.   That conference, held amid the confusion of retreat and under imminence of dire disaster, marked in a real sense the turning-point of the Great War.   The proposal for a supreme commander-in-chief, for a generalissimo of all the Allied forces, strongly put forward by Clemenceau and Milner, was welcomed by Haig and Pétain.

For the new post there could be but one choice — Ferdinand Foch.   He was by universal consent the master mind among the Allied generals.   He was the most learned and scientific soldier in Europe, and his greatness in the field had been amply demonstrated in the battles of the Marne and of Flanders in 1914, and in the battle of the Somme in 1917.   On March 26 it was announced that this short, grizzled, deep-eyed man of sixty-five had assumed supreme control of the Allied forces in the West. Haig and Pétain and Pershing became his lieutenants, and thenceforth the Allied Front in France and Belgium could be treated as a whole and reserves could be dispatched, regardless of nationality, from one sector to another, whithersoever at the moment they were most needed.

It was the unifying of the Allied command which contributed potently to checking the German offensive against the British both at Amiens and at Ypres and Hazebrouck and to preventing Ludendorff from isolating the British from the French and forcing the former back to the Channel.   But the supreme test of Foch's generalship was to come later.

THE DRIVE AGAINST THE FRENCH: THE AISNE AND THE OISE

Ludendorff had promised his fellow-countrymen that their supreme effort on the Western Front would bring decisive victory within four or six months.   So far, in the two months from March 21 to May 21, some progress had been made toward the realization of his promise.   A big salient had been driven into the British lines between Arras and La Fère, and a smaller salient had been made between Arras and Ypres.   German casualties in the offensive against the British already totaled half a million, but these were only a half or third of what Ludendorff had indicated as the price of victory.   He still had numerical superiority of effectives; he was still operating on interior lines; the advantage of the offensive was still his.   Just as he had devoted two months to demoralizing the British and compelling the French to weaken their own lines in order to send reserves to a hard-pressed ally, so now he would consecrate a month or two to denting French defenses, destroying French morale, and driving a big, broad salient into central France.   Then, when all enemies were reduced to impotence by his sudden, fearful thrusts, he could easily crown a marvelous campaign by occupying Paris and the Channel Ports.   There was intense jubilation in Germany as there was genuine alarm in Allied countries.

The terrain selected by Ludendorff as the starting-point for his decisive drive against the French was the heights of the Aisne, which had already been the scene of great battles in 1914 and 1917.[1]   This area was nearest to Paris; it was also the gate to the Marne, and an advance beyond that river would cut the Paris-Châlons railway and imperil the whole French front in Champagne and in the Argonne.   Accordingly, the armies of General von Boehn and General Fritz von Below, lying between Laon and Rheims, were rapidly raised in strength until they comprised some forty divisions, twenty-five for the first wave and fifteen in reserve.   And a great concentration of guns and munitions was effected.

Never, perhaps, during the whole campaign did the huge German war machine move so noiselessly and so fast.   On the evening of Sunday, May 26, all was quiet in the menaced area. Then at one o'clock on the morning of Monday, May 27, a staccato bombardment began everywhere from the Ailette to the suburbs of Rheims.   At four o'clock the infantry advanced, and in an hour or two had swept the French from the crest of the ridge north of the Aisne.   The odds were too desperate, and the few French divisions, taken by surprise, had no choice but to retreat.   By nightfall General von Boehn's troops had crossed the Aisne and reached the Vesle at Fismes.   They had taken large numbers of prisoners and an immense store of booty, and in the center they had advanced twelve miles.

Yet there was danger in thrusting too narrow a salient into the French lines; and advantageous further advance of the German center must depend upon the ability of the flanks to advance also.   Consequently, during the ensuing days the Germans attempted to widen as well as deepen the salient: General Foch,

---

[1] There is evidence to show that Ludendorff himself was opposed to the drive on the Aisne, preferring to press the offensive against Amiens.   He seems to have been persuaded by political factors to abandon his original plan and to strike towards Paris.

on his side, hastily threw in reserves with a view not so much to staying German progress south from Fismes as to strengthening the French positions at Rheims on the east and Soissons on the west.

After a stubborn defense, Soissons fell on May 29; and the German center rushed on from Fismes to the watershed between the Vesle and the Ourcq and Marne. By the next day the German center stood on the Marne from Château-Thierry to Dormans, a distance of about ten miles, but to the northwest the utmost difficulty was experienced by the right flank in debouching from Soissons, while to the northeast the left flank battered in vain at the gates of Rheims.

Though they failed absolutely to widen the Marne salient on the east, the Germans succeeded, after extremely bitter and sanguinary fighting, in advancing some six miles down the Ourcq, as far as the village of Troesnes; and they likewise enlarged slightly their holdings west of Château-Thierry. Early in June, however, French counter-attacks not only halted the German drive westward but actually recovered some ground. On June 6, American troops, coöperating with the French, gained two miles on a three-mile front northwest of Château-Thierry; at a most critical moment these Americans appeared as a singularly ill omen to Teutonic projects. Would they come in force before Ludendorff could bring France and England to terms?

Loudly the Germans acclaimed the achievement of their latest drive. To date they had taken 55,000 prisoners and 650 guns; they had occupied 650 square miles of territory and had established another salient, this time at French expense, thirty miles deep; they had lessened the distance of their lines from Paris from sixty-two miles to forty-four. But Ludendorff knew that the salient from the Aisne to the Marne was highly precarious; it was peculiarly exposed to a flanking movement from Compiègne; and it simply had to be widened, strongly fortified, or abandoned.

Consequently Ludendorff resorted to the plan of linking up the Marne salient with the Amiens salient which in March he had thrust into the British lines. If he could execute this plan, he would wipe out the huge bulge in his own line and capture the strategically important town of Compiègne; and the river valleys of the Aisne, Oise, Marne, and Ourcq would then be available for a final converging attack upon Paris, the nerve center of France.

General von Hutier's army, concentrated between Montdidier

and Noyon, opened an intense bombardment in the early morning of June 9, and at dawn attacked with fifteen divisions on a front of twenty-five miles. On most of the front von Hutier failed, for there was no element of surprise, and Foch was ready for him. The total advance on the first day was three miles and was only attained after frightful losses. On the next day the Germans advanced about three miles farther and captured, after grave losses, a few little villages. The Teuton penetration was now about five or six miles, and this was approximately the depth of their entire advance. The struggle was one of dogged resistance on the part of the French, and, for the Germans, the slowest and costliest progress; very different from the Aisne offensive a fortnight earlier. By June 13 von Hutier's effort on the Oise practically ceased.

In the meantime, American troops had been very active in the neighborhood of Château-Thierry. On June 10 they moved forward in the Belleau Wood and by the next day had captured all of it. They also crossed the Marne at Château-Thierry on scouting expeditions.

After von Hutier had failed to reach Compiègne and thus to widen the Marne salient on the west, General Fritz von Below on June 18 made a desperate assault upon the defenses of Rheims, hoping thereby to enlarge the salient to the east. Though encircled by assailants on three sides, Rheims held out most stoutly during the engagement, much aided by the fact that the French held the great *massif* of the Montagne de Rheims to the south and southwest.

For the better part of a month after the unsuccessful attack upon Rheims, comparative silence fell upon the Western Front. It was obvious that Ludendorff was preparing still another mighty blow. It was obvious too that the Allies were utilizing their respite to the full: their armies were growing daily as the Americans came into line, and their commanders were concerting strategy and tactics wherewith they hoped soon to transfer the initiative from the Teutons to themselves. Already the German casualties were mounting fast to the limit which Ludendorff had named as the price of victory; already three months had passed by of the four which he had set as a time-limit. The next drive would in all probability be the last for the Germans. Meanwhile, the Austrians would make their ultimate drive against the Italians.

THE DRIVE AGAINST THE ITALIANS: THE PIAVE

Externally the condition of Austria-Hungary seemed auspicious in the spring of 1918. Her own territories were free of foreign invaders not only, but she was in military possession of Montenegro, a large part of Serbia and Albania, and a liberal slice of northeastern Italy, and the treaties of Brest-Litovsk and Bucharest had relieved her of the necessity of maintaining a battle-front in Russia and Rumania. But internally the situation was growing steadily worse. Austria-Hungary had never had any true national unity, and the separatist ambitions of her subject peoples had been waxing as the central authority waned. Military and diplomatic successes had not served to feed the hungry or to save the starving, and large sections of the population of the Dual Monarchy were on the verge of starvation. Allied propaganda was doing its work: there were frequent mutinies among Czechoslovak and Jugoslav regiments; there were daily desertions both at the front and on the march.

One hope remained to the Emperor Charles and his Government. It was that the Great War might be ended before demoralization should find its sequel in disintegration and ruin. For a time in 1917 the Emperor, supported by Count Czernin, his crafty foreign minister, had hoped to end the war and save his dominion by means of separate, stealthy negotiations with the Entente. His duplicity having been discovered at Berlin, however, he was compelled to part with Czernin in April, 1918, and to reappoint as foreign minister the more strenuously pro-German Baron Burian. And lest the Entente might continue to cherish the notion that the Dual Monarchy was weakening in her loyalty to Germany, the Emperor Charles was obliged further to humble himself, to pay an ostentatious visit to the Emperor William II, and to conclude with him on May 12 a renewal and extension of the alliance between their countries. Henceforth Austria-Hungary was even more dependent than formerly on the good graces and military might of Germany; with anxiety the governing classes at Vienna and Budapest now watched the progress of Ludendorff's supreme effort in France.

But Ludendorff had told the Austrian authorities in no uncertain terms that, while he strained every nerve to overwhelm the British and the French, they themselves would be expected to put Italy out of the war. This they must do unaided, because he needed all German troops in the West; but this they could do, because they now enjoyed the great prestige and the advantage of position which had been acquired as results of the successful Teutonic drive of the preceding November from the Isonzo to the Piave, and because they were now unhampered by military exigencies on any other frontier.   If they could vanquish the Italians finally, they would confer inestimable favors upon the cause of *Mittel-Europa* and they would be promoting immeasurably the stability of the Dual Monarchy.

So the Austrians set to work preparing a supreme offensive against Italy.   They brought reënforcements from the East and collected a large store of guns and material.   They memorized and rehearsed the new German tactics of "surprise" and "infiltration."   And they worked out an admirable plan of strategy : Field Marshal von Hoetzendorf, commanding in the Tyrol, was to break through the Allied positions on the Asiago Plateau, and at Monte Grappa and Monte Tomba, and then

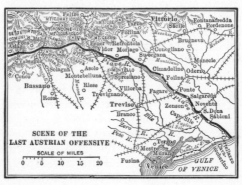

march down the Brenta valley, and take the Italian armies along the Piave on the flank or in the rear ; simultaneously, General Boroevic was to seize the hill called the Montello, which lay roughly at the angle between the north and northeastern sectors, where the Piave leaves the mountainous country for the Venetian plain, and to "infiltrate" among the Italian defenders of the Piave, thereby directly menacing Venice.

On June 15, 1918, at three o'clock in the morning, the Austrian "preparation" began on the whole front, and at seven o'clock the infantry charged, principally in two areas — in the plains on the twenty-five mile line between the Montello and San Dona di Piave, and in the hills on the eighteen miles between Monte Grappa and Canove.   But Diaz, the Italian commander, was not "surprised"; his troops were ready and also his reserves; and it soon became apparent that the Austrian generals knew the theory of "infiltration" better than their soldiers knew its practice. Hoetzendorf's advance was checked almost at the outset, and within two days the Italians, with the aid of French and British detachments, had recovered all the ground lost in the mountains and some besides.

Boroevic was a little more successful along the Piave. His troops effected crossings of the river at several points and seized the eastern end of the Montello, while lower down the Piave, in the vicinity of San Dona, they advanced five miles west of the river. On June 18, however, two events occurred of great importance. One was the arrival of Diaz's reënforcements and the resultant halting of the Austrian advance. The other was a heavy downpour of rain which rendered the Piave a swollen flood and thus cut off the Austrians on the western bank of the river and at the same time enabled Italian monitors of light draft to go up the river and shell the Austro-Hungarian positions. Five days later General Diaz inaugurated against the isolated Austrians a counter-offensive, which resulted in the capture of 4500 prisoners. By the first week in July, the Italians not only had driven General Boroevic's forces back to their old positions, but, in some places, had secured ground which had been lost in 1917, notably the delta at the mouth of the Piave.

The result of the drive against the Italians was that the Austrians had gained nothing. Actually they had been compelled to yield ground, and this with a loss to themselves of some 20,000 prisoners, seventy-five guns, and at least 150,000 casualties. They had failed grotesquely, and their offensive power was at an end. Their morale was hopelessly lowered, and domestic revolt threatened. More than ever was Germany left to continue the struggle alone.

On the other hand the Italians were jubilant. They had avenged the disastrous defeat of the preceding year, and their achievement strengthened their own morale not only, but of their allies also. Allied faith needed a sign, for at this very moment Ludendorff's Final Drive was impending.

Despite Austrian failure, the Germans had not yet lost faith in Ludendorff's ability to obtain a military decision. Only Richard von Kühlmann, the German Foreign Secretary, expressed doubt; "the end of the war," he said before the Reichstag, on June 24, "can hardly be expected through purely military decisions alone, and without recourse to diplomatic negotiations." For such faint-heartedness Kühlmann was scathingly assailed by the Pan-Germans and Junkers; he resigned on July 9, and was succeeded by Admiral von Hintze. Jove-like Ludendorff was not to be hindered by cringing diplomatists from hurling his last mighty thunder-bolt.

THE FINAL GERMAN DRIVE: THE SECOND BATTLE OF THE MARNE

At midnight on Sunday, July 14, 1918, the anniversary of the fall of the Bastille, Parisians heard the booming of great guns. At first they thought it another air raid, but the blaze in the eastern sky showed that business was afoot on the battlefield. Then they knew that the last phase had begun of the struggle for Teutonic domination of their city and of their country.

For a month and more, ever since the cessation of the drives from the Aisne and the Oise, Ludendorff had been making final preparations to achieve the victory which he had promised the German people. He had collected every reserve from every front on which there were German troops. He had overworked his whole transport system in a desperate attempt to bring up all available guns and munitions. His plan was to strike out from the uncomfortable salient in which von Boehn had been entrapped, press across the Marne, and cut the important lateral railway from Paris to Nancy. Simultaneously von Mudra (who had succeeded Fritz von Below) and von Einen, with their armies, were to advance east of Rheims between Prunay and the Argonne. In this way Rheims would be enveloped and the French front would be broken beyond hope of repair. While von Mudra and von Einen, with the aid of German armies in Lorraine and in Alsace, ground the eastern forces of the French to bits on the fortresses along the Meuse, von Boehn would march on Paris down the valley of the Marne. At the right moment, when the fate of the capital hung in the balance, von Hutier and von der Marwitz would break through the Amiens-Montdidier lines and descend on Paris from the north. Then would Haig be finally separated from Pétain, and Pétain's armies would be severed, and Foch, the generalissimo of a lost cause, would be faced by defeat complete and cataclysmic, and a German peace would be imposed on the Allies. To this end, the coming struggle was popularly styled in Germany the *Friedensturm*, the "peace offensive"; the Crown Prince Frederick William was put in nominal charge of it, and afar off the Emperor William II assumed a most theatrical pose. Everything was in readiness to resume the Battle of the Marne where it had been broken off in September, 1914. Ludendorff was a better strategist than Moltke had been, and the Germans had learned many valuable lessons in four years; on the other hand it was assumed that most of the French reserves had already been exhausted, and that what few Americans had arrived were too untrained to be dangerous.

At dawn on July 15, 1918, the German infantry advanced to the attack. Von Boehn was immediately successful. His troops crossed the Marne at various points between Château-Thierry and Dormans, reached the heights on the south bank, and in the course of the day gained one to three miles on a front of twenty-two. Yet they failed to widen the salient : on the southeast an Italian corps effectually barred the way to Épernay; on the southwest, in the vicinity of Château-Thierry, American soldiers stubbornly contested the ground. These Americans, constituting the right wing of the French army of General Dégoutte, first checked the German wave at Vaux and Fossoy, and then rolled it back, clearing that part of the south bank of the Marne and taking 600 prisoners. Such American behavior was ominous.

East of Rheims von Mudra and von Einen encountered unexpected opposition from the French under General Gouraud. Gouraud's counter-bombardment dislocated the German attack before it began, and his swift counter-attacks checked their "infiltration" before it could be set going. By dint of the utmost effort the Germans occupied the towns of Prunay, Auberive, and Tahure; further they could not go; Rheims they could not capture or isolate. By the third day of the offensive, von Einen and von Mudra were utterly exhausted.

South of the Marne and southwest of Rheims, von Boehn on July 16 and 17 pushed hard toward Épernay. Yet he too used up his reserves in vain. At the farthest point his advance was only six miles beyond his original position. On July 18 the aspect of the whole front was altered, when the French and Americans began an offensive on their own account from the Marne to the Aisne, which was highly successful, and which changed a dangerous situation for the Allies into a more dangerous one for the Germans.

Before Ludendorff had launched the final German drive, on July 15, General Foch was considering a scheme of counter-attack drawn up by General Pétain in conference with Generals Mangin, Fayolle, and Dégoutte. It was planned to take advantage of the narrowness of the German salient on the Marne, and,

Y

while von Boehn was struggling to widen it to the east, to assail it from the west between Soissons and Château-Thierry. For this purpose vast quantities of supplies were stored up in the Villers Cotterets Forest, and a great reserve army, the possibilities of which the Germans had scarcely foreseen, was gathered together.

The chief factor in General Foch's decision to inaugurate a counter-offensive at once was the unexpectedly prompt arrival and efficient training of American troops. At first the Allies as well as the Germans had been prone to overestimate the obstacles in the way of the early, active participation of the United States in the war. It was hoped by the Germans, and feared by the Allies, that the ruthless submarine warfare would hamper seriously the transportation of American troops to France and that such troops as might reach Europe could not be relied upon for front-line fighting because of their notorious lack of training and experience. As a matter of fact the submarine warfare was at no time insurmountable, and in 1918, thanks to the Anglo-American sea patrol and to German discouragement, it was becoming rapidly less effective : against losses to Allied and neutral shipping in the second quarter of 1917 totaling two and a quarter million tons must be set the combined losses of 1,150,000 tons in the first quarter of 1918, and 950,000 in the quarter from April to June, 1918, while during the same period the shipbuilding programs of Great Britain and the United States steadily grew until in 1918 the merchant vessels launched far exceeded in tonnage those destroyed. Moreover, Europe was astonished by the speed and safety with which American troops were transported across the Atlantic. During the seven months of 1917, from June to December, the number of American soldiers arriving in Europe averaged 27,000 a month; from January to March, 1918, the average was 60,000; and as soon as Germany put forth her supreme effort against the British and French, the United States performed almost a miracle in rushing men to the defense of the Allies — 117,000 came in April, 244,000 in May, and 276,000 in June. By July, 1918, more than a million American troops were in France.

No less astounding than the speedy arrival of the Americans was the quickness with which they proved themselves real warriors. Training begun in the United States was completed in Europe; and in April, 1918, the First Division had manned a sector of the front northwest of Montdidier. On May 28 this division had signalized the first American military success in the

Great War, by capturing the village of Cantigny; and in June the Second Division by their effective work in the Belleau Woods and near Château-Thierry had aided materially in checking the Teutonic drive from the Aisne to the Oise.   Even these successes, however, did not fully convince the Allied generals that the bulk of the American troops were yet fit for major operations, and it was not until the supreme effort of the Germans on the Marne in July, when the French were in dire need of reënforcements and when General Pershing insisted that his soldiers could and must be used, that General Foch, relying upon the Americans as well as upon French and British, ordered the counter-offensive.

On July 18, Franco-American troops, under the command of Generals Mangin and Dégoutte, attacked on a twenty-eight mile front from a point west of Soissons to Château-Thierry on the Marne.   The assault was made without artillery preparation, the

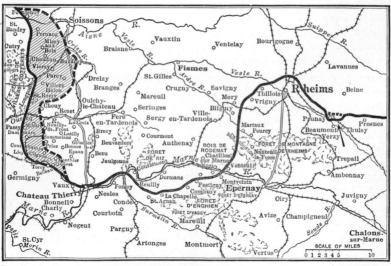

SCENE OF THE LAST GERMAN OFFENSIVE: THE SECOND BATTLE OF THE MARNE

advancing infantry being protected by large numbers of tanks and a creeping barrage.   It took the Germans by surprise, and, as a result of it, General Mangin's forces between the Aisne and the Ourcq advanced five miles and reached the heights south of Soissons, while General Dégoutte's army, between the Ourcq and the Marne, captured Torcy and threatened Château-Thierry.

Château-Thierry was evacuated on July 21, and on the same day Franco-American troops crossed the Marne and advanced three or four miles toward the Ourcq. The Germans were in retreat but they were fighting stubbornly as they went. On July 28 the Allies crossed the Ourcq and took Fère-en-Tardenois. Most bitterly did the Prussian Guards contest further advance north of the Ourcq: Sergy and Seringes changed hands several times before remaining in the possession of the victorious Americans. On August 3 the French reëntered Soissons in triumph, and on the next day the Allies recovered more than fifty villages, including Fismes. The Germans were now completely behind the Aisne-Vesle line. Their supreme effort had been a gigantic failure. In two weeks the Allies had recovered the districts of Valois and Tardenois and taken more than 40,000 prisoners. On August 6, 1918, General Foch was named a marshal of France, "in order to consecrate for the future," said Premier Clemenceau, "the authority of the great soldier who is called to lead the armies of the Entente to final victory."

The Second Battle of the Marne, like the First, was a great Allied victory. In both combats the Germans had made desperate attempts to overwhelm and crush the French armies and to occupy Paris; in both they had been decisively beaten. But to the Teutons the Second battle, in 1918, was far more disastrous than the First battle, in 1914. In September, 1914, the Allies were so exhausted that they could not press their advantage; the Germans could intrench themselves on the heights of the Aisne and hold their lines intact in France and Belgium while they proceeded to punish Russia. And the Allies, short of men and short of munitions, had to resign themselves unwillingly to a four years' vigil along a far-flung battle front. Now, however, in August, 1918, the Germans had shot their last bolt. They had suffered terrible losses; they had no more reënforcements to bring on from Russia or any other place; they were at last, thanks to their foolhardiness in bringing the United States into the war, outnumbered and outmanœuvered. Their munitions were of inferior quality; their air service, at least on the British front, was distinctly inferior; their supply system was in confusion; their generals were discredited. Henceforth there could be no more German offensives. It was, in fact, very doubtful whether the Germans could make a defensive stand.

The Allies, flushed with victory, did not rest from their labors when they had checked Ludendorff's last drive and had turned it back across the Marne. They did not stop short even with the recovery of what they had lost in his earlier drive from the Aisne. The offensive, of which they had been deprived from March to

July, 1918, they would now resume, and they would press it until *Mittel-Europa* sued for peace.   In Allied countries defeatism disappeared and martial enthusiasm ran high.   In the Central Empires, on the other hand, popular morale declined rapidly, for people who had been assured of a triumphant peace within four months had now to face the prospect of a peace imposed not by them upon their enemies but by their enemies upon them. It was a prospect hitherto almost inconceivable to the German mind.   Yet such was the amazing turn of fortune in July, 1918, that whereas four months earlier Ludendorff had appeared as the dictator of Europe, four months later he and his Hohenzollern master were to be dishonored fugitives even from the Fatherland. The Second Battle of the Marne was the beginning of the end. They that had taken the sword were about to perish by the sword.

CHAPTER XIV

THE ALLIES TRIUMPH AND CENTRAL EUROPE REVOLTS

ALLIED VICTORIES IN THE WEST

WITH the wiping out of the German salient from the Marne to the Aisne in July and early August, 1918, Marshal Foch had reaped the first fruits of the Allied offensive, but it was not his plan to allow any rest or respite to the harassed and discouraged Germans. On August 8 he struck his second great blow in an endeavor to "pinch" the extended German salient in Picardy, reaching out toward Amiens. First the British under General Rawlinson and the French under General Debeney attacked the Germans on the southern side of the salient, just south of the Somme river, and in three days drove them back fifteen miles in some places and an average of ten miles along the entire line. Montdidier was retaken on August 10, and before the end of the month Roye and Noyon were recovered. In the meantime, the French under General Mangin assailed the Germans on the line from the Oise, near Ribecourt, to the Aisne, near Soissons, while the British under General Byng successfully struck the northern side of the Picardy salient, making notable gains and inflicting heavy losses upon the enemy. Bapaume was regained on August 29, and Péronne on September 1. Farther north, in Flanders, the British army of General Plumer launched an offensive in August against the salient between Arras and Ypres and crowned its efforts on the first day of September by compelling the Germans to evacuate Mont Kemmel.

By the end of August the results of Marshal Foch's energetic offensive were already appreciable. Since the middle of July the Allies had captured 130,000 prisoners, 2000 heavy guns, and 14,000 machine guns, and had wrested from the Germans the greater part of the territory conquered by the latter in the sensational and sanguinary drives of the spring. The Teutons were now in most places back on the Hindenburg Line, and their morale had suffered a blow from which it was destined not to recover. That 300,000 fresh American troops were pouring into

France every month was the chief of the fateful factors in German defeat and Allied triumph.

The German Government was fully alive to the situation and thoroughly alarmed. A secret conference of civil and military officials, held at General Headquarters at Spa on August 14, under the presidency of Emperor William II, concluded from clear evidence at hand that, contrary to Ludendorff's earlier

PRINCIPAL CHANGES IN WESTERN FRONT FROM AUGUST, 1914, TO NOVEMBER, 1918

assurances, Germany could no longer hope to win the war; she must initiate peace negotiations with the Entente Powers. It would take time to formulate new peace proposals, to secure the sanction of Austria-Hungary, to present them through a neutral Power to the Allies, and to obtain final acceptance. During this delay attempts must be made, by means of false statements and high-flown proclamations, to buoy up the soldiers at the front and the civilians at home, for otherwise there would be real danger of a political and social revolution in Germany.

To keep the armies intact and in possession of a large part of their former conquests in Belgium and France seemed to be the best guarantees against revolution at home and against a disastrous and crushing peace abroad.   On this point Field Marshal von Hindenburg, Chancellor von Hertling, and the Emperor himself were agreed.   Ludendorff himself was inclined to be panicky.

The Allies were at this time in ignorance of the conference at Spa and of its momentous decisions.   But they were in no frame of mind to help the Teutonic authorities stave off revolution and obtain more favorable peace terms.   And Marshal Foch was not the man to give an enemy any rest.   What had been in July and August mere drives against German salients were enlarged under his direction, in September, into a vast battle covering the whole Western Front from the North Sea to the Meuse River.   It was his purpose, by means of numerous offensives at various points, to force the Teutons to evacuate the line which they had spent years in intrenching and fortifying and which, comprising successive positions that depended on one another, extended from Dixmude, through Lens, Quéant, Cambrai, St. Quentin, La Fère, north of Rheims, and across Champagne and the Argonne, to the Meuse, and was supported in the rear by the three mighty camps of Lille, Laon, and Metz.

The first days of September were utilized by the French, British, and American armies in pressing the pursuit of the Germans and in liberating the territory up to the Hindenburg Line, in Picardy, between the Oise and the Aisne, and south of the Aisne.   At the same time British troops under General Horne, east of Arras, vigorously assailed the lines between Drocourt and Quéant which constituted one of the most formidable sectors of the German front.   After some of the bitterest fighting of the war, the British broke the line and penetrated six miles along a front of more than twenty.   Quéant was taken by storm, together with a dozen towns and villages.   In this operation alone more than 10,000 prisoners were captured. Lens was evacuated by the Germans on September 4, and the British settled down to a slow but steady advance toward Cambrai.

Then quickly, at the opposite end of the long battlefield, east of the Meuse in the plain of the Woëvre, began an American offensive movement against the St. Mihiel salient, which was a relic of German successes in the early months of the war.   On September 12, after four hours' bombardment, American infantry under General Pershing assailed the southern and western flanks of the salient.   The chief resistance was in the west, where the

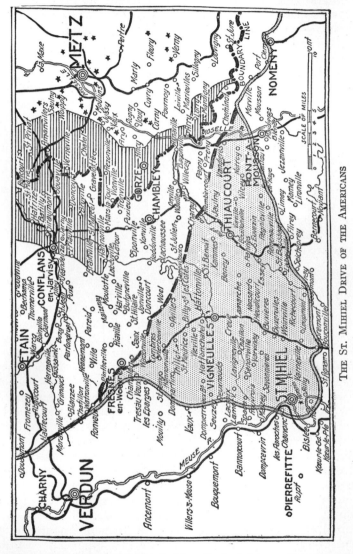

THE ST. MIHIEL DRIVE OF THE AMERICANS

German positions were defended by the heights on the edge of the Woëvre.   Nevertheless so impetuous and so unflinching was the attack, that on the second day the forces advancing from the south and from the west met at Vigneulles, and the St. Mihiel salient was no more. By this blow seventy villages were delivered and nearly 175 square miles of territory; 16,000 prisoners were taken, and 450 guns; the great French railway system running through Verdun, Toul, and Nancy was freed; a strategically important position was obtained from which subsequently an offensive might be launched against Metz and the iron fields of Briey; and the Germans were shown in most disquieting manner that the American Expeditionary Force had reached a stage of development where it could be depended upon by the Allies to take full and decisive share in the war.

Ever bolder and more determined and more varied grew the Allied offensives. The Germans could no longer risk the transfer of troops from one sector to another; everywhere they were worn out and exhausted. Hardly had the St. Mihiel salient fallen when the Teutons found themselves assailed simultaneously on five main sectors: (1) on September 18, the British army of General Rawlinson and the French army of General Debeney, under the superior command of Field Marshal Haig, inaugurated an offensive against St. Quentin, which resulted in the capture of that town on October 1; (2) on September 27, the British Generals Byng and Horne moved against Cambrai, occupying it on October 9; (3) on September 28, King Albert and his Belgians, aided by a French army under General Dégoutte and the British army of General Plumer, struck out between Dixmude and Ypres, and while the Belgians got close to Roulers, the British recovered Passchendaele, advanced on Menin, and threatened Lille; (4) on September 28, the French army of General Mangin pushed back the Germans between the Oise and the Aisne and regained the Chemin des Dames; and (5) on September 26 an offensive of the utmost significance was begun on both sides of the Argonne, from the Meuse to Rheims, American troops attacking east of the Argonne and in the valley of the Meuse, and French forces under Generals Gouraud and Berthelot coöperating with them to the west, in Champagne.

In all these sectors the Allies made rapid progress despite stubborn resistance and repeated counter-attacks on the part of the Teutons. By the end of September the Allied armies had captured from the Germans, since the turn of fortune on the Marne (July 18), 5500 officers and almost a quarter of a million men, besides enormous quantities of guns and munitions and stores. On September 30 the demoralization of Germany was strikingly manifested by the resignation of Hertling as Imperial

Chancellor and prime minister of Prussia and by the succession
to his important positions two days later of Prince Maximilian
of Baden who had been a Liberal critic of recent governmental
policies.   Under Prince Max, Dr. W. S. Solf, the colonial secretary, was named foreign secretary, and a coalition ministry was
formed of which two Socialist deputies, Scheidemann and Bauer,
and two Centrist deputies, Groeber and Erzberger, were members.   In an address to the Reichstag, the new chancellor set
forth his program as follows: adherence to the principles set
forth in the reply to the Pope's note of August 1, 1917; a declaration that Germany is ready to join a league of nations if it
comprises all states and is based on the idea of equality; a clear
statement of purpose to restore Belgium; repudiation of peace
treaties already concluded, if necessary to effect a general peace;
Alsace-Lorraine to be an autonomous state within the Empire;
radical electoral reform to be carried out immediately in Prussia;
strict observance of ministerial responsibility to the duly elected
representatives of the nation; the rules as to the state of siege
to be amended in order to assure freedom of meeting and of
press as well as all other personal liberties.

In October the new Government of Prince Max appealed
direct to President Wilson for a cessation of hostilities.   In this
course it was heartened by an address delivered by the American
president at New York on September 27, in which the purposes of
the war had been restated and five principles laid down for
the foundation of a League of Nations:

"First, the impartial justice meted out must involve no
discrimination between those to whom we wish to be just and
those to whom we do not wish to be just.   It must be a justice
that plays no favorites and knows no standard but the equal
rights of the several peoples concerned;

"Second, no special or separate interest of any single nation
or any group of nations can be made the basis of any part of the
settlement which is not consistent with the common interest of all;

"Third, there can be no leagues or alliances or special covenants or understandings within the general and common family
of the League of Nations;

"Fourth, and more specifically, there can be no special, selfish
economic combinations within the League and no employment
of any form of economic boycott or exclusion except as the power
of economic penalty by exclusion from the markets of the world
may be vested in the League of Nations itself as a means of
discipline and control;

"Fifth, all international agreements and treaties of every kind must be made known in their entirety to the rest of the world."

Throughout October a series of diplomatic notes was exchanged between the United States and Germany, the latter being gradually led to perceive that no cessation of hostilities would be recommended by President Wilson to the Entente Powers until its Government had agreed unreservedly to accept the "Fourteen Points" of the President's address of January 8, 1918, as well as his address of September 27, to put a stop to unrestricted submarine and other ruthless warfare, to evacuate occupied foreign territories, and to guarantee the destruction of autocracy and militarism in Germany.

It was both President Wilson's diplomacy and Marshal Foch's continuous military blows that eventually caused Germany to yield to the inevitable. Throughout October, while negotiations were proceeding between the American president and the German chancellor, the Allied armies forged steadily ahead and the Teutonic forces reeled back before their onsets. In Flanders the group of Belgo-Franco-British armies renewed their attacks on October 14 on a vast front from Dixmude to the Lys and in the next few days took Roulers, Menin, and Courtrai, thereby obliging the Germans to evacuate Douai, Lille, and, soon afterwards, Tourcoing and Roubaix. In Belgium the progress of King Albert's victorious soldiers continued : Ostend and Bruges were reëntered, then Zeebrugge; the suburbs of Ghent and the Dutch frontier were reached; the Lys was crossed. On October 21 the British assailed the Germans east of Denain and captured Valenciennes on November 2 and Landrecies two days later. Maubeuge fell on November 9, and on November 11, the last day of fighting, the British gained Mons, the scene of their defeat and retreat in August, 1914.

In the meantime, farther south the French under General Mangin had broken the strong "Hunding Line" of the Germans between the Oise, the Serre, and the Aisne, and by November 8 they were at the outskirts of Mézières on the Franco-Belgian frontier, while east of the Argonne Forest the Americans smashed their way through the supposedly impregnable "Kriemhilde Line," which extended across the Meuse from Grand Pré to Damvillers, and reached Sedan on November 6. At the same time General Gouraud, west of the Argonne, advanced through Champagne, capturing Vouziers and Rethel, and effecting a juncture with the forces of General Mangin near Mézières on November 11.

The Franco-American advance in the Champagne-Argonne-Meuse region threatened to cut the main line of communications between Germany and her armies in Belgium and northern France, so that even if the Allied armies had elsewhere been less successful than they actually were, Germany would have been doomed to decisive defeat in a very short time. The Germans thoroughly understood the strategic importance of the Meuse valley, and in this valley occurred during October and early November some of the fiercest fighting of the war. Much of the fighting was hand to hand, and the nature of the ground, with

THE FRANCO-AMERICAN OFFENSIVE ON THE MEUSE AND IN THE ARGONNE

its ravines and gullies and woods, made it necessary to wipe out machine-gun nests with infantry rather than with artillery. Yet the Americans, as well as the French, acquitted themselves most admirably in this difficult, last campaign of the Great War. The Americans captured 26,000 prisoners and 468 guns; the French took about 30,000 prisoners and 700 guns. It is estimated that the Germans, in their unsuccessful efforts to defend their main line of communications, lost 150,000 men.

From July 18 to November 11, 1918, Allied arms were uniformly and continuously victorious in all parts of the Western Front. The Teutons were crowded almost completely out of

France and deprived of a considerable portion of Belgium. The Great War was practically at an end, for by November all other fronts — the Italian, the Macedonian, the Turkish, and the Russian — had crumbled, and Germany's partners in the enterprise of *Mittel-Europa* had surrendered unconditionally to the triumphant Allies. Germany had staked everything on the Western Front, and Germany had lost.

ALLIED INTERVENTION IN RUSSIA

Germany, it will be recalled, had concluded the peace of Brest-Litovsk with the Bolshevist Government of Russia in March, 1918. At that time the treaty was advantageous to Germany in three ways. First, it enabled her to transfer the bulk of her armed forces from the Eastern Front and to make her supreme effort in the West. Second, it promised to supply her in the not too distant future with much needed foodstuffs and with raw materials and markets for her manufactures. Third, it afforded her the opportunity to draw into the orbit of *Mittel-Europa* a number of new quasi-independent states, such as Ukrainia, Lithuania, Esthonia, Latvia, and Finland, from which she hoped to conscript reserves of soldiers as well as to obtain economic support and political prestige.

Consequently, from March to July, 1918, while the German General Staff was devoting its chief attention and energy to preparing and launching successive mighty offensives on the Western Front against the British and the French, the German Government was not altogether unmindful of the situation in the East. In the name of upholding and enforcing the treaty of Brest-Litovsk German troops remained on Russian soil, coöperating now with the Ukrainians, now with the Lithuanians, now with the White Guards in Finland, now with the Turks in the Caucasus and the region north of the Black Sea.

In Ukrainia German soldiers backed Skoropadsky's dictatorial régime with bayonets and suppressed peasants' revolts against it. In Latvia and Esthonia, German landlords were encouraged to declare the independence of the Baltic provinces and then to beg Germany's "protection." In May Emperor William II formally recognized Lithuania as a free and sovereign state on the basis of the action of a provisional government which in the preceding December had proclaimed "the restoration of Lithuania as an independent state, allied to the German Empire by an eternal, steadfast alliance, and by conventions chiefly regarding military matters, traffic, customs, and coinage," but William's declaration significantly assumed that Lithuania would "participate in the war burdens of Germany, which secured her liberation." In June German officers took charge of the Finnish army and, after deposing General Mannerheim, the patriotic Finnish commander of the White Guards, and suppressing insurrection and imprisoning numerous socialists and radicals, prepared to transform Finland into a monarchy under a German prince and in close alliance with the German Empire.

Moreover, German army officers proceeded to collect Austrian and German ex-prisoners of war, recently released from prison-camps in Russia, and to utilize them in overrunning parts of Russia in which, according to the letter of the treaty of Brest-Litovsk, Germany had no right whatsoever to interfere. Thus, in the spring of 1918, Germans in coöperation with the Turks were rendering the Black Sea an interior lake of *Mittel-Europa*: the Turks occupied Russian Armenia, Georgia, and other districts of the Caucasus, inflicting unspeakable atrocities upon the population, while the Teutons seized the ports on the northern shore of the Black Sea and a large strip of territory adjacent thereto. And far away, in Siberia, bands of Teuton ex-prisoners were possessing themselves of the railways and other trade routes and likewise of valuable stores of munitions and foodstuffs.

Against these flagrant aggressions the Russian Soviet Government at Moscow protested bitterly and repeatedly, but in vain. By playing the lamb at Brest-Litovsk the Bolsheviki had not tamed the lion; and when the lamb attempted to lie down with the lion, a not unusual fate overtook the lamb. Germany was devouring Russia, and Russia was helpless. The Bolsheviki were confronted by chaos at home as well as in foreign relations. By their repudiation of the Russian debt, by their radical socialistic ventures, and by their separate peace with the Central Empires, they had flouted and alienated the Entente Powers, so that from the Allies they could expect little aid or sympathy in their hour of need. And constituting as they did but a minority of the Russian people, they could hope to bring order out of chaos and still maintain themselves in power only if they accepted a partnership with the Germans. The Bolshevist leaders recognized that their sycophancy to Germany invited counter-attacks upon them by the Allies, but for the present the results of German hostility appeared more real and more menacing. As Lenin stated before the Central Executive Committee of the Soviets in May: "We shall do the little we can, all that diplomacy can do, to put off the moment of attack. . . . We shall not defend the secret agreements which we have published to the world; we shall not defend a 'Great Power,' for there is nothing of Russia left but Great Russia, and no national interests, because for us the interests of the world's socialism stand higher than national interests. We stand for the defense of the socialistic fatherland." Lenin professed belief that the defense of Soviet Russia was facilitated by what he termed "the profound schism dividing the capitalistic governments," by the fact that "the German bandits" were pitted against "the English bandits," and that there were economic rivalries between "the American bourgeoisie" and "the Japanese bourgeoisie." "The situation is," he explained, "that the stormy waves of imperialistic reaction, which seem ready at any moment to overwhelm the little island of the Soviet Socialist Republic, are broken one against another."

For the present, however, Lenin had to swallow his pride and restrain his rhetoric. The Germans were still conquering territories in France, and in Russia they were still sitting squarely in the saddle. Against the potent spurs of the All-Highest German Kaiser, mere diplomacy was exceedingly thin protection to the Bolshevist brute. Under Teutonic direction and domination, and chiefly to Teutonic advantage, the Soviet Government was forced in June to sign humiliating treaties with Ukrainia and Finland. Lenin even had to acquiesce in the "self-determination" of White Russia, a few of whose people, in an assembly controlled by German agents, proclaimed (May 24, 1918) an "independent republic" in federal union with Lithuania and under the protection of the German Empire.

Yet Germany was not altogether successful in her efforts to exploit Russia politically and economically. The former empire of the Tsar was too extensive and too varied, and the Revolution had already introduced too much chaos into Russian politics and Russian industry, to admit of speedy and simple exploitation by any foreign Power. The Soviet Government might promise, under German pressure, to perform valuable services, but it was one thing to promise and another thing to perform; and with a steadily diminishing production of soil and mill and mine, the Bolsheviki had the utmost difficulty in supplying the needy population of Great Russia with the bare necessities of life, to say nothing of exporting supplies to the hateful Teutons. Besides, there were considerable groups of persons and even sizable forces of armed men in Russia who opposed both the Teutons and the Bolsheviki; this opposition would have to be overcome before Germany could expect to reap the full fruits of the peace of Brest-Litovsk.

In May, 1918, the Central Committee of the Russian Socialist Revolutionary party formally denounced the Bolshevist régime and called for a national uprising against the Germans; and in June the Central Committee of the Constitutional Democratic Party did likewise. That popular feeling throughout Russia was inflamed against the Teutons was evidenced by the assassination of Count von Mirbach, the German ambassador at Moscow, on July 6, and of Field Marshal von Eichhorn, the German commandant in Ukrainia, on July 30. About the same time, the Cossacks of the Don took the field against the Soviet Government, as did also the forces of the "Provisional Government of the Caucasus"; and in Siberia several Conservative officers, such as General Alexeiev, General Semenov, Admiral Kolchak, and Colonel Orlov, organized loyalist bands and inaugurated counter-revolutionary movements. As early as February a "Temporary Government of Autonomous Siberia" had been proclaimed at Tomsk, but subsequently when this town was captured by Bolsheviki and Teutonic ex-prisoners, the seat of the Temporary Siberian Government was transferred to Harbin, in Manchuria, and then to Vladivostok. To add to the complications, General Horvath, vice-president of the Chinese Eastern Railway, in July set up an independent anti-Bolshevist government in eastern Siberia.

But the most effective check to Teutons and Bolsheviki alike was provided by a free-lance expeditionary body of Czechoslovaks. At the time of the Bolshevist *coup d'état*, in November, 1917, there were in Ukrainia and southern Russia some 100,000 Czech and Slovak soldiers who originally had been in the service of Austria-Hungary, but who had gone over to the Russians in the hope of fighting for their national independence on the side of the Allies. Upon the conclusion of the treaty of Brest-Litovsk, an agreement was reached with the Soviet military authorities whereby these Czechoslovak troops would be allowed to proceed unmolested across European Russia and Siberia to Vladivostok, whence they would sail to join the Allies in France or Italy. At first the Czechoslovaks preserved a strict neutrality in the internal politics of Russia, and some of them actually made the journey over the Trans-Siberian railway to Vladivostok. But before their transportation had progressed far,

z

friction developed between them and the Bolsheviki and turned to open hostility; and Trotsky, yielding to German representations, sought to disarm them and to prevent them from aiding the Allies.

Armed conflict began on May 26, 1918. The Czechoslovaks opened operations against forces of Bolsheviki and Teutonic ex-prisoners simultaneously in the region of the Volga and in Siberia. In Siberia, they defeated and ousted the pro-Germans from Irkutsk and Vladivostok, occupied several towns on the Amur river, and by the middle of July were in possession of 1300 miles of the Trans-Siberian railway west of Tomsk. In the meantime, in June, they had captured Samara, Simbirsk, and Kasan on the Volga, had advanced to Ufa in the Ural Mountains, and had gained control of the chief grain routes and deprived European Russia of the Siberian food supply.[1] The Czechoslovaks thus did heroic work in preventing the consummation of Teutonic designs on Russia and in arousing national opposition to the Bolshevist régime, but they could not hope with their slender forces to retain their hold on such a vast territory unless they received active assistance from the Allies.

For several months the Allies had been discussing the advisability and practicability of armed intervention in Russia, with a view to reconstructing the Eastern Front and thereby lessening the force of Teutonic attacks in the West. But from a military standpoint the task was at any time difficult enough, and at the very moment when every available Allied soldier was needed to stay supreme German offensives on the Western Front it was peculiarly hazardous. Besides, from the political standpoint intervention in Russia was beset with difficulties, for the Allies were not at war with Russia and there were influential groups in Great Britain, and especially in the United States, who would bitterly resent any attempt to interfere in the domestic affairs of a presumably friendly Power.

Nevertheless the spectacular exploits of the Czechoslovaks and the increasingly obvious interdependence of the Germans and the

---

[1] The death of the Tsar Nicholas II was a curious and sorry incident of the fighting between the Russian Bolsheviki and the Czechoslovaks. The ex-tsar, who had been taken in August, 1917, from his palace of Tsarskoe-Selo to Tobolsk, in Siberia, and thence transferred in May, 1918, to Ekaterinburg, was killed at the latter town on July 16, 1918. The official statement issued on the subject by the Soviet Government said: "Ekaterinburg was seriously threatened by the approach of Czechoslovak bands, and a counter-revolutionary conspiracy was discovered which had as its object the wresting of the ex-tsar from the hands of the Soviet; consequently the president of the Ural Regional Soviet decided to shoot the ex-tsar, and the decision was carried out on July 16."

Bolsheviki finally caused the Allied Governments to reach a tentative accord on the question of intervention. It was decided to dispatch two expeditionary forces to Russia: the one would be landed on the Murman coast and at Archangel in order to defend the Murman railway [1] from Finnish-German attacks, prevent the establishment of submarine bases on the Arctic, and keep the large stores of munitions and supplies which had been purchased by the old Russian régime but never paid for, from falling into enemy hands; the other would be sent to Vladivostok in order to police the Trans-Siberian railway and support the Czechoslovaks. The former would comprise British troops, with detachments of French and Americans; the latter would

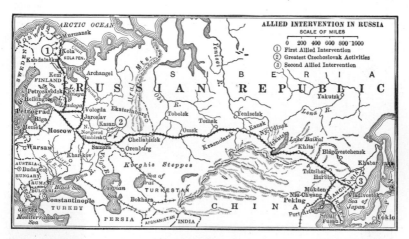

consist of Japanese troops, with smaller contingents of Americans, French, British, Chinese, and Italians. The United States Government, in embarking upon the enterprise, declared it did so "not for interference in internal affairs of Russia and not to distract from the Western Front," but "to protect the Czechoslovaks against the armed Austrian and German prisoners who are attacking them and to steady any efforts at self-government or self-defense in which the Russians themselves may be willing to accept assistance. Whether from Vladivostok or from Murmansk and Archangel, the only present object for which American troops will be employed will be to guard military stores which may subsequently be needed by Russian forces."

---

[1] The Murman railway had been built in 1916 from the ice-free port of Murmansk on the Arctic to Petrograd, in order to provide means of importing war supplies into Russia from Great Britain, France, and the United States.

A naval landing had been effected by the British in March, 1918, at Murmansk, the single ice-free port on the Arctic and the terminus of the recently constructed railway to Petrograd. Hither in June arrived the small Allied expedition, under the British General Poole, which proceeded to occupy the railway as far as Kem on the White Sea and to declare the Murman coast to be "Russian territory under Allied protection." On August 2 General Poole took Archangel, and five days later he organized, from among anti-Bolshevist Russian refugees, a regional "provisional government," headed by Nicholas Tchaikovsky. These activities of the Allies in northern Russia served alike to embitter the Bolsheviki and defeat German schemes. Finland's enthusiasm for conquest of the Arctic littoral gradually waned and Germany's increasing preoccupation elsewhere made her aid negligible. By the second half of September General Poole had advanced from Archangel fifty miles southward along the Dvina river, but farther he could not get. His forces were too few and his lines of communication too precarious. Merely to feed the starving population in the liberated region overtaxed his resources.

In the Far East the Allied Expeditionary Force, under the Japanese General Otani, landed at Vladivostok in August, 1918, and within a month cleared the regions to the north, along the Ussuri and Amur rivers, and likewise the Trans-Siberian railway as far as Lake Baikal where a juncture was effected with the Czechoslovaks operating to the westward. Communication was thus opened between Vladivostok and the Volga, and the enemy in Siberia virtually collapsed. Yet the comparative smallness of the Allied forces, their lack of unity, and their endless civil difficulties about railway control and the recognition of "provisional" Russian Governments, which sprang up in their wake like mushrooms, prevented them from utilizing their successes in Siberia for a decisive drive against the Bolsheviki in European Russia. In particular, there was dislike of the Japanese, who constituted a large majority of the whole expeditionary force and who not only treated all Manchuria and eastern Siberia as their peculiar "sphere of influence" but also blocked for several months the project of the other Allies to intrust the repair and operation of the Trans-Siberian railway to a staff of experienced American engineers headed by John R. Stevens. It was not until the signing of the armistice on the Western Front, in November, 1918, that Japan, responding to American representations, consented to reduce her army in Siberia from 73,000 to 25,000 and to turn over the whole Trans-Siberian railway to the American engineers.

Ever since Allied intervention at Archangel and at Vladivostok, in August, what amounted to a state of war had existed between the Entente Powers and the Bolshevist Government of Russia. That Moscow and Berlin were coming nearer to conciliation and united action was evidenced by the signing on August 27 of three special agreements supplementary to the treaty of Brest-Litovsk. By the terms of these agreements, Germany conceded to the Soviet Government full liberty to nationalize Russian industry; the Baltic states of Esthonia and Livonia were declared independent of Russia, though Russia was given free harbor zones in the Baltic ports of Reval, Riga, and Windau; Baku (in the Caucasus) with its rich naphtha deposits, was left to Russia with the understanding that a portion of the naphtha should be at the disposal of Germany; the Bolsheviki promised to employ all the means at their disposal to expel the Entente forces from northern Russia, while Germany guaranteed Russia against attacks by or through Finland; and Russia agreed to pay Germany an indemnity of one and one-half billion dollars, a small part of which would be assumed by Finland and Ukrainia.

As the Bolshevist Government leaned more and more toward Germany, the Allies redoubled their efforts to coördinate and unify the anti-Bolshevist factions and "governments" in Russia. In September anti-Bolshevist members of the Constituent Assembly which had been elected in the autumn of 1917, held a National Convention at Ufa and set up a new "All-Russian Government," with Nicholas Avksentiev as president and Peter Vologodsky as premier. With this government were gradually consolidated the Temporary Siberian Government, the Provisional Government of Northern Russia, and the regional administrations of the Urals and the Don, so that early in November its authority extended over the greater part of Siberia and over portions of the provinces of Samara, Orenburg, Ufa, Ural, and Archangel, and its seat seemed securely established at Omsk. On November 18, however, a counter-revolutionary *coup d'état* was executed at Omsk by Admiral Kolchak, the minister of war and marine in the All-Russian Government; President Avksentiev was "taken to an unknown place," several influential radical leaders, such as Victor Tchernov, minister under Kerensky, were imprisoned, and Admiral Kolchak assumed a dictatorship. Obviously the same factional wranglings and dissensions which had ruined Kerensky in the autumn of 1917 were disgracing and paralyzing the anti-Bolshevists in Russia in the autumn of 1918.

Nevertheless, in spite of manifold difficulties, Allied intervention in Russia, combined with the chaos in Bolshevist Russia and with the nationalistic strivings of lesser nationalities within the former empire of the tsars, effectually prevented Germany and Austria-Hungary from reaping the full fruits of the peace of Brest-Litovsk. Russia as a whole did not become a Teutonic satrapy or supply-station. And by the time that German arms were defeated on the Western Front German prestige had been quite lost in the East. Had it not been for the continued chaos in Russia to which probably the Czechoslovaks and the Allies contributed, it might have been possible for Germany to have exploited the East politically and economically and thereby to have strengthened her resistance in the West and postponed the collapse of *Mittel-Europa*. As it was, Allied intervention in Russia hastened the inevitable.

Nor should the rôle of the Bolsheviki in the final drama of Germany's downfall be passed over in silence. Whatever criminal deeds these fanatics were guilty of — and their guilt was certainly considerable — they at any rate indirectly were of great service to the Allies in paving the way for the destruction of German morale and for the overthrow of the Kaiser. If they were at times pro-German in deed, they were always in thought and word anti-Kaiser and anti-Ludendorff. From the moment of their assumption of power, in November, 1917, they had never wearied of spreading propaganda in Germany, as well as in Russia, against Teutonic militarism and imperialism. To this end they availed themselves of the negotiations at Brest-Litovsk and of their "friendly" contact with the Germans throughout the summer and autumn of 1918. Their embassy in Berlin became a center of revolutionary agitation as sinister to the Imperial German Government as it was timely to the Allies. The Teutonic crash in November, 1918, was due primarily, of course, to German military disaster in the West, but secondarily (and a little ironically) it might be traced to the Bolshevist Revolution and German "successes" in the East.

ALLIED TRIUMPH IN THE NEAR EAST: SURRENDER OF BULGARIA AND TURKEY

At the very time, in the spring of 1918, when Germany was making her supreme effort on the Western Front, her Near

Eastern confederates — Bulgaria and Turkey — were engaged in diplomatic controversies that were undignified and annoying. The greedy and grasping King Ferdinand was insisting that the whole region of the Dobrudja, recently surrendered by Rumania, should be added to Bulgaria. The Young Turk régime at Constantinople, on the other hand, was stoutly maintaining that, if Bulgaria secured Dobrudja, Turkey must have compensations not only in the Caucasus, as a charge upon Russia, but also in Thrace, at Bulgaria's expense. King Ferdinand would not agree to another rectification of the Turco-Bulgar frontier, and consequently the governments of Germany and Austria-Hungary, so as not to offend the sensitive Young Turks, decided not to hand over the Dobrudja to Bulgaria but to administer it themselves "pending final adjustment." To patriotic Bulgars this was interpreted as a threat by the Central Empires; and the relations between Sofia and Berlin were not made more cordial by the aid which the Teutons rendered the Turks in the Caucasus or by the backing which the Turks gave the Teutons in southern Russia and in the Dobrudja. The Black Sea might become an interior lake of *Mittel-Europa*, but the Bulgars feared it would become a lake dominated by a close Turco-Teutonic alliance. Bulgaria had entered the Great War three years ago, not in order to subject herself to an overlordship of sultan and kaiser, but simply to establish her own hegemony in the Near East.

And now in the spring of 1918 the Bulgarian army faced alone the Allied forces in Macedonia. The Austro-German divisions which had buttressed it from 1915 to 1917 had been called away to participate in the mighty offensives on the Western Front. There was still, indeed, the so-called Eleventh German Army, but its staff officers alone were German; the troops were Bulgarian. In Albania a few Austrian battalions were opposing the Italians. But the entire Macedonian Front from Lake Ochrida to the Ægean was held by the Bulgars with sixteen divisions, or about 400,000 men. The prolonged inaction of the Allies at Salonica, who had made only partial and limited attacks in the vicinity of Monastir, the bend of the Tcherna, and Lake Doiran, kept the Bulgars under the illusion that the war would end in reciprocal lassitude and that they would be able to retain their sensational conquests of 1915.

As a matter of fact, however, Bulgaria was rotting from within. The common people had had enough of the war; they were hungry, weary, and restless. King Ferdinand was growing unpopular. German influence was decreasing in proportion as the divisions lent for the victories of 1915 and 1916 decreased.   And the army itself, worn out by war, by insufficient food, and by long inaction, would probably be unable to resist an unexpected and sweeping attack.   Perhaps the new government of Premier Malinoff, which in June replaced the pro-German ministry of Radoslavoff at Sofia, was quite willing, before intrusting itself to the good-will of the Entente, that such an attack should come.   A defeat would justify a separate and much desired peace.

Allied confidence waxed as that of the Bulgarians waned. The composite Army of the East, better known as the Expeditionary Force at Salonica, grew ever more formidable.   In the beginning it had been formed of French and British divisions from Gallipoli, and, although its effectives had been gradually increased from 1915 to 1917 and it had been further reënforced by Italian troops and by Serbian divisions which had escaped the frightful retreat of the winter of 1915–1916, it had not become strong enough to break through the Bulgarian front and join with Rumania when that nation entered into the conflict in the autumn of 1916.

Later, however, in the winter of 1916–1917, Venizelos, having broken with the pro-German government of King Constantine, added three divisions of Greek soldiers who had rallied to his banner; and, after the deposition of Constantine, in June, 1917, the Greek army increased steadily to ten divisions, creating odds that would permit the Allies to undertake a great offensive movement in Macedonia.   In July, 1918, the Army of the East comprised some twenty-nine divisions — eight French, four British, six Serbian, ten Greek, and one Italian — or about 725,000 men.

In July and August, 1918, Marshal Foch, while raining blows on the badly shaken armies of Ludendorff in the West, did not lose sight of the Near East and of the effect which the elimination of the Bulgars and Turks would have upon the decision of the war.   With that clairvoyance and measured audacity which characterized his method of forcing victory, he planned a double operation in Macedonia and Syria, synchronizing precisely with his own smashing blows in France and Belgium, and intrusted its execution to two leaders — Allenby and Franchet d'Esperey — whose aggressive spirit he could trust.

General Franchet d'Esperey, who arrived at Salonica in July, first obtained from his predecessor, General Guillaumat, precise information regarding the situation of the Bulgars, and then set to work preparing for victory.   On September 14, 1918, the

Bulgarian lines were heavily bombarded, and on the two succeeding days infantry attacked, — British and Greek troops in the
vicinity of Lake Doiran, on the right of the Macedonian Front;
French and Serbian forces, in the center, along the Vardar and
the Tcherna; and the Italians, on the extreme left, in Albania.
So great was the Allied success, especially in the center, that
within a week the Serbians advanced forty miles and threatened
to isolate the Bulgarians operating north of Monastir.   On
September 24, French cavalry entered Prilep and found huge
quantities of abandoned stores.   The next day witnessed the
capture of Babuna Pass and Ishtip, and the opening of the way
for a quick advance upon Veles and Uskub.   Meanwhile, the
Greeks and British had overcome peculiarly stubborn resistance

MACEDONIAN FRONT AT TIME OF BULGARIA'S SURRENDER

near Lake Doiran, and on September 27 they seized the Bulgarian town of Strumnitza.   The road to Sofia was opened to the
triumphant Allies.

Then suddenly Bulgaria sued for an armistice and promptly
agreed to an unconditional surrender.   The armistice, signed at
Salonica on September 30, provided: that the Bulgarian army
should immediately be demobilized and its arms and equipment
placed in Allied custody; that all Greek and Serbian territory
still occupied by Bulgaria should at once be evacuated; that all
Bulgarian means of transport, including railways and ships on
the Danube, should be put at the Allies' disposal; that her territory should be available for their operations; and that strategic
points in Bulgaria should be occupied by British, French, or
Italian troops.   The bubble of Bulgarian pretension was pricked,
and its bursting brought consternation to the Central Empires
and to Turkey.

On October 4, tricky King Ferdinand, despised alike by the
Teutons and the Allies and threatened by his own people whom
he had misled and deceived, abdicated in favor of his son, the

Crown Prince Boris, and withdrew to his private estates in Hungary. Allied forces proceeded in triumph to the Danube, meeting with no resistance except from broken Austro-German fragments. On October 12 the Serbians entered Nish, their ancient capital. There had been a brilliant naval raid on Durazzo by Italian and British warships on October 2; on October 7 the Italians occupied El Bassan, and a week later they took Durazzo. On October 19, only about a month after the launching of the Macedonian offensive, the Allies reached the shore of the Danube. Late in October Montenegro was cleared of Austrians and Bosnia was invaded; and early in November Belgrade was reoccupied.

The liberation of the Balkan states south of the Danube had immediate consequences of far-reaching importance. It encouraged the Rumanians to disregard the peace of Bucharest which their government had concluded in March with the Central Empires and to reënter the war on the side of the Allies. It enabled General Franchet d'Esperey to carry the contest into Rumania and southern Russia not only, but also to menace the now exposed southern border of Austria-Hungary. In this way the subject nationalities of the Dual Monarchy were put in a new position of vantage in their struggle for independence. From the signing of the armistice at Salonica, the old Habsburg Empire was doomed; Austrian aggression against Serbia was transformed by the act of Austria's confederate, as by a sort of poetic justice, into Serbian triumph over Austria.

Bulgaria's surrender menaced the integrity of Austria-Hungary indirectly; directly it threatened the speedy downfall and dissolution of the Ottoman Empire. For the Balkan link in the Berlin-Bagdad Railway was now in Allied hands; Turkey was isolated from *Mittel-Europa;* and General Franchet d'Esperey was in a position to make a direct and unhampered attack by land upon Constantinople.

Already the Ottoman Empire was *in extremis.* Ever since the loss of Bagdad in March, 1917, Turkish morale had been steadily declining. Unfortunately General Allenby was unable immediately to follow up his capture of Jerusalem, in December, 1917, with a decisive campaign, by reason of the fact that his expeditionary force was depleted by withdrawal of British and French troops to reënforce the Allied lines in France which, as we have seen, were mightily assailed by Ludendorff in the spring of 1918. However, the Turks, fully engaged with the Arabs of Hedjaz, were powerless to take advantage of the temporary weakness of their most dangerous enemy; and Allenby utilized the respite afforded him by capturing Jericho and the line of the Jordan and by strengthening otherwise his hold upon Palestine.

With the turn of fortune on the Western Front and with the arrival of reënforcements from India, and at almost the same moment as General Franchet d'Esperey drove against the Bulgars, General Allenby resumed the offensive against the Turks. On September 19, 1918, he struck on a sixteen-mile front between Rafat and the seacoast, and cleared the ground for a sensational cavalry dash, which within thirty-six hours reached Beisan and

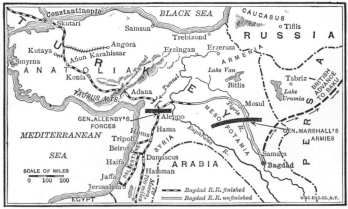

PROGRESS OF BRITISH AND ARAB OFFENSIVE IN TURKEY, OCTOBER, 1918

Nazareth, far to the north, and broke up the Turkish armies between the Jordan and the Mediterranean. Haifa and Acre were seized on September 23, and three days later the British arrived at the Sea of Galilee and occupied Tiberias. Turkish forces east of the Jordan were meanwhile being driven by the Arabs in a southerly direction and were thus hopelessly separated from their comrades west of the Jordan who were fleeing north in a mad rout.

Allenby's advance was now a rapid pursuit, without any frontal fighting on the part of the Turks. The British general, accompanied by the son of the Sultan of Hedjaz, entered Damascus on October 1; and Rayak, Beirut, Tripoli, and Homs fell in quick succession. On October 26 Aleppo was captured, and the German General Liman von Sanders, with the Turkish General Staff in his baggage train, fled to Alexandretta. In five weeks the Allies in Palestine and Syria had moved their front three hundred miles to the northward; they had taken 80,000 prisoners and 350 guns; they had destroyed whole Turkish armies; and they had cut the much prized Bagdad Railway.

To cap the climax of Turkish disaster, the British in Mesopotamia now moved irresistibly upon Mosul, while the Allies in Macedonia threatened Adrianople and even Constantinople itself. The "Sick Man of the East" was in his last throes. The Sultan Mohammed V had died on July 3, and his successor, Mohammed VI, now accepted (October 10) the resignations of Enver Pasha, Talaat Pasha, and the other Young Turks who by espousing the Teutonic cause had brought their country to ruin, and consented to sue for peace. On October 14 the Porte appealed to President Wilson to use his influence to secure an armistice. Receiving no reply from the United States, the Turkish Government released General Townshend, who had been captured at Kut-el-Amara, and sent him to the headquarters of Admiral Calthorpe, commanding the British naval forces in the Ægean, to ask that negotiations should be immediately opened for an armistice. Admiral Calthorpe outlined the conditions on which the request would be granted, and during the last week of October Turkish plenipotentiaries arrived under safe conduct at Mudros on the island of Lemnos.

Here, on October 30, was signed an armistice which went into effect on the following day. Its main terms were the opening of the Dardanelles, Bosphorus, and Black Sea, the prompt repatriation of Allied prisoners, the demobilization of the Turkish army, the severing of all relations with the Central Powers, and the placing of Turkish territory at the disposal of the Allies for military purposes.

German mastery of the Near East had lasted only three years. Throughout the Near East, in Syria, in Mesopotamia, in Persia, in Armenia, in Asia Minor, in all the Balkan states, and in Constantinople, the Allies were now masters. The solution of the Near Eastern problems rested henceforth not with the Central Empires but with the Entente Powers. For the unconditional surrender of Bulgaria and Turkey was followed straightway by the complete collapse of that keystone of *Mittel-Europa*, that Power which in 1914 had precipitated the Great War — Austria-Hungary.

THE COLLAPSE OF AUSTRIA–HUNGARY: RESURGENCE OF OPPRESSED NATIONALITIES

Long before the surrender of Bulgaria and Turkey, long before the German defeat on the Western Front, the Dual Monarchy faced disaster. Unlike her confederates, Austria-Hungary suffered less from foreign prowess than from internal weakness. Ever since the Russian Revolution, in March, 1917, the task of dominating a majority of Slavs by a minority of Magyars and German-Austrians, under any theory of democracy or national self-determination, had become utterly hopeless.

At first each of the subject nationalities, — Czechoslovaks, Jugoslavs, Poles, Ruthenians (Ukrainians), and Rumans, — clamored for autonomy within the Dual Monarchy, but as time went on they all demanded complete separation from German Austria and from Hungary. Each of the subject nationalities developed remarkable solidarity, the clergy and the university professors vying as a rule with the business-men, the peasants, and the artisans, in the furtherance of national interests. Separatist propaganda was carried on in the open and by stealth. Loyalty to the Habsburgs was undermined. In such cities as Prague, Agram, Laibach, Cracow, and Lemberg there were increasingly frequent riots and demonstrations. Mutinies in the Austro-Hungarian army were everyday occurrences; and many Czechoslovak, Jugoslav, and Polish troops deserted to the Allies and served the Allied cause in Russia or on the Western Front or in Italy. "National Councils" of the several subject nationalities were organized in Paris, or London, or Rome, or Washington; and these "provisional governments" not only fanned the flame of sedition within Austria-Hungary but strove to secure active Allied assistance in their efforts to disintegrate the Dual Monarchy.

In 1917 "disloyal" agitation had been less prevalent among Poles than among Czechoslovaks and Jugoslavs. The Poles of Galicia had always been treated rather liberally by the Habsburgs, and the erection of a kingdom of Poland by Austro-German decree of November 5, 1916, had temporarily appeased the Austrian Poles and enabled Premier von Seidler to control a majority of votes in the Austrian *Reichsrat*. But in the winter of 1917–1918 Austria lost the support of her Poles, for she was obliged to agree to Germany's policy respecting Poland, and Germany's policy was to strengthen Ukrainia at Poland's expense. Thus the Polish province of Cholm was incorporated into the new Ukrainian state, despite the vehement protests of the German-appointed Polish Regency at Warsaw (February 14, 1918) and the bitter imprecations of the Austrian Poles in Galicia. Thenceforth the Poles, as well as the Jugoslavs and the Czechoslovaks, were openly hostile to the Dual Monarchy.

General Joseph Pilsudski, a great national hero and formerly quite pro-Austrian, directed such an agitation in Poland against the Teutons that for the safety of *Mittel-Europa* he was arrested and deported to Germany. Joseph Haller, a colonel in the Austrian army, deserted after the treaty of Brest-Litovsk, with his Polish regiment, and, after joining the Czechoslovaks in Russia, made his way to Paris, where he assumed supreme command of a Polish army fighting for the Allies in France. And when the Polish deputies in the Austrian *Reichsrat* united with the already numerous opposition of Czech and Jugoslav deputies, parliamentary government in Austria became impossible. The only session of the *Reichsrat* during the Great War was closed abruptly by Emperor Charles and Premier von Seidler on May 4, 1918.

The majority of the population of the Dual Monarchy were at last becoming articulate, and, what was far more significant, they were uniting in common opposition to the continuance of the Habsburg Empire. This was the burden of the Pan-Slavic Congress held at Prague on January 6, 1918, of a second Congress held at Agram on March 2, and of a third held at Laibach in July. But greater freedom of speech naturally prevailed outside of Austria-Hungary than within; and consequently the clearest statement of the aims of the subject peoples of the Dual Monarchy was made at the famous Congress of Oppressed Austrian Nationalities convened at Rome under the auspices of the Italian Government on April 10, 1918. This Congress, which included leading representatives of the Czechoslovaks, Jugoslavs, Rumans, and Poles, unanimously adopted the following resolutions: "(1) Every people proclaims it to be its right to determine its own nationality and to secure national unity and complete independence; (2) Every people knows that the Austro-Hungarian Monarchy is an instrument of German domination and a fundamental obstacle to the realization of its free development and self-government; (3) The Congress recognizes the necessity of fighting against the common oppressors."

That the Congress at Rome faithfully reflected the sentiments of the subject nationalities in Austria-Hungary was amply demonstrated three days later by a noteworthy assembly at Prague. On this occasion the *Reichsrat* deputies of the Czech nation and those of the Jugoslav nation, the latter speaking in the name of the Croats, Slovenes, and Serbs, met and made a joint agreement, through an oath worthy of everlasting remembrance, to suffer and struggle relentlessly to free their peoples from the foreign yoke and bring down into the dust the old imperialistic Empire, covered, as they said, with the maledictions of mankind.

To the appeals of the oppressed Austrian nationalities the Allies did not turn deaf ears. Already, in 1917, France had authorized the organization of Polish and Czechoslovak armies on the Western Front and had recognized them as belligerent units; and now, on April 21, 1918, Italy recognized the Czechoslovak National Council as a *de facto* government and placed a Czechoslovak legion beside her own troops on the Piave Front. On May 29 Secretary Lansing, in behalf of the United States, declared "that the nationalistic aspirations of the Czechoslovaks and the Jugoslavs for freedom have the earnest sympathy of this Government"; and a week later the sixth session of the Supreme War Council, meeting at Versailles and attended by the prime ministers of France, Great Britain, and Italy, adopted resolutions that "the creation of a united, independent Polish state, with free access to the sea, constitutes one of the conditions of a solid and just peace and the rule of right in Europe," and that "the Allies have noted with satisfaction the declaration of the American Secretary of State, to which they adhere, expressing the greatest sympathy with the national aspirations of the Czechs and Jugoslavs for freedom." Of the complete independence of Czechoslovakia, formal recognition was accorded by France on June 30, by Great Britain on August 13, by the United States on September 2, and by Japan on September 9. No other course could honorably be taken by the Allies toward a country whose soldiers at the time were waging war against the Central Empires in France, in Italy, and most thrillingly in Russia.

Under the circumstances the Habsburg officials at Vienna and at Budapest bent all their energies to the task of preserving some semblance of order in their dominions until such time as the Germans should have won the war and come to their assistance. They proclaimed martial law in Bohemia and in Croatia. They imprisoned "seditious" persons and endeavored to suppress "revolutionary" publications. They kept a fairly large army on the Italian Front, though they discovered to their chagrin that it was no longer fit for any offensive operations. They sent some artillery and a few regiments of infantry to aid Ludendorff in his supreme effort on the Western Front. Most of all, for the success of the great German offensive in France they prayed ceaselessly and imploringly. There was little else that they could do. There was no other hope for them. German defeat would mean for Germany simply defeat; for the Dual Monarchy, it would signify dissolution.

Despairingly the Magyars and the German Austrians witnessed the quick, sharp hammer-blows with which Marshal Foch during August and September was driving Ludendorff's mighty hosts out of France and Belgium. Still more despairingly they beheld the surrender of Bulgaria and the advance of General Franchet d'Esperey's armies, in October, to the Danube and into Bosnia and Herzegovina. The nadir of their despair was reached when, on October 24, General Diaz, the commander-in-chief of the Italian armies, struck suddenly against their lines along the Piave and in the Alps. Their remaining armed forces were now so honeycombed with disaffection and sedition that they were incapable of making even a defensive stand.

Italian armies on October 24–25, 1918, smote the Austrians in the Monte Grappa region, between the Brenta and Piave rivers, while a British unit attacked along the lower Piave and a French unit took Monte Seisemol on the Asiago plateau. By October 30 the Italians had captured Monte Grappa, with 33,000 prisoners, and were driving the Austrians back along the whole front from the Alps to the Adriatic.

With the fall of Monte Grappa the enemy army in the mountains was definitely cut off from the one in the plains, and both began to flee in increasing confusion. By November 1 the one in the south was in utter rout, and the Italians were already across the Livenza river, inflicting terrific losses on the fugitives. The whole stretch of country, in the mountains and on the plains, for a distance of seventy miles, was strewn with the bodies of Austrian dead. On November 3 the Italian War Office announced that both Trent and Trieste had been captured and that Italian cavalry had entered Udine. In ten days the Austrians lost an immense quantity of material of all kinds, nearly all their stores and depots, and left in Italian hands some 300,000 prisoners and not fewer than 5000 guns.

Meanwhile, Austria-Hungary had bowed to the inevitable. On October 29, Count Julius Andrassy, who had recently succeeded Baron Burian as foreign minister of the Dual Monarchy, notified President Wilson that his Government was ready to acknowledge "the rights of the peoples of Austria-Hungary, notably those of the Czechoslovaks and the Jugoslavs," and to make a separate peace without awaiting the outcome of Germany's negotiations, and he begged the United States to urge upon the Allies the cessation of hostilities. On October 31 an official Austrian mission, under a flag of truce, visited the headquarters of General Diaz and offered unconditional surrender. An armistice was accordingly drawn up and signed on November 3, 1918; and on the following day hostilities against Austria-Hungary ceased. The principal terms of the armistice were as follows: complete demobilization of the Austro-Hungarian armies and the withdrawal of all troops operating with the Germans, half of the artillery and equipment being delivered to the Allies; evacuation of all territories invaded by Austro-Hungarian troops and likewise of all territory in dispute between the Austro-Hungarians on one hand and the Italians and Slavs on the other, such territory being occupied by the Allies; Allied occupation of strategical points in Austria-Hungary and of the transport system of the Dual Monarchy; withdrawal of all German troops from the Balkan and Italian fronts as well as from Austria-Hungary; immediate repatriation of Allied prisoners; surrender of captured Allied merchantmen; and delivery to the Allies of fifteen Austro-Hungarian submarines, three battleships, three light cruisers, nine destroyers, twelve torpedo boats, and six monitors, all other warships being disarmed; and Allied occupation of Pola and control of the Danube.

The irretrievable disaster of the Austro-Hungarian armies in Italy led swiftly, even before the conclusion of the armistice, to the dissolution of the Dual Monarchy. By the end of October the Government at Vienna had resigned and the empire was already disintegrating into independent states. Emperor Charles acquiesced in the inevitable by appointing Professor Lammasch, an anti-war Liberal, as head of a liquidation ministry to hand over the former imperial powers to the provisional governments of the several emerging nationalities.

From the ruins of the Habsburg Empire, Czechoslovakia emerged at once. On October 18 its independence had been solemnly declared at Paris; ten days later the Austrian Governor fled from Prague; and on October 29 Dr. Karel Kramarcz, the local head of the Czechoslovak National Council, proclaimed the deposition of Charles as king of Bohemia, Moravia, Silesia, and Slovakia, and the establishment of a free and united republic. At the end of October two delegations of Czechoslovak leaders — the one from Prague and the other from Paris — met at Geneva in Switzerland and drafted a constitution for the new republic, modeled in part after that of the United States, and chose Professor Thomas G. Masaryk, the "grand old man" of Bohemia, as

2 A

provisional president. A Czechoslovak National Assembly, convened in Prague in November, ratified the choice of Masaryk as president and selected Kramarcz as prime minister.

Jugoslavia was also becoming a reality. Over the Slovenes of Austria and the Croats of Croatia and the Serbs of Bosnia-Herzegovina, the Jugoslav National Council at Agram assumed control. On October 29 the Croatian Diet unanimously proclaimed the deposition of Emperor Charles and the separation of the "kingdom of Dalmatia, Slovenia and Fiume" from Hungary. At the same time the Diet expressed a desire for union with Serbia and Montenegro. "The people of Croatia, Slovenia, and Serbia wish to have nothing in common with Austria and Hungary. They aspire to a union of all the Jugoslavs within the limits extending from the Isonzo to the Vardar. They desire to constitute a free state, sovereign and independent." For the fulfillment of this desire, a provisional agreement was reached at Geneva, in Switzerland, on November 7, between Nicholas Pashitch, premier of Serbia, Dr. Anton Koroshetz, leader of the Jugoslav party in the Austrian *Reichsrat*, and Dr. Anton Trumbitch, president of the Jugoslav National Council in London. Although there were cultural and religious differences between the Croatians and Slovenes, on one hand, and the Serbs, on the other, and although the Slovenes in particular would have preferred a republic to a monarchy, nevertheless so great was the desire for national union that, in accordance with the arrangements effected at Geneva, the Jugoslav Convention at Agram on November 24 formally proclaimed the establishment of "the Unitary Kingdom of Serbs, Croats, and Slovenes." [1] Of the new kingdom — really a Greater Serbia — King Peter of Serbia became monarch, with Prince Alexander as regent, and with a coalition ministry including Pashitch as premier, Koroshetz as vice-premier, and Trumbitch as minister of foreign affairs. Against the union, King Nicholas of Montenegro alone held out; his fate was sealed by the Montenegrin Parliament, which on December 1 deposed him and voted for the incorporation of Montenegro into the Kingdom of the Serbs, Croats, and Slovenes.

Apace the disintegration of the Dual Monarchy proceeded. Transylvania fell away from Hungary and Bukowina from Austria, and both were prepared by nationalist agitators for union with Rumania. The Banat of Temesvar drifted away from Hungary and became the object of rival claims of Rumania and

[1] This action was confirmatory of the Declaration of Corfu of July 20, 1917. See above, p. 265.

Serbia.   And Galicia, the scene of conflict between Poland and Ukrainia, was a unit in repudiating Austrian rule.

Even Hungary would no longer endure any form of union with the Teutons.   Demonstrations at Budapest on October 28 inaugurated a swift and comparatively bloodless revolution which put Count Michael Karolyi and his Independence Party in power.   On November 2 Karolyi announced to the Hungarian National Council that the Emperor-King Charles had voluntarily freed the Magyars from their oath of fealty and left them free to decide their future form of government.   On November 16 Hungary was formally declared a republic, with Karolyi as governor, and assurances were given of radical democratic reform.   It was the end of the *Ausgleich* between Austria and Hungary.   The Dual Monarchy was no more.

In the meantime Vienna had become the center of a revolution which aimed to weld the Teutonic population of Austria proper and of the Tyrol into the "German State of Austria" under a national and democratic government.   The movement began on October 30 with a demonstration of students and workmen in front of the Parliament building, when the president of the German National Council announced a new administration. "But without the Habsburgs!" shouted the crowd.   An officer in uniform then called upon his fellow-officers to remove their imperial cockades, which was done "with enthusiasm"; and the imperial standard, flying before the Parliament building, was hauled down.   Even German Austria was done with the Habsburgs.

Emperor Charles was ruined by a war which he did not make and by circumstances over which he had little control.   Young, well-intentioned, and amiable, his respectable personal qualities were no proof against the vast elemental forces which took his realm from him and only left him the unenviable fame of being the last of the Habsburg Emperors.   On November 11, 1918, Charles issued his final imperial decree.   "Since my accession," he said, "I have incessantly tried to rescue my peoples from this tremendous war.   I have not delayed the reëstablishment of constitutional rights or the opening of a way for the people to substantial national betterment.   Filled with an unalterable love for my people, I will not, with my person, be a hindrance to their free development.   I acknowledge the decision taken by German Austria to form a separate state.   The people have by their deputies taken charge of the government.   I relinquish all participation in the administration of the state.   Likewise I have released the members of the Austrian government from their offices. May the German Austrian people realize harmony from the new adjustment. The happiness of my peoples was my aim from the beginning. My warmest wishes are that an interval of peace will avail to heal the wounds of this war." On November 13 the National Assembly at Vienna formally proclaimed German Austria a republic.[1]

The Great War began in July, 1914, with the attack of the Dual Monarchy of Austria-Hungary upon the little Slav state of Serbia. By the autumn of 1918, however, Serbia was free and amply avenged. Within the former confines of the Dual Monarchy were now the three independent republics of Czechoslovakia, German Austria, and Hungary, while large portions of its erstwhile territories were added to Poland, to Italy, to Rumania, and to Serbia. The Habsburg Empire was destroyed; it had taken the sword, and by the sword it had perished.

Of *Mittel-Europa* all that remained was the Empire of the Hohenzollerns, and the way was now opened for an Allied advance into Germany not only through France and Belgium but through Austria and Czechoslovakia and Poland. The Empire was tottering and the Hohenzollerns were preparing for flight. Germany, which in 1914 had not delayed to stand "in shining armor" beside her ally, could not delay in 1918 to follow Austria-Hungary in suing for peace.

THE END OF HOSTILITIES: FLIGHT OF WILLIAM II

Synchronizing with the surrender of Bulgaria and Turkey and the collapse of Austria-Hungary was the constant, forced retirement of German troops from France and Belgium. Late in October serious mutinies broke out in the German fleet, soldiers at the front refused to fight, Ludendorff resigned, Liebknecht and other Independent Socialists were inciting revolution, Emperor William was promising far-reaching democratic reforms, and Chancellor Prince Maximilian was begging President Wilson to grant an armistice.

---

[1] Austrian general elections were held on February 15, 1919, with four million men and women participating. The National Constituent Assembly, thus chosen, convened on March 4, its membership comprising 70 Social Democrats, 64 Christian Socialists (Clericals), and 91 adherents of minor groups. Karl Seitz, leader of the Social Democrats, was elected president; a coalition ministry of Social Democrats and Christian Socialists was formed under Karl Renner as chancellor; and a republican constitution for German Austria was drafted and subsequently adopted. Ex-Emperor Charles sought refuge in Switzerland in March, 1919.

Negotiations between the United States and Germany which began on October 5 ended on November 5, when President Wilson informed the Germans that Marshal Foch had been authorized to conclude an armistice with accredited German agents and that the Allies were ready to make peace according to the terms laid down "in the President's address to Congress of January, 1918, and the principles of settlement enunciated in his subsequent addresses," subject to reservations on "Point Two" (the freedom of the seas) and to an explicit understanding that "compensation will be made by Germany for all damage done to the civilian population of the Allies and their property by the aggression of Germany by land, by sea, and from the air." The next day the German Government sent a mission headed by Mathias Erzberger to receive the terms of armistice from Marshal Foch. At Rethondes, six miles east of Compiègne, the dejected German envoys on November 8 met the stern generalissimo of the Allied armies and heard from his lips the hard conditions of the victors, conditions which without amendment they must accept or reject within seventy-two hours. At five o'clock in the morning of November 11 the terms of the armistice were finally accepted and signed.

In accordance with the armistice, hostilities were to cease everywhere at eleven A.M. on November 11. Within fourteen days Germany was to evacuate Belgium, France, Alsace-Lorraine, and Luxemburg; within a month she was to evacuate all territory on the left bank of the Rhine. Allied troops would promptly occupy these areas together with the bridgeheads at the principal crossings of the Rhine (Mainz, Coblenz, and Cologne) to a depth of thirty kilometers on the right bank. The treaties of Brest-Litovsk and Bucharest were to be renounced and German troops withdrawn from Russia, Rumania, Austria-Hungary, and Turkey. German submarines and warships were to be surrendered, and likewise five thousand locomotives, five thousand motor lorries, and 150,000 railway cars in good working order. The economic blockade against Germany would remain in force.

The terms of the armistice, originally agreed upon for thirty days, were subsequently renewed from time to time and remained in effect, with minor changes, until the signing of the definitive treaty of peace at Versailles on June 28, 1919. In the meantime the Allies secured a strangle-hold upon Germany. Within ten days after German acceptance of the armistice, the Allied armies had passed beyond Brussels, had penetrated into

Luxemburg, and had reached Saarbrücken and the Alsatian line of the Rhine to the Swiss border. King Albert of Belgium formally entered Ghent on November 13, Antwerp on November 19, and Brussels on November 22. General Pétain, commander-in-chief of the French armies, who was made a Marshal of France on November 19, entered Metz the same day; and on November 25 French troops under Marshals Foch and Pétain triumphantly

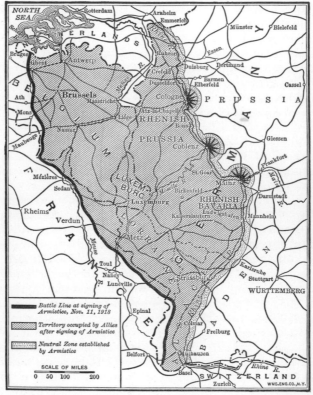

TERRITORY OCCUPIED BY THE ALLIES UNDER THE ARMISTICE OF NOVEMBER 11

occupied Strassburg. Everywhere the advancing armies were welcomed by the inhabitants. The demonstrations by the people in Belgium and in Alsace-Lorraine were marked by undisguised joy, in the one case that they were again free and independent after four years' indescribable sufferings, in the other case that they were returning to France after a compulsory separation of forty-eight years. Even in Luxemburg, which was believed to have strong German leanings, the American troops were cordially received. By the middle of December the French had advanced 170 miles, the British, 150, the Americans, 160, and the Belgians, 160. The British took over the administration of the zone around Cologne, the Americans that around Coblenz, and the French that around Mainz.

The first surrender of German naval vessels under the armistice was the delivery of twenty submarines to Admiral Tyrwhitt of the British navy off Harwich at sunrise on November 20. The following day nineteen more were delivered. The most spectacular event, however, was the surrender of the German High Seas Fleet to Admiral Beatty and the Allied armada off the Firth of Forth on the morning of November 21, the greatest naval capitulation in history. The ships surrendered were nine dreadnoughts, five battle cruisers, seven light cruisers, and fifty destroyers, representing a total tonnage of 410,000. Under British guardianship this mighty flotilla was interned at Scapa Flow in the Orkneys; the vaunted German navy was at last in British hands, and Germany was defenseless not only in Europe but on the seas and in the dominions beyond the seas.

The Teutonic debacle was complete. Sea power was gone. Land power was gone. Belgium was arising from her ruins. France was in possession of Alsace-Lorraine. Allied armies held the Rhine. To the East, Polish troops were advancing toward Posen and Danzig, while the Czechoslovaks were occupying Upper Silesia. Rumania denounced the treaty of Bucharest and reappeared as one of the Allies. Constantinople was at the mercy of the Allied fleets, and communications were opened between General Franchet d'Esperey, on the Danube, and General Denikin, commanding anti-Bolshevist forces in southern Russia. The whole dream of Teutonic mastery of Russia was dispelled. Skoropadsky, the pro-German dictator of Ukrainia, was overthrown; the pro-Ally General Mannerheim became the head of the Finnish Government; and the states of Finland, Esthonia, Latvia, Lithuania, and Ukrainia made haste to proclaim their complete independence and to appeal to the Allies for assistance against the Teutons on one side and against the Bolsheviki on the other. In Poland the German-appointed regency resigned on November 14, 1918, in favor of General Joseph Pilsudski, who had recently been released from a German prison; in January, 1919, Pilsudski reached an agreement with the Polish National Committee at Paris whereby Ignace Paderewski, the celebrated pianist, became premier and minister of foreign affairs while he himself was made president.

To the neutral countries of Europe the cessation of hostilities brought an intense feeling of relief. The Scandinavian countries, the Netherlands, Switzerland, and Spain could now reduce their armed establishments to a peace footing without fear of having their neutrality violated; they perceived the early ending of the economic distress under which they had long labored; and they promptly repressed whatever sympathies they may have had for Germany. For a time they were threatened in greater or lesser degree by the revolutionary agitation which followed in the wake of *Mittel-Europa's* collapse, but they managed to weather the storm, and Denmark was soon demanding the retrocession of northern Schleswig as her portion of the spoils of vanquished Germany.

Such a catastrophe as was overtaking the Teutons could not leave intact either the territory or the political institutions of Germany. The German Empire had been builded in the four years from 1866 to 1870 by iron and blood; by iron and blood it was destroyed in the four years from 1914 to 1918. Its subject nationalities — the Poles in Posen and West Prussia, the Czechs in Silesia, the Danes in Schleswig, and the French in Alsace-Lorraine — were now liberated from its yoke; and the German people themselves were free within their restricted territories to resume the task of creating national unity at the point where the democratically minded deputies of 1848 had laid it down and resigned themselves to the acceptance of Bismarck's substitute of militarism, autocracy, and imperialism.

On the eve of the conclusion of the armistice, when Germany first began to appreciate the extent of her defeat and humiliation, there were loud popular outcries against the Kaiser and insistent demands for his abdication. William hurriedly left Berlin and sought refuge at General Headquarters at Spa. But hither the clamor followed him. News came that Liebknecht and the Minority Socialists were inciting openly to rebellion and that mutinies were occurring in the navy. The south German states threatened to secede unless the Emperor should abdicate. Philip Scheidemann, the leader of the Majority Socialists, telegraphed that he could no longer be responsible for the actions of his followers. On November 8 the Socialists at Munich, under Kurt Eisner, deposed King Louis, transformed Bavaria from a monarchy into a republic, and served notice on Emperor William that they could not tolerate royalist institutions. Frantically Chancellor Prince Maximilian wired the Kaiser that abdication must be immediately forthcoming. To all these civilian entreaties William II might have turned a deaf ear, but when at last Field Marshal von Hindenburg and other weighty members of the General Staff bluntly told him that they could no longer insure his personal safety because the German army itself was seething with disloyalty and sedition, he hastily packed his bags and with a few faithful henchmen fled quite ingloriously on November 9, 1918, across the frontier into Holland. On the following day he took up his residence in Count Goddard Bentinck's château at Amerongen. To Holland, also, fled subsequently that other despised Hohenzollern, the Crown Prince Frederick William. It was a curious commentary upon the mutability of human fortune that the history of the German Empire was almost exclusively the history of two reigns — William the First (1871–1888), under whom the Empire had been reared in might, and of William the Last (1888–1918), under whom the Empire had fallen with a fearful crash.

On November 9, 1918, the German Imperial Chancellor, Prince Maximilian of Baden, issued the following decree: "The Kaiser and King has decided to renounce the throne. The Imperial Chancellor will remain in office until the questions connected with the abdication of the Kaiser, the renouncing by the Crown Prince of the throne of the German Empire and of Prussia, and the setting up of a regency, have been settled. For the regency he intends to appoint Deputy Ebert as Imperial Chancellor, and he proposes that a bill should be brought in for the establishment of a law providing for the immediate promulgation of general suffrage and for a constituent German National Assembly, which will settle finally the future form of government of the German Nation and of those peoples which might be desirous of coming within the empire."

A general upheaval throughout Germany quickly followed the publication of Prince Maximilian's decree. Throughout the Rhenish and Westphalian industrial regions the movement spread like wildfire. Imperial emblems were torn down and red flags hoisted. With Socialists coöperated Catholic Centrists and Protestant Liberals. Hamburg, Bremen, and Leipzig went over to the revolution. While contested in some places, on the whole it was accomplished with an astonishing lack of disorder. In Berlin only a few hours on Sunday, November 10, sufficed for its complete triumph. Here a general strike was started at nine o'clock in the morning, and shortly afterwards thousands of soldiers, carrying red flags and accompanied by armed motor cars, began to pour into the center of the city. With them came workingmen from outlying factories, and a little later trains arrived bringing 3000 sailors from Kiel. Presently all these arrivals broke up into detachments and occupied the bridges, public buildings, street corners, and railway stations. Almost as by magic red flags appeared everywhere, and officers on the streets and barracks stripped off their cockades and epaulettes — in very few cases was compulsion required — and threw them away. Hundreds of Iron Crosses could be picked up from the gutters. The announcement from the front of the Reichstag building that Friedrich Ebert, a conspicuous leader of the Social Democratic Party, had become Chancellor and had chosen a popular ministry, was greeted with thunderous cheers. From the official news agency a message of democratic triumph was transmitted to the whole world. "The revolution has gained a glorious and almost bloodless victory."

In those November days of 1918 German crowns fell like over-ripe fruit in late autumn. The flight of the king of Bavaria on November 8 and of the king of Prussia on November 9 was followed immediately by the abdication or deposition of the kings of Württemberg and Saxony, the grand dukes of Baden, Oldenburg, Mecklenburg, and Saxe-Weimar, the dukes of Brunswick and Anhalt, and all the lesser princes. By the end of November every German state possessed a republican form of government.

It was not until Chancellor Ebert was firmly established in power and Germany seemed thoroughly committed to republicanism that Emperor William II, at Amerongen, on November 28, 1918, signed a formal abdication of the crowns of Prussia and the German Empire, and that Crown Prince Frederick William, at Wieringen in Holland, on December 1, definitely renounced all claims to the succession. On November 30 the Ebert Government decreed a provisional electoral law, by which a National Assembly should be elected by secret ballot of all Germans over twenty years of age, men and women alike, and this Assembly would determine the country's future political institutions.

In the meantime Germany was tormented by economic distress and torn by partisan strife. On the one hand a considerable number of Junkers, pan-Germans, and confirmed militarists, blaming the radicals for the disasters which had overtaken the nation and fearing the revolution would deprive them of their rights and privileges, conducted an agitation in behalf of a monarchical restoration. On the other hand the "Spartacus" group of Socialists, led by Karl Liebknecht and Rosa Luxemburg, were unwilling that the German Revolution should stop short with the establishment of a democratic republic; in imitation of the Russian Bolsheviki they held that there should be no National Assembly and that the body politic, as well as the Government, should consist of one class, the proletariat, while the intellectual class should be hired to work for it, and the capitalists and landlords should be eliminated altogether. With the "Spartacans," the Minority Socialists, led by Hugo Haase, Eduard Bernstein, and Karl Kautsky, were inclined to coöperate. The Spartacans were aided, moreover, by the ambassador of the Russian Soviet Government in Berlin, Karl Radek, and to a certain extent by Kurt Eisner, the Socialist premier of Bavaria; they championed "direct action" and fomented strikes and disorders. For a while it was feared in Allied countries that Germany — and all *Mittel-Europa* — would follow Russia into Bolshevism.

The Majority Socialists, however, under Ebert and Scheidemann steered a middle course, suppressing the reactionaries on one hand and discountenancing the activities of the Spartacans on the other. They were resolved to erect a democratic republic by orderly processes, and in their resolution they were supported by the bulk of trade-unionists throughout Germany as well as by the Catholic Center Party, recently rechristened the "Christian People's Party," and by the "Democratic Party," which represented a fusion of the radicals of the old Progressive Party and the left wing of the old National Liberal Party.

On the eve of the elections to the National Assembly, in January, 1919, the Spartacans and other extremists, abetted by the chief of police at Berlin, made a desperate effort to seize the Government and introduce a reign of terror. The insurrection was sternly suppressed by Ebert's Government: several hundred rioters were slain; Karl Liebknecht and Rosa Luxemburg were killed by loyalist mobs on January 15; and on January 19 the elections to the National Assembly passed off without untoward incidents.[1]

At Weimar, on February 6, 1919, the German National Assembly was opened. It included 164 Majority Socialists, 91 Centrists, and 77 Democrats, — a total Government *bloc* of 332, — while the Opposition was confined to 34 Nationalists (former Conservatives and reactionaries) and 24 Minority

---

[1] Subsequently there were spasmodic outbreaks of disorder in Germany. The assassination of Kurt Eisner by reactionaries on February 21 precipitated fairly serious civil war in Bavaria; and in March there were menacing situations elsewhere in the country. Ebert's Government managed, however, to retain the upper hand and to restore order.

Socialists (more or less in sympathy with soviet principles). Some seven "Independents" brought up the total membership of this historic body to 397.   Among the members were twenty-eight women — veritably a remarkable sign of the new democratic era.

On February 11, 1919, the National Assembly adopted a provisional constitution for republican Germany and elected Friedrich Ebert as Provisional State President.   At the same time Philip Scheidemann became chancellor, with a coalition ministry comprising seven Majority Socialists, three Centrists, three Democrats, and one Independent, and including such well-known men as Mathias Erzberger, Gustav Noske, Eduard David, and Count von Brockdorff-Rantzau.

The flight of Emperor William II and the ensuing establishment of a democratic republic in Germany aroused Teutonic hopes that the Allies in dictating final peace-terms would be specially considerate and merciful.   But such hopes were soon blasted.   The Allies had suffered too much and too long from Hohenzollern militarism and imperialism and had had too many proofs of popular German devotion to that imperialism and militarism, to be impressed by a twelfth-hour conversion of the German people to pacifism and democracy.   As recently as March, 1918, Germany had dictated an outrageous peace to Russia and to Rumania, and if her armies on the Western Front had been as successful in the summer of 1918 as Ludendorff had predicted, she would have shown no consideration and no mercy to France or Great Britain or the United States.   And in this event the bulk of the German people would probably have been as mute and as acquiescent as they had been in the negotiations at Bucharest and Brest-Litovsk.   Knowing these things the Allies proceeded in much the same manner as they would have done if Kaiser Wilhelm were still in power: the German people might revolt and become republican if they liked — that was little or no business of the Allies; it was the business of the Allies to refashion the map of Europe and dictate the peace-settlement in their own interests.   "To the victors belonged the spoils," and the Allies were the victors.

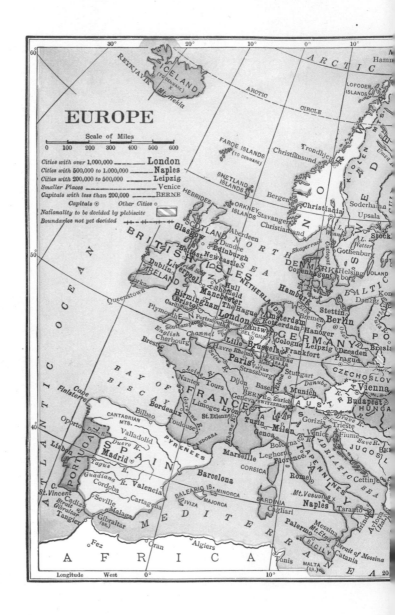

EUROPE

Scale of Miles

0 100 200 300 400 500 600

Cities with over 1,000,000 _____ **London**
Cities with 500,000 to 1,000,000 _____ Naples
Cities with 200,000 to 500,000 _____ Leipzig
Smaller Places _____ Venice
Capitals with less than 200,000 _____ BERNE
     Capitals ⊙   Other Cities ○
Nationality to be decided by plebiscite
Boundaries not yet decided

CHAPTER XV

A NEW ERA BEGINS

THE SETTLEMENT

No series of events in the whole recorded history of mankind had proved so cataclysmic, in a like period of time, as the Great War, which began on July 28, 1914, with Austria's attack on Serbia and virtually closed on November 11, 1918, with the armistice between Germany and the Allies. In politics, in economics, in society, Europe had undergone a revolution and the entire world was in ferment. Yet out of the chaos must come order, out of war must come peace. Just as the Great War had put an end to an epoch of international anarchy and fear, so the peace-settlement must serve to inaugurate a new era of international coöperation and hope. Upon the sanity of the settlement would depend the happiness of men and the true welfare of nations in future generations.

The nature of Allied victory possessed for the peace-settlement an advantage and a disadvantage. On the one hand, that the victory was complete and overwhelming made it possible for the Allies, if they chose to do so, to liquidate *Mittel-Europa* and settle once for all the litigious estates of the Ottoman Turks, the Habsburgs, and the Hohenzollerns. That the victory was achieved by a large number of nations, held together in a loose and informal federation, was disadvantageous, however, for each victorious Power had its own particular interests to subserve, and peace was likely to partake less of the character of ideal justice than of selfish compromise.

Among the masses in all countries were large numbers who entertained the fondest and most glorious expectations of what the Peace Congress would do. According to them, it should lay broad and deep the foundations of a new world-order; it should conduct its proceedings in the light of open day; it should recognize to the fullest degree the right of every people to decide its own fate; it should treat great and small nations alike; truly it should "make the world safe for democracy"; it should finally end not only the Great War but all wars.

But the diplomatists and statesmen of the several Powers, while professing the utmost devotion to these altruistic principles, had to face melancholy facts as well as roseate rainbows. They had to recognize, and make allowance for, certain very earthy, practical circumstances. In the first place, the war had been so long and so exceedingly bitter and the Teutons had been guilty of such heinous offenses against public and private morality that naturally in Allied countries there was a feverish and nightmarish horror, in which some members of the governments and the bulk of the people shared, and which gave rise to an almost hypnotic fear of what Germany might do in the future if she were not crushed and terribly punished at the present. Doubtless in some quarters this psychosis went so far as to confuse justice with vengeance.

Secondly, the war had entailed such grave economic losses and hardships that many Allied citizens, aware of the downright inability of Germany to make adequate financial reparation, clamored all the more for some tangible compensation from her in the form of territories and rights.

Thirdly, the Allied Governments, though originally taking the sword in order to rescue civilization from destruction, had come in the course of the protracted conflict to wield that sword for a great variety of specific ends: France, to regain Alsace-Lorraine and to secure guarantees against subsequent German aggression; Great Britain, to destroy the menacing sea-power of Germany and to strengthen her own empire; Italy, to obtain *Italia irredenta* from Austria-Hungary and to assure a commanding position for herself in the Adriatic and eastern Mediterranean; Japan, to extend her sway in the Far East and to establish a sort of "Monroe Doctrine" for China; Serbia, Rumania, Czechoslovakia, and Poland, to secure independence and in each instance to annex any lands in which its nationality was represented; Greece, to obtain southern Albania, and Thrace and Smyrna — all the coasts and islands of the Ægean. Upon these specific ends the peoples of the several countries had set their minds, and their representatives at Paris could not afford to disappoint them. The United States was the only Great Power associated with the Entente which had no territorial ambitions and whose motives in this respect could be described as absolutely disinterested.

Then too, the temporary league of free nations, which had

finally destroyed *Mittel-Europa* and crushed the German Empire, had been builded up and strengthened by means of promises held out to prospective members at various times when the Entente was hard pressed. These promises were usually made in the form of "secret treaties," such as those of 1915 by which Italy had been brought into the war, or those of 1916 which had induced Rumania to join the Allies. In 1917 a whole series of secret engagements had been entered into, guaranteeing definite territorial or economic gains to Great Britain, Russia, France, Italy, and Japan. To none of the "secret treaties" was the United States a party; of the existence of some of them she was actually kept in ignorance until after the cessation of hostilities; yet one of the celebrated "fourteen points" of President Wilson, on which the Allies consented to negotiate peace, was "open covenants openly arrived at." Here was a circumstance most trying even to experienced and calloused diplomatists.

Between the actual situation imposed upon Allied statesmen by circumstances of the preceding four years and the hopes of enlightened public opinion in Allied countries there was obviously a wide chasm. Between the aims and ambitions of the several Allied Powers there was patent divergence and potential cause of conflict. To prevent the chasm from becoming unbridgeable and the national divergences from leading to armed strife — either of which would surely redound to Germany's advantage and might easily enable the Teutons to escape just punishment for their transgressions — it was decided soon after the cessation of hostilities (November 11, 1918) to exclude Germany from the Peace Conference until the Allies themselves should have agreed upon the provisions of the final treaty of peace, until their own differences should have been amicably adjusted and the demands of their diplomatists squared as far as possible with the dictates of popular conscience. It was decided also, quite appropriately, that the Preliminary Conference among the Allies should be held in Paris, and the Definitive Peace Congress with the Germans at Versailles, the two historic capitals of France, — France which, perhaps of all the Allies, had contributed most, alike in suffering and in glorious deed, to the cause of Allied victory.

January 18 was the date in 1871 when the Hohenzollern king of Prussia, in the midst of a successful war against France, and surrounded by his triumphant generals and statesmen, had stood in the Hall of Mirrors at Versailles and been proclaimed German Emperor. Forty-eight years had since elapsed, and now at the close of an overwhelmingly victorious war against Germany, Allied statesmen and Allied generals assembled at Paris to undo the work of Bismarck and the Hohenzollerns. On January 18, 1919, the Peace Conference held its first session.

It was a brilliant assemblage of the foremost men of those countries which had banded together to resist Teutonic aggression. There was Clemenceau, the grizzly and sagacious veteran of French Republican politics, the "Tiger" of his country and of the Alliance; there was Marshal Foch, the organizer and winner of victory; there was President Wilson, who had played a major rôle in the past two years of the war and who, in coming to Europe, had established a wholly new precedent for American executives; there was Lloyd George, the "little Welsh attorney," who from being the most feared and hated radical social reformer in Great Britain had become the most conspicuous patriot in all the dominions of King George V; Orlando, the Italian premier; Marquis Saionji, twice prime minister of Japan; Venizelos, the greatest statesman of modern Greece; Kramarcz, premier of Czechoslovakia; Bratiano, premier of Rumania; Pashitch, premier of Serbia; Stephen Pichon, French minister of foreign affairs; Jules Cambon, who was French ambassador at Berlin when war broke out in 1914; Arthur J. Balfour, British foreign secretary and once upon a time attendant at the Congress of Berlin; General Botha and General Smuts, erstwhile Boer warriors against Great Britain but now stalwart defenders of the British Union of South Africa; William Hughes, premier of Australia; William Massey, premier of New Zealand; Sir William Lloyd, premier of Newfoundland; Sir Robert Borden, premier of Canada; the Maharajah of Bikaner and Sir S. P. Sinha, representing India; Prince Feisal, the son of the Sherif of Mecca who had become the sultan of the new Arab kingdom of Hedjaz; Robert Lansing, American Secretary of State; Colonel House, special friend and confidential adviser of President Wilson; Henry White and General Bliss, representing the diplomatic and military traditions of the United States; Baron Sidney Sonnino, Italian foreign minister continuously since 1914 and an uncompromising advocate of Italian imperialism; Epitacio Pessoa, president-elect of Brazil and one of the foremost jurists of Latin America; Paul Hymans, Belgian foreign minister; Van Der Heuvel, Belgian envoy to the Pope; and Émile Vandervelde, the patriotic Belgian Socialist. Attending all these celebrities were a host of more obscure but no less important "experts" — professors and publicists and

cartographers and financiers and secretaries — a host as necessary
to the Peace Conference as privates to an army. And waiting
upon them were numerous "missions" and ".envoys" from
racial or religious groups throughout the world, who sought
favors or aspired to freedom: Russians, Koreans, negroes,
Irishmen, Abyssinians, *etc.*

The formal assembling of the Peace Conference on January 18
had been preceded by almost daily conferences of the Inter-
allied Supreme War Council and by several informal meetings
of the President of the United States with the premiers and
foreign ministers of Great Britain, France, and Italy, assisted
by the Japanese ambassadors in Paris and London. At these
meetings and conferences the procedure and general scope of
the Peace Conference had been planned.

The Preliminary Peace Conference, as organized, included
seventy delegates from thirty-two states, distributed as follows:
United States, Great Britain, France, Italy, and Japan, five
each; Belgium, Brazil, and Serbia, three apiece; Canada,
Australia, South Africa, India, China, Greece, Hedjaz, Poland,
Portugal, Rumania, Siam, and Czechoslovakia, two apiece;
and one each from New Zealand, Bolivia, Cuba, Ecuador,
Guatemala, Haiti, Honduras, Liberia, Nicaragua, Panama,
Peru, and Uruguay. At the opening session of the Conference
in the Peace Hall of the Ministry of Foreign Affairs, just across
the Seine from the Place de la Concorde, President Poincaré
of the French Republic welcomed the delegates with felicitous
phrase, and then Premier Clemenceau of France was chosen
president, while honorary vice-presidencies were bestowed upon
Secretary Lansing of the United States, Premier Lloyd George
of Great Britain, Premier Orlando of Italy, and Marquis Saionji
of Japan.

Thenceforth, until the presentation of the draft of the completed treaty to the Germans on May 7, the Conference met
on rare occasions, and even its sessions were largely perfunctory
and ceremonial. The real work of the Conference was carried
on by special committees of diplomatists and "experts" selected as needs arose for the consideration of such matters as
"league of nations," "responsibility for the war," "reparations,"
"labor legislation," "international regulation of waterways,"
"financial questions," "economic questions," "territorial questions," *etc.* Most of the work was conducted in privacy and
secrecy, and only such committee reports were passed on to the
plenary Conference as met the approval of the spokesmen of

2 B

the Great Powers. At first the Great Powers maintained a "Supreme Council," consisting of the two ranking delegates from the United States, Great Britain, France, Italy, and Japan, to which was subordinated all the machinery of the Conference and before which all conflicting claims were presented. But the Supreme Council of Ten proved too unwieldy, and it gradually gave way to an informal Council of Five, including Japan; then Japan was dropped from the inner circle, and Premiers Clemenceau, Lloyd George, Orlando, and President Wilson, known as the Council of Four, carried on the discussions on the most important issues among themselves; finally, when on the eve of the conclusion of the treaty with the Germans Italy became temporarily alienated by the proposed settlement of Adriatic claims, and Orlando withdrew, the chief responsibility for the Conference devolved upon the "Big Three" — Wilson, Clemenceau, and Lloyd George.

It was no easy task to reconcile differences of opinion and policy among the thirty-two delegations and to preserve a united front on the part of all the Allied and Associated Governments. President Wilson, who had set his heart upon fashioning a League of Nations, felt himself obliged to make repeated concessions to his associates in order to enlist their support for his pet project. For example, "freedom of the seas," of which he talked much before he went to Europe, quite disappeared from polite conversation — it was a concession to British susceptibilities, and a concession gratefully received, for the British delegates at Paris, as soon as they were assured of the unquestioned control of the seas by Great Britain, and British management, through a "mandatary" system, of the bulk of the German colonies, became enthusiastic champions of the League of Nations and devoted friends of President Wilson. To France President Wilson found it convenient to yield not only Alsace-Lorraine and various economic privileges in Germany but special financial and political rights, for a term of fifteen years, in the strictly Teutonic Saar basin and the extraordinary guarantee of a new defensive alliance between France, the United States, and Great Britain — an alliance which in spirit if not in letter was contrary to earlier declarations against group alliances within the League of Nations. Furthermore, the German rights and privileges in Shantung, instead of being surrendered to China, were transferred to Japan, and the secret treaties which had been concluded in 1917 between Japan and the Entente were recognized and upheld, because otherwise Japan threatened to withdraw from the Conference and to disrupt the League of Nations; in this way the United States departed radically from her traditional Far Eastern policy of protecting China and permitted one of the weaker Allies to be despoiled by one of the stronger. In the case of Italy, which had the audacity to demand the cession, at the expense of Serbia, not only of all the territory pledged her by the secret treaties but the Adriatic port of Fiume also, President Wilson stood his ground better, but the Italian delegates actually withdrew temporarily from the Conference and subsequently secured a compromise.[1]

In addition to these difficulties, the diplomatists at Paris were confronted with perplexing boundary disputes among the lesser Powers. So intermingled were different nationalities in various parts of the ruined empires of Russia, Austria, and Turkey, that it was well-nigh impossible to draw frontiers for Poland, Czechoslovakia, Rumania, Serbia, Greece, and Armenia, which would satisfy the ambitions of their own peoples and which at the same time would not outrage their neighbors. So conflicting, moreover, were the interests of Japan, on one hand, and of Australia and New Zealand, on the other, that it required much tact to arrive at a territorial settlement in the Pacific. Over all these questions the negotiations were protracted, and it was almost miraculous that a general agreement was finally reached. Only the weariness of the European peoples and the dictatorial attitude of the representatives of the five Great Powers prevented some of the Allied states from engaging in open war with each other, and even then there were hostile clashes in Central Europe between Poles and Czechoslovaks, between Poles and Ukrainians, between Rumanians and Jugoslavs, and between Jugoslavs and Italians.

After four months of unremitting labor on the part of the Allied diplomatists the draft of the proposed treaty with Germany, containing about 80,000 words, was agreed to by the Council of Five and accepted by the Preliminary Peace Conference in plenary session assembled on May 6;[2] and the Pre-

---

[1] Against the excessive imperialism of Orlando and Sonnino, protests had been made in Italy, and at the close of 1918 the Socialist Leonida Bissolati and the Clerical Francesco Nitti had resigned their posts in the Orlando cabinet as ministers respectively of pensions and finance. As an outcome of the controversy with the Jugoslavs and President Wilson over Fiume, a new ministry was formed in July, 1919, with Nitti as premier and Tommaso Tittoni as foreign secretary. Nitti was somewhat more conciliatory than his predecessor, but not even he could be deaf to vociferous demands of his countrymen for extensive territorial annexations. For the settlement subsequently proposed, in January, 1920, see below, p. 385.

[2] This plenary session on the afternoon of May 6 was secret; and the treaty draft was accepted without its details being fully and generally known. The reading

liminary Peace Conference was then transformed into the Definitive Peace Congress, in which Germany was to be represented. Already, on May 1, the German plenipotentiaries, headed by Count Brockdorff-Rantzau, the foreign secretary of the republican government at Berlin, had been formally received at Versailles and had presented their credentials to the Allies. Now, on May 7, 1919, which by a curious coincidence was the fourth anniversary of the sinking of the *Lusitania*, Premier Clemenceau, in the presence of the plenipotentiaries of France, Great Britain, Italy, Japan, the United States, and the lesser Allied belligerents, and in their behalf, submitted the final peace-terms to Count Brockdorff-Rantzau and his associates in the great dining hall of the Trianon Palace Hotel at Versailles. The terms were stringent; they testified eloquently to Germany's degradation.

Throughout the next six weeks the world's attention was centered upon the desperate efforts of Count Brockdorff-Rantzau and his fellow-delegates to induce the Council of Five to modify the stringent peace-terms. As oral discussion had been barred, the Germans continued submitting notes of protest and argument until May 29, when they finally produced an elaborate set of counterproposals in a document aggregating some 60,000 words. To this the Council of Five on June 16 made an almost equally extended reply, chapter for chapter; it was in effect an ultimatum calling for Germany's final acceptance or refusal on or before Monday, June 23. It offered a number of concessions, but none of vital import.

During the seven-day interval that followed, while the German Government and National Assembly were in agitated discussion as to whether to sign or refuse to sign, the Franco-Anglo-American armies of occupation, under Marshal Foch, made all necessary preparations, in case of refusal, to cross the Rhine in force and march on Berlin, and the whole world awaited the outcome calmly but with intense interest. Would Germany sign? German newspapers, German statesmen, the Scheidemann ministry, and President Ebert said "No." The masses of war-weary people, led by the Minority Socialists, said "Yes." The first result in Germany was a cabinet crisis: Chancellor Scheidemann resigned and was succeeded by Gustav Adolf Bauer, a Majority Socialist, with a colorless and obviously transitional ministry which was

of a 10,000-word digest constituted the first and only knowledge of the treaty vouchsafed by the Council of Five to the smaller Powers. Several Powers such as Portugal, France, China, and Italy, made "reservations." The complete text of the treaty was not printed until later.

inclined to sign. Simultaneously the *bloc* parties — the Majority Socialists, the Catholic Centrists, and the Democrats, — fearful lest continued refusal to sign would aid the program of the Minority Socialists and of the Spartacan extremists, decided to support the new government; and on June 23, the last day of grace, the German National Assembly at Weimar voted to accept unconditionally the Allied terms.

Dr. Hermann Müller, the foreign secretary in the new German government, and Dr. Johannes Bell, colonial secretary, were finally prevailed upon by Chancellor Bauer to perform the distasteful duty of signing a most humiliating treaty of peace. And on June 28, 1919, in the Hall of Mirrors in the stately old palace of Louis XIV, the Peace of Versailles was signed by the plenipotentiaries of Germany and by those of thirty-one [1] nations leagued against her. The scene was that in which in 1871 the militaristic German Empire had been born. The date was that on which in 1914 the Archduke Francis Ferdinand of Austria-Hungary had been assassinated. The Great War thus formally closed on the fifth anniversary of the immediate occasion of its outbreak, and its close officially registered the death of the German Empire.

With the signing of the treaty of Versailles, the principal purpose of the Peace Congress was achieved; and President Wilson and many of the premiers and "experts" returned home. Nevertheless, Paris remained throughout 1919 and well into 1920 the center of most significant international negotiations. The Supreme Allied Council, now consisting of diplomatic agents of the five Great Powers, continued to hold sessions and to fashion peace-treaties with Austria, Bulgaria, Hungary, and Turkey, as well as to work out numerous details of the settlement as it affected the lesser Allied Powers and particularly as it concerned the new states which the Great War had brought into existence.

The final settlements of 1919–1920 may now be rapidly sketched, beginning with the outstanding provisions of the treaty of Versailles between the Allies and Germany. This treaty, as ratified by the German National Assembly at Weimar on July 7, 1919, revolutionized the international position of Germany, territorially, economically, and militarily. By the terms of the treaty, Germany ceded Alsace-Lorraine to France, Eupen and

---

[1] Of the total thirty-two delegations included in the Allied Conference, the Chinese alone refused to sign, because of the special concessions to Japan. It should be remarked that General Smuts in attaching his signature on behalf of South Africa protested bluntly against what he conceived to be the illiberality of the victors to the vanquished.

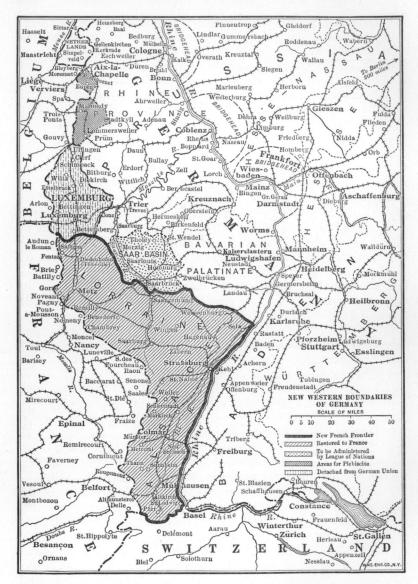

NEW WESTERN BOUNDARIES
OF GERMANY
SCALE OF MILES
0 5 10   20   30   40   50

New French Frontier
Restored to France
To be Administered
by League of Nations
Areas for Plebiscite
Detached from German Union

Malmédy to Belgium, Memel to Lithuania,[1] and a large part of
the provinces of Posen and West Prussia to Poland; to Poland,

[1] The treaty merely provided for the detaching of Memel from East Prussia;
the understanding was that subsequently it would be awarded to Lithuania.

moreover, she agreed to cede Upper Silesia, the southern part of East Prussia, and a strip west of the Vistula, if the population

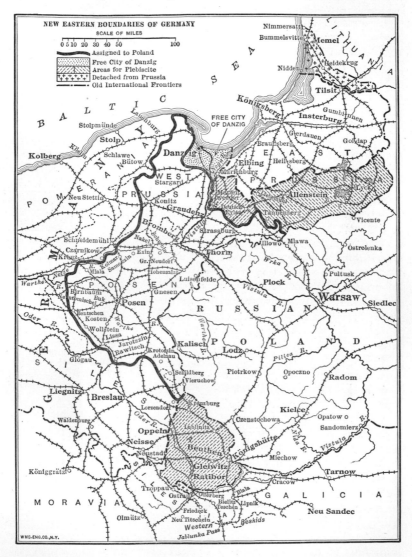

of these districts should express the desire, in a plebiscite conducted under international auspices, for incorporation within the Polish Republic, and in order to provide Poland with a convenient access to the Baltic she consented to the establishment of Danzig as an internationalized free city; furthermore, she would acquiesce in the cession to Denmark of such districts of Schleswig as should vote accordingly in a similar plebiscite; and likewise she would submit for fifteen years to the economic exploitation by France, and the political control by an international commission, of the rich Saar basin, and would undertake to abide by the decision reached by popular plebiscite at the end of fifteen years as to whether the Saar region should thereafter remain permanently under international government or revert to Germany or be ceded outright to France.

In addition to territorial cessions in Europe, Germany surrendered all her overseas colonies and protectorates. Her lease of Kiao-chao and other privileges in the Chinese province of Shantung as well as her Pacific islands north of the equator went to Japan; her portion of Samoa, to New Zealand; her other Pacific possessions south of the equator, to Australia; German Southwest Africa, to the British Union of South Africa; German East Africa, to Great Britain; and Kamerun and Togoland were partitioned between Great Britain and France. In most cases the Powers receiving German colonies did so not as absolute sovereigns but as "mandataries" of the projected League of Nations, to which they would be required from time to time to give an account of their stewardship. Besides, Germany renounced all special rights and privileges in China, Siam, Liberia, Morocco, and Egypt.

Politically, Germany recognized the complete independence and full sovereignty of Belgium, and likewise of German Austria, Czechoslovakia, and Poland; she denounced the treaties of Brest-Litovsk and all other agreements entered into by her with the Bolshevist government of Russia and gave the Allies *carte blanche* to deal as they would with Russia not only, but with Turkey, Bulgaria, Hungary, and Austria.

Militarily, Germany promised to reduce her army to 100,000 men, including officers; to abolish conscription within her territories; to raze all forts fifty kilometers east of the Rhine; to stop all importation, exportation, and nearly all production of war material; to reduce her navy to six battleships, six light cruisers, and twelve torpedo boats, without submarines, and a personnel of not more than 15,000; to surrender or destroy all other armed vessels; and to abandon military and naval aviation within three months. Moreover she agreed to demolish fortifications at Heligoland, to open the Kiel Canal to all nations, to refrain from building forts on the Baltic, and to surrender her fourteen submarine cables. She specifically agreed to the trial of her War Lord, the ex-Kaiser, by an international high court for a supreme offense against international morality,[1] and of other Germans for violation of the laws and customs of war.

By way of reparation and economic settlement, Germany accepted full responsibility for all damages caused to the allied and associated governments and nationals, and promised to reimburse all civilian damages, beginning with an initial payment of five billion dollars, subsequent payments being secured by bonds to be issued at the discretion of an International Reparation Commission. Germany agreed to pay shipping damage on a ton-for-ton basis by cession of the bulk of her merchant, coasting, and river fleets, and by new construction; to devote her economic resources to the rebuilding of the devastated regions; in particular, to deliver enormous quantities of coal and coal-products to France, Belgium, and Italy; to return works of art removed from Belgium and France; and to deliver manuscripts and prints equivalent in value to those destroyed at Louvain. She pledged herself, moreover, to return to the 1914 most-favored-nation tariffs, without discrimination of any sort; to allow allied and associated nationals freedom of transit through her territories; and to accept highly detailed provisions as to pre-war debts, unfair competition, internationalization of roads and rivers, and other economic and financial clauses.

Until reparation should be made and the treaty fully carried out, Allied occupation of the left bank of the Rhine and of the bridgeheads at Cologne, Coblenz, and Mainz, would continue, although provision was made that if Germany should be duly fulfilling her obligations, Cologne would be evacuated at the end of five years, Coblenz at the end of ten years, and Mainz at the end of fifteen years.

In the destruction of militaristic Germany, the peace removed a chief menace to the free development of democratic peoples. But the treaty of Versailles went further, and in two significant and novel respects attempted to deal with the social unrest and international anarchy which had hitherto prevailed throughout

[1] In accordance with this provision, Great Britain, France, and Italy, in January, 1920, asked the Netherlands Government to surrender William II for trial on the charge of "moral" offenses, such as the breaking of a treaty by the invasion of Belgium, the authorization of ruthless submarine warfare, and the use of poisonous gas. Queen Wilhelmina's advisers refused to comply with the request on the ground that no existing international court had legal jurisdiction and that the Dutch people "could not betray the faith of those who have confided themselves to their free institutions."

the world. One section of the treaty sought to eradicate many of the evils inhering in the old individualistic doctrine and selfish practice of coequal sovereign states, by establishing a League of Nations. Another section recognized the relations between capital and labor everywhere as matters of international concern. These provisions were designed quite as much for the Allies themselves, and even for neutral Powers, as for Germany.

Thus, the treaty of Versailles provided for the formation of a permanent world-organization of labor, consisting of an annual International Labor Conference and an International Labor Office. The former was to be composed of four representatives of each state, two from the government and one each from the employers and the workingmen, and to act as a deliberative body, its measures taking the form of draft conventions or recommendations for legislation, which, if passed by two-thirds vote, must be submitted to the law-making authority in every state participating. Each government was left free to enact such recommendations into law; approve the principle, but adapt them to local needs; leave the actual legislation in case of a federal state to local legislatures; or reject the recommendations altogether without further obligation. The International Labor Office was to be conducted at the seat of the League of Nations; its chief functions would be the collection and distribution of information on labor throughout the world, the preparation of agenda for the Labor Conferences, and the oversight of the enforcement of labor conventions between states.

Nine principles of labor conditions were specifically recognized by the treaty of Versailles on the ground that "the well-being, physical, moral, and intellectual, of industrial wage-earners is of supreme international importance." With exceptions necessitated by differences of climate, habits, and economic development, the most significant of these principles were affirmed to be: (1) that labor should not be regarded merely as a commodity or article of commerce; (2) right of association of employers and employees; (3) a wage adequate to maintain a reasonable standard of life; (4) the eight-hour day or forty-eight hour week; (5) a weekly rest of at least twenty-four hours, which should include Sunday wherever practicable; (6) abolition of child labor and assurance of the continuation of the education and proper physical development of children; (7) equal pay for equal work as between men and women; (8) equitable economic treatment of all workers, including foreigners; and (9) a system of inspection in which women should take part.

In accordance with the treaty, the first meeting of the International Labor Conference was held at Washington, in October and November, 1919, and the new labor era was ushered in by discussions at that time of the prevention of unemployment, the extension and application of the international conventions adopted at Berne in 1906 prohibiting night work for women and the use of white phosphorus in the manufacture of matches, and the employment of women and children at night or in unhealthy work.

Recognition of the international importance of labor questions was one of the most promising achievements of the Paris Peace Congress of 1919. Another, even more sensational, was the recognition of the evils inherent in pre-war international anarchy and the resulting determination on the part of President Wilson and his associates at Paris to institute a new world-order of international coöperation. The Covenant of the League of Nations,[1] as proposed and adopted by the Preliminary Peace Conference, appeared in the treaty of Versailles as Section One; and with the Covenant the whole settlement of 1919 was inextricably bound up.

As established by the Covenant, the League of Nations comprised all the allied and associated powers and most neutrals, excluding (at the start) only Germany, Austria, Hungary, Bulgaria, Turkey, Russia, Mexico, and Costa Rica. In the future any state, dominion, or colony might be admitted to membership by two-thirds vote of the Assembly, and any state upon giving two years' notice might withdraw if it had fulfilled its international obligations. The organs of the League were to be: (1) a permanent Secretariat, with headquarters at Geneva in Switzerland; (2) an Assembly, consisting of representatives of the several members of the League (each member having one vote and not more than three representatives), and meeting at stated intervals; and (3) a Council, composed of representatives of the five Great Allied Powers, — the United States, Great Britain, France, Italy, and Japan, — together with representatives of four other members selected from time to time by the Assembly, and normally taking decisions by unanimous vote.

The members of the League undertook "to respect and preserve as against external aggression the territorial integrity and existing political independence" of one another. Furthermore, the members pledged themselves to submit matters of dispute to arbitration or inquiry and not to resort to war with

[1] See Appendix, below, p. 413.

one another until three months after the award. Awards might take the form of judicial decisions or simply of advisory opinion; normally they would be rendered by a Permanent Court of International Justice, for the establishment of which the Council should forthwith formulate plans. Members not submitting their case to this Court must accept the jurisdiction of the Council itself or of the Assembly; in the former instance, the Council would make award by unanimous vote (not counting the parties to the dispute); in the latter instance, the Assembly would make award by unanimous vote of its members represented on the Council and a simple majority of the rest (not counting the parties to the dispute). Members agreed to carry out arbitral awards, and not to go to war with any party to a dispute which should comply with the award. If a member should fail to carry out an award, the Council would propose "the necessary measures." Members resorting to war in disregard of the Covenant would immediately be debarred from all intercourse with other members, and the Council would in such cases consider what military or naval action could be taken by the League collectively against the offending party. Similarly, upon any war or threat of war by any outside Power against any member of the League, the Council would promptly meet to consider what common action should be taken.

The Covenant formally abrogated all obligations between members of the League inconsistent with its terms, but expressly affirmed "the validity of international engagements, such as treaties of arbitration or regional understandings like the Monroe Doctrine, for securing the maintenance of the peace of the world." It especially provided, also, that all treaties or international engagements concluded after the institution of the League should be registered with the Secretariat and published, and that the Assembly might from time to time advise members to reconsider treaties which had become inapplicable or involved danger to peace. To the Council was intrusted the important function of preparing plans for a general reduction of armaments; these plans were to be revised every ten years, and, once adopted, no member must exceed the armaments fixed, without the Council's concurrence.

Under the general supervision of the League of Nations were placed the International Labor Organization and its activities, the execution of agreements for the suppression of traffic in women and children and for the control of trade in arms and ammunition, the assurance of equitable treatment for commerce of all members of the League, and the international prevention and control of disease. International bureaus and commissions already established were subordinated to the League, as well as all those to be established in the future.

In addition to its general duties, the League of Nations was intrusted by the treaty of Versailles with several specific duties in connection with the German settlement. Thus, the League might question Germany at any time for a violation of the neutralized zone east of the Rhine; it would appoint three of the five members of the Saar Commission, oversee its régime, and conduct the plebiscite; it would designate the High Commissioner of Danzig, guarantee the independence of the Free City, and arrange for treaties between Danzig and Germany and Poland; it would work out the mandatary system to be applied to the former German colonies; it would act as a final court in the plebiscites in Schleswig and on the Polish frontiers, and in the disputes as to the Kiel Canal; and it would decide certain of the economic and financial problems arising from the war.

The French Government, still fearful of a German "war of revenge," would have preferred to have obtained further military guarantees from Germany and to have strengthened the Covenant by providing for a permanent international General Staff which should direct the military action of the League of Nations in resisting any attempted German aggression in the future. To mollify the French and meet their criticisms, President Wilson and Premier Lloyd George concluded on June 28 special treaties respectively between the United States and France and between France and Great Britain, by the terms of which the United States and Great Britain would be bound to come immediately to the aid of France if any unprovoked act of aggression should be made against her by Germany. It was specifically provided that these treaties should be submitted to the Council of the League of Nations, which would decide whether to recognize them as engagements in conformity with the League Covenant; in the meantime, the Franco-American treaty should be submitted for approval to the United States Senate and the French Parliament.

The treaty of Versailles, including the Labor Convention and the Covenant of the League of Nations, was ratified by Germany on July 7, by France on October 13, by Great Britain and Italy on October 15, and by Japan on October 30. China accepted it, with reservations concerning the cession of Shantung to Japan, on September 24; and most of the other signatories ratified it promptly. In the case of the United States, President Wilson encountered extraordinary opposition from the Republican majority in the Senate and even from certain members of his own political party. Among his opponents were those who specially objected to the Covenant of the League of Nations as tending to impair American sovereignty and vitiate certain constitutional powers of the American Congress, or as tending further to entangle the United States in the meshes of Old-World diplomacy; there were those likewise who were bitterly disappointed with the terms of peace with Germany, particularly the concessions to Japan and to Great Britain, and who were unwilling that the United States should underwrite a "vicious" and "unjust" peace; and there were doubtless those who felt that President Wilson had treated the Senate altogether too cavalierly, as well as those who were fearful lest a Democratic President should derive political capital from a radical change in American foreign policy. For months a deadlock ensued between the President and the Senate Majority, the latter insisting upon "reservations" which the former would not accept. The Senate in November, 1919, adopted, by majority vote, some fifteen drastic reservations to the treaty of Versailles, but failed to secure the necessary two-thirds vote for the ratification of the treaty with these reservations. Thenceforth various efforts were made to reach a compromise; and in February, 1920, it looked as though the United States would shortly ratify the treaty with somewhat milder reservations than those originally adopted by the Senate in November.[1] As yet it was extremely doubtful whether the United States Senate would ratify the Franco-American Alliance Treaty, although its complement had already been ratified by Great Britain.[2]

The Allies delayed for some time to put the treaty of Versailles into effect, hoping that the United States would join them in ratifying the document. At length, however, on January 10, 1920, representatives of all the Powers which to date had approved the Versailles Treaty deposited their certificates of ratification at Paris and signed the *procès-verbal* which put the treaty into effect. This ceremony, which formally ended the Great War, was discharged in the Clock Hall of the French Ministry of Foreign Affairs. Fourteen allied and associated

---

[1] For these Senate Reservations of November, 1919, see Appendix II.
[2] For the proposed treaty of Triple Alliance between France and Great Britain, and France and the United States, see Appendix III.

Powers on the one hand, — France, Great Britain, Italy, Japan, Belgium, Bolivia, Brazil, Guatemala, Panama, Peru, Poland, Siam, Czechoslovakia, and Uruguay, — and Germany on the other, made peace and again became "friendly nations." The United States did not participate, nor did China, Greece, or Rumania.

On January 16, 1920, pursuant to the call of President Wilson, the first meeting of the Council of the League of Nations was held in Paris. It comprised representatives of Great Britain, France, Italy, Japan, Spain, Belgium, and Brazil. Léon Bourgeois, the French representative, was elected chairman, and Sir Eric Drummond was installed as permanent secretary; and the Council prepared to arrange for the convocation of the League Assembly, and to take up and continue the manifold labors of the Supreme Council of the Peace Conference, which formally disbanded on January 20.

The settlement of 1919–1920 was effected not only by the Covenant of the League of Nations, by the proposed new Triple Alliance of France, Great Britain, and the United States, by the novel Labor Convention, and by the drastic terms of the treaty of Versailles with Germany, but also by the series of peace treaties concluded by the Allies in turn with Austria, with Bulgaria, with Hungary, and with Turkey, and likewise by a vast number of special engagements entered into among the allied and associated Powers themselves.

Austria, by the treaty signed at St. Germain on September 10, 1919, and ratified by the Austrian National Assembly on October 17, was required to recognize the complete independence of Hungary, Czechoslovakia, Poland, the Serbo-Croat-Slovene State (Serbia), and to cede various territories which previously, in union with her, composed the Dual Monarchy of Austria-Hungary. Austria was left thereby a small independent German republic, with an area of five thousand to six thousand square miles and a population of between six and seven millions. She was deprived of seaports and her army was restricted to 30,000 men.

From Bulgaria were taken, by the treaty signed at Neuilly, near Paris, on November 27, 1918, most of the territories which she had appropriated in the Balkan wars of 1912–1913 and all her conquests in the Great War; the Dobrudja went to Rumania; the greater part of Macedonia, to Serbia; and the Thracian coast, to the Allies, who seemed disposed to award it eventually to Greece with an understanding that Bulgarian goods might be transported across it duty-free. Bulgaria was obliged to pay an indemnity of approximately $445,000,000, and to reduce her army to 20,000 men, with a police-force not exceeding 10,000.

With Hungary, the Allies encountered exceptional difficulties in making peace, for a radical Socialist revolution at Budapest on March 21 overthrew the government of Count Karolyi and set up a Soviet government under Bela Kun, a former associate of Lenin and Trotsky, the Russian Bolshevist leaders; and Bela Kun pursued most dilatory and annoying tactics in dealing with the Allies. It was not until Rumanian troops invaded the country and approached the capital, in August, that Bela Kun was driven from power and replaced by a Provisional Government under Archduke Joseph, which resumed negotiations for peace. As ultimately arranged, Hungary was stripped of non-Magyar peoples as completely as Austria had been shorn of non-German peoples: Slovakia went to Czechoslovakia; Transylvania was ceded to Rumania; Croatia was incorporated into the Kingdom of the Serbs, Croats, and Slovenes; and the Banat was divided between Rumania and Serbia. Hungary itself shrank from a maritime, imperialistic country of 125,000 square miles and twenty-two million inhabitants into a landlocked national Magyar state of nine millions with a trivial army of 30,000 men.

The conclusion of peace with the Ottoman Empire was an even slower process. Allied diplomatists obviously did not know what to do with Constantinople, now that Russia had collapsed, and they were embarrassed by protracted disputes between France and Great Britain over Syria, and between Italy and Greece over Asia Minor. By February, 1920, however, the general outlines of the probable settlement in the Near East were becoming clear: the Arab state of Hedjaz, embracing the territory east of the Red Sea and the River Jordan and the towns of Damascus and Aleppo, would become autonomous, under a British mandate; Armenia would become a free Christian republic, under international auspices; and, probably as mandataries of the League of Nations, Great Britain would take Palestine and Mesopotamia, France would secure Syria and Cilicia, Italy would appropriate Adalia, and Greece would obtain Smyrna and adjacent territory on the coast of Asia Minor. It appeared certain that the Dardanelles and the Bosphorus would be internationalized and that Turkey's future would be that of a small national state confined mainly to Asia Minor.

Among the Allied and Associated Governments various other territorial and commercial matters were the subject of negotiation in 1919–1920. Thus, in November, 1919, Poland was given a twenty-five year mandate to Eastern Galicia, with its sixteen million inhabitants, a majority of whom are Ruthenians (Ukrainians); and arrangements were made for a plebiscite in Teschen, to determine whether that district should go to Poland or to Czechoslovakia. Furthermore, Greece and Italy agreed to settle their outstanding differences: Italy would yield to Greece southern Albania and the twelve islands in the Ægean which had been under Italian rule since the Tripolitan War of 1911–1912; in return, Greece would lease to Italy the site of a coaling station in the Ægean islands and would recognize an Italian protectorate over the greater part of Albania. Then, too, in November, 1919, the Arctic archipelago of Spitzbergen, hitherto a "no man's land," was ceded to Norway. And a special convention between Belgium and the Netherlands, concluded in 1920, freed navigation on the Scheldt from onerous Dutch restrictions and otherwise relieved Belgium of burdensome disabilities imposed upon her by the treaty of 1839, which had recognized her independence.

To draw a boundary-line along the eastern coast of the Adriatic between Italy and Jugoslavia (Serbia) proved peculiarly troublesome. So long as the Orlando cabinet was in power at Rome, Italy vehemently demanded the cession to her, not only of the Adriatic islands and that part of Dalmatia pledged her by the secret treaties of 1915 and 1917, but the important port of Fiume also, — a demand stubbornly rejected both by the Jugoslavs and by the American President. With the advent to power of the more conciliatory Italian cabinet of Francesco Nitti in July, 1919, the outlook for a mutually acceptable compromise grew brighter, only to be overcast, however, in September, by the forcible seizure of Fiume by a free-lance Italian expedition under Gabriele d'Annunzio, the ultra-patriotic poet-soldier-adventurer. D'Annunzio posed as a twentieth-century Garibaldi, and even surpassed his illustrious prototype in rhetorical exuberance and likewise in creating embarrassment for the Italian Government. D'Annunzio won a plebiscite in Fiume and raided the town of Zara in Dalmatia; but the general Italian election, in November, 1919, registered an overwhelming majority of the Italian people as disposed to support Nitti rather than D'Annunzio, and late in January, 1920, the Italian Government agreed to a compromise proposed by the

2 C

Allied Supreme Council, by which both Fiume and Zara would be internationalized under the auspices of the League of Nations; Italy would secure the eastern Adriatic coast as far south as Fiume, the greater part of Albania, and the Adriatic islands of Lissa and Lesina; and Serbia would obtain the other Adriatic islands, Dalmatia, and a northern strip of Albania. Against this compromise, however, the Jugoslavs protested, and in February the deadlock still persisted.

A whole series of treaties was concluded by the Great Powers with the several states which had recently come into existence — Poland, Czechoslovakia, Finland, *etc.*, — and likewise with those lesser Powers whose national unifications had been achieved in the course of the Great War — Rumania, Serbia, and Greece. These treaties contained provisions relating to boundaries, to the assumption of debts of annexed regions, and to commercial affairs. In most instances, moreover, they contained provisions guaranteeing certain rights and privileges to racial or religious minorities within these states. In the case of Poland, and in that of Rumania, special protection was deemed necessary for the Jews; in the case of Serbia, it was the Catholics; in the case of Czechoslovakia, it was the German minority in Bohemia.

In all these cases much the same phraseology was utilized as in the treaty concluded by the Allies with German Austria: "Austria undertakes to bring her institutions into conformity with the principles of liberty and justice and acknowledges that the obligations for the protection of minorities are matters of international concern over which the League of Nations has jurisdiction. She assures complete protection of life and liberty to all inhabitants of Austria, without distinction of birth, language, race, or religion, together with the right to the free exercise of any creed. All Austrian nationals without distinction of race, language, or religion are to be equal before the law. No restrictions are to be imposed on the free use of any language in private or public, and reasonable facilities are to be given to Austrian nationals of non-German speech for the use of their language before the courts. Austrian nationals belonging to racial, religious, or linguistic minorities are to enjoy the same protection as other Austrian nationals, in particular in regard to schools and other educational establishments and in districts where a considerable portion of Austrian nationals of other than German speech are resident; facilities are to be given in schools for the instruction of children in their own language and an equable share of public funds is to be provided for the purpose.

These provisions do not preclude the Austrian Government from making the teaching of German obligatory. They are to be embodied by Austria in her fundamental law as a bill of rights, and provisions regarding them are to be under the protection of the League of Nations."

Such were the salient points in the settlement effected in 1919–1920 by the host of statesmen, diplomatists, and "experts." There were still a vast number of intricate and perplexing problems to be faced and solved by the Great Powers before the world could properly be pronounced "normal" and "settled." There were treaties to be ratified and put in force. There was the League of Nations to be provided with machinery and precedents. There was the dilatory and doubtful action of the United States. There was the uncertain status of Esthonia, Latvia, Lithuania, and Ukrainia. There were no defined eastern boundaries of Poland. There were outstanding imperialistic difficulties in Asia, in Africa, and in America. There were the grievances of China against Japan, and of Ireland against Great Britain.[1] Above all, there was Bolshevism in Russia, chaos in one of the largest countries on the surface of the globe.[2]

[1] As a result of the unwillingness or inability of the British Government to carry into effect the Home Rule Act of 1914, Ireland had grown steadily more restive, until the general election of December, 1918, returned from the unhappy island 26 Ulster Unionists, 6 Nationalists, and 73 Sinn Feiners. Sinn Fein thus secured an overwhelming majority of Irish votes, and, by a sort of referendum, Ireland declared in no uncertain terms for the right of independent, national self-determination. The Sinn Feiners who were elected to Parliament, refusing to take part in the proceedings of the British House of Commons at Westminster, assembled in Dublin, proclaimed the independence of their country, drafted a democratic constitution, elected Eamonn de Valera president and appointed plenipotentiaries to the Peace Congress. The British Government would not treat with the "provisional government" at Dublin or allow the Irish Question to be discussed at Paris. President Wilson, it is true, received a committee representing Irish-Americans and listened to their pleas in behalf of Ireland, but Premier Lloyd George declined even to receive them. Subsequently, in September, 1919, the "Irish Parliament" was suppressed by the British Government; and throughout 1919 Ireland was ruled with a rod of iron. At the end of the year a new project for Irish Home Rule was put forward by the British Government, involving the creation of separate parliaments for Ulster and for the rest of Ireland and of a joint "Council of Ireland," but it was opposed both by the Ulster Unionists and by the Sinn Feiners.

[2] The Allies failed signally in 1919 to solve the "Russian Question." In January they proposed a conference of all Russian factions and "governments" on Prinkipo Island, in the Sea of Marmora, under their auspices; the Bolsheviki accepted, and likewise the Esthonians, Letts, Lithuanians, and Ukrainians, but the opposition of anti-Bolshevist Russians was so acute and the Allies themselves were so irresolute that the project was soon dropped. The Allies could not bring themselves to recognize the Bolshevist régime at Moscow, although Lenin assured them that the Soviet Government would agree to assume the foreign indebtedness of previous Russian governments. On the other hand, they did not give sufficient aid to Admiral Kolchak or other anti-Bolshevist Russian leaders to bring about the

Yet at the beginning of 1920 enough of a settlement had already been reached, and the settlement was sufficiently revolutionary, to justify us in hailing it as the beginning of a new era. In the following section we shall undertake roughly to estimate what the settlement had cost Europe and the world in the five years of warfare from the assassination of the Archduke Francis Ferdinand, on June 28, 1914, to the signing of the treaty of Versailles, on June 28, 1919. Then, in the concluding section, we shall make bold to state wherein, as we think, lies the significance of the new era, the real meaning of the Great War.

THE LOSSES

The Great War was indeed a cataclysm; and commensurate with the revolutionary peace settlement which followed it were the gigantic losses in life and property which attended it. Sixteen established states — Germany, Austria-Hungary, Russia, France, the British Empire, Italy, the United States, Japan, Belgium, Turkey, Serbia, Montenegro, Bulgaria, Rumania, Greece, and Portugal, — and three new ones which the war brought forth — Poland, Czechoslovakia, and Hedjaz, — assembled their human powers for the conflict — fifteen on one side and four on the other. Against one or more of the four, eleven other nations also declared war, but engaged in it less actively, — Brazil, China, Costa Rica, Cuba, Guatemala, Haiti, Honduras, Liberia, Nicaragua, Panama, and Siam. Of the remaining twenty independent nations of the world, five — Bolivia, Ecuador, Peru, Santo Domingo, and Uruguay — severed diplomatic relations with one or more of the four original aggressors, and one — Persia — became a battle-ground of contending forces. Only fourteen independent states on the earth's surface preserved neutrality — Abyssinia, Argentina, Chile, Colombia, Denmark, Mexico, Netherlands, Norway, Paraguay, Salvador, Spain, Sweden, Switzerland, and Venezuela. All states, neutral as well as belligerent, were seriously affected by the Great War.

The toll of human life taken by the Great War was simply astounding. The table printed below gives the most reliable estimates regarding the man-power employed and the casualties

downfall of Lenin by force of arms. While declaring that their intervention in Russia was aimed at relieving the distress and suffering of the Russian people, they enforced with great rigor an economic blockade against the Bolsheviki, thereby inflicting no slight hardship upon the most populous regions of Russia. It was not until January 16, 1920, that the Allied Supreme Council raised the blockade.

suffered by the sixteen nations which were officially mobilized for the war and took an active part in it.

MOBILIZED STRENGTH AND CASUALTY LOSSES OF THE BELLIGERENTS [1]

Central Powers

NATION	MOBILIZED	DEAD	WOUNDED	PRISONERS OR MISSING	TOTAL CASUALTIES
Germany	11,000,000	1,611,104	3,683,143	772,522	6,066,769
Austria-Hungary . .	6,500,000	800,000	3,200,000	1,211,000	5,211,000
Turkey	1,600,000	300,000	570,000	130,000	1,000,000
Bulgaria	400,000	101,224	152,399	10,825	264,448
Total	19,500,000	2,812,328	7,605,542	2,124,347	12,542,217

Allied and Associated Powers

NATION	MOBILIZED	DEAD	WOUNDED	PRISONERS OR MISSING	TOTAL CASUALTIES
Russia	12,000,000	1,700,000	4,950,000	2,500,000	9,150,000
France	7,500,000	1,385,300	2,675,000	446,300	4,506,600
British Empire . . .	7,500,000	692,065	2,037,325	360,367	3,089,757
Italy	5,500,000	460,000	947,000	1,393,000	2,800,000
United States . . .	4,272,521	67,813	192,483	14,363	274,659
Japan	800,000	300	907	3	1,210
Belgium	267,000	20,000	60,000	10,000	90,000
Serbia	707,343	322,000	28,000	100,000	450,000
Montenegro	50,000	3,000	10,000	7,000	20,000
Rumania	750,000	200,000	120,000	80,000	400,000
Greece	230,000	15,000	40,000	45,000	100,000
Portugal	100,000	4,000	15,000	200	10,000
Total	39,676,864	4,869,478	11,075,715	4,956,233	20,892,226

It has been estimated that the Polish combatants with the Allies numbered 150,000; that the Czechoslovak armies in Siberia, France, and Italy included 180,000 nationals; that the sultan of Hedjaz fought the Turk with 250,000 Arabs. These three new nations, therefore, employed a combatant force of 580,000 men, which was joined to the Allies' 39,676,864 against the Central Powers' 19,500,000.

Nearly sixty million men at war! Of this huge number nearly eight millions died and approximately six millions (or thirty per cent. of the wounded) became human wrecks. But

[1] Much of this statistical information is taken from an interesting article by Walter Littlefield in *The New York Times Current History* for February, 1919, pp. 239 *et sqq.*

this only refers to the soldiers and sailors who died or were irreparably maimed. Civilians suffered even more grievously, not only by engines of war, but by famine, disease, and massacre. There were those who were killed by direct military causes; those who died from indirect causes.

In the first category we have: 692 Americans slain on the high seas; 20,620 British subjects slain on the high seas; 1270 English men, women, and children, the victims of air raids and bombardment; 30,000 Belgians butchered or deprived of life in various ways; 40,000 French similarly destroyed; and 7500 neutrals slain by submarines and mines; a total of over 100,000. In the second category we have: four million Armenians, Syrians, Jews, and Greeks, massacred or starved by the Turks; four million deaths beyond the normal mortality as the result of the influenza and pneumonia induced by the war; one million Serbian dead through disease or massacre. All this gives a military and civilian mortality, directly or indirectly the product of the Great War, of about seventeen millions.

And this is not all. Who can even estimate the millions of human beings whose bones whitened the roads of Poland, Ukrainia, and Lithuania, and the other millions who were starved throughout the length and breadth of Europe by blockades, malnutrition, and revolutionary disorders?

It should be remembered, moreover, that the gigantic human losses were bound to be an even greater debit to the following generation than to the present, for the soldiers killed were mostly youthful, the ablest, strongest, most spirited, and most promising members of the race, and among civilians the mortality was highest of children and of child-bearing women. Furthermore, while Europe was most grievously affected in this respect, many regions in other continents received serious set-backs. For example, in the total armed strength and casualties of the British Empire were included millions of stalwart young men from Canada, Australia, New Zealand, South Africa, and India; in the case of Canada, out of an aggregate population of seven and a half million, nearly one million went to war, and of this number over one hundred thousand never returned; even India supplied almost a million native troops who suffered enormous losses in Mesopotamia, in Arabia, and in East Africa. In the French totals likewise were embraced at least 900,000 colonials, chiefly black, who did their full share of fighting and suffered proportionately.

Throughout the world there was a noticeable decline in the

birth-rate. In France, for illustration, official statistics showed that civilian population in the four years of the war decreased by considerably over three-quarters of a million, without including the deaths in occupied Northern France or the losses due directly to the war. In 1913 the births in France outnumbered the deaths by 17,000, but in the following year this excess disappeared and thereafter the deaths considerably outnumbered the births — in 1914 by more than 50,000, and in 1915, 1916, 1917, and 1918 by nearly 300,000 in each year. Births, which numbered approximately 600,000 in 1913, dropped to 315,000 in 1916, while the deaths increased, but not in comparable proportions, so that the total decrease in population was due less to any great increase in deaths than to a great diminution in births. It seemed as though mothers despaired of bringing children into a world the prey to the horrors and terror of war. And what was true of France was true, only in lesser degree, of other belligerents.

If during the four years of the Great War blood flowed like water, money was poured out similarly. From August, 1914, to August, 1918, — thereby excluding the final stage of the war and the whole period of settlement and readjustment, — the principal belligerent nations increased their public debts as follows:

PUBLIC INDEBTEDNESS [1]

Central Powers

NATION	AUGUST, 1914	AUGUST, 1918	INCREASE
Germany	$ 1,165,000,000	$ 30,000,000,000	$28,835,000,000
Austria	2,640,000,000	13,314,000,000	10,674,000,000
Hungary	1,345,000,000	5,704,000,000	4,359,000,000
Total	$ 5,150,000,000	$ 49,018,000,000	$43,868,000,000

Allied and Associated Powers

NATION	AUGUST, 1914	AUGUST, 1918	INCREASE
Great Britain	$ 3,458,000,000	$ 30,000,000,000	$26,542,000,000
Rest of British Empire .	1,454,000,000	3,000,000,000	1,546,000,000
Russia	5,092,000,000	25,383,000,000	20,291,000,000
France	6,598,000,000	25,227,000,000	18,629,000,000
United States. . . .	1,208,000,000	15,008,000,000	13,800,000,000
Italy.	2,792,000,000	7,676,000,000	4,884,000,000
Total	$20,602,000,000	$106,294,000,000	$85,692,000,000

[1] These statistics are taken from an article by D. G. Rogers in *The New York Times Current History* for August, 1918, pp. 227 *et sqq.*

Among the Allies, Great Britain showed the largest increase of indebtedness : her total of twenty-six and a half billions included some eight billions advanced by her to the Entente and to the British Dominions and likewise some four billions loaned her by the United States.   In the same category with the eight billions advanced by Great Britain, chiefly to Russia and Italy, should be put American loans totaling eight and a half billions, of which four billions went to Great Britain, two and a half to France, one and a quarter to Italy, and the rest was distributed in smaller amounts among Russia, Belgium, Greece, Cuba, Serbia, Rumania, Liberia, and Czechoslovakia.   In the case of the Central Empires, their increased indebtedness included large financial advances to Bulgaria and Turkey.

Increase of public indebtedness, staggering though it appeared, was only part of the cost of the Great War to the belligerent states.   Vast sums of money were taken in direct and indirect taxes, — heavy income taxes, taxes on war profits, taxes on luxuries, *etc.*, *etc*.   No human being escaped the necessity of contributing something to the military decision.   In France, for example, the civilian population paid in taxes in 1918 thirty-eight dollars per capita.   Hand in hand with this universally burdensome taxation and with the floating of gigantic loans went naturally enormous issues of paper-money and a dangerous inflation of currency.   Thus, while the amounts of gold and silver in the banks of the warring countries of Europe changed but little in the aggregate from August, 1914, to November, 1918, the ratio of these amounts to their liabilities decreased from 54.3 to 9.4. The result was a stupendous increase in the cost of living throughout the world.

Then, too, the Great War served to diminish the production of food-staples and thereby to bring Europe to the verge of starvation.   Mr. Herbert Hoover, who as Director General of the International Relief Organization made a tour through the Continent shortly after the signing of the armistice, cabled in January, 1919, to the United States a brief statement of conditions as he had found them :

"Finland — The food is practically exhausted in the cities. While many of the peasants have some bread, other sections are mixing large amounts of straw.   They are exhausted of fats, meats, and sugar, and need help to prevent renewed rise of Bolshevism.

"Baltic States — The food may last one or two months on a much reduced scale.   They sent a deputation to our Ministry at Stockholm imploring food.

"Serbia — The town bread ration is down to three ounces daily in the north not accessible from Salonica. In the south, where accessible, the British are furnishing food to the civil population. We are trying to get food in from the Adriatic.

"Jugoslavia — The bread ration in many towns is three or four ounces. All classes are short of fats, milk, and meats.

"Vienna — Except for supplies furnished by the Italians and Swiss, their present bread ration of six ounces per diem would disappear. There is much illness from the shortage of fats, the ration being one-and-one-half ounces per week. There is no coffee, sugar, or eggs, and practically no meat.

"Tyrol — The people are being fed by Swiss charity.

"Poland — The peasants probably have enough to get through. The mortality in cities, particularly among children, is appalling for lack of fats, milk, meat, and bread. The situation in bread will be worse in two months.

"Rumania — The bread supply for the entire people is estimated to last another thirty days. They are short of fats and milk. The last harvest was sixty per cent a failure.

"Bulgaria — The harvest was also a failure here. There are supplies available for probably two or three months.

"Armenia — is already starving.

"Czechoslovakia — There is large suffering on account of lack of fats and milk. They have bread for two or three months and sugar for six months."

The havoc wrought by the Great War can never be fully estimated. For France, one of the grievous sufferers, a few statistics are available,[1] and from these perhaps we may form a faint notion of the cost of the war. French agriculture was hard hit: the soil of the entire country, having been tilled for four years mainly by women, elderly men, and young boys, was greatly impoverished; the number of cattle, which in England decreased by four per cent., decreased in France by eighteen per cent.; the production of milk decreased by sixty-three per cent.; the number of sheep diminished by thirty-eight per cent., and of swine, by forty per cent. In the invaded region alone the damage caused directly by the Germans to the soil, to live-stock, to crops, tools, etc., was estimated conservatively at two billion dollars.

Furthermore, the part of France occupied by the Germans produced before the war four-fifths of the coal and iron supplies of the whole country and included three-fourths of the nation's

[1] In a report prepared in December, 1918, by Mr. George B. Ford, head of the Research Department of the American Red Cross in France.

spinning and weaving industries. During the four years of their occupation the Germans willfully and methodically destroyed all that was in their power to destroy. In the cotton industry, the French lost more than two and a quarter million spindles and twenty thousand looms. Iron works, machine works also, were looted, the useful equipment — engines, rolling mills, machine tools, even structural steel — having been taken away and utilized again in the iron works in Germany. Mines were flooded, the surface plants dynamited, the workmen's dwellings destroyed. It was estimated that altogether four billion dollars' worth of machinery would be needed to replace that destroyed or carried away.

Another two billion dollars would be required to replace the 250,000 destroyed buildings in France and to repair the 500,000 damaged buildings. Yet another two billions would have to be spent in repairing and replacing the used or destroyed public works in northern France: the Northern Railway alone had lost 1731 bridges and 338 stations. According to figures submitted by the Budget Committee to the Chamber of Deputies in December, 1918, the total damage in the north of France, including public works, buildings, furniture, industry, agriculture, and forestry, was estimated at sixty-four billion francs, or close to thirteen billion dollars.

Little Belgium had suffered at least two billion dollars' worth of outright destruction, and in addition there were two billions in thefts and taxes imposed by Germany. Of this amount, one and one-half billions represented the loss of machinery, tools, and stock. And if to the special losses of France and Belgium were added those of Poland, Russia, Rumania, Serbia, and Italy, a financial amount could be computed that would surpass human powers of comprehension. No financial amount could compensate the world for the destruction of such monuments as the cathedral of Rheims or the library of Louvain.

Finally, in sketching the cost of the Great War, we must not lose sight of the enormous destruction of the world's shipping. The total losses of the world's merchant tonnage from the beginning of the war to the end of October, 1918, through belligerent action and marine risk, was 15,053,786 gross tons, of which 9,031,828 were British. In December, 1918, Sir Eric Geddes, First Lord of the British Admiralty, stated that 5622 British merchant ships had been sunk during the war, of which 2475 had been sunk with their crews still on board and 3147 had been sunk and their crews set adrift. Fishing vessels to the number of

670 had been destroyed, and more than 15,000 men in the British merchant marine had lost their lives through enemy action. Emergency building had contributed much to the replacement of lost tonnage, but it had been accomplished at heavy expense.

The United States bore its share of the losses. According to official figures published by the Bureau of Navigation, a total of 145 American merchant vessels, of 354,449 gross tons, with 775 lives, was lost through enemy acts from the beginning of the war to the cessation of hostilities on November 11. Nineteen of the 145 vessels and sixty-seven of the 775 lives were lost through German torpedoes, mines, and gunfire prior to the entrance of the United States into the Great War.

LANDMARKS OF THE NEW ERA

The Great War could not do otherwise than close one era in human history and inaugurate another. Its expenditure of man-power and of natural resources was too prodigious to allow the world to be the same in 1920 as it had been in 1914. To be sure, much remained unchanged, for the human animal is too instinctively conservative, too naturally a victim of habit, to permit even a cataclysm like the Great War to wrench him quite loose from the institutions and customs of the past. Besides, many of the changes which attracted most attention during the five years' conflict were destined possibly to be only temporary, and others would seem perhaps to future generations humorously insignificant.

Yet after making full allowance for the numerous and important respects in which the world was not changed by the Great War, or was altered only temporarily, sufficiently striking novelties had already appeared in society and in government in 1920, as a direct or indirect outcome of the struggle, to justify us in describing them briefly as landmarks of a new era. In these landmarks is found the significance of the Great War.

What was accomplished by five years' unprecedented outpouring of blood and treasure? The most obvious achievement, certainly the most universally impressive to contemporaries, was the staggering defeat of Germany and her associates. Germany, a militaristic Power *par excellence*, after frightening Europe for two generations by swashbuckling words and rattlings of heavy armor, had finally essayed by dint of methods most truly anarchic and by aid of confederates most terribly unscrupulous to impose her will and her *Kultur* upon the world; she had ultimately taken the sword and sought to substitute for the system of free sovereign states and for the Balance of Power a world-order established and maintained on the basis of a *Pax Romana Germanica*. She had failed. The slogan of her Bernhardi — *Weltmacht oder Niedergang* — had been answered with *Niedergang*. Her dream of a Teutonized *Mittel-Europa* was dispelled. Turkey and Austria-Hungary were disrupted; Bulgaria and Germany herself were overwhelmed and crushed. The Great War, in this respect, confirmed an historical lesson of modern times, that no one state could or would be suffered to revive a Roman Empire; and William II of Germany proved to be but a shadow following the fated footsteps of Emperor Charles V, of Philip II of Spain, of Louis XIV of France, and of Napoleon Bonaparte. And with the downfall of the German Empire in the twentieth century, the free nations of the world breathed more easily.

Other achievements, incidental to this major one, deserve more extended consideration, for they, in the main, are positive and constructive, while the defeat of Germany in itself was merely destructive and negative. If we contrast the world in 1919 with the world in 1914, we discover the following facts and tendencies, significant outgrowths of the Great War and prophetic landmarks of a new era:

I. *Nationalism.* The Great War marked the all but universal triumph of the principle of nationalism, the doctrine that people who speak the same language and have the same historic traditions shall live together under a common polity of their own making. This principle, this doctrine, made rapid headway during the five years' strife; the Germans utilized it against Russia, and the Allies invoked it against the Central Empires. Generally the prophets and seers of the new era, unlike those of the eighteenth century, did not decry nationalism in behalf of an utopian "cosmopolitanism"; they extolled nationalism alike as desirable in itself and as a starting-point on the promised road to "internationalism." Nor did the peacemakers of 1919–1920 repeat the mistake of their predecessors at Vienna a century earlier and ignore the unmistakable popular longings for national self-determination; on the other hand, they consecrated nationalism and wrote it into the public law of Europe.

Four great non-nationalistic states were dismembered — Austria-Hungary, Turkey, Russia, and Germany, — and one small state — Montenegro — disappeared. From the ruins emerged nine newly independent national states — Poland, Czechoslovakia, Hedjaz, Armenia, Finland, Ukrainia, Lithuania, Latvia, and Esthonia, — while, through annexations and consolidations, the national unification was virtually completed of Italy, of Jugoslavia (Serbia), of Rumania, and of Greece; and the return of Alsace-Lorraine to France and of the Danish-speaking portion of Schleswig to Denmark redressed long-standing national grievances. Germany, deprived of Danes, French, and Poles, became for the first time in history genuinely a national state. Similarly, Russia became a homogeneous state of Great Russians; Hungary, a national state of Magyars; the Ottoman Empire, a small national state of Mohammedan Turks; and Austria, a minor but homogeneous Teuton colony on the Danube. Had German Austria been permitted to unite formally with Germany, all central Europe, except Switzerland, would have been completely reorganized on a national basis.

In recognizing the new nationalistic order of things, the diplomatists had the farsightedness to try to correct its intolerant tendencies by eliciting pledges from the new national states to preserve and respect religious, cultural, and economic rights of dissentient nationalities within their territories. In this war the Jews especially were, in Central Europe, placed more or less under international protection. What with the encouragement of Zionism in Palestine and with the international guarantee of their status in Europe, the Jews were signal gainers by the Great War.

In certain quarters of the world, particularly in Allied territories, national self-determination was temporarily checked or suppressed. Such was the situation in Ireland, where, though conditions were not essentially different from those in Czechoslovakia, the British Government thwarted the undoubted desire of the majority of the people to found a national republic and successfully combated their every effort to obtain a hearing at the Peace Congress. In Egypt, too, the British suppressed a national insurrection by force of arms in the spring of 1919. And in Albania the Italians set to work deliberately to stifle the spirit of independent nationalism. Yet in all these regions nationalistic agitation went forward; it troubled to an unusual degree the British in India and in Persia, the Japanese in Korea, and to some extent the Americans in the Philippines.

II. *Change in Relative Importance of States.* As an outcome of the Great War there was, on the one hand, a considerable increase in the number of small independent states in the world.

and, on the other, a reduction in the number of Great Powers.   Of the eight recognized Great Powers in 1914, Austria-Hungary had ceased to exist by 1919, and Germany and Russia, at least temporarily, had been outclassed. Russia had become a pariah among the nations, thanks to her embracing of extreme socialism; and Germany had lost her navy, her colonies, and her merchant marine and had declined from a position as the foremost military state in the world to virtual disarmament and impotence.

In theory at any rate the new state-system was unlike the old. The old, as was pointed out in the opening pages of this book, was essentially anarchic; it rested on the fancied self-sufficiency of each of its members, on series of alliances and ententes formed for selfish ends, and on balances of power and threats of war. The new system had gradually evolved from the exigencies of the Great War and had been enshrined in the Covenant of Versailles; it was based on the concept of a League of Nations in which no state should presume to set its own interests above those of mankind at large, and on a contract according to which certain activities were recognized as of international concern rather than as within the restricted purview of individual nations. If the League of Nations flourished, if the new order became a reality,— and only the lapse of many years could tell, — then the old ascription of absolute and unrestricted sovereignty to each and every independent state would in time be revised, and out of the anarchic welter and chaos of modern times would succeed an organized Inter-Nation capable of preserving the peace of the world and of promoting the orderly development of human life. To the realization of such a dream the Great War pointed posterity.

Without some sort of a League of Nations, the growth of nationalism during the war and its recognition by the Peace Congress might readily become a curse rather than a blessing. Merely to add ten or a dozen new national states to forty or fifty already existing, merely to "Balkanize" Central Europe, would render confusion worse confounded, if the new ones like the old should not receive a striking object-lesson, which unfortunately at the outset they seemed all too prone to ignore, in the necessity of restraint and humility and coöperation, in uprooting the weeds of nationalism and cultivating only its best fruits.

The League of Nations, as actually established in 1920, was none too strong.   Excluded from its membership were not only Germany, Austria, Hungary, Bulgaria, and Turkey, but also

Russia and most of the states newly detached from the old Russian Empire; and the United States seemed unwilling to adhere to it without "reservations" which further weakened it. Furthermore, between the multitude of small states included in the League and the four Great Powers which at first practically controlled it, — Great Britain, France, Italy, and Japan, — there was a wide divergence of power and prestige. There were adverse critics a-plenty who insisted that the Covenant was primarily a cloak for the further aggrandizement of the four Great Powers at the expense of the rest.

III. *Imperialism.* Superficially, at any rate, the Great War gave zest and zeal to the game of capitalistic imperialism. As nationalism was the goal of the smaller states, so imperialistic gains seemed to be the stakes of most of the Great Powers. Great Britain emerged from the war as the foremost maritime and colonial and industrial Power in the world; she had humbled Germany, her latest rival, as completely as in earlier eras she had overcome the Spaniards, the Dutch, and the French; to her already far-flung empire were now added, in one form or another, some of the wealthiest provinces of the old Ottoman Empire, — Mesopotamia and Palestine,[1] — and the bulk of the German overseas possessions, — East Africa, Southwest Africa, parts of Kamerun and Togoland, and the Pacific islands south of the equator. She could now complete the construction of the Cape-to-Cairo railway exclusively on British soil, and by bringing Persia[2] within her orbit of influence she could dominate economically and politically the vast expanse of land and water from Cairo and Damascus to Rangoon and Singapore. The richest regions of Asia and of Africa were hers. To be sure, these gains were shared by Great Britain with South Africa, Australia, and New Zealand, for the British Empire, it should be remembered, was less a unitary state than an alliance of mother-country and self-governing dominions; nevertheless, they redounded to Anglo-Saxon prestige throughout the world and most substantially to the economic advantage of British capitalists within the United Kingdom.

France emerged from the Great War as the foremost military state on the Continent of Europe. She was exalted as Germany was abased. Against the possibility of the military resurrection

---

[1] Great Britain also now exercised a veiled protectorate over Hedjaz and a greatly strengthened protectorate over Egypt.

[2] A treaty concluded in 1919 between Persia and Great Britain virtually recognized the former as constituting a "sphere of influence" of the latter.

of Germany she was now insured by possession of Strassburg and Metz, by a fifteen-year occupation of Mainz, and, she hoped, by a special defensive alliance with Great Britain and the United States. Moreover, she enjoyed a paramount influence alike in the military and in the economic policies of Poland, Czechoslovakia, Rumania, Jugoslavia, and Greece; most of the smaller states of Europe were her satellites. And outside of Europe, France maintained her position as a colonial and imperialistic Power second in importance only to Great Britain. To the French Empire.were added "mandates" for Syria, Cilicia, and portions of Kamerun and Togoland, and a greatly strengthened protectorate of Morocco.

Italy not only completed her national unification but assumed a leading imperialistic rôle in the Adriatic and in the eastern Mediterranean. She obtained a hold on Albania and Adalia and counted upon extensions of her territories and privileges in Tripoli, Cyrenaica, and Somaliland.

Japan asserted and maintained a kind of Monroe Doctrine for China, that no European Power might increase its holdings in the Far East but that she herself might freely act as sponsor and guardian for the entire Chinese Empire. Specifically, she annexed the former German Pacific islands north of the equator and acquired the German rights and concessions in the Chinese province of Shantung. Less directly, she obtained at least a temporary hold on eastern Siberia.

The United States gained nothing directly. Indirectly, however, her participation in the Great War and her probable underwriting of the various treaties which concluded it marked her coming-of-age as a Great Power and as a World Power. On the one hand, she gained from Europe a formal recognition of the Monroe Doctrine; on the other hand, she set a precedent for subsequent interference in the affairs of Asia not only but of Europe likewise. She departed from her traditional policy of avoiding "entangling alliances" with Old-World Powers; and if she should ratify either the Covenant of the League of Nations or the defensive treaty of alliance with France, or both, she would obviously have entered into novel international engagements and assumed new international obligations of far-reaching import.

In fine, while Germany and Russia were turned from imperialistic paths by the Great War, four of the five victorious Great Powers, and possibly the fifth, paved wide and deep the highways of their own imperialism. One concession was made, how-

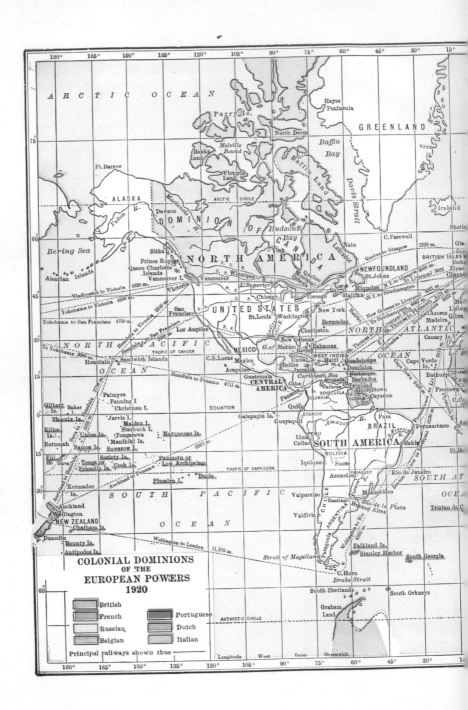

COLONIAL DOMINIONS
OF THE
EUROPEAN POWERS
1920

British
French
Russian
Belgian
Portuguese
Dutch
Italian

Principal railways shown thus ————

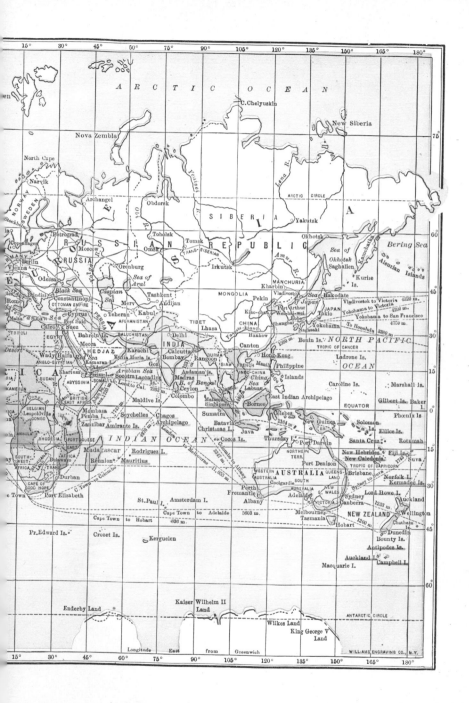

ever, to critics of imperialism, for most of the former German colonies were ceded to the several Allies not in full sovereignty but as "mandataries" of the League of Nations. In other words, the five Great Powers recognized the international, rather than the strictly national, character of capitalistic imperialism. The very phrasing of one of the sections of the Covenant was eloquent of the new point of view and of promise for the future: "To those colonies and territories which as a consequence of the late war have ceased to be under the sovereignty of the state which formerly governed them and which are inhabited by people not yet able to stand by themselves under the strenuous conditions of the modern world, there should be applied the principle that the well-being and development of such peoples form a sacred trust of civilization and that securities for the performance of this trust should be embodied in this Covenant. The best method of giving practical effect to this principle is that the tutelage of such peoples should be intrusted to advanced nations who by reason of their resources, their experience or their geographical position can best undertake this responsibility, and who are willing to accept it, and that this tutelage should be exercised by them as mandataries on behalf of the League.

"The character of the mandate must differ according to the stage of the development of the people, the geographical situation of the territory, its economic conditions and other similar circumstances. Certain communities formerly belonging to the Turkish Empire have reached a stage of development where their existence as independent nations can be provisionally recognized subject to the rendering of administrative advice and assistance by a mandatary until such time as they are able to stand alone; the wishes of these communities must be a principal condition in the selection of the mandatary. Other peoples, especially those of Central Africa, are at such a stage that the mandatary must be responsible for the administration of the territory under conditions which will guarantee freedom of conscience and religion, subject only to the maintenance of public order and morals, the prohibition of abuses such as the slave trade, the arms traffic and the liquor traffic, and the prevention of the establishment of fortifications or military and naval bases and of military training of the natives for other than police purposes and the defense of territory, and will also secure equal opportunities for the trade and commerce of other members of the League. There are territories, such as Southwest Africa and certain of the South Pacific islands, which, owing to the sparseness of their population or their

2 D

small size, or their remoteness from the centers of civilization, or their geographical contiguity to the territory of the mandatary, and other circumstances, can be best administered under the laws of the mandatary as integral portions of its territory, subject to the safeguards above mentioned in the interests of the indigenous population.

"In every case of mandate the mandatary shall render to the Council [of the League of Nations] an annual report in reference to the territory committed to its charge.   The degree of authority, control, or administration to be exercised by the mandatary shall, if not previously agreed upon by members of the League, be explicitly defined in each case by the Council.   A permanent commission shall be constituted to receive and examine the annual reports of the mandataries and to advise the Council on all matters relating to the observance of the mandates."

IV. *Republicanism.*   The Great War was as advantageous to republicanism throughout the world as it was disastrous to monarchy.   In 1914, six of the eight Great Powers were monarchical; in 1919, only three remained monarchical and these three — Great Britain, Italy, Japan, — had reconsecrated their political institutions by military victory.   The three most famous dynasties — the Habsburgs, the Romanovs, and the Hohenzollerns — had been worsted and had ceased to reign.   From German lands had been chased out all those lesser historic sovereign families — the Wittelsbachs, the Wettins, the Guelfs, *etc.*[1]   Republics had replaced monarchies in Russia, in Germany, and in Austria; and in the states newly created in Central Europe republican forms of government prevailed — in Poland, Czechoslovakia, Ukrainia, Lithuania, Latvia, Esthonia, and Finland.   Not only were the American continents almost wholly republican, but Europe was now predominantly so, and even in Asia the vast Chinese Empire was nominally republican.   Divine-right monarchy was at last extinct, except possibly in Japan; even constitutional, liberal monarchy was on the decline.

V. *Political Democracy.*   Within most of the belligerent countries radical political reforms of a democratic nature were fostered and hastened by the war.   Throughout Central Europe, in Germany, in Austria, and in Hungary, as well as in the newly

---

[1] Individual kings were forced out of Greece and Bulgaria, but in both these countries monarchy survived.   In the case of Montenegro, King Nicholas was deposed in favor of King Peter of Serbia.   In 1918 there were ineffectual anti-royalist demonstrations in the Netherlands, in Sweden, and in Spain.   A royalist uprising in Portugal against the republican government was easily put down.   Only in Hungary was there, in 1920, a popular drift from republicanism back to monarchy.

erected states of Poland, Czechoslovakia, and Finland, a host of new constitutions were written providing pretty uniformly for representative government, ministerial responsibility, and guarantees of personal liberties. In Germany and in Austria full woman suffrage on the same basis as that of men was accorded by the new constitutions; it was an appropriate recognition of the significant rôle which women had played in the Great War as well as a logical interpretation of the spirit of political democracy. In Great Britain, too, the franchise was granted to most women, while in the United States a constitutional amendment providing for general woman suffrage was approved by the Congress and submitted to the federated States for ratification. In France, a bill granting the franchise to women passed the Chamber of Deputies and barely missed passage through the Senate. In Italy, a woman-suffrage bill was pending in 1920.

In Great Britain the electoral reforms of 1832, 1867, and 1884–1885 were consolidated and supplemented by an important Electoral Reform Bill enacted in 1918. Anomalies of former acts were effaced and much-needed uniformity was secured. Hereafter, a general election was to be held everywhere on the same day; no person could vote in more than two constituencies; the franchise was extended to all men who were twenty-one years of age and had maintained a residence or place of business for six months, to all women who were thirty years of age and had owned or tenanted premises for six months or were married to men who owned or tenanted premises, and to veterans of the war who were nineteen years of age; the principle of proportional representation was to be applied to university constituencies returning two or more members; and a redistribution of seats was effected, whereby there would be one member for every 70,000 of the population in Great Britain, and one for every 43,000 in Ireland, so that the total membership of the House of Commons would be increased from 670 to 707.[1]

In France, a long-debated Electoral Reform Bill, which had been repeatedly passed by the Chamber and as repeatedly blocked by the Senate, was finally enacted in 1919. Under its terms, the *scrutin de liste* was substituted for the *scrutin d'arrondissement*,

---

[1] The first general elections, under this Reform Act, were held in December, 1918, and gave a decisive verdict in favor of the Lloyd George Coalition Government. The distribution of seats in the new House of Commons was as follows: Coalitionists, 471 (334 Unionists, 127 Liberals, 10 Laborites); Opposition, 236 (46 Unionists, 37 Asquith Liberals, 65 Laborites, 1 Socialist, 7 Irish Nationalists, 73 Sinn Feiners, 7 Independents). In Great Britain the position of the Conservative Unionists was greatly strengthened, and in Ireland that of the Sinn Fein.

and the principle of proportional representation was recognized and adopted.   In Belgium likewise the year 1919 witnessed an electoral reform, by which the system of plural voting was abolished and that of one-man-one-vote was introduced.   In Rumania,[1] too, universal suffrage was substituted for the undemocratic device of the three-class system which in earlier years had been borrowed from Prussia.

VI.   *Temporary Impatience with Popular Government.*   Though the outcome of the Great War was distinctly favorable to the cause of republicanism and of political democracy, temporarily at least there was not unnatural impatience with popular government.   In the midst of the war, when the fortunes of the Central Powers reached full-tide and those of the Allies appeared to ebb, many persons felt and expressed doubt of democracy and liberty; they pointed to Teutonic success as proof positive of the inherent superiority, at any rate in times of stress and strife, of autocracy over democracy, of obedience over freedom; they complained bitterly of the inefficiency of popular government and of the license of popular criticism; and they sought to destroy Autocracy by resorting to methods quite autocratic.   In part the Allied Governments responded to these feelings and complaints; everywhere the machinery of political democracy was supplemented, and in some instances well-nigh supplanted, by a bureaucracy of "experts," dependent upon a dictatorial "War Cabinet"; parliaments became chiefly "rubber-stamps" for registering and recording the decisions of the Government; and individual liberties were substantially abridged.   In all belligerent countries a censorship, open or veiled, was rigorously maintained; and constitutional guarantees of the freedom of association, meeting, and publication, were practically set aside, either by formal statutory restriction, or, more often, by direct action on the part of outraged patriots.   In the passions and hysteria of the Great War, majorities proved themselves utterly intolerant of minorities, and even majorities were impatient of the slow and ponderous workings of the usual engines of orderly political democracy.

How much of this was merely episodical to the war, time alone will tell.   Undoubtedly most of it arose out of military exigencies and will disappear with them.   But it may not be idle to conjecture that in the age-long struggle between the principle of

---

[1] The disasters which overtook Rumania from 1916 to 1918 led not only to political reform but also to a noteworthy social transformation, for the large landed estates were broken up and distributed, with compensation to their former owners, among the numerous and needy peasantry.

governmental authority and that of personal liberty, the Great War aided the former to the detriment of the latter.[1]   Nor might it be wholly beside the point to hazard the guess that the political democracy of the future would undergo a noteworthy transformation in letter if not in spirit : democracy might be rendered more real and more effective if it were based on social groupings rather than on territorial divisions, if "experts" were accorded a more honorable and appropriate place within it, and if its machinery were simplified and applied less reservedly to social ends, to the well-being of a whole community.   To reform political democracy and to extend its operation to industry and commerce was a burden imposed upon progressive nations by the Great War.

VII. *Habit of Resorting to Force.*   In the Great War, Germany had employed armed force in order to impose her peculiar *Kultur* upon the world, and the Allies had developed and utilized a superior armed force in order to curb Teutonic ambitions and to preserve their own freedom and independence.   For four years and more the fate of the bulk of mankind had hung, not upon orderly, peaceful evolution, but upon violence and force, — "force to the utmost, force without stint or limit."   And men who had been taught by the most practical examples and experiences that force was the righteous arbiter in the gravest of all international questions were dangerously but naturally inclined to resort to a forceful and illegal settlement of domestic differences.   "Direct action" was too frequently invoked during the Great War, and at its close, both by ultra-conservatives and by ultra-radicals.

In economic matters as well as in purely political questions revolutionary aims and revolutionary methods were increasingly championed.   On one side, reactionary statesmen and reactionary capitalists counseled the governments to refuse popular demands for political and economic reforms and to employ soldiers, if necessary, to back up their refusal.   On the other hand, groups of fanatical agitators preached class-warfare and the violent overturn of "bourgeois" government and society.   The career of the Bolsheviki in Russia was made possible only by a condition and a state of mind engendered by the Great War.   And only the habitual resort to force explained fully the policy which the Allies pursued in 1919 of attempting to overthrow the Bolsheviki by foreign intervention.

With the passing of war-psychology, the human mind will probably return gradually to a quieter and more normal state.

[1] A case in point is the enactment of permanent prohibition of alcoholic beverages throughout the United States (1918).

But in the meantime, for at least a generation, the world will be laboring to throw off the inherited incubus of terrorism and violence. In all countries, particularly in those which have suffered most in the Great War, a high degree of character, intelligence, and self-restraint will be required of the whole citizenry if, as a final outcome of the Great War, liberty is not to degenerate into license and civilization into barbarism.

VIII. *Social Tendencies*. The Great War strengthened certain tendencies which had been developing in the social order of the preceding era and inaugurated new ones:

(*a*) There was a marked increase of state socialism and of state intervention in labor disputes. Systems of transportation and communication were pretty generally taken over and managed by the governments; hours of labor were regulated, as were also in many instances wages and profits; and in some cases whole war-industries were maintained and operated by public authorities. In Great Britain, the Labor Party demanded (January, 1918) the permanent nationalization of land, railways, and mines.

(*b*) There was an increased influence, on the one hand, of bankers and great financiers, and, on the other hand, of labor organizations. "Profiteering" on the part of producers of war *matériel* and of dealers in foodstuffs was accompanied by unusual prosperity of farmers and by an unprecedented rise of wages of day-laborers. Salaried and professional men suffered disproportionately from the parallel rise in the cost of living. Trade-unionists enormously increased their influence both by reason of the greater demand for their individual service and by reason of their perfected organization and their consequent gain in collective bargaining.

(*c*) There was a new vogue of Marxian Socialism. Socialists controlled Russia from the time of the Bolshevist Revolution in November, 1917; they played prominent rôles in the revolutionary movements in Germany, Austria, and Hungary, in 1918, and they were more vocal than ever in Italy, in France, in Great Britain, and in the United States. Nevertheless they were much divided among themselves on aims and tactics: generally, in Allied countries, they had learned to coöperate loyally with bourgeois governments, while in Germany and Austria the majority of them found no great difficulty in sharing responsibility for the new revolutionary governments with Catholic parties; in Russia, the Bolshevist Socialists in attempting to carry the teachings of Marx into practice, profoundly modified the historic traditions of their party and succeeded in alienating not only the mass of non-Socialists throughout the world but the majority of Socialists in foreign countries and a large number of Russian Socialists. It seemed as though the Great War had cleft Marxian Socialism asunder : one wing was so fully committed to force and violence as to nullify Marx's political doctrines; the other wing was so completely given to compromise as to postpone indefinitely the realization of Marx's economic program. Socialism might be the goal of the future, but it was likely to be attained, if at all, through middle-class coöperation rather than by the unaided efforts of old-fashioned doctrinaire Marxian Socialists.

(d) Over against the manifest tendency toward state socialism appeared, curiously enough, a counter-tendency toward what for lack of a better phrase may be termed gild socialism. By this term is meant all those expedients, such as profit-sharing, shop-stewards, joint management, *etc.*, by which the workers would gradually gain control, and then ownership, of industries, and thus secure direct industrial democracy without the interposition of the state except as a regulator and accelerator of the process and as a protector of the interests of the public. Certainly considerable progress was made in Great Britain, in the United States, in France, in Italy, and in Germany, in 1918 and in 1919, toward admitting representatives of the workers to boards of directors of various industrial establishments and toward sharing profits between capitalists and workingmen.

Many persons professed to see in gild socialism the most practicable solution of the perplexing but all-important problem of improving the condition of the working classes without decreasing production, and at the same time the most promising antidote alike to state socialism, with its dangerous bureaucracy, and to Marxian Socialism, with its destructive class-hatred. Gild socialism in industry, taken in conjunction with an agricultural program of small holdings and of coöperation in production, buying and selling, might provide the basis for a significant social transformation during the ensuing century. It should be remarked in this connection that among many groups espousing such an evolution the Social Catholics were particularly active at the close of the Great War : it was the burden of the platforms of the Center Party in Germany, of the Christian Socialist Party in Austria, of the Democratic Party in Poland, of the Clericals in Belgium, of the *Action Libérale* in France, and of the newly formed Catholic Popular Party in Italy; it received the endorsement of the Catholic War Council of the United States.

(e) Whatever might be thought of the relative value of schemes of state socialism and gild socialism, there was certainly in the popular mind at the close of the Great War a firmer conviction than ever before that social reforms and readjustments were imperatively needed, that coöperation must be substituted for competition.   Just how this conviction would be translated into action, none could predict with assurance; that it would involve an eclectic choice of the best points in all existing social theories — capitalism, socialism, state-intervention, trade-unionism, profit-sharing, and industrial democracy — admitted of little doubt.   At any rate it was evident that the world was quite done with the economic individualism of the preceding century.   As the British Labor Party said in its famous "reconstruction" pronouncement of January, 1918: "The individualist system of capitalist production . . . may, we hope, have received a death-blow.   With it must go the political system and ideas in which it naturally found expression.   We of the Labor Party, whether in opposition or in due time called upon to form an administration, will certainly lend no hand to its revival.   If we in Britain are to escape from the decay of civilization itself we must insure that what is presently to be built up is a new social order, based not on fighting, but on fraternity, — not on the competitive struggle for the means of bare life, but on a deliberately planned coöperation in production and distribution for the benefit of all, — not on the utmost possible inequality of riches, but on a systematic approach toward a healthy equality of material circumstances for every person, — not on an enforced dominion over subject nations, subject races, subject colonies, subject classes, or a subject sex, but, in industry as well as in government, on that equal freedom, that general consciousness of consent, and that widest possible participation in power, both economic and political, which is characteristic of democracy.   We do not, of course, pretend that it is possible, even after the drastic clearing away that is now going on, to build society anew in a year or two of feverish 'reconstruction.'   What the Labor Party intends to satisfy itself about is that each brick that it helps to lay shall go to erect the structure that it intends, and no other."

IX. *Science and Education.*   The Great War gave an impetus to certain applications of experimental science.   Thus, there was an extraordinary development not only of strictly military weapons such as heavy artillery, machine guns, poisonous gases, tanks, airplanes, and submarines, but also of devices and implements which could be put to important commercial uses in the subsequent era of peace. To this category belonged the gradual perfecting of all sorts of aircraft, so that in 1919 government mails were being regularly transported by airplane between chief cities in the United States, and British and American air pilots were crossing the Atlantic in their frail, high-powered bird-ships. To this category belonged also the development of wireless telephony and of devices for detecting sounds in water. Likewise Great Britain and the United States were forced by circumstances of the war to improve their chemical and dyeing industries and to bring them up to a par with those of Germany.

In their endeavors to return wounded men to something like their former condition army surgeons accomplished marvels, and surgery developed in the course of the war to a point which ordinarily would have taken many years to attain. Considerable progress was made, moreover, in the sciences of sanitation and preventive medicine, in the age-long struggle against venereal disease, and in psycho-analysis and other methods of treating mental disorders. Psychology of groups as well as of individuals was studied scientifically; and in colleges and universities everywhere there was an immensely magnified interest in the social sciences — in politics, in economics, in sociology, and in recent history.

To the thousands of young men of every nation who participated in the Great War and survived it the experiences in camp and on the field possessed undoubted educational value. Most of these young men had formerly not traveled far from home, but during the war they were perpetually on the move, and they must have received a tremendous number of significant impressions which they could have received in no other way. The barbarian migrations of early centuries and the Crusades of the Middle Ages have long been pointed to as educational tours of the greatest importance; yet neither the Crusades nor the barbarian migrations affected nearly so many persons or embraced such extended regions as did the Great War. In the Great War, whole nations were in arms; millions of Russians sojourned in Germany, millions of Austrians in Russia, millions of Germans and Englishmen in France; and the trip of two million young Americans to Europe surpassed any educational tour ever planned by Cook's or other commercial firm.

The influence of education upon the development of a nation's ideals as well as upon the efficiency of an army was clearly perceived in the case of Germany; and one Allied government after another sought while the war was still in progress to supplement the work of the public schools at home by conducting school-classes among the troops at the front.   In Great Britain, a radical and far-reaching Education Bill, sponsored by Herbert Fisher, the secretary of education in the Lloyd George cabinet, was enacted in 1918.

X. *Religion*.   The Great War produced no spectacular religious "revival," as had been predicted.   It did promote, however, closer coöperation than had ever before obtained among Catholics, Protestants, Jews, and even Mohammedans.   In the case of the United States, the joint endeavors of the Young Men's Christian Association, the Knights of Columbus, the Jewish Welfare Board, and the Salvation Army served both to maintain the high morale of the troops at the front and to promote among the civilian population at home a greater interest in religious organizations.   In the case of all countries, neutrals as well as belligerents, the International Red Cross Society performed great and noble service for mankind.   Among Christians outside of the Roman communion there were renewed efforts to secure some sort of organic church unity.

On the whole, though Pope Benedict XV was denounced by some Allied citizens as pro-German and by some Germans as too pro-Ally, the Catholic Church was ably guided during the Great War and remained true to its high ideals.   Politically it occupied a better position at the close of the struggle than at the beginning; without materially impairing the prestige of the Catholic Center Party in Germany, Catholic Belgium had been vindicated, Catholic Poland had been reborn, Portugal had resumed diplomatic relations with the Holy See, Great Britain had sent an envoy to the Vatican, and a more cordial attitude toward the Church had been evinced by both France and Italy.   Though the Italian Government successfully prevented the pope from raising the "Roman Question," the Vatican obtained from the Peace Congress a solemn guarantee of the inviolability of the property of Christian missions abroad.   The ardor with which Catholics supported the new national movements and espoused programs of social reform was a tribute to the continuing vitality of their faith.

If the Great War did not immediately redound to the advantage of any particular ecclesiastical system, it at any rate dealt a body-blow at those doctrines of materialism and determinism which had been taking root everywhere throughout the nineteenth century and which had flourished and flowered mightily and poisonously in Germany on the eve of the final conflict.   Once more "spiritualism" came to the fore; man grew interested again in the phenomena of the "unseen"; and again absolute standards of right could be referred to with no more cynical smiling than was occasioned by mention of relative standards of might. Not the struggle for existence between each two specimens of the human species was to be the "natural" rule for the future, but the natural order was to be one with the supernatural, that all men are brothers and that in unselfish coöperation lies the hope of humanity and civilization.

Coöperation was the chief lesson taught by the Great War. No divine-right monarch could henceforth set his will above that of the nation — such was the moral of the first Russian Revolution. No single social class could henceforth dominate a whole community — such was the moral of the two Russian Revolutions and likewise of the upheavals throughout Central Europe. No one nation could henceforth set itself above all others and dominate the whole world — such was the moral of the defeat and collapse of Germany. Coöperation between social classes, coöperation between nations — these were to be the watchwords and countersigns of the new era. From the ruinous competition in industrial life and the mad anarchy in international relations, which held sway in 1914, to the coöperative enterprise and the League of Nations of 1920 was a far cry. The revolution was due to the turmoil and terrors and travail of the Great War.

APPENDIX I

THE COVENANT OF THE LEAGUE OF NATIONS

THE high contracting parties, in order to promote international coöperation and to achieve international peace and security by the acceptance of obligations not to resort to war, by the prescription of open, just, and honorable relations between nations, by the firm establishment of the understandings of international law as the actual rule of conduct among governments, and by the maintenance of justice and a scrupulous respect for all treaty obligations in the dealings of organized peoples with one another, agree to this covenant of the League of Nations.

ARTICLE 1. — The original members of the League of Nations shall be those of the signatories which are named in the annex to this covenant and also such of those other States named in the annex as shall accede without reservation to this covenant. Such accession shall be effected by a declaration deposited with the secretariat within two months of the coming into force of the covenant. Notice shall be sent to all other members of the League.

Any fully self-governing State, dominion, or colony not named in the annex may become a member of the League if its admission is agreed to by two-thirds of the assembly, provided that it shall give effective guarantee of its sincere intention to observe its international obligations, and shall accept such regulations as may be prescribed by the League in regard to its military, naval and air forces and armaments.

Any member of the League may, after two years' notice of its intention so to do, withdraw from the League, provided that all its international obligations and all its obligations under this covenant shall have been fulfilled at the time of its withdrawal.

ARTICLE 2. — The action of the League under this covenant shall be effected through the instrumentality of an assembly and of a council, with a permanent secretariat.

ARTICLE 3. — The assembly shall consist of representatives of the members of the League.

The assembly shall meet at stated intervals and from time to time as occasion may require at the seat of the League or at such other place as may be decided upon.

The assembly may deal at its meetings with any matter within the sphere of action of the League or affecting the peace of the world.

At meetings of the assembly each member of the League shall have one vote, and may have not more than three representatives.

ARTICLE 4. — The council shall consist of representatives of the principal Allied and Associated Powers, together with representatives of four other members of the League. These four members of the League shall be selected by the assembly from time to time in its discretion. Until the appointment of the representatives of the four members of the League first selected by the assembly, representatives of Belgium, Brazil, Spain, and Greece shall be members of the council.

With the approval of the majority of the assembly, the council may name additional members of the League whose representatives shall always be members of the council; the council with like approval may increase the number of members of the League to be selected by the assembly for representation on the council.

The council shall meet from time to time as occasion may require, and at least once a year, at the seat of the League, or at such other place as may be decided upon.

The council may deal at its meetings with any matter within the sphere of action of the League or affecting the peace of the world.

Any member of the League not represented on the council shall be invited to send a representative to sit as a member at any meeting of the council during the consideration of matters specially affecting the interests of that member of the League.

At meetings of the council, each member of the League represented on the council shall have one vote, and may have not more than one representative.

ARTICLE 5. — Except where otherwise expressly provided in this covenant or by the terms of the present treaty, decisions at any meeting of the assembly or of the council shall require the agreement of all the members of the League represented at the meeting.

All matters of procedure at meetings of the assembly or of the council, including the appointment of committees to investigate particular matters, shall be regulated by the assembly or by the council and may be decided by a majority of the members of the League represented at the meeting.

The first meeting of the assembly and the first meeting of the council shall be summoned by the President of the United States of America.

ARTICLE 6. — The permanent secretariat shall be established at the seat of the League. The secretariat shall comprise a Secretary General and such secretaries and staff as may be required.

The first Secretary General shall be the person named in the annex; thereafter the Secretary General shall be appointed by the council with the approval of the majority of the assembly.

The secretaries and staff of the secretariat shall be appointed by the Secretary General with the approval of the council.

The Secretary General shall act in that capacity at all meetings of the assembly and of the council.

The expenses of the secretariat shall be borne by the members of the League in accordance with the apportionment of the expenses of the International Bureau of the Universal Postal Union.

ARTICLE 7. — The seat of the League is established at Geneva.

The council may at any time decide that the seat of the League shall be established elsewhere.

All positions under or in connection with the League, including the secretariat, shall be open equally to men and women.

Representatives of the members of the League and officials of the League when engaged on business of the League shall enjoy diplomatic privileges and immunities.

The buildings and other property occupied by the League or its officials or by representatives attending its meetings shall be inviolable.

ARTICLE 8. — The members of the League recognize that the maintenance of peace requires the reduction of national armaments to the lowest point consistent with national safety and the enforcement by common action of international obligations.

The council, taking account of the geographical situation and circumstances of each State, shall formulate plans for such reduction for the consideration and action of the several governments.

Such plans shall be subject to reconsideration and revision at least every ten years.

After these plans shall have been adopted by the several governments, the limits of the armaments therein fixed shall not be exceeded without the concurrence of the council.

The members of the League agree that the manufacture by private enterprise of munitions and implements of war is open to grave objections. The council shall advise how the evil effects attendant upon such manufacture can be prevented, due regard being had to the necessities of those members of the League which are not able to manufacture the munitions and implements of war necessary for their safety.

The members of the League undertake to interchange full and frank information as to the scale of their armaments, their military and naval program and the condition of such of their industries as are adaptable to warlike purposes.

ARTICLE 9. — A permanent commission shall be constituted to advise the council on the execution of the provisions of Article 1 and 8 and on military and naval questions generally.

ARTICLE 10. — The members of the League undertake to respect and preserve as against external aggression the territorial integrity and existing political independence of all members of the League. In case of any such aggression or in case of any threat or danger of such aggression the council shall advise upon the means upon which this obligation shall be fulfilled.

ARTICLE 11. — Any war or threat of war, whether immediately affecting any of the members of the League or not, is hereby declared a matter of concern to the whole League, and the League shall take any action that shall be deemed wise and effectual to safeguard the peace of nations. In case any such emergency should arise the Secretary General shall on the request of any member of the League forthwith summon a meeting of the council.

It is also declared to be the friendly right of each member of the League to bring to the attention of the assembly or of the council any circumstances whatever affecting international relations which threaten to disturb international peace or the good understanding between nations upon which peace depends.

ARTICLE 12. — The members of the League agree that if there should arise between them any dispute likely to lead to a rupture, they will submit the matter either to arbitration or to inquiry by the council, and they agree in no case to resort to war until three months after the award by the arbitrators or the report by the council.

In any case under this article the award of the arbitrators shall be made within a reasonable time, and the report of the council shall be made within six months after the submission of the dispute.

ARTICLE 13. — The members of the League agree that whenever any dispute shall arise between them which they recognize to be suitable for submission to arbitration and which cannot be satisfactorily settled by diplomacy, they will submit the whole subject-matter to arbitration.

Disputes as to the interpretation of a treaty, as to any question of international law, as to the existence of any fact which if established would constitute a breach of any international obligation, or as to the extent and nature of the reparation to be made for any such breach, are declared to be among those which are generally suitable for submission to arbitration.

For the consideration of any such dispute the Court of Arbitration to which the case is referred shall be the court agreed on by the parties to the dispute or stipulated in any convention existing between them.

The members of the League agree that they will carry out in full good faith any award that may be rendered, and that they will not resort to war against a member of the League which complies therewith. In the event of any failure to carry out such an award, the council shall propose what steps should be taken to give effect thereto.

ARTICLE 14. — The council shall formulate and submit to the members of the League for adoption plans for the establishment of a Permanent Court of International Justice. The court shall be competent to hear and determine any dispute of an international character which the parties thereto submit to it. The court may also give an advisory opinion upon any dispute or question referred to it by the council or by the assembly.

ARTICLE 15. — If there should arise between members of the League any dispute likely to lead to a rupture, which is not submitted to arbitration in accordance with Article 13, the members of the League agree that they will submit the matter to the council. Any party to the dispute may effect such submission by giving notice of the existence of the dispute to the Secretary General, who will make all necessary arrangements for a full investigation and consideration thereof.

For this purpose the parties to the dispute will communicate to the Secretary General, as promptly as possible, statements of their case with all relevant facts and papers, and the council may forthwith direct the publication thereof.

The council shall endeavor to effect a settlement of the dispute, and if such efforts are successful, a statement shall be made public giving such facts and explanations regarding the dispute and the terms of settlement thereof as the council may deem appropriate.

2 E

If the dispute is not thus settled, the council either unanimously or by a majority vote shall make and publish a report containing a statement of the facts of the dispute and the recommendations which are deemed just and proper in regard thereto.

Any member of the League represented on the council may make public a statement of the facts of the dispute and of its conclusions regarding the same.

If a report by the council is unanimously agreed to by the members thereof other than the representatives of one or more of the parties to the dispute, the members of the League agree that they will not go to war with any party to the dispute which complies with the recommendations of the report.

If the council fails to reach a report which is unanimously agreed to by the members thereof other than the representatives of one or more of the parties to the dispute, the members of the League reserve to themselves the right to take such action as they shall consider necessary for the maintenance of right and justice.

If the dispute between the parties is claimed by one of them, and is found by the council to arise out of a matter which by international law is solely within the domestic jurisdiction of that party, the council shall so report, and shall make no recommendation as to its settlement.

The council may in any case under this article refer the dispute to the assembly. The dispute shall be so referred at the request of either party to the dispute, provided that such request be made within fourteen days after the submission of the dispute to the council.

In any case referred to the assembly all the provisions of this article and of Article 12 relating to the action and powers of the council shall apply to the action and powers of the assembly, provided that a report made by the assembly, if concurred in by the representatives of those members of the League represented on the council and of a majority of the other members of the League, exclusive in each case of the representatives of the parties to the dispute, shall have the same force as a report by the council concurred in by all the members thereof other than the representatives of one or more of the parties to the dispute.

ARTICLE 16. — Should any member of the League resort to war in disregard of its covenants under Articles 12, 13, or 15, it shall *ipso facto* be deemed to have committed an act of war against all other members of the League, which hereby undertake immediately to subject it to the severance of all trade or financial relations, the prohibition of all intercourse between their nationals and the nationals of the covenant-breaking State, and the prevention of all financial, commercial, or personal intercourse between the nationals of the covenant-breaking State and the nationals of any other State, whether a member of the League or not.

It shall be the duty of the council in such case to recommend to the several governments concerned what effective military, naval or air force the members of the League shall severally contribute to the armed forces to be used to protect the covenants of the League.

The members of the League agree, further, that they will mutually support one another in the financial and economic measures which are taken under this article, in order to minimize the loss and inconvenience resulting from the above measures, and that they will mutually support one another in resisting any special measures aimed at one of their number by the covenant-breaking State, and that they will take the necessary steps to afford passage through their territory to the forces of any of the members of the League which are coöperating to protect the covenants of the League.

Any member of the League which has violated any covenant of the League may be declared to be no longer a member of the League by a vote of the council concurred in by the representatives of all the other members of the League represented thereon.

ARTICLE 17. — In the event of a dispute between a member of the League and a State which is not a member of the League, or between States not members of the League, the State or States not members of the League shall be invited to accept the obligations of membership in the League for the purposes of such dispute, upon such conditions as the council may deem just. If such invitation is accepted, the provisions of Articles 12 to 16 inclusive shall be applied with such modifications as may be deemed necessary by the council.

Upon such invitation being given the council shall immediately institute an inquiry into the circumstances of the dispute and recommend such action as may seem best and most effectual in the circumstances.

If a State so invited shall refuse to accept the obligations of membership in the League for the purposes of such dispute, and shall resort to war against a member of the League, the provisions of Article 16 shall be applicable as against the State taking such action.

If both parties to the dispute when so invited refuse to accept the obligations of membership in the League for the purposes of such dispute, the council may take such measures and make such recommendations as will prevent hostilities and will result in the settlement of the dispute.

ARTICLE 18. — Every treaty or international engagement entered into hereafter by any member of the League shall be forthwith registered with the Secretariat and shall as soon as possible be published by it. No such treaty or international engagement shall be binding until so registered.

ARTICLE 19. — The assembly may from time to time advise the reconsideration by members of the League of treaties which have become inapplicable and the consideration of international conditions whose continuance might endanger the peace of the world.

ARTICLE 20. — The members of the League severally agree that this covenant is accepted as abrogating all obligations or understandings *inter se* which are inconsistent with the terms thereof, and solemnly undertake that they will not hereafter enter into any engagements inconsistent with the terms thereof.

In case any member of the League shall, before becoming a member of the League, have undertaken any obligations inconsistent with the terms of this covenant, it shall be the duty of such member to take immediate steps to procure its release from such obligations.

ARTICLE 21. — Nothing in this covenant shall be deemed to affect the validity of international engagements, such as treaties of arbitration or regional understandings like the Monroe Doctrine, for securing the maintenance of peace.

ARTICLE 22. — To those colonies and territories which as a consequence of the late war have ceased to be under the sovereignty of the States which formerly governed them and which are inhabited by peoples not able to stand by themselves under the strenuous conditions of the modern world, there should be applied the principle that the well-being and development of such peoples form a sacred trust of civilization and that securities for the performance of this trust should be embodied in this covenant.

The best method of giving practical effect to this principle is that the tutelage of such peoples should be intrusted to advanced nations who by reason of their resources, their experience or their geographical position can best undertake this responsibility, and who are willing to accept it, and that this tutelage should be exercised by them as mandataries on behalf of the League.

The character of the mandate must differ according to the stage of the development of the people, the geographical situation of the territory, its economic conditions and other similar circumstances.

Certain communities formerly belonging to the Turkish Empire have reached a stage of development where their existence as independent nations can be provisionally recognized subject to the rendering of administrative advice and assistance by a mandatary until such time as they are able to stand alone. The wishes of these communities must be a principal consideration in the selection of the mandatary.

Other peoples, especially those of Central Africa, are at such a stage that the mandatary must be responsible for the administration of the territory under conditions which will guarantee freedom of conscience and religion, subject only to the maintenance of public order and morals, the prohibition of abuses such as the slave trade, the arms traffic and the liquor traffic, and the prevention of the establishment of fortifications or military and naval bases and of military training of the natives for other than police purposes and the defense of territory, and will also secure equal opportunities for the trade and commerce of other members of the League.

There are territories, such as Southwest Africa and certain of the South Pacific islands, which, owing to the sparseness of their population or their small size, or their remoteness from the centers of civilization, or their geographical contiguity to the territory of the mandatary, and other circumstances, can be best administered under the laws of the mandatary as integral portions of its territory, subject to the safeguards above mentioned in the interests of the indigenous population.

In every case of mandate the mandatary shall render to the council an annual report in reference to the territory committed to its charge.

The degree of authority, control, or administration to be exercised by the mandatary shall, if not previously agreed upon by the members of the League, be explicitly defined in each case by the council.

A permanent commission shall be constituted to receive and examine the annual reports of the mandataries and to advise the council on all matters relating to the observance of the mandates.

ARTICLE 23. — Subject to and in accordance with the provisions of international conventions existing or hereafter to be agreed upon, the members of the League :

(*a*) will endeavor to secure and maintain fair and humane conditions of labor for men, women, and children, both in their own countries and in all countries to which their commercial and industrial relations extend, and for that purpose will establish and maintain the necessary international organizations;

(*b*) undertake to secure just treatment of the native inhabitants of territories under their control;

(*c*) will intrust the League with the general supervision over the execution of agreements with regard to the traffic in women and children and the traffic in opium and other dangerous drugs;

(*d*) will intrust the League with the general supervision of the trade in arms and ammunition with the countries to which the control of this traffic is necessary in the common interest;

(*e*) will make provision to secure and maintain freedom of communications and of transit and equitable treatment for the commerce of all members of the League. In this connection the special necessities of the regions devastated during the war of 1914–1918 shall be borne in mind;

(*f*) will endeavor to take steps in matters of international concern for the prevention and control of disease.

ARTICLE 24. — There shall be placed under the direction of the League all international bureaus already established by general treaties if the parties to such treaties consent. All such international bureaus and all commissions for the regulation of matters of international interest hereafter constituted shall be placed under the direction of the League.

In all matters of international interest which are regulated by general conventions but which are not placed under the control of international bureaus or commissions, the secretariat of the League shall, subject to the consent of the council and if desired by the parties, collect and distribute all relevant information and shall render any other assistance which may be necessary or desirable.

The council may include as part of the expenses of the secretariat the expenses of any bureau or commission which is placed under the direction of the League.

ARTICLE 25. — The members of the League agree to encourage and promote the establishment and coöperation of duly authorized voluntary national Red Cross organizations having as purposes the improvement of health, the prevention of disease, and the mitigation of suffering throughout the world.

ARTICLE 26. — Amendments to this covenant will take effect when ratified by the members of the League whose representatives compose the council and by a majority of the members of the League whose representatives compose the assembly.

No such amendment shall bind any member of the League which signifies its dissent therefrom, but in that case it shall cease to be a member of the League.

ANNEX

I. Original members of the League of Nations signatories of the treaty of peace.

United States of America
Belgium
Bolivia
Brazil
British Empire
   Canada
   Australia
   South Africa
   New Zealand
   India
China
Cuba
Ecuador
France
Greece
Guatemala

Haiti
Hedjaz
Honduras
Italy
Japan
Liberia
Nicaragua
Panama
Peru
Poland
Portugal
Rumania
Serb-Croat-Slovene State
Siam
Czecho-Slovakia
Uruguay

States invited to accede to the covenant.

Argentine Republic
Chile
Colombia
Denmark
Netherlands
Norway
Paraguay

Persia
Salvador
Spain
Sweden
Switzerland
Venezuela

II. First Secretary General of the League of Nations. The Honorable Sir James Eric Drummond, K.C.M.G., C.B.

APPENDIX II

AMERICAN RESERVATIONS TO THE TREATY OF VERSAILLES

(Adopted by majority vote of the United States Senate on November 8, 1919, and again, with minor modifications, in March, 1920. President Wilson consistently opposed them, however, and on both occasions their proponents failed to muster the necessary two-thirds vote of the United States Senate to assure American ratification of the treaty of Versailles with these Reservations.)

THAT the Senate advise and consent to the ratification of the treaty of peace with Germany concluded at Versailles on the 28th day of June, 1919, subject to the following reservations and understandings, which are hereby made a part and condition of this resolution of ratification, which ratification is not to take effect or bind the United States until the said reservations and understandings adopted by the Senate have been accepted by an exchange of notes as a part and a condition of this resolution of ratification by at least three of the four principal allied and associated powers, to wit, Great Britain, France, Italy, and Japan:

1. The United States so understands and construes Article I. that in case of notice of withdrawal from the League of Nations, as provided in said article, the United States shall be the sole judge as to whether all its international obligations and all its obligations under the said covenant have been fulfilled, and notice of withdrawal by the United States may be given by a concurrent resolution of the Congress of the United States.

2. The United States assumes no obligation to preserve the territorial integrity or political independence of any other country or to interfere in controversies between nations — whether members of the League or not — under the provisions of Article X., or to employ the military or naval forces of the United States under any article of the treaty for any purpose, unless in any particular case the Congress, which, under the Constitution, has the sole power to declare war or authorize the employment of the military or naval forces of the United States, shall by act or joint resolution so provide.

3. No mandate shall be accepted by the United States under Article XXII., Part I., or any other provision of the treaty of peace with Germany, except by action of the Congress of the United States.

4. The United States reserves to itself exclusively the right to decide what questions are within its domestic jurisdiction and declares that all domestic and political questions relating wholly or in part to its internal affairs, including immigration, labor, coastwise traffic, the tariff, commerce, the suppression of traffic in women and children, and in opium and other dangerous drugs, and all other domestic questions, are solely within the jurisdiction of the United States and are not under this treaty to be submitted in any way either to arbitration or to the consideration of the Council or of the Assembly of the League of Nations, or any agency thereof, or to the decision or recommendation of any other power.

5. The United States will not submit to arbitration or to inquiry by the Assembly or by the Council of the League of Nations, provided for in said treaty of peace, any questions which in the judgment of the United States depend upon or relate to its long-established policy, commonly known as the Monroe Doctrine; said doctrine is to be interpreted by the United States alone and is hereby declared to be wholly outside the jurisdiction of said League of Nations and entirely unaffected by any provision contained in the said treaty of peace with Germany.

6. The United States withholds its assent to Articles CLVI., CLVII., and CLVIII., and reserves full liberty of action with respect to any controversy which may arise under said articles between the Republic of China and the Empire of Japan.

7. The Congress of the United States will provide by law for the appointment of the representatives of the United States in the Assembly and the Council of the League of Nations, and may in its discretion provide for the participation of the United States in any commission, committee, tribunal, court, council, or conference, or in the selection of any members thereof and for the appointment of members of said commissions, committees, tribunals, courts, councils, or conferences, or any other representatives under the treaty of peace, or in carrying out its provisions, and until such participation and appointment have been so provided for and the powers and duties of such representatives have been defined by law, no person shall represent the United States under either said League of Nations or the treaty

of peace with Germany or be authorized to perform any act for or on behalf of the United States thereunder, and no citizen of the United States shall be selected or appointed as a member of said commissions, committees, tribunals, courts, councils, or conferences except with the approval of the Senate of the United States.

8. The United States understands that the Reparations Commission will regulate or interfere with exports from the United States to Germany, or from Germany to the United States, only when the United States by act or joint resolution of Congress approves such regulation or interference.

9. The United States shall not be obligated to contribute to any expenses of the League of Nations, or of the secretariat, or of any commission, or committee, or conference, or other agency, organized under the League of Nations or under the treaty or for the purpose of carrying out the treaty provisions, unless and until an appropriation of funds available for such expenses shall have been made by the Congress of the United States.

10. If the United States shall at any time adopt any plan for the limitation of armaments proposed by the Council of the League of Nations under the provisions of Article VIII., it reserves the right to increase such armaments without the consent of the council whenever the United States is threatened with invasion or engaged in war.

11. The United States reserves the right to permit, in its discretion, the nationals of a covenant-breaking State, as defined in Article XVI. of the covenant of the League of Nations, residing within the United States or in countries other than that violating said Article XVI., to continue their commercial, financial, and personal relations with the nationals of the United States.

12. Nothing in Articles CCXCVI., CCXCVII., or in any of the annexes thereto or in any other article, section, or annex of the treaty of peace with Germany shall, as against citizens of the United States, be taken to mean any confirmation, ratification, or approval of any act otherwise illegal or in contravention of the rights of citizens of the United States.

13. The United States withholds its assent to Part XIII. (Articles CCCLXXXVII. to CCCCXXVII. inclusive) unless Congress by act or joint resolution shall hereafter make provision for representation in the organization established by said Part XIII. and in such event the participation of the United States will be governed and conditioned by the provisions of such act or joint resolution.

14. The United States assumes no obligation to be bound by any election, decision, report, or finding of the Council or Assembly in which any member of the League and its self-governing dominions, colonies, or parts of empire, in the aggregate have cast more than one vote, and assumes no obligation to be bound by any decision, report, or finding of the Council or Assembly arising out of any dispute between the United States and any member of the League if such member, or any self-governing dominion, colony, empire, or part united with it politically has voted.

APPENDIX III

AGREEMENT BETWEEN THE UNITED STATES AND FRANCE

(Signed at Versailles, June 28, 1919, but not ratified by the United States Senate.)

WHEREAS the United States of America and the French Republic are equally animated by the desire to maintain the peace of the world so happily restored by the treaty of peace signed at Versailles the 28th day of June, 1919, putting an end to the war begun by the aggression of the German Empire and ended by the defeat of that power; and,

WHEREAS the United States of America and the French Republic are fully persuaded that an unprovoked movement of aggression by Germany against France would not only violate both the letter and the spirit of the Treaty of Versailles to which the United States of America and the French Republic are parties, thus exposing France anew to the intolerable burdens of an unprovoked war, but that such aggression on the part of Germany would be and is so regarded by the Treaty of Versailles as a hostile act against all the powers signatory to that treaty and as calculated to disturb the peace of the world by involving inevitably and directly the states of Europe and indirectly, as experience has amply and unfortunately demonstrated, the world at large; and,

WHEREAS the United States of America and the French Republic fear that the stipulations relating to the left bank of the Rhine contained in said Treaty of Versailles may not at first provide adequate security and protection to France on the one hand and the United States of America as one of the signatories of the Treaty of Versailles on the other;

Therefore, the United States of America and the French Republic having decided to conclude a treaty to effect these necessary purposes, Woodrow Wilson, President of the United States of America, and Robert Lansing, Secretary of State of the United States, specially authorized thereto by the President of the United States, and Georges Clemenceau, President of the Council, Minister of War, and Stephen Pichon, Minister of Foreign Affairs, specially authorized thereto by Raymond Poincaré, President of the French Republic, have agreed upon the following articles:

ARTICLE I. — In case the following stipulations relating to the left bank of the Rhine contained in the treaty of peace with Germany signed at Versailles the 28th day of June, 1919, by the United States of America, the French Republic and the British Empire among other powers:

"Article 42. Germany is forbidden to maintain or construct any fortifications either on the left bank of the Rhine or on the right bank to the west of a line drawn 50 kilometres to the east of the Rhine.

"Article 43. In the area defined above the maintenance and assembly of armed forces, either permanently or temporarily, and military manœuvres of any kind, as well as the upkeep of all permanent works for mobilization are in the same way forbidden.

"Article 44. In case Germany violates in any manner whatever the provisions of Articles 42 and 43, she shall be regarded as committing a hostile act against the powers signatory of the present treaty and as calculated to disturb the peace of the world."

may not at first provide adequate security and protection to France, the United States of America shall be bound to come immediately to her assistance in the event of any unprovoked movement of aggression against her being made by Germany.

ARTICLE II. — The present treaty, in similar terms with the treaty of even date for the same purpose concluded between Great Britain and the French Republic, a copy of which treaty is annexed hereto, will only come into force when the latter is ratified.

ARTICLE III. — The present treaty must be submitted to the Council of the League of Nations, and must be recognized by the Council, acting if need be by a majority, as an engagement which is consistent with the Covenant of the League. It will continue in force until on the application of one of the parties to it the Council, acting if need be by a majority, agrees that the League itself affords sufficient protection.

ARTICLE IV. — The present treaty will be submitted to the Senate of the United States at the same time as the Treaty of Versailles is submitted to the Senate for its advice and consent to ratification. It will be submitted before ratification to the French Chambers for approval. The ratification thereof will be exchanged on the deposit of ratifications of the Treaty of Versailles at Paris or as soon thereafter as shall be possible.

In faith whereof the respective plenipotentiaries, to wit: On the part of the United States of America, Woodrow Wilson, President, and Robert Lansing, Secretary of State, of the United States; and on the part of the French Republic, Georges Clemenceau, President of the Council of Ministers, Minister of War and Stephen Pichon, Minister of Foreign Affairs, have signed the above articles both in the English and French languages, and they have hereunto affixed their seals.

Done in duplicate at the City of Versailles, on the twenty-eighth day of June, in the year of our Lord one thousand nine hundred and nineteen, and the one hundred and forty-third of the Independence of the United States of America.

[Seal]   WOODROW WILSON.
[Seal]   ROBERT LANSING.
[Seal]   G. CLEMENCEAU.
[Seal]   S. PICHON.

SELECT BIBLIOGRAPHY

I. General Historical Background

MANUALS: C. J. H. Hayes, *A Political and Social History of Modern Europe*, 2 vols. (1916); L. H. Holt and A. W. Chilton, *The History of Europe from 1862 to 1914* (1917); J. S. Schapiro, *Modern and Contemporary History* (1918); C. D. Hazen, *Fifty Years of Europe* (1919); E. B. Krehbiel, *Nationalism, War and Society* (1916).

DIPLOMATIC HISTORIES: F. M. Anderson and A. S. Hershey (editors), *Handbook for the Diplomatic History of Europe, Asia, and Africa, 1870–1914* (1918); Charles Seymour, *The Diplomatic Background of the War* (1916); W. S. Davis, *The Roots of the War* (1918); Arthur Bullard, *The Diplomacy of the Great War* (1916), a survey of international politics from 1878 to 1914; W. M. Fullerton, *Problems of Power*, 2d ed. (1915); H. A. Gibbons, *The New Map of Europe, 1911–1914* (1914), *The New Map of Africa, 1900–1916, a History of European Colonial Expansion and Colonial Diplomacy* (1916), and *The New Map of Asia, 1900–1919* (1919); A. C. Coolidge, *The Origins of the Triple Alliance* (1917); E. J. Dillon, *From the Triple to the Quadruple Alliance, Why Italy went into the War* (1915); B. E. Schmitt, *England and Germany* (1916); André Tardieu, *France and the Alliances, the Struggle for the Balance of Power* (1908); E. D. Morel, *Ten Years of Secret Diplomacy* (1915); Gilbert Murray, *The Foreign Policy of Sir Edward Grey 1906–1915* (1915); Ernst (Graf) zu Reventlow, *Deutschlands Auswärtige Politik 1888–1913* (1914).

GERMANY: W. H. Dawson, *The German Empire (1867–1914) and the Unity Movement*, 2 vols. (1919); R. H. Fife, Jr., *The German Empire between Two Wars, a Study of the Political and Social Development of the Nation between 1871 and 1914* (1916); J. Ellis Barker, *Modern Germany, its Rise, Growth, Downfall, and Future* (1919); C. D. Hazen, *Alsace-Lorraine under German Rule* (1917); P. E. Lewin, *The Germans and Africa* (1915), and *The German Road to the East, an account of the "Drang nach Osten" and of Teutonic Aims in the Near and Middle East* (1917); F. A. J. von Bernhardi, *Germany and the Next War*, Eng. trans. by A. H. Powles (1913).

II. General Works on the War

DOCUMENTS: A vast amount of material has been published by the Governments of the several belligerents, both diplomatic and military; many documents of signal importance have been published in convenient form by the American Association for International Conciliation (New York), by the World Peace Foundation (Boston), by *The Nation* (New York), and by *The New Europe*, a valuable weekly review of foreign politics (1917–1920); *Current History*, a monthly magazine issued

431

since 1914 by *The New York Times*, is a store-house of documents, special articles, and illustrations; *The Times Documentary History of the War*, published by the London *Times*, is similarly useful. SECONDARY WORKS: John Buchan, *Nelson's History of the War*, 24 vols. (1915–1919); F. H. Simonds, *History of the World War;* Hilaire Belloc, *Elements of the Great War;* Arthur Conan Doyle, *A History of the Great War; Mr. Punch's History of the War* (1919); Louis Raemaeker, *Raemaeker's Cartoon History of the War;* F. W. T. Lange and W. T. Berry, *Books on the Great War*, an annotated bibliography.

III. Diplomacy and Apologetics of the War

DIPLOMACY: J. B. Scott (editor), *Diplomatic Documents relating to the Outbreak of the European War*, 2 vols. (1916); E. R. O. von Mach, *Official Diplomatic Documents relating to the Outbreak of the European War, with photographic reproductions of the official editions of the documents published by the Governments of Austria-Hungary, Belgium, France, Germany, Great Britain, Russia, and Serbia* (1916); F. Seymour Cocks, *The Secret Treaties;* O. P. Chitwood, *The Immediate Causes of the Great War* (1917); J. W. Headlam, *The History of Twelve Days, July 24th to August 4th, 1914* (1915); J. W. Headlam, *The German Chancellor and the Outbreak of War* (1917); E. C. Stowell, *The Diplomacy of the War of 1914* (1915); Munroe Smith, *Militarism and Statecraft* (1918). APOLOGETICS: E. R. Bevan, *Method in the Madness, a fresh consideration of the case between Germany and Ourselves* (1917); Yves Guyot, *The Causes and Consequences of the War*, Eng. trans. by F. A. Holt (1916); G. Lowes Dickinson, *The European Anarchy* (1916); J. M. Beck, *The Evidence in the Case* (1914); E. J. Dillon, *A Scrap of Paper* (1914); *I Accuse*, by a German, Eng. trans. by Alexander Gray (1915); *Modern Germany in relation to the Great War*, by various German writers, notably Professors Meinecke, Oncken, Schumacher, and Erich Marcks, trans. by W. W. Whitelock (1916); H. T. W. Frobenius, *The German Empire's Hour of Destiny* (1914); E. R. O. von Mach, *What Germany Wants* (1914) and *Germany's Point of View* (1915); Paul Rohrbach, *Germany's Isolation, an Exposition of the Economic Causes of the War*, Eng. trans. by P. H. Phillipson (1915); Friedrich Naumann, *Central Europe*, Eng. trans. by Christabel M. Meredith (1917); Ernst (Graf) zu Reventlow, *The Vampire of the Continent*, Eng. trans. by G. C. Hill (1916); G. M. C. Brandes, *The World at War*, Eng. trans. by Catherine D. Groth (1917). CRITICISM AND COMMENT: J. W. Gerard, *My Four Years in Germany* (1917), and *Face to Face with Kaiserism* (1918); D. J. Hill, *Impressions of the Kaiser* (1918); M. F. Egan, *Ten Years near the German Frontier* (1919); Henry Morgenthau, *Ambassador Morgenthau's Story* (1918); Henry van Dyke, *Fighting for Peace* (1917); Émile Prüm, *Pan-Germanism versus Christendom, the Conversion of a Neutral* (1917); T. Tittoni, *Who is Responsible for the War, the Verdict of History* (1917); Count Julius Andrassy, *Whose Sin is the World War* (1915); Christian Gauss, *The German Emperor as Shown in his Public Utterances* (1915); S. Grumbach, *Germany's Annexationist Aims*, Eng. trans. by J. E. Barker (1917); J. P. Bang, *Hurrah and Hallelujah, the Teaching of Germany's Poets, Prophets, Professors and Preachers*, Eng. trans. by Jessie Bröchner

(1917); William Archer, *Gems (?) of German Thought* (1917); Edwyn Bevan, *German Social Democracy during the War* (1919); H. N. Brailsford, *Across the Blockade* (1919); T. L. Stoddard, *Present Day Europe, its National States of Mind* (1917).

IV. Special Works on Particular Countries

BELGIUM: Brand Whitlock, *Belgium, a Personal Narrative*, 2 vols. (1919); Hugh Gibson, *A Journal from our Legation in Belgium* (1917); Cardinal Mercier, *Pastorals, Letters, Allocutions 1914–1917*, with a biographical sketch by Rev. J. F. Stillemans (1917); Léon van der Essen, *The Invasion and the War in Belgium, with a Sketch of the Diplomatic Negotiations preceding the Conflict* (1917); C. P. Sanger and H. T. J. Norton, *England's Guarantee to Belgium and Luxemburg, with the full text of the treaties* (1915); *Reports on the Violations of the Rights of Nations and of the Laws and Customs of War in Belgium, by a Commission appointed by the Belgian Government*, 2 vols. (1917); Charles De Visscher, *Belgium's Case, a Juridical Enquiry*, Eng. trans. by E. F. Jourdain (1916); K. A. Fuehr, *The Neutrality of Belgium, a Study of the Belgian Case under its aspects in Political History and International Law* (1915), the German case; Erich Erichsen, *Forced to Fight, the Tale of a Schleswig Dane* (1917); A. J. Toynbee, *The German Terror in Belgium, an Historical Record* (1917); Charles Sarolea, *How Belgium Saved Europe* (1915); Émile Waxweiler, *Belgium, Neutral and Loyal, the War of 1914* (1915).

AUSTRIA-HUNGARY: H. W. Steed, *The Hapsburg Monarchy* (1913); R. W. Seton-Watson, *Racial Problems in Hungary* (1908), *The South Slav Question and the Hapsburg Monarchy* (1911), *Corruption and Reform in Hungary* (1911), *German, Slav, and Magyar, a Study in the Origins of the Great War* (1916); E. Ludwig, *Austria-Hungary and the War* (1916).

THE NEAR EAST: N. E. and C. R. Buxton, *The War and the Balkans* (1915); L. II. Courtney, 1st Baron Courtney, *Nationalism and War in the Near East* (1916); J. A. R. Marriott, *The Eastern Question, an Historical Study in European Diplomacy* (1917); Marion I. Newbigin, *Geographical Aspects of Balkan Problems in relation to the Great European War* (1915); Fortier Jones, *With Serbia into Exile, an American's Adventures with the Army that Can Not Die* (1916); V. R. Savic, *Southeastern Europe* (1918); *Greece in her True Light, her position in the world-wide war as expounded by El. K. Venizelos, her greatest statesman, in a series of official documents*, trans. by S. A. Xanthaky and N. G. Sakellarios (1916); Historicus (pseud.), *Bulgaria and her Neighbors* (1917); G. J. Shaw-Lefevre, 1st Baron Eversley, *The Turkish Empire, its Growth and Decay* (1917); Henry Morgenthau, *Ambassador Morgenthau's Story* (1918); André Chéradame, *The Pan-German Plot Unmasked* (1917); C. Snouck, *The Revolt in Arabia* (1917).

ARMENIA: Viscount Bryce, *Treatment of Armenians in the Ottoman Empire 1915–1916, Documents presented to Viscount Grey* (1917); H. A. Gibbons, *The Blackest Page of Modern History* (1916); A. J. Toynbee, *The Armenian Atrocities, the Murder of a Nation* (1916); Abraham Yohannan, *The Death of a Nation, or the Ever Persecuted Nestorians or Assyrian Christians* (1916).

2 F

ZIONISM: Paul Goodman and A. D. Lewis (editors), *Zionism, Problems and Views* (1917).

EAST-CENTRAL EUROPE: I. D. Levine, *The Resurrected Nations, a Popular History* (1919); Ralph Butler, *The New Eastern Europe* (1919); Stephan Rudnicki, *The Ukraine* (1915); C. Rivas, *La Lithuanie sous la joug allemande* (1918); H. A. Gibbons, *The Reconstruction of Poland and the Near East, Problems of Peace* (1917); E. H. Lewinski-Corwin, *A Political History of Poland* (1917); F. E. Whitton, *A History of Poland* (1918).

RUSSIA: H. W. Williams, *Russia of the Russians* (1914); Gregor Alexinsky, *Modern Russia* (1914), *Russia and the Great War* (1915), and *Russia and Europe* (1917); Leo Wiener, *An Interpretation of the Russian People* (1915); R. W. Child, *Potential Russia* (1916); I. F. Marcosson, *The Rebirth of Russia* (1917); I. D. Levine, *The Russian Revolution* (1917); Gen. Basil Gourko, *War and Revolution in Russia, 1914-1917* (1919); A. F. Kerensky, *The Prelude to Bolshevism* (1919); A. S. Rappoport, *Pioneers of the Russian Revolution* (1919); John Reed, *Ten Days that Shook the World* (1919); Émile Vandervelde, *Three Aspects of the Russian Revolution* (1919); John Spargo, *Bolshevism versus Democracy* (1919); Arthur Ransome, *Russia in 1919;* A. R. Williams, Arthur Ransome, and Col. Raymond Robins, *Lenin, the Man and his Work* (1919); J. V. Bubnoff, *The Coöperative Movement in Russia, its history, significance, and character* (1917).

THE FAR EAST: K. S. Latourette, *The Development of China* (1917); S. K. Hornbeck, *Contemporary Politics in the Far East* (1916); Jefferson Jones, *The Fall of Tsingtau, a Study of Japan's Ambitions in China* (1915); G. H. Blakeslee (editor), *Japan and Japanese-American Relations* (1912); T. F. F. Millard, *Our Eastern Question, America's Contact with the Orient and the Trend of Relations with China and Japan* (1916), and *Democracy and the Eastern Question* (1919); Naoichi Masaoka (editor), *Japan to America, a symposium of papers by political leaders and representative citizens of Japan and on the relations between Japan and the United States* (1915); B. L. Putnam Weale, *The Fight for the Republic in China* (1917), and *The Truth about China and Japan* (1919).

V. Great Britain and the War

BRITAIN AND THE EMPIRE: David Lloyd George, *Through Terror to Triumph, speeches and pronouncements,* arranged by F. L. Stevenson (1915); W. S. M. Knight, *A History of Great Britain during the Great War* (1916); André Chevrillon, *England and the War 1914-1915,* with a preface by Rudyard Kipling (1917); J. C. Smuts, *War-Time Speeches, a compilation of public utterances in Great Britain* (1917); G. L. Beer, *The English-speaking Peoples, their Future Relations and Joint International Obligations* (1917); Sinclair Kennedy, *The Pan-Angles, a Consideration of the Federation of the Seven English-speaking Nations* (1914).

IRELAND: W. B. Wells and N. Marlow, *The History of the Irish Rebellion of 1916* (1917); F. P. Jones, *History of the Sinn Fein Movement and the Irish Rebellion of 1916* (1917); G. W. Russell (pseud., A. E.), *National Being, Some Thoughts on an Irish Policy* (1916); L. R. Morris, *The Celtic Dawn, a Survey of the Renascence in Ireland 1889-1916* (1917); Shane Leslie, *The Celt and the World, a Study of the Relation of Celt and Teuton in History* (1917); Francis Hackett, *Ireland, a Study in Nationalism* (1918); E. R. Turner, *Ireland and England* (1919); Lord Ernest William Hamilton, *The Soul of Ulster* (1917).

VI. The United States and the War

GENERAL NARRATIVE: J. B. McMaster, *The United States in the World War*, 2 vols. (1918–1919); J. S. Bassett, *Our War with Germany, a History* (1919); Florence F. Kelly, *What America Did* (1919); Colonel De Chambrun and Captain De Marenches, *The American Army in the European Conflict* (1919); L. P. Ayres, *The War with Germany, a statistical summary*, 2d ed. (1920).

PRESIDENT WILSON: J. B. Scott (editor), *President Wilson's Foreign Policy, messages, addresses, papers* (1918); William Archer, *The Peace President, a brief appreciation of Woodrow Wilson* (1919); Daniel Halévy, *President Wilson* (1919).

MISCELLANEOUS: W. F. Willoughby, *Government Organization in War Time and After, a Survey of the Federal Civil Agencies created for the Prosecution of the War* (1919); Lt.-Col. J. C. Wise, *The Turn of the Tide, Operations of American Troops* (1919); Committee on Public Information, *War Information Series;* Ida C. Clarke, *American Women and the World War* (1918).

VII. Detailed Military and Naval Operations

MILITARY: In addition to the General Works on the War, listed above, there are innumerable accounts of various campaigns. Chief among these are official reports of the commanding generals and narratives by press correspondents and reminiscences of soldiers engaged. The books of Philip Gibbs are probably the most important journalistic narratives. Special mention should be made of "*1914*"; *the Memoirs of Field Marshal Viscount French* (1914); Maj. Gen. Sir F. Maurice, *The Last Four Months, How the War Was Won* (1919); E. A. Powell, *Italy at War* (1917); G. Gordon-Smith, *Through the Serbian Campaign* (1916); John Masefield, *Gallipoli* (1916); John Reed, *The War in Eastern Europe* (1916); Stanley Washburn, *The Russian Campaign* (1915); A. T. Clark, *To Bagdad with the British* (1917); J. H. Morgan (translator), *The War Book of the German General Staff, being "The Usages of War on Land" issued by the Great General Staff of the German Army* (1915); Gen. Erich von Ludendorff, *Ludendorff's Own Story, August, 1914, to November, 1918*, 2 vols. (1920); Raymond Recouly, *A Life of Marshal Foch* (1919); H. A. Atteridge, *Marshal Ferdinand Foch* (1919); S. Lauzanne, *Fighting France* (1918); Mario Alberti, *Italy's Great War* (1918); Field Marshal Sir Douglas Haig, *Despatches, December, 1915–April, 1919* (1920).

NAVAL: Admiral Viscount Jellicoe of Scapa, *The Grand Fleet, 1914–1916* (1919); A. S. Hurd and H. H. Bashford, *The Heroic Record of the British Navy, a Short History of the Naval War, 1914–1918* (1919); Grand Admiral von Tirpitz, *My Memoirs*, 2 vols. (1919).

MISCELLANEOUS: C. R. Gibson, *War Inventions and How They Were Invented* (1917); I. F. Marcosson, *The Business of War* (1918); P. Azan, *The Warfare of To-day* (1918); W. J. Abbot, *Aircraft and Submarines*

(1918); E. Middleton, *Aircraft of To-day and of the Future* (1918); H. P. Davison, *The American Red Cross in the Great War* (1919); Evangeline C. Booth and Grace L. Lutz, *The War Romance of the Salvation Army* (1919); W. L. Mallaber, *Medical History of the Great War* (1916); Romain Rolland, *Above the Battle* (1916); H. G. Wells, *Mr. Britling Sees it Through* (1916); Henri Barbusse, *Under Fire* (1917); Bruce Bairnsfather, *Bullets and Billets* (1917).

VIII. The League of Nations and the Peace

PEACE PROPOSALS: R. S. Bourne (editor), *Towards an Enduring Peace, a Symposium of Peace Proposals and Programs, 1914–1916* (1916); *Documents and Statements relating to Peace Proposals and War Aims, December, 1916, to November, 1918* (1919).

THE LEAGUE OF NATIONS: S. P. Duggan (editor), *The League of Nations, the Principle and the Practice* (1919); Mathias Erzberger, *The League of Nations, the Way to the World's Peace*, Eng. trans. by Bernard Miall (1919); D. S. Morrow, *The Society of Free States* (1919); T. J. Lawrence, *The Society of Nations* (1919); D. J. Hill, *The Rebuilding of Europe* (1917); J. A. Hobson, *Towards International Government* (1915); J. S. Bassett, *The Lost Fruits of Waterloo* (1918); F. B. Sayre, *Experiments in International Administration* (1919).

THE PEACE CONGRESS: Walter Lippmann, *The Political Scene* (1919); H. M. Hyndman, *Clemenceau, the Man and his Time* (1919); J. M. Keynes, *The Economic Consequences of the Peace* (1920); E. J. Dillon, *The Inside Story of the Peace Conference* (1920).

POLITICS AND ECONOMICS: F. A. Ogg and C. A. Beard, *National Governments and the World War* (1919); J. L. Laughlin, *Credit of the Nations* (1918); E. J. Clapp, *Economic Aspects of the War* (1915); F. W. Hirst, *The Political Economy of War* (1915); A. D. Noyes, *Financial Chapters on the War* (1916); H. L. Gray, *War-Time Control of Industry* (1918); E. L. Bogart, *Direct and Indirect Costs of the Great World War* (1918); D. C. McMurtrie, *The Disabled Soldier* (1919); P. W. Kellogg and A. H. Gleason, *British Labor and the War* (1919); F. A. Cleveland and Joseph Schafer (editors), *Democracy in Reconstruction* (1920); E. M. Friedman (editor), *American Problems of Reconstruction* (1919); Bertrand Russell, *Proposed Roads to Freedom, — Socialism, Anarchism, and Syndicalism* (1919).

INDEX

Printed in the United States of America.